I0754209

SULTAN SOUK AND FAMILY.

ORIENTAL

AND

WESTERN SIBERIA:

A NARRATIVE OF

Seven Years' Explorations and Adventures

IN

SIBERIA, MONGOLIA, THE KIRGHIS STEPPES, CHINESE TARTARY, AND PART OF CENTRAL ASIA.

BY

THOMAS WITLAM ATKINSON.

WITH A MAP AND NUMEROUS ILLUSTRATIONS.

NEW YORK:
HARPER & BROTHERS, PUBLISHERS,
FRANKLIN SQUARE.
1858.

TO

His Imperial Majesty, Alexander the Second,

EMPEROR OF ALL THE RUSSIAS,

ETC., ETC.,

THIS VOLUME,

BY SPECIAL PERMISSION,

IS GRATEFULLY DEDICATED

BY

HIS IMPERIAL MAJESTY'S

MOST HUMBLE AND OBEDIENT SERVANT,

THE AUTHOR.

PREFACE.

WHEN the journey narrated in the following pages was undertaken, it was not with the intention of publishing either a book of Travels or any other work. My sole object was to sketch the scenery of Siberia, scarcely at all known to Europeans. While thus employed, I passed out of the Emperor of Russia's Asiatic dominions, having been provided with an especial passport by command of his imperial majesty, Nicholas the First, which enabled me to cross the frontier, as well as to re-enter the empire at any other points to which my rambles might lead me.

I have brought back faithful representations of the scenery, without taking any artistic liberties, preferring Nature in her own attractions to snatching a grace within the reach of Art.

Mine has been a tolerably wide field, extending from Kokhan on the west to the eastern end of the Baikal, and as far south as the Chinese town of Tchin-si, including that immense chain Syan-shan, never before seen by any European, as well as a large portion of the western part of the Gobi, over which Genghis Khan marched his wild hordes toward the west—scenes on which no pencil has previously been employed—comprising a distance traversed of about 32,000 versts in carriages, 7100 in boats, and 20,300 on horseback—in all, 59,400 versts (about 39,500 miles) in the course of seven years. Neither the old Venetian nor the Jesuit priests could have visited these regions, their travels having been far to the south; nor am I aware that they brought back any pictorial representations of the scenes through which they wandered. Even the recent travelers Huc and Gaby, who visited "the land of grass" (the plains to the south of the great Desert of Gobi), did not penetrate into the country of the Kalkas, and the illustrations to their works were evidently fabricated in Paris.

Mine is a simple narrative of facts, taken from journals kept with scrupulous care during the whole journey, often under the influence of great fatigue, and amid the pressure of numerous difficulties. I suffered much both from hunger and thirst, have run many risks, and on several occasions have been placed in most critical situations with the tribes of Central Asia, more particularly when among the convicts escaped from the Chinese penal settlements—desperate characters who hold the lives of men cheap. I have several times looked upon what appeared inevitable death, and have had a fair allowance of hair-breadth escapes when riding and sketching on the brinks of precipices with a perpendicular depth of 1500 feet below me.

With these accompaniments, I traversed much of the hitherto unexplored regions of Central Asia, and produced 560 sketches of the scenery, executed with the moist colors made by Winsor and Newton, invaluable to an artist employed under such circumstances. I have used them on the sandy plains of Central Asia in a temperature of 50° Réaumur (144° Fahrenheit), and in Siberia have had them frozen as solid as a mass of iron when the temperature was 43° Réaumur of frost, 11° below the point where the mercury became solid, when I could make it into balls in my bullet-moulds. Some of my largest works have been painted with colors that have stood these severe tests, and for depth and purity of tone have not been surpassed by those I have had fresh from the manufactory. With cake colors all my efforts would have been useless.

I am deeply indebted to the late Emperor of Russia, for without his passport I should have been stopped at every government, and insurmountable difficulties would have been thrown in my way. This slip of paper proved a talisman wherever presented in his dominions, and swept down every obstacle raised to bar my progress. I have also to thank her imperial highness, the Grand-

Duchess Helen, for many acts of kindness and condescension. Nor have I forgotten my obligations to the Baroness Rahden and Miss Euler, a worthy descendant of the mathematician. To Count Nesselrode I offer my thanks for many obliging acts. From Mr. Buchanan, our late minister in Denmark, I received much assistance in procuring the emperor's permission, for which I take this opportunity of recording my gratitude. Prince Gertchikoff, the Governor-General of Western Siberia, rendered me most essential service by forwarding my sketching materials to far-distant Cossack posts, for which I return my acknowledgments. I will not attempt to particularize the mining officers of the Altai, from all of whom I received assistance and attention. My thanks are equally due to the peasants, from many of whom I received a crust of black bread when sorely pressed by hunger—to my Cossack companions, who freely shared my toils and dangers—to the brave Kalmucks, who led me through difficult mountain regions, and suffered both hunger and thirst in my service, with the prospect of certain captivity in case of our being overpowered. To General Mouravieff, the Governor-General of Eastern Siberia, I wish also to express my cordial acknowledgments. He is one of the most faithful servants of his imperial majesty, and has done much, and would do more, for the good of his country, were he permitted. My other friends in Eastern Siberia I remember with the kindest feelings, and sincerely hope that I have not been forgotten by them.

CONTENTS.

LIST OF ILLUSTRATIONS.

ORIENTAL AND WESTERN SIBERIA, AND CHINESE TARTARY.

CHAPTER I.

ST. PETERSBURG TO EKATERINEBURG.

SOON after my arrival in St. Petersburg I made the acquaintance of the late Admiral Rickardt, and from him gathered much information about Siberia, or, rather, the route through the country to Kamtschatka, the southern regions being unknown to him. He had only traveled by the great post-road from St. Petersburg to Ochotsk, a very monotonous journey. The road never approaches the Altai, being usually carried along the great Siberian plain at a distance of five or six hundred versts from this mountain chain. I was told that the authorities would only give a passport to travel from one town to another, and that this would have to be changed at every government town, causing great trouble, expense, and delay. After due consideration, I determined to apply to the emperor for especial permission to travel and sketch, feeling certain that if this were granted there would be no difficulties; if refused, I would not make the attempt. I wrote a letter, which was most kindly laid before his imperial majesty by Mr. Buchanan, Chargé d'Affaires, and in three days received an answer from Count Nesselrode, informing me that the emperor had granted my request, and that orders had been issued to the Minister of the Interior, and other authorities, to prepare for me all the necessary papers. Having received these, I commenced making inquiries about the country. The Minister of Finance very kindly put me in communication with a mining-engineer officer who had been engaged in the Altai, and from him I collected much valuable information relative to my route.

I found the road between St. Petersburg and Moscow very bad, the great traffic between the two capitals having cut it into such deep holes that the sledge went down every few minutes with a fearful shock. This I considered a good breaking in for the long journey before me. On the evening of the third day I reached Moscow in a great snow-storm, which rendered my entry into the ancient city any thing but pleasant. I was provided with letters to several Russian families, who did every thing they could to render my short stay agreeable. About a week after my arrival, there was a great festival to commemorate the anniversary of the founding of Moscow, seven hundred years ago. Through the kindness of some friends I was enabled to join in these festivities; but I shall not attempt to describe either dinners or balls; suffice it to say, they were on a grand scale. What interested me most was a series of *tableaux vivants* given in the "Nobility's Hall" (Assembly Rooms) before his imperial majesty and most of the court. Some of these were highly interesting, as they were representations of life seven centuries back. Old furniture, armor, and plate were brought from the Kremlin; these and the antique dresses gave a most faithful character to the pictures. During the evening a *tableau* was given representing the four elements, Air, Earth, Fire, and Water, which were represented by four beautiful young ladies, whose appearance called forth immense applause. Without dropping the curtain, this picture was changed by suddenly drawing off the dresses, which was done by some one beneath the stage. One young lady (whether of earth or heaven seemed difficult to determine) was kneeling on one knee on a piece of rock, and when the signal was given, was jerked from her place and turned feet upward on the floor, a position for which she was evidently not prepared. Many of the spectators began to laugh, but this was very properly hushed by his imperial majesty in an instant; in the next, the lady was divested of her first costume, and again took her place on the rock, with the additional charm of a deep blush spreading over her face.

Another very interesting event took place during my stay: this was the jubilee given to Professor Fischer. I had previously made his acquaintance, and he was much interested in my journey. I found afterward, on reaching the Altai, that he had written to his friend, Dr. Gabler, recommending me to his peculiar care. I remained at Moscow fifteen days, most of which were stormy, with heavy falls of snow and violent winds.

An order from the minister in St. Petersburg procured me a postillion from the post-office in Moscow to travel with me to Ekaterineburg, and on the 6th of March we started. There was now no time to spare; already the roads were reported bad, and I had a journey of 1707 versts before me. My only companion in the vashock was a large deer-hound; the postillion sat with the driver. It is, perhaps, necessary to say that a vashock is a long, box-like machine, placed on a sledge; in fact, a sort of half-grown omnibus. When the roads are worn into "oukhabas" (deep holes), this conveyance is too long, for the horses drag it over the ridges, going at a good speed, and jerk it beyond the centre; then down it goes with a tremendous thump, which sends the head of the unfortunate inmate against the top with terrible force. In fact, after the second day's traveling, I came to the conclusion that my head was well-nigh bullet-proof.

We passed through Vladimir early in the morning, when I saw the Cathedral with its five domes, which has a very imposing appearance. This is a small town, and has, I believe, fourteen churches, with several other public buildings. From one point of the road there was a pretty view of the place, with its numerous domes and towers, which gave it a very picturesque appearance. With the thermometer standing at 12° R. of frost, this was not the time to stop sketching any town, so on we galloped through snow and storm, and reached Nijne-Novgorod at nine o'clock the following morning. Having a letter to the governor, Prince Ourousoff, I determined to stay a few hours and deliver it, also to stroll through this ancient city, held in melancholy remembrance as the one where Ivan Vassilievitch the Cruel committed some of his most barbarous atrocities. Entering the lower town, I was taken to a sort of inn on the banks of the Volga; but as my stay was to be short, it mattered little what accommodation it afforded. All those travelers who expect to find a Russian host very attentive to his guests will be disappointed. My postillion led the way up stairs, and showed me a whole flat of pens or private boxes in a filthy condition, and with very little furniture: these were formed by dividing large rooms with inch and a half boards. My luggage was brought up stairs, as it could not be left with safety in the sledge. After a wash, my man succeeded in getting (with some difficulty) a breakfast. Having dispatched this meal, I got into a sledge and paid my visit to the governor, who received me with much kindness, and insisted on my dining with him. I urged the necessity of my pushing forward without delay as an excuse, but this was overruled, he assuring me that the present intense cold would prevent the roads being destroyed, and that, as I was proceeding to a colder clime, I need be under no apprehension on that score.

Being free until four o'clock, I sallied forth to stroll through the upper town, and visited some of the churches, of which there are a great number; several are very ancient, and possess considerable architectural merit. There is one that stands on the banks of the Volga—a very curious composition, which I was anxious to transfer to my sketch-book, but this was impossible. A little before the dinner-hour I again left my lodging, got into a sledge, and drove to the upper town. The wind had now increased to a gale, and it was with difficulty the man made his horse face the clouds of snow. On reaching my point of observation, I found a party of eight assembled, and, what was still more agreeable to me, the Princess Ourousoff spoke excellent English. Having spent a few pleasant hours, I returned to my dirty room, intending to get, if possible, a good night's rest, and start at daylight. At this place they provided neither bed, mattress, pillows, nor sheets; a bedstead there was with a boarded bottom, and on it I rolled myself up in my fur, and prepared for sleep. I had no sooner done this than I discovered that I had neighbors on one side of me, and by their voices I found they were of different sexes. At first they appeared to be in a very angry mood, as I supposed from the tone of their voices, which induced me to wish them on the other side of the Styx. Either I was dreadfully tired, or the chatterers became quiet, for I remember no more until roused up just at daylight; on looking out, I saw it was a clear, cold, and calm morning, a good prospect for our onward progress.

Our road was along the ice nearly all the way to Kazan, a distance of about 380 versts. Having reached the track, the four horses were turned toward the east, and away we went at a slashing pace. Temporary or winter stations are made on the banks of the river. I found them wretched and dirty, often mere hovels, into which it was loathsome to enter. After leaving Novgorod, the south bank of the Volga is in many places very abrupt, and rises 150 to 200 feet above the stream. In summer, when the trees are clothed in their varied foliage, and reflected on the broad bosom of the river, many of these scenes will be exceedingly beautiful. Station after station was passed, and still our course was onward. An exhilarating gallop brought us to one of these stations about two o'clock, where we were informed that at fifteen versts' distance we must leave the river, as the ice was unsafe for several versts beyond this point. In rather less than an hour we reached the place, when the yemstchick (driver) drove up the steep bank in an oblique direction. About thirty or forty feet below the summit the horses came to a dead stand, when our united efforts could not get us out of the difficulty. After lifting and pulling for nearly an hour without gaining a yard, the shades of evening fast coming on, I began to suspect our only hope was to send to the next station, ten versts distant, and get other horses. While the man was repairing some broken traces, the postillion and myself ascended to the top of the bank to look out for assistance, when we discovered a long caravan of sledges at a considerable distance, coming toward us; this relieved our anxiety, and just at dusk they came up, when three of their horses were unyoked, and dragged us to the summit.

Presently we again started forward, driving over a flat tableland to another part of the river. Having gone some five or six versts, I was roused up by a great shout from the two men, when we discovered that we were on the brink of a steep bank; almost instantly the horses lost all power over the machine, and down we went with fearful speed. Suddenly a great crash occurred, every square of glass was broken, out leaped my dog much alarmed, while I was driven with such force against the side of the carriage that I thought my shoulder was dislocated; the door was wrenched open by the concussion, and I sprang out into the snow, which I found very deep. On looking round I could not see either of the men, but, forcing my way to the other side of the vashock, discovered a pair of legs sticking out of the snow: getting hold of these, and tugging away for a moment, out floundered the postillion. We now looked for the driver, and discovered him lying among his horses in the deep drift; we dragged him out, and found him unhurt. Getting up the horses was a more laborious work; however, in due time they were extricated, but the vehicle was a wreck. Fortunately, we had a good stock of rope, and the two men set about repairing damages. At last the conveyance was pronounced strong enough to take us to the station. I sat down, when we were dragged slowly along in a most shattered condition, till we reached our destination, where I was detained four hours while the vashock was repaired. During the time I examined into the state of affairs inside, when, to my horror, I discovered that my two mountain barometers were broken, and other things damaged. A bad beginning the first day on the Volga! The accident had been caused by the driver going out of the track, and, to avoid the stumps of some trees, had pulled his horses sharp round over the brink of the bank, which was hidden by deep snow.

After this affair my journey along the river was smooth and agreeable, and we reached Kazan at half past four o'clock on the morning of the second day since leaving Novgorod. Having letters to the governor, General Baratinsky, and his lady, I presented them, and was very kindly received. I met several of the professors of the University, and in their company two days were most advantageously spent. The Kremlin at Kazan stands on high ground commanding the valley toward the Volga, and has a very picturesque effect when approached from the river. In 1844 nearly one half of the town was burned down, and even at this time many parts have a most desolate and wretched appearance. Several of the churches had been seriously damaged, and it was really distressing to see so many blackened skeletons of fine buildings, and heaps of ruins in other places.

I was advised to delay my journey as little as possible, as a few stages farther I should find no snow; therefore at five o'clock in the afternoon of the second day I was again *en route*, and soon met with symptoms of a rapid thaw. Indeed, so bad was the road that I was only able to travel three stations during the night. At seven o'clock in the morning I had made but sixty-nine versts in fourteen hours. While taking my breakfast it began to rain, and continued for several hours. The postillion ordered six horses to drag us over the country. I soon found we had left the road, and it was a hunt for a track the whole time. Snow was still lying in the woods, and wherever this was found our pace was increased to a gallop. Near the end of the second station I had another break-down. Ropes were again resorted to, and another hour was spent in tying up the broken limbs of the machine. While taking my tea I was joined by a traveler, a Russian officer, who, after speaking to the postillion, addressed me in German on the insecurity of my sledge. He remained with me for more than an hour, then left, promising to dine with me at the next station, where he was going, but, before leaving, gave some instructions to my man.

Again we had six horses, which took us off at a rattling pace. I began to feel great doubt as to our reaching Malmouish, the sledge was so bad; there, I felt certain, it must be left. However, at last we entered the town, when the man drove into a large yard, belonging to a very good house, which I was certain was not the station. On stepping out of the vashock, the Russian officer and an old gentleman met me, who, I was told, was the father of my new friend. They led me into the house, and shortly a good dinner was placed before the officer and myself, the family having dined before his arrival. I spent several hours with these kind people; my baggage was taken out of the vashock and packed into a kebitka, and nowhere at this place would they allow me to pay for any thing I needed. They urged me to stay a day or two, but this was impossible; I remained until midnight, when, after expressing my obligations, I was once more galloping along the road, now hard frozen. Fortunately the weather remained cold, and a heavy fall of snow, which continued for two days, rendered the road good again, though it prevented me seeing the country.

I was now on the western slopes of the Oural, and very anxious to see the chain, but in this I was disappointed, and entered Perm at half past two o'clock on the third morning after leaving Malmouish without having seen a mountain. From hence our road was over the Oural, and in twenty hours we should cross the boundary and be in Asia. We only remained here to change horses, as the master at the station said it was doubtful if we could reach Ekaterineburg in a sledge. About half past three o'clock in the morning we left Perm in a drenching rain and as dark as Erebus. How the yemstchick found his way was to me a mystery; but he did so, and at a most rapid speed. We had four horses, and traveled the twenty-five versts in an hour and a half.

The people at this station said I must leave the sledge and go on in a post-carriage on wheels; however, after a long discussion between my postillion and the men, besides a taste ot a heavy whip to give weight to his argument, six horses were at last harnessed to the sledge, and we started, the rain still pouring down, and every hour making the road worse; indeed, in many places, it was with great difficulty that the horses could drag us along. About midday we reached Coungour, celebrated for its tanneries and its thieves. Of the attainments of the latter in their particular vocation they gave me a specimen. A considerable number of men were assembled around the sledge in which I sat, but my deer-hound leaped out, and the postillion gave him some water. The horses were quickly put in. Observing that the dog evidently wished to run, I let him do so, and we started off; after going about two hundred yards, I looked for him, but could see him nowhere. In a moment the horses were stopped and turned back toward the station; still no dog was visible. Several groups of men were standing about, but they all swore, in answer to the postillion's questions, that they had not even seen the animal. At this moment I perceived two men walking off toward the back of some old buildings. My man had taken his pistol and gone in another direction. I took one of mine from the sledge, put it in my pocket, and followed quickly through some ruined wooden buildings into a large yard, surrounded by stables, where I found a third man; all three turned toward me, and said something I did not understand. Being convinced I had got on the right track, I gave a whistle, which the animal replied to, first by a whine, and then by a loud bark that directed me to his prison. I now walked toward the door; the three black-looking scoundrels stepped forward to prevent my opening it; but my two barrels suddenly pointed toward them, and the click of the lock, spoke a language they perfectly understood. Unresisted, I pushed open the door, and out bounded the deer-hound with a leathern thong on his neck. When he saw the three fellows he set up a loud growl, evidently thinking we should have a fight; but they did not attempt to bar our passage out. My man was delighted to see the dog again, and we soon turned our backs on this den of thieves. There are several stations along this part of the road notoriously bad, demanding unceasing vigilance from the traveler.

Near the end of the third station from Coungour I passed a very heavily-loaded vashock, which the horses, notwithstanding flogging, coaxing, and swearing, could scarcely move along. The evening was just drawing in when I reached the station, where, after a twelve hours' fast, I found it necessary to take some refreshment I had brought with me, as nothing but hot water can be obtained at these places. While doing this the vashock I had passed came up, and in walked an officer, two ladies, and a little boy. We made some attempts at conversation, and succeeded in a trifling degree with German. My provisions were nearly exhausted, so that I had none to offer them. I had, however, some very old "Kirschenwasser," given me by a friend to drink on the road. The ladies looked so cold, hungry, and miserable, that I could not help offering it to them as a cordial; age, perhaps, had taken off its fiery edge, for one of them drank nearly a tumbler; the gentleman also partook of it freely. He was a mining-engineer proceeding to Barnaoul.

We left them at the station, and traveled on, over frightful roads, now almost impassable; even with six horses my progress was slow. Early on the following morning we crossed the boundary into Asia, and at the first station took my breakfast—only seventy-six versts to the end of my present journey. A thick fog, with heavy rain, obscured all the country — a most unpleasant mantle. The last part of the road was fearful; we were fourteen hours traveling it. Between twelve and one o'clock on the Wednesday morning we got into Ekaterineburg, having been ten days making the journey.

After a good night's rest, I called and delivered my letter from the Minister of Finance to the chief of the Oural. His reception was most cordial, and having placed me under the care of a countryman who had been in the Russian service ten years, I felt at home, being able to talk in my own tongue. To this gentleman, and to his amiable little wife, I am indebted for many pleasing recollections of Ekaterineburg. This was the last week of the great fast, and Sunday next was Easter. The general-in-chief invited me to dine, and see the ceremony of kissing; and at his house I found some fifty officers assembled. I spent three weeks among these kind and hospitable people, acquiring much useful information respecting the regions I intended to visit. My Siberian friends reached Ekaterineburg two days later. We met frequently during my stay, and then separated, they going 2500 versts eastward, and I turning to the north, but hoping to meet again in the summer when I reached the Altai.

CHAPTER II.

IRON MINES.

THE ice on the River Tchoussowaia broke up last night: this was the signal for my departure. I started at twelve, with an officer of the mines, to Outkinskoï *Pristan* (port). The roads were very bad—in some places almost impassable. Even with five horses yoked to a very light carriage, we were five hours traveling twenty versts. We arrived at Bilimbawsky at eight o'clock, and went to the iron-works of Count Strogonoff. The director gave us a hearty welcome, and entertained us most sumptuously. His supper was good and his wine excellent. He also gave me some English porter, which I enjoyed much more than his Champagne. We spent a very pleasant evening; my two friends smoked and talked until one o'clock, and then I was taken to my sleeping apartment—the drawing-room, where I passed the night upon the same sofa on which the Emperor Alexander had rested the evening of his visit to these works.

Having slept well, I turned out early in the morning, and walked over the iron-works, with which I was greatly interested. They are well conducted, and produce a large quantity of very good metal. Our host gave us a most substantial breakfast, after which we were taken in his carriage to the pristan on the Tchoussowaia, about three versts from the iron-works, where a small boat and three men were ready to take us down the river. At this port numbers of workmen were busily engaged loading thirty-six barks with bar and sheet iron to send to the fair at Nijne-Novgorod, where they were expected to arrive in July: each carries a cargo of 9000 poods, or about 144 tons.

At nine o'clock we bade adieu to our hospitable host, stepped into the boat, and were soon floating down the stream at a great speed. The view from this part of the river is not very interesting; in most places there is forest to the water's edge on both banks, rising high on the south side, but at some distance from the river; yet the scenery is pretty in some parts. Though the sun was shining brightly, the masses of ice and snow piled up in the valley rendered the atmosphere exceedingly cold; nor were there any indications of spring. We descended the river rapidly, making the thirty versts in two hours, and arrived at Outkinskoï Pristan at eleven o'clock. This is the place where most of the barks are built to convey the produce of the Oural mines and iron-works, belonging to the crown, to Nijne-Novgorod, Moscow, and St. Petersburg. It was now a scene of great activity, there being four thousand men in this small village, brought from various places (some from villages five and six hundred versts distant), all diligently engaged in loading the vessels with guns of large dimensions, made in Kamenskoi Zavod; also with shot, shell, and other munitions of war from the different works in the South Oural, destined for Sevastopol and the forts on the Black Sea. These munitions of war are made with great care and accuracy under the superintendence of very intelligent artillery officers.

The barks are built on the bank of the Tchoussowaia with their sides to the stream; they are flat-bottomed, with straight sides 125 feet long, have a breadth of twenty-five feet, and are from eight to nine feet deep; the head and stern are formed by a sort of obtuse angle, the ribs of birch-trees selected for the purpose, and the planking of deal: there is not a nail or an iron bolt in them, they being put together with wooden pins; and they must be built the year before they are launched. The decks are formed with strong boards framed together, but not fastened to the bark; a precaution absolutely necessary, as they are often sunk in deep water after striking the rocks. When this happens, the deck floats, by which the men are saved. Each bark, whose cargo has a weight of 9000 poods, requires thirty-five men to direct it; and one with a cargo of 10,000 poods has a crew of forty men. Oars, usually of forty-five to fifty feet long, with strong and broad blades, guide it at the head and stern, and a man stands upon a raised platform in the middle to look out and direct its course.

I saw several of these vessels launched: it was a curious spectacle. On the top of the craft there were about twelve men; two gave, or rather sang, the words of command, which was followed by the others. About 400 men and numbers of women stood ready with long poles to push the vessel toward the stream, which was done most lustily, all singing a chorus, and each verse bringing the vessel nearer the water. The first I saw launched occupied more than three hours, much of the physical force of the operators having been spent in singing.

Launching a Bark on the Tchoussowaia.

On the 15th of April there was an earthquake at forty minutes past twelve o'clock at noon, which caused a great sensation throughout the Oural, although no damage was done. A large boat had been built for me at the pristan, and was to have a crew of five men and a boy. Unfortunately, there was a marked change in the weather; we had rain and a strong wind, which caused a great flood, that swept large masses of ice down the river at a fearful speed, producing much confusion and anxiety at the port, as the barks were in danger of being cut through by the blocks of ice as they floated past. Not far from the government pristan I saw seven belonging to a merchant in Ekaterineburg, laden with tallow, and ready to float down the Tchoussowaia to the River Kama, and two were seriously damaged by the ice. I received an invitation, which I accepted, to go on board and see the priest bless them before starting on their voyage. I found the ceremony highly interesting, and it was attended to with much solemnity by every person on board. After this the company began feasting on the various good things provided by the merchant. The *wodky* (brandy) soon performed its part, for in an hour they had forgotten their toil, and were embracing each other with the fervor of brothers after twenty years' separation.

The flood having subsided, the storm of wind, snow, and rain was followed by a bright sunny morning, which induced me to hasten my departure. The water had risen 6 feet 4 inches higher than since 1830, and much damage had ensued. My friends at the pristan provisioned me, and added some bottles of Madeira and rum, believing it probable we might have a storm that would compel us to seek shelter in the woods. Having thanked my hospitable host and wife, I stepped into the boat; my crew, by direction of the steersman, offered up a prayer for our safe voyage down this rocky and rapid river; this ended, they pulled out into the stream, and we were soon floating with the current at a great speed. From information I had received, I did not expect to find much fine scenery for the first twenty-five or thirty versts; still, there were some parts very pretty; indeed, if this river were in England, every point of it would be sketched.

The valley for the first twenty versts is not wide; on one side the hills rise from the stream, but not abruptly; they are covered with a pine forest to their summit, but the trees are small. On the opposite bank there is meadow-land—at least such it appears, although no cattle graze there excepting near the villages, and these are very far apart. We traveled thirty and forty versts without seeing even a cottage. On this low land there are fine clumps of pine and birch trees, often so beautifully arranged that I fancied they had been planted with the greatest care; Nature alone, however, has been the landscape gardener. I was told there were many elks in these valleys, but saw none, nor did I make any attempt to get at them, it being impossible at this season to penetrate the forests, as the mountain streams are pouring down with great fury. Bears are also numerous, which I do not wonder at, for they are never disturbed, the inhabitants in these parts being few in number. There are many places containing thousands of acres, upon which it is probable man has never set his foot. In summer it would be impossible to penetrate these gloomy forests, on account of the extensive morasses, which no one would dare to cross; and in winter, the certainty of being frozen to death in these wilds is a sufficient check upon any daring spirit.

In some places I passed masses of rock most curiously thrown up and broken, affording abundant proof that at some very remote period volcanic agency had been at work. In many parts the strata, which had once been horizontal, were now turned up, and curved into most extraordinary forms, and other substances forced

Jasper and Limestone.

through them. I saw in the limestone rocks several apparently large caverns, but it was impossible to enter them in the then state of the flood. Had our boat touched the rocks, she would have gone to pieces in a minute, and no one would have been left to tell the tale.

We had been nine hours on the river, and had descended about thirty-five versts, and it was now dark and snowing fast. On turning a mass of rock I distinguished a light from a furnace in the forest: we pushed on, and soon came to a small stream, and at the distance of a verst I beheld the iron-works. Our boat was turned to enter this torrent, as it proved to be, but we found it impossible to ascend with the oars. The men, therefore, landed, and, having obtained assistance, hauled the boat up the stream with a rope, which was not effected without some difficulty; at last we came to a part that stopped our progress. Here I jumped ashore, and my steersman walked with me to the house of the director.

After a walk of about twenty minutes, almost up to the knees in mud and water, I was taken into a yard and shown at my request the door of the director's house. Door I ought not to call it, for it was not more than four feet high by two feet six wide. Thinking the man had made a mistake, or had misunderstood me, I turned round and repeated my question. "Dome Nachalnik?" he exclaimed, still pointing to the door; so in I went, regardless of pitfalls, and found the place so dark that I could see nothing. I began to feel for a door. At last I heard some voices, and, walking toward the sound, reached another room, the sole occupant of which proved to be a large dog, who began to bark and growl furiously.

This seemed to rouse up the family, as a woman opened another door, which let in some light from the lamp, and then I found that I was in a Russian bed-room: to retreat was useless, so I put a good face on the matter and went forward. What the woman thought of my intrusion it is impossible to say; however, her husband quickly appeared, and then I handed him my papers, which at once procured me every attention.

I had at last found the director of the works. He sent men with a horse and cart to bring my luggage up to his house, and very shortly a boy brought me some hot tea and preserved fruit. When my things arrived I got a pair of dry boots; the other clothing I could not change, as the good lady kept passing in and out of the room every minute.

Through one of the doorways I observed some six or seven pairs of eyes twinkling and staring at me, wondering, no doubt, what sort of animal it was that had invaded their quiet abode. After a sight of their little faces, I determined to establish myself in the good opinion of the mother by making friends with the children. I succeeded in persuading one little boy to come forward. She then left the room, returning in a few minutes with her youngest son, whom I presently tossed in my arms, to the great astonishment of the family and the gratification of the mother.

Conversation beyond a few words could not be attempted, as I was obliged to resort to my Russian and English dictionary every few minutes, and this made it exceedingly tedious; however, all went on well and in good humor. About ten o'clock they began to set out a table, and in due time supper appeared. I was placed at the head of the table, the good man at one side, and I naturally expected his amiable spouse would take a seat opposite to me, instead of which she walked to the end of the room and sat down; but, having refused to partake of their hospitality unless she would sit by us, the lady was induced to make one of the party, after which every thing went on well. To describe the dishes would be useless; I can only say that some of them were very good—at least I thought so after the sharp, frosty blast I had encountered. My host placed several sorts of wine on the table, and both he and his wife urged me to eat and drink.

In Siberia, each good housewife makes from the wild fruit, of which there is a great variety, several sorts of *nalifka* (cordial). A bottle of this was produced, and a glass of it handed to me; it was the color of claret, but the flavor vastly superior. I took a second glass, to their particular satisfaction. Immediately four other bottles of different sorts were ordered in, from all of which I was obliged to drink a "wee drap" during supper; and most delicious nailifkas they were. Finally, as a finish to our repast, my host brought in a bottle of Champagne and *two* glasses on a tray, evidently intending that he and I should drink it alone; but here I was forced to disappoint him, for, as soon as he had filled a bumper for me, I could not help presenting it to his wife, evidently to her great surprise and pleasure. Another glass was brought for me, and we then very deliberately proceeded to finish the bottle.

When this was disposed of, I thought all concluded for the

night, but was mistaken; my hostess left the room, presently returning with other varieties of Siberian liquors, all of which she insisted on my tasting: this, with them, means finishing a glass; I had no sooner taken one than she had another ready. At last I got through the tasting process, or, at least, supposed that I had; but judge my astonishment when my host walked in with another bottle of Champagne, which, in spite of all opposition, my friends compelled me to join in drinking. I was then provided with a sofa to sleep on, and turned in for the night.

At seven o'clock next morning a boy brought me tea and bread, of which I partook; I then went with my host to the iron-works. Bar iron in large quantities is made here, and is sent in barks to the Kama. Having spent three hours in looking over the works, I returned to breakfast. Tea formed no part of this meal: it was Siberian fare—fish-pasty, meat, several sorts of game, and tarts made of preserved wild strawberries, with plenty of their excellent nalifka; and it finished with a bottle of Champagne.

All the children were brought into the room to wish me a safe voyage. I felt it necessary to say something to each—the daughter twelve years old, the others, boys, varying from a baby to a lad of nine years. I presented to the girl one of my illustrated English books, and wrote my name in it to satisfy all hands: this will be preserved with great care, and most probably handed down to the next generation. The whole family sat down, and I followed their example: two or three minutes were spent, as I supposed, in silent prayer, and then all rose up. My host advanced and kissed me three times; I then kissed his wife's hand, and she my cheek: similar salutations were exchanged between myself, the daughter, and boys, all of whom I kissed most heartily. I am sure I left this family on the strongest terms of friendship. I then renewed my journey. My host told me that himself and a friend were going three versts down the Tchoussowaia, if I would take them in the boat. I was glad of the opportunity to oblige him, and off we started. We had not proceeded more than two versts when he ordered my boy to give him the glasses and a bottle. It is only necessary to add that the Champagne flowed again. His sledge was waiting on the bank of the river, and his only object in going with me was to show his hospitality. My friends landed, got into the sledge, and returned home.

After passing Outkinskoï, I found the rocks on one side of the river very high and craggy; in one part there were two large caverns in the face of the rock, about one hundred feet above the water. I called to the boatmen "*Stoi!*" (Stop!), that I might ex-

Entrance to a Cavern.

amine them. Although they immediately obeyed, the stream was so strong it forced us past, and, notwithstanding all their efforts, we could not pull back to the place. At last they succeeded in putting me ashore lower down, where I began to climb over the rocks, hoping to reach the caverns. After an hour's hard labor and some tumbles, I was compelled to give it up, as I found ropes and ladders were indispensable to enable me to scale the rocky parapet. I dared not attempt the slippery ledges close to the boiling flood; it would have been certain destruction. What these caverns contain I can not tell; I did not expect to find either gold or precious stones, but something in their dark recesses on which I might employ my pencil, and I left the place with great reluctance. Again I noticed most singular contortions in the strata—some forced up in curves, others in triangles; and some rose almost perpendicular, giving great variety and picturesque beauty to these wild gorges.

A snow-storm, that continued for several hours, prevented my sketching many of the scenes I passed, which I much regretted, as they are interesting from being named after some of the celebrated Tartar chiefs, "men terrible in battle." After a very cold and unpleasant voyage, we arrived at Chaitanskoï Pristan at half past seven o'clock. There I found some friends from Verkne Issetzskoï, by whom I was most cordially welcomed. They were engaged dispatching the barks to Nijne-Novgorod with the produce of their several iron-works. About three hours before I arrived six poor men were drowned in attempting to cross the river in a small boat, and although several hundred people saw the accident, they could render no assistance. Shortly afterward, at a point two versts farther down the river, another accident occurred. A little before eight o'clock the church bell began to ring most violently, which induced me to think it was an alarm of fire; both men and women, carrying small poles in their hands and running fast, were making for the scene of danger or misfortune. It appeared, however, that, instead of a fire, an accident had happened to one of the large barks laden with iron, which had struck on a rock and sunk immediately, excepting the deck part, that floated and saved the crew.

From the window at which I am now sitting I can see the higher ridge of the Oural, covered with snow. Though only seven versts distant, it would require a day to ascend it on horseback. Had it been possible, I should have gone there; but the streams dashing from the mountains forbade such an attempt at this season of the year.

CHAPTER III.

EXCURSIONS ON THE TCHOUSSOWAIA.

ALL was prepared for my departure at eight o'clock this morning, but a great snow-storm approaching from the higher region of the Oural, I was told that I must on no account leave till this had passed. It was well I remained, as it commenced to blow most furiously, and the snow fell so thick that we could not have descried objects a boat's length before us. The storm continued without intermission until past three, when the weather cleared up. I then determined to walk along the north bank of the river, and take a sketch of some fine rocky masses about a verst distant; but in this I was disappointed. I had proceeded a short distance only, when the snow-storm began again with redoubled vigor, which compelled me to seek shelter in the nearest dwelling. I turned back and entered a respectable cottage, where I found two women, who treated me with extreme kindness. It was difficult to make them understand a word of my Russian; however, I suppose the storm spoke for me. When they had given me a seat, one of them brought some preserved fruit and a plate of small nuts, which I was entreated to eat: the nuts were from the Siberian cedar, and are much liked here. After remaining two hours and the storm moderating, I thanked these kind people and hastened back to my quarters, as I saw that we should have a stormy night.

I crossed the Tchoussowaia to the east bank, telling the men to follow me up the stream with the boat; I then walked on, and in about half an hour arrived at a fine rocky gorge; the precipices on either side are limestone broken into very beautiful forms, with small pine and larch trees growing from the fissures. Here I sketched two views, each displaying some curious geological features.

My companions, having come up, rowed me across the river, and I continued my walk along the bank about six versts. Here I sketched another beautiful scene—a splendid mass of limestone, with the river rushing past its base, and nearly filling up a cavern in the rocks, which, as I am informed, can be entered in summer when the water is low. These scenes must be exceedingly beautiful in June and July, when the shrubs and flowers of numerous species are in bloom. After great labor, my men succeeded in hauling the boat to this place; farther they could not go, as the rocks rose up 100 to 150 feet nearly perpendicular on both sides of the river, and the water rushed through the gorge with extraordinary force. Seating myself in the boat and pointing up the river, the crew began to pull in good earnest, but our progress was very slow, and it soon became evident that it was utterly impossible to propel the boat against the rapid current of the narrow passage. With all our efforts, we had only ascended the river about fifteen versts in eleven hours, but we glided down to the pristan in less than an hour. While eating my dinner, I was told that a gentleman had been waiting for me several hours; that he had just gone out, and would return in a quarter of an hour. I could not imagine who this could be; however, the mystery vanished when my kind and hospitable host of Outkinskoï walked into the room. He had heard that I was weather-bound at Chaitanskoï, and determined to see me once more, even if he could not induce me to return to his house. He urged me strongly and in the most friendly manner to accompany him, promising to send me back in a boat with a crew of five men who would stop at any point I directed. I readily availed myself of his kindness, as it would enable me to sketch the scenes I had passed through in the storm. We started a little before eight o'clock to ride through a Siberian or Ouralian forest, as this part of the Tchoussowaia is in Europe. My friend's tarantass was a light carriage placed on four wheels, and four long poles which rest on the axle-trees; thus it is rendered elastic (patent axles and springs would be useless in this region). To make it more comfortable, a quantity of straw was put into the bottom, covered with a rug, and several pillows were placed at the back.

To this machine we had six horses, four yoked to it, managed by a driver sitting in front, while a boy had charge of the two leaders. The speed at which we started was kept up through the village to the foot of a steep hill, where commenced the toils of a forest drive. A more wild and gloomy road I had never entered upon. The first hour we had daylight, and then a dusky twilight, gradually shading into darkness, crept over every thing. In some parts of our road I saw magnificent pine trees, that might be called giants of the forest: there they stood in all their vigor and strength, bidding defiance to the storm; others were observed which, like these, had once equally defied the tempest, but now showed the marks of lightning in their shattered limbs, which trembled with every blast. Hundreds lay around in all stages of decay, convincing proofs of the ravages of time, while young plants and saplings were growing of every age, from a seedling to a tree.

Our pace was almost reduced to a walk in consequence of the darkness, which had been increased by the dense character of the forest. At times I could see neither the men nor the horses; all around was shrouded in impenetrable gloom. On looking upward, I could just perceive, through the dim obscurity, gnarled and twisted branches extending over us, looking like huge serpents ready to seize their prey. About ten o'clock the moon rose slowly, and shed her silvery light over wood and glen, giving the different objects in one direction a spectral appearance; while to our right, where her rays touched the summits of the rugged crags, a deeper shade settled along their base. As the light became stronger, our drivers pushed on their horses, and soon we were going at a great speed along a more even track. Suddenly a man rode out from a dark mass of rock directly toward us, which caused the drivers to stop our vehicle. My host said something to the man, which caused him to gallop away at full speed, and the clatter of his horse's hoofs was soon lost in the distance. He was my friend's servant, ordered to be waiting about half way, that he might speed on and announce our approach, that supper might be ready for us on our arrival. The latter part of our journey was slow and over very rugged ground. Despite all the care taken by our drivers, we had some narrow escapes; twice we were nearly tumbled out; and in one case, had we actually turned over, we should have been precipitated into a very deep glen; but incidents like these are common enough in these wild regions. At a quarter past twelve o'clock I again entered the hospitable dwelling of my Russian friend, whose wife, daughter, and servants rivaled each other in giving me a warm welcome.

I walked out early the next morning, and observed a boat preparing for me, and at ten o'clock left my kind friends, although they used every means to induce me to remain a few days. We had a bright sunny morning, quite warm, which made every thing look gay, and gave a warm tone to the forest scenes. When I had got into my boat, the men plied their oars well, and sent the little shallop rapidly along. All at once the wind began to roar as it rushed through the narrow valley, a certain harbinger of a coming storm. "No morning sun lasts a whole day." The sun was soon obscured, and dark clouds came rolling over the hills, pouring down rain and sleet, which almost blinded us. We pulled up and got into shelter under some large pines—a poor protection against the icy blast, which made us all shiver. After waiting more than an hour, my crew urged me to go on, as the storm would continue all day. They were right. When we arrived in Chaitanskoï we were completely drenched, and almost frozen with sitting eight hours in an open boat. Again my wishes had been frustrated.

At four o'clock this morning the thermometer stood at 15° R., with a keen cutting wind from the north. I had been told that some magnificent scenery might be met with near one of the mountain torrents, about ten versts distant, which could only be reached by walking over the mountain. An Ouralian hunter having consented to be my guide, I started at five o'clock to penetrate the forest: road or track there was none. We descended, in the first place, the bank of the Tchoussowaia about a verst, then began the ascent of a very steep and rugged hill toward the north: this was a work of difficulty, and occupied two hours. Here we observed both new and old snow, in some places very deep. My guide pointed out the ravine to which we were going, which appeared distant not more than a verst, but we found that this was the most laborious part of our walk. The snow often broke through with us, and many times we were to the middle in the upper crust, and as frequently floundering about among fallen trees, half buried in the snow.

At times I almost feared we must give in, but my English spirit said No, and on I went, determined not to be beat by my woodsman; besides, I had good reason to think that my friends in Ilimskoï supposed that no one but a Russian or Ouralian could accomplish the journey at this time of the year. I did, however, and was not disappointed in the scenery. I came to a deep and narrow gorge, formed most probably when the Oural was upheaved; the rocks have been rent asunder, and dolomite peaks are forced into rugged and picturesque forms. Occasionally a torrent of water pours through this ravine, which must add much to its grandeur; at this time there was scarcely any thing of a stream, the frost having closed up the supply; but later in the day, when the snow is melting on the mountains, the water will come down in a perfect flood; from two o'clock until eight o'clock its roar will be tremendous.

Having made a sketch and collected some shells from the limestone rocks, we began to retrace our steps, which we found much more difficult, as the snow was already very soft. This compelled us to seek another route through a more dense part of the forest, not yet touched by the sun's rays. After a most fatiguing walk, we arrived at the village at one o'clock, to the great astonishment of my friends, who never expected that I should succeed.

I decided to remain a day or two in Ilimskoï and sketch several fine scenes on the river; to some I must walk, to others go in my boat. On one of these excursions up the river I noticed a remarkable change in my men, and that my orders were obeyed with great reluctance; this induced me to watch their conduct more closely. The result was the discovery of a mutiny on board my little craft, having for its chief the servant-boy, who seemed to have imbibed the idea that, as I understood little of their language, he could direct the men. During my stay in Ilimskoï I had made a small map of the river, with the names of all the villages, and had marked those at which I ought to stop for the night. For some cause unknown to me, the lad had decided with the boatmen that they should stop at other places, which probably they liked better, supposing this could easily be done without my knowledge. I was not slow in showing him that the best-conceived plans will sometimes fail.

There are some remarkable rocky scenes between Chaitanskoï Pristan and Ilimskoï; the limestone rocks are broken and twisted into every variety of form, rising in many parts 300 or 400 feet in height.

In some places the strata are forced into a vertical position, with jagged peaks. The following view shows one of these disruptions, to which has been given the name of the *Four Brothers*, after some celebrated robbers who (as the people say) once lived in a large cavern near these rocks.

The Robbers, or Four Brothers.

Ilimskoï is a small village, pleasingly situated at a sweep of the river, where another stream, after winding through a rocky valley, joins the Tchoussowaia. In summer, when the birch and aspens are in full leaf, with wild flowers growing among the rocks from every cleft, and flowering shrubs in blossom, this little spot would, no doubt, be beautiful. Now it is one where much care is necessary to avoid being swallowed up in its mud and water; even the cattle have great difficulty in dragging their legs out of the mud pools.

When we arrived here the first evening it was near dusk, and I tried some of these pools on my walk from the boat to the house of the first man in the village. On entering his dwelling I was not impressed with a very favorable idea of the domestic management. The sight of two not particularly cleanly-looking women past the bloom of youth somewhat impaired my admiration of the sex. Each of them was nursing a child, and the two children appeared far too advanced for such indulgence. Then came into the room mine host, of whom I desired to know if he would be kind enough to give me quarters for the night. He seemed rather surprised at my request, and said something to one of the females which I did not understand. She left the room, and returned in a few minutes with a young girl, who was also one of the nursing mothers; then followed two other women-servants and a man, who flanked the party.

All stood looking at me with a broad stare of astonishment, evidently wondering how I could venture to ask their lord and master to give me a night's lodging. I had given the gentleman my papers, on which he, having read, rose, made me a very polite bow, took my hand, and led me to a sofa. He then gave his orders in a very decided tone, when all scampered off, a new light having evidently burst upon them. In about a quarter of an hour I was shown into a small room, where I changed my wet garments. During this necessary operation I found that I could not consider the room entirely private, for one of the damsels, having opened a door, stood gazing at me. Having finished my toilet as well as I could do in the presence of scrutinizing eyes, I hurried to my host.

I might with truth call him a great man, not so much in stature as in vast circumference. He seemed, however, to have much good-nature in his composition, and was most urgent in inducing me to drink a large quantity of tea with rum to counteract the bad effects of the wet, which had been so liberally applied externally. When tea was ended, his wife came into the room; in size she proved to be a good match for her husband; indeed, such *a* pair I had never seen before. I was presented to her in due form, after which supper was served, which I found excellent. We sat sipping Ouralian wine and trying to talk until twelve o'clock, and then separated, mutually satisfied, I believe, with each other.

Having sketched the most interesting and picturesque scenes around Ilimskoï, I wanted to depart, but my host and hostess would not consent to my leaving their hospitable dwelling so soon. My colored sketches were examined by them, and as they recognized the views on the river, they were greatly interested. Shortly before dinner the old gentleman came to me with a small silver cup in his hand, and insisted on my accepting it as a token of his esteem. At the same time his wife brought me a netted comforter for my neck—the work of her own hands! It was plain enough that to refuse these little tokens would give pain; I could do no less, therefore, than accept them. After dinner the mistress of the house took my arm and accompanied me to the boat, which was waiting to bear me from them; we were followed by her husband and his daughters, also by the nurses with the other children. Having bid them a last farewell, I sat down in my boat and pushed off into the stream, the women waving their handkerchiefs, and the men-servants firing a salute of musketry.

I descended the river for about an hour and a half, when I came to a splendid scene. The stream runs winding through a limestone gorge, in which cliffs of every varied form rise 400 feet,

Curious Rocks on the Tchoussowaia.

some resembling the ruins of old castles, their deep chasms separating other masses of peculiar shape. In other parts the rocks are perpendicular, extending regularly along the water side like a wall; elsewhere in the same vicinity I found them broken in huge masses, like buttresses supporting the ruins of some former world.

Among these precipices there are many large caverns, some extending far into the mountains, and branching off into different galleries. I explored one of these by the aid of pine torches carried by two of my men, and found the entrance not more than fifteen feet high and eight feet wide. At about thirty feet from the external opening the cavern extended into a circular room twenty-eight feet in diameter, and apparently forty-five to fifty feet to the top of the dome: I could not perceive any stalactites. A narrow opening led the way farther into the rocks. I followed this about one hundred feet, which brought me to an aperture that rose nearly perpendicular from where I stood, till lost in gloom which our feeble lights failed to penetrate. About twenty feet above me there were two apertures leading in different directions, but these I could not enter without other aid.

About a verst lower down the river I explored another cavern: the external opening was small, and the gallery low and narrow. Taking four men with me, and each of us having a bundle of long pieces of split pine, we entered the narrow gallery extending into the mountain about 120 paces, when it opened into a cavern very irregular in form, but of large dimensions, and branched off in two directions. We turned into the left branch, which in some places was eight, and in others twelve paces wide, and about forty or fifty feet high. This terminated in a large cleft almost filled up with fallen rocks, that stopped our further progress. The floor was perfectly dry, and this portion was 143 paces long. I now turned into the right branch, and found it much larger; in some parts the width was twenty paces, in others considerably more. With our lights I could not see the roof. We went on about 300 paces farther, and then found the floor covered with fallen blocks of limestone, some of large size. Huge buttresses jutted from the sides of the cavern, forming deep recesses; these I examined, but found no openings. After scrambling over the fallen rocks, we reached a smooth floor; here the width was about nine paces: it was a cleft in the mountain, with a sharp angular roof. A little beyond this point it turned to the right, and ended in a narrow chasm, down which came tumbling a small waterfall, our light making the spray sparkle like diamonds. The chasm was very deep; I threw in several stones, and could hear them bound from side to side for several seconds. This point is between 500 and 600 paces from the entrance. I found neither stalactites nor animal remains: the floors are dry limestone.

Not far below these caverns I found a mass of rock under which a man was buried when it fell from the high pine-fringed cliffs above. It is a solitary spot, well suited to such a tragic event. At the foot of the cliffs there is a small plot of fine green sward, and in the middle stands the fatal stone that first crushed its vic-

Rocky Tomb.

tim deep into his grave, and now remains immovable as his monument. This place is seldom visited: the bear and the wolf rest here unmolested.

I had plenty of employment for my pencil to-day, having met with many attractive scenes. Pulling the boat ashore, my traps were taken out and carried a short distance into the forest to some large pine-trees, where they were piled up to keep off the cold blast. A large fire was soon kindled, which rendered our berth exceedingly comfortable. Presently the singing of the tea-kettle was heard above the crackling of the logs, and in due course followed a most appetizing repast, to which a basket of cold game, placed in the boat by my thoughtful friends, largely contributed.

After this I took my rifle, and rambled into the forest to some distance from our encampment, but found no game. I, however, beheld what was more agreeable to me, flowers pushing through the thick brown grass—the first indications I had met with of spring, and I hailed them with delight.

My crew, having also enjoyed themselves, were singing merrily. I listened for a while to their songs, then wrote up my journal by the light of our blazing fire, drank off a goblet of Ouralian wine, wrapped myself in my cloak, and, lying down with my feet toward the glowing embers, passed away into the land of dreams.

At dawn of day I awoke, thoroughly refreshed after my first night's sleep in the open air. My people were lying round the fire, evidently enjoying peaceful slumbers. I picked up a log and threw it on the embers; this roused them, and in a few minutes they were all in motion. A part of them commenced making up the fire, one started with the kettle to the river for water, and another began spreading my tea-things on the brown sward. My breakfast was soon ready; it did not detain me long, and I returned to the boat.

From this point I found the river had lost its rugged character; it was now winding through a forest of pines, birches, and aspens, which grew to the water's edge. In many parts thick masses of underwood covered the ground, extending apparently for many miles up the mountain sides. Toward noon we stopped for dinner, and then pushed on up a mountain torrent. Having walked along the bank more than an hour, and found no point worth sketching, I returned to my boat, and again descended the stream.

At eight o'clock we arrived at Outkinska-Demidoff, a pristan belonging to the works at Tagilsk, where the whole produce of

Demidoff's mines is put on board the barks, and forwarded to Nijne-Novgorod and St. Petersburg.

At this port the valley of the Tchoussowaia extends from two to three versts in width. On the west bank of the river there is a considerable extent of meadow-land; on the eastern side the land is partly cultivated, and a fine crop of rye was springing up. This is a warm and sheltered situation, having high wooded hills to the north, which keep off the cold and cutting blasts from that quarter. The meadows looked beautifully green, and were already adorned with many flowers, and the birch-trees bursting into leaf every hour. The change in this region from winter to summer is so rapid that it seems almost magical. Last night, for example, I slept on grass browned by the frost, under trees showing no buds; to-night I could take up my quarters beneath birches half in leaf, and awake to-morrow morning under a splendid green canopy.

The change is so delightful, I have already decided to spend to-morrow (Sunday) at this place.

This is a glorious morning—a bright sun, and a sky without a cloud, while a gentle breeze is wafting the sweet scents from the larch and birch trees, now almost in full leaf. Still I see in the distance large masses of snow stretching along the mountain sides, and extending down into the forests, which tell me winter is not yet past. The Outka is a small mountain stream flowing into the Tchoussowaia at this place. I determined to take a long walk up its banks, toward the mountains, as this would take me in the direction of the higher ridge of the Oural. The small open valley in which the little stream winds its course extends northward about two versts, and is then lost in the forest.

Along this valley my walk was exceedingly agreeable. I found many flowers quite new to me, and collected specimens for drying. Having entered the forest, there was a great change: large patches of snow were lying under the trees, and in some places the remains of drifts covered up the brook, giving a very wintry appearance to the scene. I was soon plunged to the knees in a morass; and, getting out of it, gave up my morning ramble. These valleys can only be examined later in the summer, when the snow has melted and the water has drained off.

I returned to the pristan by another path, and gathered other flowers to add to my collection. I had not been long in my room when the men came in a body, and begged me to go down the river about fifteen versts this afternoon, and then stay over night. The spokesman of the party said I should find excellent quarters at that distance, and every thing I could desire; besides which, our voyage on Monday would be a very long one. The reason assigned had great weight with me; and, being anxious to arrive early in the morning at a part of the river which had been described as the best scenery on the Tchoussowaia, I consented to go on. We left Outkinska-Demidoff at five o'clock, dropping slowly down the river, no interesting scenery presenting itself on the way. At seven o'clock we reached Kageka.

My steersman and the boy went with me to a large house about one hundred paces from the river, into which, after a little delay, we gained admittance. I was taken into a spacious room by my chief man, who left me to seek the owner of the apartment I had thus taken possession of. The room contained four or five chairs, a long bench placed against the wooden wall, a large table covered with papers, and a strong arm-chair on one side of the table, across which lay a pipe long enough for the Grand Turk. The room was dirty, heated to 25° R., and redolent of any thing but roses.

After sitting a few minutes, three women of Amazonian proportions passed through the room. I had just time to notice that their garments were what might be called scant, scarcely reaching to the knees. In fact, the dress of each consisted of one "cutty-sark," as Tam O'Shanter would have called it, with a blue body over; add to this a red handkerchief tied on the head, and the costume is complete. The door into the adjoining room was left open, so that I could see the movements of these very stately persons, and have them within call; but, as I had no particular desire to follow their motions or claim their assistance I remained quiet.

In about half an hour my man returned with the master of the house, to whom I handed my papers, which he examined. I requested permission to pass the night under his roof, to which he consented, and, seating himself beside me, called to the women to bring in tea: this was instantly done, leading me to think that it had been prepared immediately after my arrival. A friend of my host's, who had just dropped in, joined our tea-party, and between us three glass after glass disappeared from the board. The tea-drinking continued a long time, which gave my two companions the opportunity of putting a series of questions, few of which I could understand. They talked very fast, however, and I listened attentively, saying ("*Dah!*" "*Neate!*") Yes or No, in Russian, as the case appeared to require. At length I got tired of this, and began an oration in English, speaking as fast as I could, by which I got the advantage, for they ceased immediately. But the moment I left off addressing the chair, one or other began to catechise me again. As a last resort, I was driven to try some snatches of poetry, which fairly silenced them.

About ten o'clock supper was announced as ready for us in another room. I was taken through a bed-room to the supper-table, and in passing beheld one of the bare-legged females stretched full-length on the floor, covered up for the night. On coming to the table, one of these damsels placed before us a large basin of soup and three spoons, intimating that *I* must try my luck in the same dish. I could endure hunger for a long time, could eat black bread and salt without difficulty, but take broth with my two friends from the *same* soup-bowl I could not. The next course—a great number of boiled eggs—suited me better; from these I managed to make a good supper. My companions drank a large quantity of *wodky*, and tried to induce me to follow their example, but I declined. Leaving them, I went to my room, where I found nothing better to sleep on than a wooden bench. I, however, was used to hard fare and hard beds, and content with whatever turned up.

I was up at half past four o'clock this morning, had one cup of tea, without either bread or milk, and at five o'clock was floating down the river, which here winds through a more open valley, with meadow-land along its banks. At twelve we reached another gorge, through which the river runs, in some places very rapidly. On one side of the entrance into this rocky scene a small plot of level land extends along the water, about 300 yards by about 25 yards wide, from the latter to the forest, where it rises very abruptly in broken masses of rock, covered with flowering shrubs and bushes. There are also larches, pines, and birches growing out of the clefts. On the opposite side of the river, rocky masses rise from the water to a great height, nearly perpendicular, their summits crowned with a fine growth of the pine and birch.

Near the centre of this little glade stands a simple cross, raised on three steps, which excites at once the curiosity of the traveler. It was erected to mark the site on which the great-grandfather of the present Prince Demidoff first saw the light. His mother, on

Demidoff's Birth-place.

her way down the River Tchoussowaia, in a bark, along with those which were conveying the produce of the mines to Russia, was prevailed on to encamp here for the night. Perhaps a more appropriate spot could not have been found for the birth-place of one who was destined to become, in after years, a powerful agent in the development of the mineral wealth of these vast regions.

A strip ot canvas sheltered the new-born infant, and protected alike the mother and her child from the inclemency of the season. It was he who subsequently, by superior genius and indefatigable industry, left imperishable monuments of his greatness in the different works established by him in many parts of the Oural.

While I was sketching this scene, my men were tapping the birch-trees and drawing off the sap. Having finished my labors, I sat down on a rock, and my steersman brought me a piece of black bread with a little salt, and a bottle of sap drawn from a tree near the cross—a sweeter morsel or a better draught I thought I had never tasted.

We continued our voyage, and in about an hour I stopped to sketch another fine scene—some isolated masses of rock standing in the bed of the river. This was the last of twenty-eight sketches I had made on the Tchoussowaia. While at work I observed that there were +18° R. in the shade at half past two o'clock—a wonderful change within the last few days. After descending the stream, now running through a thickly-wooded forest, we arrived at Cynowskoï Zavod, iron-works belonging to Count Strogonoff. Here I found excellent quarters in the house of a gentleman who spoke German, with whom I spent a most agreeable evening.

The earthquake which occurred on the 15th of April was felt severely at these works. A terrible growling sound, like subterranean thunder at a great depth under ground, was instantly followed by a violent motion of the earth, causing great alarm to every one. I was told that the horses trembled as it passed.

It was from this Zavod, and under the protection of the Strogonoffs, who then possessed nearly all this region, that Yermak the Cossack commenced his expedition for the conquest of Siberia. His battle-fields are on the other side of the Oural; but it was at this place, and in the caravans on the Tchoussowaia, that he found a safe retreat after his first defeats in Asia.

During the night the water in the Tchoussowaia had risen three feet, caused by the snow melting so rapidly yesterday, and apparently it will be still warmer to-day. I was induced to remain and visit the works in this Zavod. A great quantity of wire, both strong and fine, is drawn here, which produces a very good price in the fair at Novgorod on account of its superior quality. Bar iron is also made. After visiting the iron mines we returned to the house of my host, and sat down to an excellent dinner, well cooked and well served. It would be impossible in England to give the different varieties of game placed on the table. We had also English porter, Scotch ale, and Champagne, with several sorts of Ouralian wine; of the last I tasted one kind for the first time made from cedar-nuts: it equaled the best Maraschino.

A great change had taken place in the weather: at four o'clock there were $-5°$ R. with a strong wind; at five I left the Zavod, and away we went at a good speed down the river. It was exceedingly cold, with dark clouds rolling over the tops of the mountains; in less than half an hour we had a tremendous snow-storm, which gave to every thing a winter clothing, and rendered my last day's voyage on the Tchoussowaia cold and unpleasant. After sitting nine hours in an open boat, the snow falling the whole time, we arrived at Oslanskoï at two o'clock in the morning. Such are the changes of temperature in this region, and I am told this will not be the last of the winter.

The river has a most tortuous course, winding about among the mountains in a very singular manner. It has happened to me more than once that, after descending it sixty or seventy versts, I have found, on inquiry, that the place I started from in the morning was not more than sixteen or twenty versts distant across the mountains. Having finished my voyage on the Tchoussowaia, my men were obliged to return home. I parted with them on excellent terms; a few rubles had rendered them happy, and kissing my hand, they all declared they would go any where with me. At three o'clock I left Oslanskoï in a carriage; the road, passing through a thick forest, was bad, owing to the fall of snow, which lay deep on the ground. At five I found myself comfortably lodged in new quarters at the house of the director of the iron-works in Serebrianskoï, a Zavod belonging to the crown on the small river Serebrianka.

CHAPTER IV.

ASCENT OF THE KATCHKANAR.

A LARGE lake has been made at great expense by a very high embankment across this little valley, by which water-power is obtained for the iron-works. About fifteen versts below Serebrianskoï the river runs through a deep, narrow, and winding ravine, containing some very picturesque scenery, which furnished me with several subjects for my pencil. Both the Tchoussowaia and Serebrianka also afford many highly interesting studies to the geologist, by the numerous sections of strata exposed in these rugged defiles, the characteristics of which are well described by Sir R. I. Murchison.*

I shall now bid farewell to the Tchoussowaia and to Europe, and cross the Oural into Asia, where my wanderings will be far and wide. Still, I carry along with me many pleasing recollections of this region, and the kind people I found there. I have a remembrance also of a different sort, occasioned by a cut on my knee from a fall among the rocks of this wild river, which it seems likely I shall retain through life.

During my stay in Serebrianskoï, the director, who was a great

* See his valuable work, "The Geology of the Oural." He speaks also of their picturesque beauties in terms of high praise at page 125: "No description of the geologist, still less a mere sectional drawing, can convey an adequate idea of the contortions and pictorial beauty of these wild gorges. The flexures on the Meuse may, in some respécts, be compared with them, but the channel of the Tchoussowaia being narrower, the rocks more rugged, and diversified with foliage, and the defiles highly intricate, the Russian scene appeared to us more striking than that in Belgium." Again at page 388: "A more picturesque river gorge was certainly never examined by geologists. Between the hamlet of Kinish and Ust-Koiva we passed through scenes even surpassing in beauty those higher up the stream, and to which it would require the pencil of a professed artist to do justice. The river runs in a limestone gorge, in which are cliffs of every variety of form, occasionally exposing large caverns along their vertical faces, with trees and flowers grouped about in the clefts—rocks varying in color from black to white."

sportsman, wished to give me a day's repchick (tree-partridge) shooting. It was arranged that we should start early in the morning, as a few hours before ten o'clock, and in the evening after four, are the best times to find this game. We were both armed with pea-rifles, with which they are usually shot when sitting on the branches. Each sportsman is provided with a quill, formed into a whistle, and with this he imitates so well the call of the birds that they instantly respond. By this means they are easily found in the thick forest, and fly from tree to tree, always approaching their supposed mate, when they shortly find their way into the game-bag. A good woodsman was appointed to attend me, who imitated them with so much success that we soon had numbers on the trees around us, affording me plenty of sport. He was also my instructor in the use of the whistle, which I learned, and before the day's shooting was over had employed successfully. In after times this accomplishment enabled me to obtain many a meal I could not otherwise have procured. When I met the director at the appointed place for dinner, I had ten brace and a half, and he turned out sixteen brace of repchicks and a black cock. He considered that mine was good sport, but his own was usually better.

When I left Serebrianskoï, the director and several other friends accompanied me a few versts on the road to a place in the forest where tea and other good things had been provided, that we might take our leave in the true Siberian fashion. The eating and drinking being over, we shook hands and parted. I then continued my journey toward the crest of the Oural. The country across this part of the chain has no striking features: there are no rugged mountain summits to break the monotony of the well-rounded hills covered with pine and larch. Some of the valleys are cultivated, and the new-grown rye was now looking fresh and green. I found many flowers I had not seen before, which I added to my collection. At three o'clock I stood on the summit of the chain: it does not rise to a great elevation, and no very extensive views are seen from this portion of the road; but the whole of these rounded summits are clothed with a luxuriant growth of pines of different varieties. The descent into Asia is somewhat more abrupt than would be the descent to the European side. The country between Serebrianskoï and Barantchinsk is exceedingly plain and uninteresting, but on approaching to within ten or fifteen versts of Kooshwinsk the scenery improves.

During the latter part of this journey I was suffering much from my knee; I also began to feel the effects of a violent cold, caught during the storm on the Tchoussowaia, and was apprehensive that I should be laid up with a fever. On entering the director's room after my arrival at the Zavod, noticing my indisposition, he immediately ordered tea; his next step was to send for a physician. In the course of half an hour the latter arrived, and, seeing the condition I was in, directed that I should at once go to bed, while a Russian bath should at once be prepared for me. This was commencing business in earnest. In due time the bath was got ready, to which I was carried by two sturdy Cossacks. Having laid aside my last clothing, the body-guard placed me on the top shelf of the bath-room, within an inch of the furnace, if I may so call it, and there *steamed* me till I thought my individuality well-nigh gone. After about forty minutes of drubbing and flogging with a bundle of birch twigs, leaf and all, till I had attained the true color of a well-done crawfish, I was taken out, and treated to a pail of cold water, dashed over me from head to foot, that fairly electrified me. I found myself quite exhausted and helpless, in which condition I was carried back to bed. I had scarcely lain down ten minutes when a Cossack entered with a bottle of physic of some kind or other, large enough apparently to supply a regiment. The doctor followed instead of preceding the apothecary, and instantly gave me a dose. Seeing that I survived the experiment, he ordered the man in attendance to repeat it every two hours during the night. Thanks to the Russian bath, and possibly the quantity of medicine I had to swallow, the fever was forced, after a struggle of eight days, to beat a retreat.

At the expiration of this time a returning desire for green fields and mountain scenery convinced me that I might safely resume my journey, which I was soon enabled to do.

The director of the iron-works at Nijne Toura arrived in Kooshwinsk. This morning we dined at the same table, and on my name being mentioned, he addressed me: "I have received instructions to aid you in visiting the Katchkanar. If you will take a place in my carriage to-night to Nijne Toura, I will then make arrangements for you to ascend the mountain, which is about 120 versts from here." Although still very weak, I gladly accepted this kind offer, and presently we started on our way to the Zavod of Tourinsk with five horses and two drivers at great speed.

To this place it was a short and pleasant drive of nine versts along the valley of the Toura. Large lakes have been made in this valley, which supply the water-power to the iron-works. It was a most splendid evening; the sun went down below the Oural Mountains, tinging every thing with his golden hues. From one part of the road we had a view of the Katchkanar, and some other mountain summits to the north, clearly defined against the deep yellow sky in a blue-gray misty tone; a nearer range of hills was purple as seen through a misty vapor rising from the valleys; while nearer to us rose some thickly-wooded hills, their outlines broken by rocky masses of a deep purple color. From these to the lake in the valley there is a dense forest of dark pines, gradually sloping down to the water, and now partially lost in the deep shadow. The lake reflected the sky in all its golden splendor, giving a deeper tone to surrounding objects, and rendering more obscure the dark forest beyond it.

We remained two hours with the officers in Tourinsk, where we supped, and at eleven o'clock were once more galloping along toward our destination. My companion was soon fast asleep. He had gone over this road so often that no charms were left for him. With me the case was different; each step in advance presented some agreeable novelty, consequently I watched every turning of the road with great interest. At some points I had a distant view of parts of the Oural chain, at others a peep over those interminable forests which clothe the lower range of hills, now seen by me for the first time under the effect of the peculiar twilight of these regions, where at this season it is never dark. A partial gloom and solemn stillness as of death spread over these scenes, filling me with strange sensations. All nature seemed wrapped in eternal sleep, which I almost feared to disturb by the rattling of our wheels.

We had now entered a forest region which led us up high hills, then down into deep valleys filled with white vapor, through which the tops of lightning-blasted pines stood out like the shivered masts of a wreck above the sea. A little lower, and all was lost in fog and indistinctness, which checked our speed, moistened and chilled me. Then again we emerged from the misty cloud, and galloped up another wooded height, from the summit of which I saw the Katchkanar looming over the forest beneath, and apparently quite near, although fifty or sixty versts distant.

From this point we began to descend rapidly into the valley of the Toura. Here my companion woke up and pointed out the

Valley of the Toura.

Zavod. All was calm and still in the town, which stands on the south side of the lake, while below and near the rock named "Shaitan," to the north, there were continuous clouds of black smoke, through which tongues of flame and a long line of sparks shot up high into the pure air: these, and the heavy rolling of the forge-hammers that now broke on our ears, are truly characteristic of this igneous region. After crossing the head of the lake, we were in a short time snugly seated in the director's house.

Nijne Toura is a Zavod belonging to the crown, in which a large quantity of excellent bar iron is made from the magnetic ores of Blagodat. It is beautifully situated on the shore of a large lake formed in the valley of the Toura, from which the fall for the water-power used in the iron-works is obtained. On the north side of this fine sheet of water a large rugged mass of pinkish-colored rock, "said to be true syenite," rises 350 to 360 feet high, possessing some remarkable magnetic qualities; one small space of only a few feet in extent was pointed out to me, on which the needle of a compass will turn round. To the east and west of this bare mass there are luxuriant pine and larch woods, extending down into the valley.

The director informed me that it will require a few days to make the necessary preparations for my journey through the forest to the Katchkanar, which has induced me to make some sketches in the valley of the Toura, more particularly on the lake. There are two or three points whence the Katchkanar is seen rising high above all the other mountains, presenting his rugged crest sometimes against a deep blue sky, at others encircled by clouds black as night.

I found a fine view from the forest at the head of the lake, about eight versts distant from the Zavod. This I determined to sketch, although the musquitoes were here in millions. Our horses had been taken to some high ground clear of wood, where the wind compels these pests to seek shelter from the breeze: they are now taking a most savage revenge upon me for their loss. I have tried various means to keep them at a distance, in vain. The last plan I adopted is one much used by the woodmen: it consists of a small sheet iron box, seven inches long, four wide, and five deep, with small holes pierced in the bottom. This is secured to a leather strap, which passes over the shoulder, and lets it hang down like a soldier's cartridge-box at the back of the hip. Some hot charcoal is placed in the bottom, and upon this moist decayed wood, which smoulders and keeps up a cloud of smoke that drives off the bloodthirsty insects. Although successful enough, I soon found that it was, if any thing, a little worse than the evil it was intended to avert. Indeed, the continued smoke affected my eyes to such a degree that I could not see to sketch: many of the woodmen suffer from the same cause. I was obliged, therefore, to abandon the smoking process, at the risk of being devoured.

About a verst below the Zavod I found another good view, which I sketched from some rocks at the west end of Shaitan, where I could look over the valley of the Toura to the Katchkanar. At this point the river winds through meadow-land, twisting and turning in every direction. Fine clumps of birch and pine trees skirt its banks. From the opposite side of this narrow valley to the Katchkanar there appeared to be one dense forest, covering all the lower range of hills. While sketching, I perceived a sudden change at the Katchkanar; clouds began to collect around the summit, sweeping downward till the whole mountain was enveloped in a shroud of inky blackness, presenting here and there on its dark ground whitish streaks, as if jets of steam had been forced up from below. Part of the lower chain soon became obscured also by clouds, which showed signs of much inward commotion. Meanwhile the advancing storm put on its most threatening look. I could now see the lightning, flash on flash, stream from the clouds to earth, but heard no thunder. After about an hour the storm turned toward the south and followed the mountain chain, leaving me in calm and sunshine to pursue my occupation. It was not long before the Katchkanar became visible, and the sun was once more shining upon these riven crags in all his splendor.

On Sunday morning, an Englishman who has the direction of some large iron-works on the west side of the Oural, near Perm, arrived in Nijne Toura. He had heard at Serebrianskoï (115 versts distant) that I was going to ascend the Katchkanar, and particularly desired to accompany me, to which I made no objection. During the week three other gentlemen decided to go with me. All was arranged; but when we met at dinner to-day, and I told them we should leave for the Katchkanar at eight o'clock to-morrow morning, they made excuses, and finally gave up the journey, not one apparently having courage to attempt difficulties they had often described.

At the appointed time the horses were brought into the yard, accompanied by three men. One was a sturdy old hunter, about fifty years of age, who had been selected on account of his knowledge of the forests we had to ride through; the two others were younger men—one quite tall, with a good, manly countenance; his comrade a shorter man, with a good-natured, smiling face nothing could put out of humor. Each carried a rifle slung across his shoulder. My companion from the West Oural was a thin, spare man, capable of enduring any fatigue, who had been accustomed to Ouralian life about seven years. He feared neither storms nor forests, and cared no more for a bear than he would for a stray pig. He had a perfect dread, however, of the insect tribe which feast on blood.

For the first eight versts we traveled over a moderately good road, which brought us to a small stream not more than sixty feet wide. The bridge had been carried away by the ice, and was lying partly across the stream a little farther down, but this it was impossible to cross. One of my men rode into the stream and crossed very well, but as he attempted to ascend the opposite bank his horse sunk under him till nearly overhead; the other men hastened to his assistance, crossing the stream as he had done, but their horses got fast also, which prevented them from giving any aid. Seeing how matters were likely to end, I sprang from my horse, throwing the reins to my companion, ran to the wreck of the bridge, and managed with great difficulty to get across. I found my man in a complete quicksand, in which I also was near sinking. Fortunately, he was not indifferent to the law of self-preservation; for, tying a cord of sufficient length to his bridle, he tossed the end of it to me, and by this means I was enabled to get both horse and rider on to solid ground. As he was shivering with cold, I gave him a tumbler of raw wodky; some one flung a sheepskin over him, and every thing being put in good condition again, we rode on.

At a short distance from this place we entered a thick forest, passing through it for several versts; at length we rode out into a beautiful glade, and on the opposite side, at no great distance, beheld a man approaching on horseback, at sight of whom the men instantly exclaimed, "Egor Stepanish has killed a bear." When we met, I observed a fine black skin hanging over his horse. He had been watching the greater part of the night for the bear, who did not come; and shortly after daylight, giving up all hopes of meeting him for that time, had left his hiding-place to return to his horse, which had been secured in the forest. He had not gone far, however, when, while passing a huge lump of rock, the bear stood before him at twenty yards distance. The rifle was instantly unslung, the prongs in the ground, and the deadly weapon leveled, while Bruin, apparently no way alarmed, rose upon his hind legs and marched on, intent upon a grapple. When within fifteen paces the fatal ball was sent on its mission, and the shaggy monster fell dead, the skin adding one more trophy to the spoils of Egor.

About two versts farther we came to a broad and rapid river, apparently not very deep. There being no means of getting over the stream except by fording it, we plunged boldly in, and soon found the water, which was extremely cold, up to our boots, and frequently as high as our knees: happily, it proved no deeper. We shortly reached the opposite shore and struck into the forest, pursuing a mere track, along which we proceeded slowly, sometimes nearly up to the saddle-flaps in mud and water, at others riding over large stones and trunks of trees, which lay across the path in every direction.

This was a most dreary ride—nothing but dense forest, without a single opening to afford so much as a glimpse of the surrounding country. Toward noon we had a thunder-storm, which echoed loudly through the forest, accompanied by heavy rain. Some large Siberian cedars afforded us shelter during the storm, which continued more than an hour. When it was over we rode on, but were soon completely drenched by the droppings from the trees. Portions of the forest were so thick that the light of day was entirely excluded; indeed, it was frequently necessary to cut our way through the branches, which rendered our progress very slow.

Although there are many bears and other dangerous animals in these wilds, strange to say we did not meet with any. Our great risk was a fall in the midst of rocks and prostrate trees, which might be attended with painful consequences. After a while our veteran hunter, who became a sort of leader of the party, left the track we had been pursuing for some time, and struck off toward the southwest. Forcing our way through thick underwood for about an hour, we emerged at last from the dark forest at the foot of a steep ascent overlaid with huge blocks of stone. Rough as this appeared, it was more agreeable than the woods and morass we had been floundering in for so many hours. Both patience and great care were required in riding up this rugged hill. As we ascended the height, we heard the roaring of water, and supposed by the sound there must be a fall not far distant. From the great noise we expected to find a large stream; but, on approaching, it turned out to be a small one, tumbling down a steep and rocky bed in a succession of snow-like waterfalls. This we had to cross: no very pleasant prospect, as a false step might pitch both horse and rider into the foaming water. Our steeds, however, stepped carefully, placing one foot firmly down before lifting the other. The difficulty being soon overcome, we continued our course upward, and at eight o'clock reached the Katchkanar, after a tedious ride of eleven hours on horseback. The old hunter proposed stopping for the night at the foot of some high rocks: this I was not unwilling to do, and accordingly we dismounted, wet and stiff enough. All hands set to work and made a great fire, which blazed up fiercely. After this I gave each man a glass of brandy, my companion and myself taking a little also to qualify the water we had received during our ride. The musquitoes being here in abundance, my friend took his post on the smoky side of the fire, obstinately refusing to leave it on any account.

Although tired, I could not rest without taking a look at the upper part of the mountain. Seizing my rifle, I began to ascend the rocks, and in about half an hour stood on their summit. When there, a most rugged scene burst upon my view: the jagged top of the Katchkanar was towering far above into the deep blue vault of heaven; the rocks and snow were tinged by the setting sun; while lower down stood crags overtopping pine and cedar trees, and lower still, a thick forest sloped along till lost in gloom and vapor.

I now turned toward the west, and walked to a high crag overlooking the valley; here I seated myself to watch the great and fiery orb descend below the horizon, and a glorious sight it was. Pavda, with its snowy cap, was lighted up, and sparkled like a ruby; the other mountains were tinged with red, while in the deep valleys all was gloom and mist. For a few minutes the whole atmosphere appeared filled with powdered carmine, giving a deep crimson tint to every thing around. So splendid was this effect, and so firm a hold had it taken of my imagination, that I became insensible to the hundreds of musquitoes that were feasting on my blood. Excepting their painfully disagreeable *hum*, no sound, not even that of the chirping of a bird, was to be heard: it was truly solitude.

Soon after the sun went down a white vapor began to rise in

the valleys to a considerable height, giving to the scene an appearance of innumerable lakes studded with islands, as all the mountain tops looked dark and black. I was so riveted to the spot by the scene before me that I remained watching the changes until near eleven o'clock, when that peculiar twilight seen in these regions stole gently over mountain and forest. The effect I can not well describe; it appeared to partake largely of the spiritual.

I now thought it was quite time to return to our camp-fire, and, arriving there a little before twelve o'clock, found the people sleeping and my companion lying near the fire covered over with a cloak, as he said, "to keep the devils off." He had neither slept nor dared to look out. The humming sound of millions of musquitoes was something awful: the high rocks sheltered them from the wind, so that we soon found we had got into the very regions of torment. As it was utterly impossible to endure this, I proposed to remove our encampment to the top of the rocks, where the current of air might relieve us of our tormentors and let us rest in peace; this was at once acceded to by all. So, taking up a burning brand, I clambered to a spot a little higher up, where I pitched on a desirable location. I soon had a fire blazing, having selected the neighborhood of plenty of fallen timber, and the men came round with the horses and our traps. In this place, where the breeze kept fanning us, not a musquito dared show his proboscis.

Once more settled down, we found time to be hungry, and accordingly ordered tea. Who could paint our despair when the men proclaimed that there was neither tea, nor a kettle to boil water, both having been left behind. We had plenty of provisions, with brandy and Ouralian nalifka, and these enabled us to make a meal. There is, however, nothing which can be compared to the beverage "that cheers but not inebriates," and makes the traveler supremely comfortable after a day of hard toil. We sat talking over our misfortune and the anticipated pleasures of the morrow till past one o'clock, then lay down on the rocks and wrapped ourselves up for the night; but the joint effects of wine and smoke had given me a violent headache, which prevented me sleeping. A little before three o'clock I was up, and my toilet made by rubbing the smoke out of my eyes and giving myself a shake.

Day was rapidly dawning over those boundless forests of Siberia. Long lines of pale yellow clouds extended over the horizon; these became more luminous every few minutes, until at length they were like waves of golden light rolling and breaking on some celestial shore. I roused up my fellow-traveler that he might partake with me in my admiration of the scene, and a most splendid one it was. The sun was rising behind some very distant hills, and tipping all the mountain tops with his glorious rays: even the dark pines assumed a golden hue. We sat silently watching the beautifully changing scene for an hour, until hill and valley were lighted up: my friend could no longer repress his feelings. "This is a glorious sight!" he exclaimed; "if it were not for these d—d musquitoes, I should like to spend a month here."

Having broken our fast with a crust of bread and a glass of Ouralian, we prepared for our ascent to the summit. Our rifles were first examined, as they might be required should Bruin feel disposed to dispute our right of way through his domain, this being his summer residence. All was found right; so, strapping my sketching traps across my back, and with rifle over my shoulder, we marched off, my old hunter pointing out the way. The other two men were left in charge of the horses.

A short distance from our encampment we found a confused mass of rocks thrown about in the wildest disorder, evidently having tumbled from the upper part of the mountain. Some were of such huge dimensions that it is difficult to comprehend the colossal power that had hurled them from their rocky beds. We scrambled over this labyrinth to a small valley; on the other side of this the Katchkanar reared his jagged crest.

This little valley was carpeted with short grass and numerous plants, in flower or just budding. A month later, and this will be a garden of iris, geraniums, roses, and peonies, amid scenes of the wildest grandeur. Here also were growing clumps of magnificent pines and Siberian cedars (*Pinus cembra*). From a high, decayed branch of one, I brought down with my rifle a "gluckaree"—a splendid male bird, which my old hunter said weighed thirty pounds: there are many of them in this region. Having reloaded, we proceeded across the valley, and then began the real ascent.

It was a chaotic mass of large loose rocks, with snow filling up many of the cavities; in other places we passed under huge blocks, over which it would have been no easy task to climb. Farther up we met with large patches of snow, and walked over them without difficulty; at length we were at the foot of the high crags of the Katchkanar. We found many of these crags standing up like crystals, some not less than 100 feet high, composed of regular courses, with pure magnetic iron ore between their beds, varying from one inch to four inches thick. In some places cubes or crystals of iron project from the solid rock three and four inches square; and again, in other portions of these rocks the whole mass seems to be of iron, or some other mineral substance.

Summit of the Katchkanar.

I now determined to ascend one of the highest crags. Selecting one, I put down my rifle and all other things, excepting a small sketch-book, and commenced climbing. I found it exceedingly difficult; but, after much labor and some risk, I sat on one of the highest pinnacles with my feet dangling over, in which position I began writing a note to a friend. The view to the east, looking into Siberia, is uninterrupted for hundreds of versts, until all is lost in fine blue vapor. There is something truly grand in looking over these black and apparently interminable forests, in which no trace of a human habitation, not even a wreath of smoke, can be seen to assure us that man is there. Turning to the north, and about 100 versts distant, Pavdinsky Kamen rises out of the dark forest (this is one of the highest points in the Oural chain); it is partly covered with snow, and shines like frosted silver in the bright sun. All the mountains near are blue, purple, and misty, with a rugged foreground of rocks of great height, broken into all shapes and forms. In fact, the summit of the Katchkanar is evidently a mountain in ruins, the softer parts having been removed or torn away by the hand of Time, leaving the harder portion, or vertebræ of the mountain, standing like a huge skeleton, which, seen at a distance, often assumed the most fantastic and picturesque shapes.

Having finished my small epistle, and made a few notes in my journal, I began to descend, which I found much more difficult than climbing; indeed, having descended about thirty feet, I was stopped; however, by reascending a little, and by taking a turn round the jutting points of some of the windings of my late "bad eminence," I got down, to the great joy of both my companions, who had been much alarmed for me. We now scrambled over fallen rocks toward the south, every hundred paces bringing us upon another wild and rugged scene. After walking, tumbling, and climbing for about an hour, we turned our steps down the mountain in a new direction toward our encampment. This brought us to a large patch of ice and snow, surrounded by fallen rocks and dwarf pines. The sun was intensely hot; this and the fatiguing walk made us both hungry and thirsty. As my hunter carried in his bag a bottle of Ouralian and some bread, also brandy for himself, we determined to lunch. A large rock projecting from the snow formed our table and chairs; above us the high crags of the Katchkanar rose to the height of six hundred feet. In this solitary spot I commenced a new occupation. I filled a tumbler nearly full of hard frozen snow, then poured the strawberry nalifka upon it, and in the course of a very few minutes it was turned into ice equal to any ever made by Gunter; our spoons were cut out of a branch, and a delicious dessert repaid me for my trouble.

Having rested a short time, we continued our descent through some magnificent rocky scenes. I made several sketches, and at seven o'clock we were sitting at our camp-fire, having had twelve hours' hard walking. Later in the evening, the old hunter predicted a change with bad weather before morning, and advised our moving under the shelter of the rocks below. To this proposition we objected, rain or storm being nothing in comparison with the torments in store for us there. Stooping a little to listen, we could hear the everlasting hum of the myriads of insects from which we had escaped: they would have devoured us. Contenting ourselves, therefore, with our new position, we lay down on our exposed and rocky beds, where we slept soundly and in peace till near three o'clock in the morning, when we were awakened by a gale of wind, its icy blast making us shiver. Before our traps were packed we had rain and sleet; at length our horses were saddled, and we descended the mountain to seek for shelter in the forest. At six o'clock we were sitting under some cedars, completely protected from the storm, before a huge blazing fire.

The wind became stronger and the rain poured down; the tops of the mountains were covered with clouds—bad omens in these regions. My companion and all my men said we should have some days of bad weather, and urged me to return. I consented, and at ten o'clock we were on our march back to Nijne Toura, where we arrived at half past ten o'clock at night, completely saturated.

CHAPTER V.

MINERAL TREASURES OF THE OURAL.

After three days' incessant rain I left Nijne Toura with the director of the iron-works, and arrived at Kooshwinskoï at nine o'clock, where I found my former acquaintances assembled for a dance. It was a name's-day, and the officers had come to Kooshwinskoï from all the Zavods around. They were, indeed, a gay party; dancing was kept up until half past two o'clock, and then we supped and separated.

Monday was also a great festival at the adjoining Zavod Tourinsk, and every one was going there. I received an invitation to dine, and accepted it with pleasure, intending to make some sketches on my way. I started early in the morning across the country, and made two views in the valley of the Toura looking over the lake to the Oural; then rode on, and arrived at the Zavod some hours before dinner: this enabled me to see how the workmen and their families passed their holidays. Not far from the iron-works several large swings with boxes were erected, and many females and children were riding in them. At a little distance the men were wrestling: some got very ugly falls. Each man stripped off his coat, and tied his long sash tight round his waist; this was grasped fast in the right hand of his antagonist, while the left hand was placed on his shoulder; then the struggle began; the feet, however, were not employed for tripping. One strong man seemed to be the champion, and laid every one low who entered the lists against him. Some time passed, and no one would accept his repeated invitations to take a tumble or try his prowess. He was in the act of picking up his coat, when a man stepped into the circle, and said, if no one else accepted the challenge, he would try one fall. The speaker was much slighter built, but exceedingly active, and was evidently a stranger. He was heartily laughed at for his daring, but appeared to enjoy the mirth he created, and very coolly prepared himself for the combat. The champion looked at him rather contemptuously; indeed, from the manner in which he tied on his sash, and eyed his supposed victim, there seemed a determination on his part to give him a terrible "fling." Presently they went at it. The struggle was a long one—to the great surprise of the spectators. The wrestler tried every artifice of the craft on his supple opponent, but without effect. He now made a desperate effort to throw him by his superior strength; this failed; in another moment he was laid prostrate on the ground, when a great shout of joy greeted him from those he had lately defeated. Springing hastily to his feet, he challenged the victor to another trial; it was instantly accepted, and the two men clinched each other again. This second struggle was soon over, and the late champion received a second defeat and a most fearful fall. No one would now risk a contest with the stranger.

In another part of the Zavod the young girls were occupied in more peaceful games. They were in groups, dressed in their holiday costume, of very bright colors, which was pleasing and picturesque. Others were walking round them with their hands linked together, singing very plaintive songs; indeed, many of these melodies were extremely beautiful. Near these several young women were engaged in another game; they had a small plank or board, about seven feet long, placed on a block in the centre, six inches high. Two girls play at this game, one at each end, standing upright. One springs up and alights again on the board; the force of her descent causes her companion to spring higher every time. I have seen a couple continue this game for twenty minutes, standing perfectly straight, and bounding up three feet, and three feet six inches. This play, which requires a little practice, is quite a pretty one, as well as a healthful exercise. The day was very fine, and I was much interested with their rural pastimes, which reminded me of sports on the village green in the days of my childhood.

Girls playing at Skakiet.

I remained several days sketching in the vicinity of Kooshwinskoï, as there are many points highly interesting to both the geologist and artist. The two hills, named the Great and Little Blagodat, are the most remarkable; the Great Blagodat is about twelve hundred feet above the level of the sea.

During the last century large quantities of magnetic iron ore have been extracted from this place; and it has been clearly proved by Helmersen, and other mining engineers, from the appearance of fissures on the sides of these hills, that there have been two distinct eruptions of magnetic ore in this place; and, further, that the first great masses of this ore have since been cut through, and intersected by similar matter.

Blagodat rises considerably above the Zȧvod and the surrounding country. To the north and west the Oural Mountains are seen at a distance of sixty or eighty versts; to the south and east there is a flat country, covered with dense forests, extending for several thousand versts toward and into Eastern Siberia, over which the eye searches in vain for some indication of the residence of man: nothing but dark pine-trees and a few small lakes are seen.

One of my sketching expeditions was to Blagodat. I started at eight o'clock in the morning in an open carriage, and was driven to within half a verst of the summit; from this point I sent the servant back to the Zavod, with orders to return for me at seven in the evening, as I had decided to devote the whole day to sketching in this remarkable region. After ascending a short distance, I found a point which afforded a very good view, and in a little time I was occupied in transferring the scene to my paper, all the while a clear blue sky and a bright sun shining over my head. About ten o'clock I fancied that I heard something like the rumbling of distant thunder, but above me all was so clear and sunny that I concluded this must be fancy, and went on with my work. Shortly, however, I heard the sounds again, a little more distinct than before; this induced me to ascend a high rock, from which I saw, sure enough, at a great distance, a storm gathering in the southeast, casting, as it approached, a dark shadow over the whole landscape. After watching it a short time, I conjectured it would pass to the east without disturbing me, and so, letting myself down to the place where I had begun sketching, I resumed my labor, listening betimes to the thunder, which seemed approaching nearer every moment. In about two hours the distant part of the view I was sketching became enveloped in thick clouds, down which slanting lines of a lighter shade, cutting the bosom of the dark mass of vapor, showed that it had burst in a deluge of rain. Several storms passed without touching me, till about two o'clock, when some large drops suggested that it would be prudent to seek shelter from the coming tempest as soon as possible. On the summit of the great Blagodat there is a small wooden chapel and a tomb erected to the memory of a Vogul chief, "Tchumpin," who was sacrificed and burned on these metallic rocks by his ferocious countrymen as a penalty for his crime in discovering the mines of magnetic iron ore to the Russians. A more appropriate spot could not have been selected for this horrible immolation. The summit of Blagodat is seen as far as the eye can reach, and when the smoke of that fearful sacrifice curled up around it in black and crimson wreaths, thousands of these wild men made the hills and rocks resound with shouts of vengeance and execration.

To these bloodstained rocks I ascended, and placed my sketches and colors in the chapel, a small octagon building about ten feet in diameter, built to appease the manes of one who is regarded as a traitor to his race. The rugged igneous rocks on which the sacrifice was offered up make a more characteristic memorial of the event than the cast iron urn erected upon them.

Having secured my papers from wet, I proceeded to the edge of the rocks, when I perceived that the storm had in its progress obscured the Oural chain in a thick black mass of clouds tinged with red, from which the lightning leaped forth in wrathful flashes. I watched its onward course with intense anxiety, feeling certain that Blagodat would soon be enveloped in this fearful vapor. For a few minutes a great dread came over me, knowing that I was standing alone on a huge mass of magnetic iron far above the surrounding country. The thunder echoed among the distant hills until at length it became one continued roll, every few minutes bringing the storm nearer. The Zavod was obscured by these dark and dreadful clouds, completely isolating me from the human race. In the valley beneath, where I had left my friends, the vapor appeared billowing and swelling up in huge surges, and in great commotion. I could also hear the wind roaring over the forest; then came a blast, which forced me to cling fast to the monument of Tchumpin, and made the little chapel tremble to its base. The cold gust of wind was instantly followed by a terrific flash of lightning, which struck the rock below me, and tinged every thing with red; at the same moment a crash of thunder, at first like the discharge of a brigade, burst into a tremendous roar, which shook the rocks beneath my feet. The rain now rushed down in torrents, from which even the little chapel did not afford me protection, for through its roof the water poured in streams. This was a truly sublime and awful scene: the lightning and thunder were incessant; indeed, I saw the rocks struck several times. The storm undoubtedly revolved round the mountain, no unfit accompaniment to the dreadful sacrifice once offered up on its summit. About four o'clock the clouds began to clear off. The director of the Zavod sent his carriage and some men to seek me, nor was I sorry to leave the spot. The following day I returned, and spent several hours finishing my sketches; after this I went into some of the excavations from which the iron ore has been obtained, and then left this singular and interesting place.

My next point of interest was Barantchinsk; these are iron-works belonging to the crown, about twelve versts from Kooshwinskoï, standing in a small picturesque valley near the foot of "Seene Gora," or Blue Mountain, an elevation which forms a fine object looking over the valley at Kooshwinskoï from Blagodat. Seene Gora stands out from the Oural in a rugged and bold mass, and when seen from a distance appears to be of a deep blue color, from which it takes its name. It is almost wholly composed of hornblende. The road to the Zavod runs along a fine valley, in many parts richly wooded with pine, birch, and larch trees of very large growth. In some places they are growing singly, in others they may be seen prettily grouped together; these clumps, with their variegated foliage, form beautiful objects in the landscape. The wild roses were now in full bloom—some of a deep crimson, others a pale pink, and some white; there were also white, yellow, lilac, and blue anemones covering the ground. The *Clematis Siberica* was twining among the leaves with its pendent and graceful creamy-white flowers, while under the bushes and in the shade were *Cypripedium calceolus*, *C. guttatum*, *C. macranthum*, *C. ventricosum;* these, and the deep orange *Trollius Asiaticus*, gave the appearance of a beautiful garden to this valley; indeed, it was one of Nature's own planting. My ride to the Zavod was most agreeable, as well as highly interesting, and enabled me to add several new flowers to my collection.

The director, an intelligent man, accompanied me over the works. Here large quantities of shells are made, no expense being spared in the manufacture of missiles; the cost to the crown, however, is very great. It is to be regretted that so much excellent iron should be thrown away on such objects, more especially as it is so much wanted in this country for other—I suppose I may say, more useful purposes. During the evening all was arranged for an excursion to Seene Gora; and, to give me a long day for sketching, it was decided we should dine there. The director, with his wife, several other ladies, and four officers, had determined to have a picnic, and spend the day on the summit.

Our party consisted of four ladies in one telaga, three gentlemen followed in another, with two men and myself on horseback. Our path was along the bank of the small river Baransha for a short distance, and then across the valley to a thick wood skirting the foot of the mountain, through which we rode over a good track until we came to an open space with some deep, wet, marshy ground. Having passed this, we entered another wood, and found the ground covered with, and our passage blocked by, large massct of stone fallen from the rocks above, lying in great confusion.

I left my friends, and proceeded forward on horseback, accompanied by one man. Our ride was among great boulders of rock, with trees growing around them, and out of the clefts in the large blocks, often rendering it very difficult to sit our horses, as the branches almost dragged us to the ground. After an hour's ride we reached the summit, or place of our encampment, where men sent in advance had cleared a small space, and made a fire, and a great smoke, to keep off the musquitoes. Having given up my horse, I walked about a verst to some rugged rocks, rising to a great height above the valley, quite detached from the precipices. These formed a fine foreground to the view looking over the valley toward the Katchkanar, and farther northward along the Oural chain. I sketched this scene, then returned to our camp, and found all my friends had arrived and dinner ready: carpets were spread on the ground, and various dishes served up to guests whose appetites had been sharpened by the ascent to the dinner-table. We all did ample justice to the repast.

After this I continued my ramble through the thick forest of the south, where I found another beautiful view. Here I descended a spur of the mountain which juts out into the valley, and scrambled over a great mass of hornblende and other rocks into a most rugged ravine, where I made an additional sketch, exceedingly wild in its character. The dark purple and greenish metallic colors of these fragments were quite in keeping with a stormy twilight, and the deep shades of evening creeping over the valley beneath. Having finished, I returned to my friends, who were drinking tea, and when our repast was ended we began our descent into the valley. This was rather difficult, owing to the fallen rocks, which could not well be seen for the darkness of the thick forest. At length we got to the open ground, placed the ladies in their telaga, and started them on the track to the Zavod. One of my men proposed that we should ride across the valley a much nearer way, but we had not ridden half a verst when we came upon some very marshy ground. Our guide said it was nothing; however, we soon found he had lost the track, and a few paces farther were floundering in a deep and dangerous morass. My horse sunk at once up to the saddle-flaps; I succeeded in turning his head to some clumps of rough grass, where I leaped from the saddle. After much difficulty, I dragged my horse up, and at last out of the fen, but with the loss of a stirrup. My two companions did not fare much better. Having once more reached hard ground, we were obliged to retrace our steps, and now found our guide's short cut was the longest way home; besides which, we were wet and covered with mud. It was past twelve o'clock when we reached the Zavod, long after our friends had become comfortable at home.

From this place I desired to cross the Oural to Vissimo Chaitanskoï, a Zavod belonging to Anatole Demidoff, near the crest of the Oural, on the western side. In doing this I should have to ride along the higher ridge of the chain. At ten o'clock I started on my way to Verkne Barantchinsk, where horses had been ordered to be ready for me at daylight the following morning. The ride up this valley was very agreeable, the ground being covered with flowers; and the little river Baransha, winding its course among the trees, gave a pleasing variety to the scene. I sketched two views during my ride, and arrived at the Zavod at four o'clock. Here I was obliged to remain for the night, it being too late to begin our mountain ride. This induced me to visit the iron-works, and afterward to walk to Lime-tree Hill, which the director informed me was a mass of greenstone. My labor was not rewarded. I observed nothing either picturesque or interesting around the Zavod; nevertheless, I spent a very pleasant evening with the director, and then prepared for my ride over the mountains.

At half past three o'clock, four men, with five horses, came into the yard: these were to be my companions to Vissimo Chaitanskoï Zavod. It was a splendid morning, with every prospect of a fine day. I had been prepared at Kooshwinskoï for a rough ride, but this did not deter me. During the first two hours we had a good track or road, along which timber, firewood, and charcoal were carted to the Zavod. After this we found a mere track, in many places overgrown with underwood and bushes. We were now ascending to the crest of the chain through a dense forest of pines, in some places so thick that it was impossible to pass between them; in others, huge rocks were standing up far above the tops of the trees, while still higher up some bold crags overtopped the forest like watch-towers. To the summit of these rocks I determined to ascend; I therefore dismounted, and, leaving two men in charge of the horses, accompanied by the rest, soon reached the top, the way to which was neither difficult nor dangerous. From the summit the scene around us appeared one interminable forest, extending far beyond the reach of vision. To the north were seen some precipitous peaks, standing like mighty fortresses guarding this vast solitude. We did not remain long on these crags, as I saw to the southward, and apparently near to us, the rugged crest of a mountain much higher than the rocks on which we stood. Having taken the bearings with my compass to enable me to direct our course through the thick forest, we descended to our horses, mounted, and rode away. I now took upon myself the duties of guide in this dense and tangled wood, as no vista whatever could be obtained through it. Trunks of trees, with fallen rocks, were the only objects in view, while a thick canopy of foliage above our heads almost shut out the light of heaven, and rendered the place dark and dismal. Although the mountain appeared so near, I was quite certain that we should have a difficult ride. We had not gone above three hundred paces when we got among large loose stones that were very dangerous to ride over; our progress, therefore, was slow. At last we were compelled to dismount. Even then it was a most perilous task taking our horses across this belt of stone, about five hundred paces in width, and extending far down the mountain. After passing these loose rocks, we descended into a small and more open valley, in which large pines and Siberian cedars were growing most luxuriantly, with a thick mossy turf beneath, in many places covered with flowers; among them were large beds of geranium, and fine clumps of peony in full bloom.

Having crossed this lovely little spot, quite park-like in its appearance, we began to ascend a steep and rugged hill, and in about half an hour were at the foot of the granite crags, to the summits of which I soon climbed. They were cut or split into several pinnacles; some had been struck with lightning, and their fragments scattered around; and others appeared ready to topple over and bound into the valley below. Dwarf cedars and young pines were growing out of the clefts. There were also large patches of dark green and yellow moss, with tufts of white and purple flowers, contrasting beautifully with the dark red of the granite.

To the north the jagged top of the Katchkanar was seen; also Pavdinska Kamen. Still farther away, and almost lost in the distance, were three other peaks, covered with snow; below these desolate, rocky summits was a dark, solitary, and apparently trackless forest, undisturbed by any sound except the shrill voice of the large, red-crested woodpecker. Having sat on these rocks about half an hour, contemplating this grand and gloomy scene, we returned to our horses, and rode down the west side of the mountain into a deep and thickly-wooded valley. At the bottom we found a small stream, and, following its course downward, at length came upon a fine open space, with plenty of grass for our horses. Here we dismounted, and turned them loose to feed, while we sat down on the bank under some large trees and partook of the good things provided for us. Any lover of the gentle craft would have found excellent sport on this little stream. The grayling were very numerous, and constantly springing at the flies playing over the pool at our feet. One of my men caught three with a loop of horse-hair. Our horses had a rest of two hours, and then we started again, still following the stream, until we entered a dark and gloomy valley. Our ride was now over bog and fen, in which our horses floundered amid fallen trees in all stages of decay, often sinking to the saddle-flaps in mire. In about two hours we got through this terrible morass, with our steeds completely jaded. At length we were once more on hard ground near a rapid stream, which ran tumbling and roaring over large stones.

One of my men now discovered where we were, and said we could not ride to the Zavod, even with fresh horses, before sunset. A short rest was absolutely necessary for our tired animals before pushing on farther.

The musquitoes were here in millions: this compelled us to make a fire and a great smoke to keep them at a distance. The poor horses stood with their heads in the smoke also, as a protection against these pests. To remain long on this spot would have subjected us to a degree of torment neither man nor beast could endure, so we were soon obliged to retreat. I wish I could say that we left the enemy in possession of the field. Not so; they pursued us with bloodthirsty pertinacity until we reached some open meadows, when they were driven back into their fenny region by a breeze—I hope to prey on each other. Our tired horses pricked up their ears, we saw the smoke at no great distance, and a little after nine o'clock rode into the Zavod, to the great joy of the entire cavalcade, after seventeen hours in the forests. The director of these works received me most kindly, freely giving me, as usual, every possible accommodation, and treating me with the greatest liberality.

The next morning I took leave of my hospitable host, and commenced my journey toward the upper ridge of the Oural. From this Zavod to Nijne Tagilsk a new road is being formed, almost in a straight line across the mountains, and must now be completed. It is a great work, and will make a splendid road from Nijne Tagilsk quite across the Oural Mountains to Outkinska-Demidoff Pristan, on the Tchoussowaia. The whole produce of the mines at Tagilsk, and of the other zavods belonging to Demidoff, are conveyed to the pristan along this road, but the greater part is taken during winter on sledges.

After riding a few versts in this direction, we turned off to visit the platinum mines near the crest of the Oural. The alluvium is found in small ravines or depressions running up toward the summit of the mountain in masses of detritus, composed principally of fragments of serpentine, and small portions of greenstone, drifted down from the higher peaks. The platinum has of late years been found in small grains; formerly it was obtained in fragments of different sizes, weighing from one to twelve ounces, and even more. There is one rare example, a piece weighing near ten pounds. I was exceedingly fortunate in procuring a curiously formed specimen weighing more than a quarter of a pound.

From these mines I determined to cross the high ridge, ride through the forest, and strike the road on the eastern side of the chain. My men thought we should encounter many difficulties; still, they did not hesitate to comply with my wish; so we turned our horses' heads up the ravine. A ride of one hour and a half brought us to the summit, which was covered with thick forest; but there were no rocks or crags from which we could obtain even a peep into Asia. The descent was much more precipitous than on the western side; in some places it was very abrupt; indeed, it gave us so much trouble that we were compelled to turn to the south and ride toward the new road. In rather more than an hour we emerged from the forest, and were glad to turn our horses toward Tagilsk. We had not gone more than a verst when we found the road extended over a wooden bridge for several versts across a deep morass. Had we continued our course in the forest, this would have given us much trouble, and stopped us most probably at a time when our horses would have been tired out, and then we should have had to remain in this morass exposed to the attacks of our late tormentors. After crossing the bridge and riding a short distance, we descended into a beautiful little valley, down which the Tchernoy winds its course. From this point our road was still through woods, and most uninteresting. At seven o'clock we arrived at Tagilsk, and I was delighted to enter the hospitable house appointed for strangers, where I received from the director the greatest kindness and attention, with every facility to enable me to sketch the scenery in and around the Zavod. Horses and men were placed at my service, and a gentleman who had spent several years in England was appointed to accompany me wherever I wished to go.

Nijne Tagilsk, the principal Zavod of the Demidoff family, is a large town, with a population of about 25,000 souls, and stands in a picturesque situation in the valley of the River Tagil, comprising many elegant buildings of brick and stone; among them is a fine church, containing some beautiful paintings; also a splendid edifice of large dimensions, in which the administration of the mines is carried on; capacious and well-conducted hospitals for the workmen; large and excellent schools for the education of youths and younger children; vast warehouses for copper, iron, and other materials, with corn, flour, groceries, clothing, and every thing required for the population; good and spacious houses for the directors and chief managers, and very comfortable dwellings for the workmen and their families.

Tagilsk.

The smelting furnaces, forges, rolling mills, machine shops, and other works, with their machinery, are on a magnificent scale. The various machines and tools are of the best description, some being from the first manufactories in England. Others are made in the works, under the superintendence of a very talented young engineer, a native of Tagilsk, who had spent several years in one of the best establishments in Lancashire. The manner in which these works are conducted reflects the highest credit on the director and his assistants in every department.

Anatole Demidoff spares no expense in educating those young men of Tagilsk, or of any other of his Zavods, who show any talent for geology, mineralogy, or mechanics. He has sent several to England and France, allowing them ample means, and affording them every opportunity of pursuing their studies; to some he has already given their freedom, and many of his people in Tagilsk have become wealthy. He has also employed some of the most eminent scientific men of Europe to survey and examine the mines and minerals in these regions.*

Both iron and copper are worked in this Zavod on an extensive scale. About two versts from the works, Vessokgora, or high hill, rises up from three to four hundred feet above the valley; near the top, and on the sides of this hill, magnetic iron ore has been extracted from a very remote period, most probably ages before the first Demidoff planted his foot on the Oural. The greater quantity is met with in a small valley on the western side of the hill, where it is being worked in an open quarry. Here lies an inexhaustible supply of this valuable mineral. The enormous mass of iron ore found on this spot is about eighty feet thick, and extends about four hundred feet in length. There is material for these iron-works for ages yet to come. Formerly a great difference of opinion was entertained among scientific men about the origin of this mound of mineral. My attendant from the works, a good practical geologist, informed me that there was no doubt these masses of ore have flowed into the valley from fissures in the adjacent hill.

About one and a half verst distance from the iron quarry the copper mines exist; the latter ore is obtained by sinking shafts to near three hundred feet deep. It was in the year 1812 that the copper was first discovered at Tagilsk; since that period the mines have been found very productive, and worked to great advantage. The most singular and beautiful product of these mines is the malachite. The doors, vases, and other works displayed in the Great Exhibition of 1851, made of this mineral, sufficiently attest its varied color and beauty as a material for works of ornament. On visiting this region I expressed a wish to see this mineral in its natural state, and the director immediately gave orders that I should descend and see the men at work in the mines.

A few years before my arrival in the Oural Mountain an enormous mass of malachite had been discovered at Tagilsk, and men

* Sir R. I. Murchison says, in his "Geology of the Oural," "At Nijne Tagilsk, and the country around, to which Anatole Demidoff is now applying so much scientific research, we doubt not he will render it a school where some of the most curious metallurgical processes of nature can be best studied."

were now engaged extracting this mighty metallic stalagmite, the deposit of ages. In the company of one of the managers I visited the mine, and found that a large quantity had already been taken away from this mass, and the miners were engaged in breaking up the remainder. Could this have been removed in its perfect state, it would have been one of the greatest natural curiosities ever exhibited. I was told that the whole mass was likely, when extracted, to produce about 20,000 poods, or 720,000 pounds of beautiful and solid malachite, worth at least £170,000. Such is the mineral wealth of some of the Ouralian mines, in a region where it is supposed Nature carried on her latest metallurgical operations.*

On this vast estate of the Demidoffs, containing 3,095,700 acres, nearly equaling Yorkshire, Nature has been most bountiful. Iron and copper ore appear to be inexhaustible. Platinum and gold are in the upper valleys, and malachite is found there also in enormous quantities, with porphyry and jasper of great beauty, and various colored marbles. Their forests extend over more than ten thousand square versts, and are thickly covered with timber. These woods are under the supervision of intelligent officers, whose

* Sir R. I. Murchison beheld this wonder of nature before the wedge and hammer had mutilated its form. He says: "The copper ground we have been describing having been excavated by shafts, an enormous mass of malachite was recently detected at the depth of 280 feet. Thin strings of green copper ore occurring at intervals were followed downward, when, increasing in width and value, they were found to terminate, at the base of the present mines, in an immense, irregularly-shaped botryoidal mass of solid malachite. . . . . The base of this valuable mass has not yet been traced, but when we examined it the surrounding matrix had been cleared away from its summit and sides; and if our notes taken on the spot are accurate, the summit alone has a length of about eighteen feet and a width of about nine feet, an enormous bulging mass being exposed beneath, the extent or base of which was not fully ascertained. The whole of the surface, however, which had been uncovered was calculated to contain not less than 15,000 poods, or upward of half a million pounds of pure and solid malachite.

"The geological interest attached to this mass lies in the indication it affords that the substance called malachite has been formed by a cupriferous solution, which has successively deposited its residue in the stalagmitic form.

"When we examined this mass of malachite, much of the surrounding matrix had been removed, and it presented precisely the aspect of having been deposited in a depression of the limestone and schaalstein. On the whole, we are disposed to view it as having resulted from copper solutions emanating from all the porous, loose, surrounding mass, and which, trickling through it to the lowest cavity upon the subjacent solid rock, have in a series of ages produced this wonderful subterranean incrustation."

duty it is to have them cut down in proper succession. It requires a space of eighty years to reproduce timber suitable for the use of the Zavods.

Formerly was carried on in Tagilsk a large manufactory of sheet-iron articles, such as oval tables, boxes, large and small, tea-trays, and various other wares. This was at one time a very important branch in the works, as these articles were almost indispensable in every Siberian dwelling. The Demidoffs were ever in advance of the age in which they lived. They saw the great advantage that would accrue by educating their workmen, and giving them a knowledge of the fine arts. There was a School of Design in Nijne Tagilsk seventy years ago. Several men from Nijne Tagilsk were sent into Italy, and placed with eminent artists, under whom they studied for several years; some possessed considerable talent, and returned home fully qualified to impart their knowledge to others. I have seen five or six oval tables, four feet six inches long, painted by them, that would do credit to any establishment in Europe at the present day.

Most probably they got the art of japanning from the Chinese: the process is accomplished with a composition that resists the action of hot water, and many of their early works are still perfect.

My next points were Tchernoistotchinsk iron-works, belonging to Demidoff, twenty-five versts distant from Nijne Tagilsk, and "Bielaya Gora," or White Mountain. The director had sent and desired the manager to make the necessary preparations to enable us to ascend Bielaya Gora, as well as to afford me every facility for sketching either on the lake or elsewhere. It was also arranged that the manager who had attended me in Nijne Tagilsk should be my companion on this journey. He had decided that this should be a party at pleasure, and that his wife should join us and visit her friends in the Zavod. We left in a carriage at one o'clock, taking a southwesterly direction for about three versts, when we began to ascend a very steep hill. Then our road was through thick forests, with a few spots of open ground, which were genuine flower-gardens. We visited one of the platinum mines a few versts out of our road. It is in a small ravine, but is no longer worked. I found some small grains of the mineral, from which the detritus had been washed away by the rains. After a very pleasant ride through these forests, we arrived at Tchernoistotchinsk at five o'clock. There is a fine lake near the Zavod, extending up to the foot of Bielaya Gora, about twelve versts in length, and varying from four to six versts in width. The lake is bounded on one side by some very rugged rocks of greenstone, and contains seven small islands. On one of these there was formerly a building named "The Castle," erected by one of the Demidoffs, where it is said he coined the silver he obtained from the Altai.

The view of the lake, looking up toward Bielaya Gora, with its islands and hilly shores, is very pretty; formerly it was thickly wooded on the north side, but the timber was cut down a few years ago for the use of the Zavod. In fifty or sixty years this will be again a dense forest, and that, too, without planting. I was told there are several parts of this lake that are never frozen in the most severe winters, not even with 25° or 30° R. of frost. This, it is supposed, is caused by springs at the bottom of it; and in consequence of such large pieces of open water remaining accessible, many kinds of water-fowl are induced to winter here, a rare phenomenon in these cold regions.

During the evening I went with the manager over the works, and found that they were in full activity, making bar iron, considered the best in the Oural. I was told that it is well known even in England by the name of "old sable iron;" and the people here were delighted to show me the material from which our best English steel is manufactured.

The manager and his three daughters proposed to accompany their friends from Nijne Tagilsk, and to go with us to Bielaya Gora. Early in the morning there had been a thick fog hanging over the lake and hills; this had gradually cleared off, and we had at starting a brilliant sunshine, and every prospect of fine weather. The men and cooks had been sent on at five o'clock with the necessary instructions. Three telagas, each drawn by three horses, were provided to take us as far as possible up the mountain, from whence we must walk to the summit. We mustered for this trip four ladies and four gentlemen, divided into three parties—two ladies and a gentleman in each of the first telagas, and two gentlemen in the last, thus equalizing the weight.

Our track was along the western shore of the lake, over low hills and undulating ground for several versts; many of the views were extremely beautiful, the open ground being covered with flowers, and the trees and bushes clothed with the richest foliage, while small islands studded the lake, and were reflected in water scarcely moved by a ripple. It was, indeed, a calm and most lovely scene.

We turned to the west, crossing some low hills so thickly wooded that we could not even get a peep at the country around. Farther on we were driving through rich park-like scenery, with magnificent timber, in some parts quite clear of underwood, with short mossy grass beneath the trees, and fine clumps of peony in full bloom. Here and there large Siberian cedars were growing, with their rich green tufted branches; in other places stood gigantic pines, towering up from a hundred to a hundred and fifty feet; and these were often so well grouped that the effect appeared to have been produced by the genius of some Paxton of by-gone ages. After a ride of about four hours we were at the foot of the mountain, and began to ascend; on this side it is a fine grassy slope, very easy to drive up. We still continued our course to the westward, gradually rising until we had attained a considerable elevation, when we turned to the south, up a rather steep ascent to a belt of pines and larches. Beyond this point the telagas could not proceed. We now began to ascend on foot, and, after passing the belt of timber, were among great masses of rock, which stand up to the height of a hundred and fifty feet. In some places huge blocks, which had fallen from above, lay strewn at the base of these rocks, occasionally pines of large dimensions growing up among them. After walking about an hour, we arrived, at five o'clock, very hungry, at a beautifully sheltered spot, which our men had selected for our night's encampment. A huge fire was burning; and a balagan, as it is called, was prepared for the ladies, made with small poles, and covered with birch bark and branches. This primitive kind of shelter is open on three sides, and, simple as it is in its structure, will keep off the rain very well. Carpets and a table-cloth were spread on the grass, and we were soon partaking of the good things the manager and the cooks had provided; both dinner and wines were excellent, and the London porter as fresh and foaming as the most tired traveler would wish to have it.

Having rested about an hour, and finding my companions inclined to sleep (a universal custom after dinner in these regions, indeed throughout Russia), I desired one of the men to take my sketching materials and go with me. Shouldering my rifle, I started off about a verst from our night's encampment, where there was a very picturesque mass of rocks and trees, forming a beautiful foreground to the valley beneath, with purple and blue mountains in the distance.

Here I sat down to my work, sketching and contemplating; at length I came to a full conviction that the entire upper peaks of the Oural must have been much higher at some very remote period. They are now shattered, broken, and tumbled about in every direction. Wind and storms can not have uprooted such stupendous masses as I beheld lying around me, nor can I suppose that they have been thrown down by earthquakes. Although earthquakes as well as faith can remove mountains, still I think these have stood on too broad and firm a base to be tossed out of their places by such convulsions, terrible as they are. Another power must have caused this tremendous devastation. Ages ago a mighty sea rolled over the crests of these mountains, probably during the great convulsion which heaved them up, and water apparently has been the agent, with its irresistible force, which has first rent their top asunder, and then hurled the huge masses from their beds.

I had not quite finished my sketch when all my friends came up and told me we should drink tea on the highest summit, at a short distance to the east of us, where the men were already waiting with the necessary apparatus. We walked toward this pile of rocks, and ascertained that they rose into a peak about two hundred feet high, small, and rather abruptly terminating near the top, on which a signal-post has been erected. We ascended without difficulty, and found room for the ladies around the framework of the post, the rest of the party hanging on as best they could. Water was brought to the summit, and the *somervar*, or urn, was soon boiling, when we drank our tea, and watched the sun sink below the mountains. This was the signal for our departure, and we descended without accident.

We had a walk in the dusk of the evening, and at half past eleven o'clock were sitting at supper in our camp. The men had built a large fire about fifty paces distant, and were singing in

Tea-party on the summit of Bielaya Gora.

chorus some beautiful Russian melodies. After a short time the ladies were stowed away under the balagan, and each of us adopted his own plan for sleeping. Some made beds of branches, but mine was composed of two logs of timber placed near the fire, with my cloak for a covering. In a few minutes after I had lain down I was fast asleep.

About two o'clock in the morning I awoke, shivering with cold; the fire had nearly burned out, and, on looking round, I began to wonder what had happened, every thing appeared so changed. Having got up, I felt the grass crisp under my feet, and on taking up a piece of wood found it frozen, so much so that I could scrape the ice from it. I threw some wood on the fire, hoping to get warm, but failed: this induced me to look for the sunrise. After taking my rifle from a branch on which it hung, I strolled away, leaving every one fast asleep. Having proceeded about two versts into some long grass, I got sight of a fine buck, who bounded past me at full speed at about a hundred and fifty yards distance. I fired, and, unluckily, missed him. Notwithstanding my disappointment, I kept on my course. At fifty minutes past two o'clock I was sitting on a high ledge of rock watching for the sun. Presently a visible token of his approach crept along the distant horizon. My friends were at least three versts away, and no signs of life were visible except a solitary bird sitting on a birch-branch chanting his matin song.

The sun was rising fast, his yellow rays were thrown far up into mid-heaven, and in a short time the rocky peaks above me were tipped with golden light. Soon he was shining upon me in his full glory, while all beneath was undefined and misty. Presently the tops of the lower hills caught the light, and every few minutes new objects seemed starting into life from out the gloomy shroud which overhung the valleys. I sat watching the changes for an hour. It was, indeed, a glorious sight. Hill after hill was breaking into view; each ridge, as it receded, was more aerial, until, at length, they appeared like golden mists; while the nearer rocks stood out grim, dark, and rugged, as if the spirits of darkness were trying to penetrate the mysteries of heaven.

The towns and zavods in the far-off distance were now touched with the sun's rays, and sparkled in yellowish white against the dark purple-gray forests by which they were surrounded, shining out like specks of light on the vast extent of wood and mountain. Although there are no great mountain masses in this region rising far into snowy space, to strike the beholder with wonder, this country has a grandeur peculiarly its own, which it is difficult to describe. The interminable forests, with their rounded hilly sweeps vanishing far into misty distance, until they appear to dissolve into thin air, and the oppressive solitude reigning over these vast scenes, create feelings of astonishment and melancholy.

I retraced my steps, arrived at the balagan at half past five o'clock, and found the cooks preparing the morning meal. After breakfast it was agreed that two men should accompany me to the northeast side of the mountain, where we could descend toward the lake, cross over a most rugged part, and meet our friends in the forest at the bottom. A brisk walk of an hour brought us to the brink of a precipice, and stopped our progress toward the lake, which we now looked down upon. Though apparently quite near, it was, in reality, several versts distant. It was shining like polished silver, its seven small islands appearing almost black on its bright surface. From the foot of the precipice on which we stood, down to the lake, there was a thick forest extending all along its shores. We were compelled to descend a little, and then cross toward the west; this brought us to a bed of loose rocks, at least half a verst in width, extending up to the summit and far down the mountain. They were difficult to cross, but not dangerous. In some places they were piled up very steep, without even a blade of grass on them; in other parts, lower down, trees and shrubs were growing between the stones; again, toward the middle of the bed, there were deep holes formed by blocks being heaped up in the utmost confusion. In many places the rocks are of enormous dimensions. I measured several, and found one 43 feet long by 12 feet wide, with an average thickness of 8 feet: this could not weigh less than 500 tons. Heavy as this is, it seems to have been tumbled about without difficulty: these ponderous blocks, being tossed up into a confused and shadowy mass, suggest thoughts of "Chaos and old Night."

There is every appearance of a mighty torrent having swept over this place, tearing up solid rocks—indeed, every thing in its course. Since I examined this spot I have spent six years among the mountains of Asia, ascending many of great elevation, and in no instance have I ever found these rocky and torrent-like beds near the summits. I have walked up the track of the avalanche where snow, ice, and rocks have torn up the mountain and carried devastation into the valleys, but these fearful roads of Nature's making bear no resemblance to the masses of rock on Bielaya Gora.

A walk of six hours brought us to our friends and to dinner, most acceptable after a fatiguing ramble. We rested some time, then got into our telagas, and returned to Tchernoistotchinsk, where we arrived at eight o'clock, much delighted with our journey.

CHAPTER VI.

PRECIOUS STONES OF SIBERIA.

On leaving this Zavod the road passes round "Lessetsia Gora," or Fox Hill, and enters a pretty valley with isolated masses of rock in many parts, and fine clumps of trees. After passing Chaitansk it is one continuous forest to Neviansk, where I arrived at two o'clock in the morning, and was taken to the castle.

This is one of the oldest Zavods in the Oural; it was built on the small river Neva under the direction of Nikite Demidoff. Sent from Tula by Peter the Great, about the year 1701 or 1702, to examine the mines in these regions, near which he soon after established himself, Demidoff may truly be considered the founder of the iron and other works in the Oural. He did more toward developing the mineral wealth of these mountains than any other man. His sound practical knowledge and untiring industry in examining this country enabled him to select those parts best suited for mining, smelting, and other operations, and he has left the stamp of his foresight and genius on several Zavods.

The castle, as it is called, was partly built by the first Demidoff, and was long the family residence; it was extended by his successor into a magnificent mansion. The rooms have all groined ceilings in brick-work; some of them with ribs, and bosses at the intersections, in very good taste, and admirably executed. In a room which I may now call my bed-room, there is a fine arched recess, in which stood an iron bedstead elegantly fitted up. The furniture had once been splendid, but is now somewhat faded. In front of the recess a beautiful painted iron table was standing, and iron chairs were round the room. There is a large saloon with fresco paintings on the walls, as well as several other apartments which have been richly furnished. The whole are now kept for the accommodation of travelers, and every thing is provided for the table free of expense. Much used to be thought of the "horn of ale" given at some of the noble mansions in England, but in this

Zavod the traveler takes up his abode, and at whatever hour he may arrive, night or day, he is certain to find a welcome. His table is covered with excellent fare and delicious wines—Port, Sherry, Rhine wine, and Champagne. Such is the generous hospitality of the Oural, evidence of which may be found in every private Zavod.

It is said that the castle was once much more extensive, but that a part of it was destroyed by one of the Demidoffs, many years ago, out of caprice. The government had some suspicion that Demidoff was working other metals than iron in this Zavod, and sent a certain Count —— to examine into the matter. On his return the two met at the palace in St. Petersburg, when the count congratulated Demidoff on the taste and splendor of his noble mansion in the Oural. Demidoff asked if his excellency was as well satisfied with the hospitality as with the appearance of the mansion; the reply was, "Enchanted with both:" this sealed its doom. Demidoff wrote immediately to his agent at the Zavod to pull down the rooms which had been occupied by the count. They were demolished immediately, and no member of the family has ever resided at the Zavod since.

About two hundred paces from the castle stands a very fine brick tower, much out of the perpendicular; there is a subterraneous passage to it, now closed up. In this building the silver brought from the Altai was refined, and afterward coined on the island in the lake at Tchernoistotchinsk. It is also said that the first Demidoffs concealed here the fugitives who escaped from Tobolsk and other regions of Siberia, employing them in the mines and iron-works; if true, it was a grave offense, considering the formidable injunctions of the emperor.

Very good bar iron is made from a mixture of iron ore obtained here with a portion of magnetic iron ore from Nijne Tagilsk. The manufacture of painted iron-ware, which was once carried on extensively in Nijne Tagilsk, has long been removed to this Zavod, and is now a very important branch of its industrial operations. Large quantities of various articles are produced, which find their way through the fair at Irbit to every part of Siberia; also a peculiar kind of iron-bound wooden boxes, mostly painted red or blue, the iron-work black and ornamented. These are necessary appendages in every cottage; are made by free people, and thousands

Leaning Tower, Neviansk.

are sent to the fair at Irbit every year in February. An immense number of rifles are also turned out by them, the iron manufactured here being considered good for the purpose; the barrels are bored out of the solid metal, and rifled with five grooves, having one and a quarter turn in the length of the barrel: they are usually made very heavy. The stocks are of birch-wood; the locks obtained from Nijne-Novgorod, and are exceedingly rough; nevertheless, this is a most deadly weapon. No rifle made by Purday will carry its ball with more certainty than these: each is sold for 31*s.* 8*d.*

Two were manufactured especially for me, by order of the director, with more care than is usually bestowed on them, and the barrels were made lighter, and better stocked. One was a small bore or pea-rifle, carrying balls sixty-four to the pound: this was for the feathered race and small animals; the other was a large bore, carrying balls thirty-two to the pound, for deer, stags, elks, wolves, bears, or even the tiger: with both of these I could shoot with perfect accuracy, and I seldom failed procuring game for a dinner when once within range of bird or beast. These two rifles cost me, complete, with cases and all the necessary apparatus, £4 15*s.*

The Zavod and mines of Neviansk have been the property of Yakovlif for about a century: the population amounts to near 18,000, a great number of whom are free. A dispute arose between Yakovlif and the Demidoffs about the boundary of this property, the former claiming the iron mines in Nijne Tagilsk. It ended in a lawsuit, and as both parties were rich, it has, of course, been carried on for a great number of years. On my visit to Nijne Tagilsk in 1847, a new boundary was being formed between the two estates. Formerly stone pillars had been set up to mark the division of the property, but these were found insecure, as the strict injunction laid down in Scripture touching "thy neighbor's land-mark" was unknown in these regions. A most excellent plan has now been adopted—a deep trench has been dug along the boundary, and filled up with small charcoal; this is almost indestructible, and to move it without immediate detection impossible.

On leaving Neviansk my route was southward, nearly parallel to the high ridge of the Oural, about thirty or forty versts distant, and through what was once a densely-wooded country, but the forests have long been cut down for the use of the adjacent Zavods. The woods are in various stages of growth, according to the years in which each division fell under the woodman's axe; they are now springing up again from a sapling of one year to trees of sixty years' standing, which will soon be swept away to smelt the ores under them. The first village on the road is Shaidurikha. Here there is a little open country, also occasional patches as far as Mostovaia; from hence to Ekaterineburg it is one continued forest, affording no points of interest to the artist. To the geologist, mineralogist, and miner, the case is different; gold alluvium has been found on the little streams in most, if not in all the valleys, and extensively worked, in many instances most profitably. To the east of the road around Mursinsk lies the region in which the following precious stones of the Oural are found—emerald, amethyst, beryl, christoberyl, topaz, rose tourmaline, and garnets, all highly interesting to the crystallographer in their natural state, and much more so to the ladies when cut into gems.

Ekaterineburg is the capital of the Oural, and on entering the town from the north a church and some large mansions are seen on a high hill to the left overlooking the lake, a beautiful sheet of water, which extends several versts in a westerly direction, until hid behind the woods of Issetzskoï. One of these mansions, built by a very rich man who accumulated his immense wealth from gold mines, is of enormous dimensions, and from its elevated situation has a most imposing effect, commanding views of the Oural far to the north and west, until lost in distant haze. The Zavod of Verkne Issetzskoï, with its churches and public buildings, stands out beautifully in the centre of the view, while in the foreground and beneath is the lake, with several public and private edifices on its shores. The gardens belonging to this mansion, with the green-houses and hot-houses, are extensive and well laid out: they are open to the public in summer, and form a pleasant promenade. Formerly there was a splendid and choice collection of plants in the green-houses, but for many years past they have been neglected. The owner, notwithstanding his enormous wealth and elegant mansion, was banished and punished for flogging some of his people to death; another man implicated in this crime shared the same fate. Both had risen from peasants.

There are many honorable exceptions to these men in Ekaterineburg—merchants and owners of mines who would do credit to any country. They have accumulated very large fortunes, and have built themselves mansions equal to any found in the best European towns; the rooms are spacious, lofty, and beautifully finished; their decorations executed with excellent taste; they are also splendidly furnished—indeed, supplied with almost every luxury as well as comfort. With many of these fortunate persons, their mode of living equals the splendor of their habitations. Attached to most of their dwellings are large conservatories, in some of which are very choice collections of tropical plants and flowers, such as few would expect to find in so severe a climate.

There is a charming view of the town from the lake; the towers, spires, and domes of its eight churches, a monastery, and a convent, rising over the numerous public and private buildings, produce a most pleasing effect. The ground on which Ekaterineburg is built is thrown up into hills, on the crests of which are several good edifices. These are again overtopped by a rocky mount, clothed with dark green foliage, and on its summit stands the observatory, used mostly for magnetic observations. The churches, convents, public buildings, and large houses are all built of brick, covered with cement, and, when seen among the pine-clad hills of the Oural, have a very imposing appearance.

Nearly in the centre of the town a high embankment is carried across the valley of the Issetz, and at this point stand the mechanical works belonging to government. They are built upon an enormous scale, and fitted up with machinery and tools from the best makers in England. Here are found Nasmyth's steam-hammer, large lathes, planing machines, with punching, drilling, grooving, and slotting machines for every purpose. The entire arrangement of this establishment has been carried out, regardless of expense, under the superintendence of a good practical English mechanic, who has served the government for about fifteen years. He executed the whole of the excellent machinery of the Mint, in which copper money to a large amount is coined annually and sent into Russia. The furnace for smelting gold is in a building connected with the Mint, to which all the precious metals found in the Oural are brought. Here they are smelted and cast into bars, and sent to St. Petersburg.

Near these works stands the Granilnoï Fabric, the building in which the jaspers, porphyries, aventurine, and other stones found in the Oural are made into columns, pedestals, vases, and tables, unrivaled in workmanship either in ancient or modern times; the lathes, saws, and polishing machines used are turned by water-power. The whole establishment belongs to the crown, and is worked by peasants.

The jaspers are found in a great variety of colors—the most beautiful a deep green, dark purple, dark violet, gray, and cream-color; also a ribbon jasper with stripes of reddish-brown and green. The porphyries are equally fine and varied, some of most brilliant colors. Orlite is also a splendid stone of a deep pink color, with veins of yellow and black; when made into vases it is semi-transparent. Malachite is also used in making tables and various other articles. The vases are usually of a most classic design: this, with the rich materials in which they are executed, gives them a most magnificent effect; but to be able fully to appreciate such works, they must be seen in the splendid collections at the imperial palaces in St. Petersburg. I have frequently found and painted huge masses of these splendid rocks, of which I have now seventy-two varieties.

Most magnificent jasper tables are made in this Zavod, inlaid with different colored stones in imitation of birds, flowers, and foliage. In 1853 I saw one of them in Ekaterineburg on which four or five men had been employed for six years—not an uncommon circumstance; indeed, some examples have occupied a longer period. The cost of labor alone in England (provided the material were found there) would effectually prevent such work ever being executed in our country. Here wages are almost nothing. I have seen a man engaged carving foliage on some of the jasper vases, in a style not excelled any where in Europe, whose wages were *three shillings and eightpence per month*, with two poods, or thirty-six pounds of rye flour per month to make into bread; meat he is never supposed to eat. I have seen another man cutting a head of Ajax, after the antique, in jasper of two colors—the ground a dark green, and the head a yellowish cream-color—in very high relief, and intended for a brooch. It was a splendid production of art, and would have raised the man to a high position in any country in Europe except Russia. *He* also, poor man! received his three shillings and eightpence per month, and his bread. There are many men employed in these productions possessing great genius; were they free to use their talents for their own benefit, this country might send into civilized Europe numerous works of vast merit. A married man with a family receives two poods of black flour for his wife and one pood for each child, on which they live and look stout.

I have watched men cutting the emerald, topaz, amethyst, aquamarina, and other stones into different shapes, which they do with perfect accuracy and in good taste. Some of these brilliant gems have no doubt, ere this, adorned imperial majesty. These men also receive a like remuneration.

The following is the rate of wages paid to the superintendents and workmen employed in the cutting and polishing works. Two superintendents or master workmen, each of whom receives 240 rubles banco per annum, about £11 sterling, and their "black flour" (rye). There are also 160 workmen employed, divided into four classes:

A first class workman receives	4	rubles banco	per month	=	3*s*. 8*d*.
A second class ditto	3	ditto	ditto	=	2*s*. 9*d*.
A third class ditto	2	ditto	ditto	=	1*s*. 10*d*.
A fourth class ditto, or boys,	1	ditto	ditto	=	11*d*.,

and their black bread.

Ekaterineburg being the capital of the Oural and the centre of the mining districts, here is established the *Gornoï-pravlania*, or General Board for the Direction of the Mines, which consists of a great number of officers who live in Ekaterineburg with their families. At present the chief of the Oural is a general of artillery, most probably appointed to this position in consequence of nearly all the iron-works belonging to the crown having been employed for many years past in casting and boring large guns, casting shot and shells, and in preparing other munitions of war. There is another general of artillery stationed in Ekaterineburg, who is independent of the chief, and holds his appointment from the Minister of War. His duty is the general supervision and a close inspection of all the guns and arms of whatever kind made in the Zavods of the Oural. This gentleman has artillery officers resident in many of the Zavods to watch every process in the manufacture of these destructive implements.

There is also a Berg inspector, or chief Director of Mines, a most important office, filled during my visit by one of the most intelligent mining engineers in the empire; not only eminent for his talents, but also for his kind disposition and gentlemanly conduct. To him and his amiable wife I am deeply indebted for many acts of kindness, as well as for some of the most agreeable days I spent in the Altai. May it please Heaven to preserve them, and give lasting prosperity to their family! Many other mining engineers are employed in the Zavod with whom I am personally acquainted, and from whom I have received much attention.

To the director of the Granilnoï Fabric, or polishing works, I am greatly indebted for permitting me to see the processes used in cutting and polishing the different jaspers and porphyries; also for allowing me to examine those elegant productions of the lathe and chisel which adorn the imperial palaces, and confer so much credit on his taste and skill. To the Natchalnic of 1852 I offer my thanks for his valuable assistance; the kind attentions of his wife will be long remembered. The Inspector of Hospitals I would not omit; although mentioned the last, he is not the least; to him and his amiable family I am indebted for many pleasing recollections of Ekaterineburg. It would ill become me were I to forget other inhabitants of the town. The Golova, or Mayor of 1853, and several of the merchants, I shall ever remember with pleasure.

A traveler from the most civilized parts of Europe, who should come here to gratify his curiosity, would not find a very remarkable difference between the style of living in this region among the wealthy and that of the same class in his own country. He would find the ladies handsomely clad in dresses made from the best products of the looms of France and England, and would be welcomed at the fireside, and on all occasions, with a generous hospitality seldom met with elsewhere. If asked to dinner, he would find placed on the board a repast that would not disgrace the best hotels of the same countries. Fish and game of every kind are most abundant here, and luxuries from far distant regions are not wanting. Wines of the finest quality, and in great variety, are ever found at their tables, the only drawback to comfort being the quantity of Champagne the traveler is obliged to drink.

Their balls are elegant, and conducted with great propriety, and they dance well. The elder members of society spend their time at cards, risking much money in this way. It is deeply to be regretted that the young men are also much addicted to gambling, a pursuit which often ends in ruin here as elsewhere. During my stay in the Oural a young officer shot himself on account of his losses at cards.

Even the fair sex in Ekaterineburg pass much of their time in card-playing. I am acquainted with one family where there are no less than eleven children; there is not a day in the year during which their mother spends less than five or six hours at cards, unless prevented by sickness; and when once she sits down to the card-table, husband, children, and all are forgotten. I know another lady here, the principal business of whose life is card-playing. She has a moderate income, and passes her days and most of her nights at cards; she has her daily rounds, and goes with as much exactness to her haunts as the most punctual merchant to his office. Ten o'clock in the morning is her hour of business; the tables are opened and the cards placed. If no one call before this hour, she goes forth to her usual occupation, and seeks some one among her friends who will sit down and play, if only for an hour. The game over at one place, she goes to another, till she finds some one who will indulge her in a second rubber, and so the time passes until dinner. After dining she sleeps a couple of hours, and wakes quite fresh for her favorite pursuit. In the evening she has no difficulty, for many are willing to play: thus the time is spent until a late hour.

At one of the large mining towns in the Altai there lives a man who has become rich from gold mines, and is a celebrated card-player. It is no unusual circumstance for him to visit St. Petersburg; and as Ekaterineburg is about midway between the capital and his place of residence, he is sometimes obliged to stop on the way to repair carriages, after a run of more than two thousand versts—in fact, it is often absolutely necessary. This man's fame having spread far and wide, his detention in the town for the first time was an event which afforded the lady I have just alluded to the utmost delight: she could not permit such an opportunity to pass without trying a rubber with so renowned a champion. At her particular request, a friend arranged that they should meet at dinner. She has been heard to say, no hours ever dragged on so slowly as on that forenoon; still, the sun ran his course, and, directly dinner was over, down they sat to cards. The evening went on with varied success, the lady was enraptured, and rose from the table the winner of a large sum. She invited her opponent to play the next day; after some demur he consented, and the following day the contest was renewed, and continued until she had lost all. Nothing daunted, she urged him again to defer his journey for four-and-twenty hours, as her half year's income would arrive by the post the following morning. But then came a difficulty about getting the money at once, as there was some formality which would delay it a day or two. After much trouble, she persuaded the person to whom it was consigned to waive the usual form, and let her have the money immediately. She got it, and so strong was her ruling passion, that every moment seemed lost until seated at the card-table. In a few hours she left it without a kopek—her half year's income entirely gone!

Speaking with some of the most intelligent men on this subject, their reply was, "In England you have the daily papers, the monthly periodicals, a literature unequaled, and the liberty of discussing every subject with freedom; if we had such things to occupy our minds, we should not care for cards."

The government employs a great number of its serfs in this Zavod in the machine shops and on other works. None of them can be said to be "poor," if by this word is meant want of bread; black bread they have, and salt; these, with a draught of quass (a drink made from rye), is the food of hundreds who work hard for twelve hours in the day, and receive for their labor *fourpence.* The Russian peasants have most undoubtedly great imitative genius, and nothing daunts them. Men are brought from a village, never having seen any mechanical operations before, and are taken into the Zavod. One is told he must be a blacksmith: he goes to his anvil without the least hesitation, and begins his work; another is ordered to be a fitter in the machine-shop: he seats himself at his bench, looks at the work his neighbor is doing, takes up his file, commences his new, and, to him, wonderful occupation: so they go on through many branches.

There is one great drawback to the efficiency of the machine works in Ekaterineburg—at present there is no practical head to direct. It is not, as the authorities suppose, sufficient that a man has been educated in the School of Mines in St. Petersburg, and that, after serving a few years in the Altai or the Oural mines, he is sent to England, and visits the different mechanical engineering manufactories, walking through them occasionally, and taking notes during a period of twelve or eighteen months. This is not the training necessary to fit a man to direct efficiently and practically a great establishment. He must acquire the requisite knowledge by the toil of his own hands. Great mechanics are not made in any other way, nor is it in the power of epaulettes, of whatever size or material, to accomplish this object. In all our great machine works there are good practical mechanics able to direct, who have worked with their own hands. The great men of England have all done so; there are Fairbairn, Roberts, Nasmyth, Whitworth, and a host of others, as distinguished examples. How much better it would be to select a hundred youths, and send them as apprentices for seven years into different establishments, either in England or elsewhere; they would learn something, and return competent to take charge of the different departments: his imperial majesty and the country would then profit by their acquirements. I have been induced to make these remarks, as I have not been an idle spectator on my rambles through the Zavods. On the other hand, I have seen and deeply regret being compelled to admit that, in some of the works near the Oural, certain departments have been conducted by my own countrymen who were evidently quite incompetent, as the Russian government have learned to their cost.

The lapidaries of Ekaterineburg deserve most honorable mention: they have brought their art to great perfection in cutting the various stones found in Siberia, and some of them may vie with the best in Europe.

About twenty-five or thirty years ago, several fine crystals of emerald were discovered by some children while playing near the village of Takovaya, and were tossed about in the cottage for a considerable time before their character was recognized. At length they were sent to Ekaterineburg, and were most splendidly cut in the Granilnoï Fabric. They proved to be gems of rare beauty and great value. As all precious stones, wherever found in Siberia, are the property of the emperor, these ought to have been sent to the imperial palace in St. Petersburg; but they never reached the imperial jewel-case. They were sent into Germany, where they were bought by a prince of one of the first reigning families. Some years afterward, his consort, on some great occasion, visited the Emperor of Russia, and, while staying in St. Petersburg, wore these magnificent and rare gems. They were of such surpassing beauty as to attract the notice of the empress, who admired them very much, and inquired whence they were obtained. To the great astonishment of her imperial majesty, she was told they came from Siberia. This caused a great sensation. Without giving time for any communication to be made to Ekaterineburg, the emperor sent an officer to search the works, and the houses of all persons connected with the Granilnoï Fabric. He found in the house of the director several gems of great value, which the latter declared were there for safe custody. This was thought somewhat strange, as other gems and valuable works were lying at the museum in the Fabric. The director was, without any investigation, sent to prison, and, after many years' confinement, died there; nor is it known to this day by whom these emeralds were stolen. In Siberia it is still believed that the man was innocent, but that, for the safety of persons of more consideration, it was absolutely necessary he should be imprisoned; in short, it has been hinted that the offense was committed by parties much nearer his imperial majesty. Since this period few emeralds of value have been discovered.

Amethysts are still found at Tushakalva, a village near Mursinsk: these stones are far superior to the Brazilian amethyst, have a much greater brilliancy, and are more valuable. Beryl is found in several parts of the Oural—some crystals exceedingly fine, of a blue, yellow, and rose color; those of the latter kind are rare, and, when perfectly transparent, of considerable value. I have seen some splendid specimens in Ekaterineburg most beautifully cut. Chrysoberyl is met with in the same locality as the emerald; occasionally very fine crystals are obtained, and cut into beautiful gems. Topaz is found at Alabaska and near Maïas; some of these magnificent crystals have been discovered six inches long, perfectly transparent, and sold at a very great price. I have seen fine specimens cut as gems, and exceedingly brilliant. Pink topaz is rare: up to this time only five small crystals have been met with at one of the gold mines in the South Oural; one of these was presented to me: I deeply regret to say that it is either mislaid or has been lost on the journey.

Rose tourmaline is found at the village of Sarapulsk, near Mursinsk. This is also a rare mineral; I have seen but one crystal pure and transparent. Small specimens cut into gems are sometimes to be got in Ekaterineburg under the name of "malina sherl." Smoke topaz is met with in many places in the Oural—some beautifully transparent, which they cut into seals of most elegant form. Pure transparent quartz also passes under the name of topaz: large quantities of seals are made of this, and sold in Ekaterineburg, on which the lapidaries cut figures, coats of arms, or ciphers at a very moderate cost. This forms quite a trade, as the workmen employed in the Granilnoï Fabric cut these articles at home in the evenings and holidays, using a small foot-lathe. Malachite is also worked into a variety of beautiful ornaments, such as vases, work-boxes, tables, paper-weights, brooches, and beads, for which they find a ready sale.

Aquamarina is brought to Ekaterineburg from Eastern Siberia. It is obtained near Nertchinsk, sometimes in very fine crystals of great value; these are cut into bracelets, brooches, ear-rings, stones for pins, rings, and other ornaments, and have a most sparkling and brilliant effect. Besides gems and seals, the lapidaries make tables, small vases, and paper-weights, in great numbers, of the different jaspers and porphyries, many of great beauty both in design and color. Some of the jasper paper-weights have a bunch of grapes in amethyst, with foliage on the top, beautifully executed.

An extensive manufactory of stearine has recently been established near Ekaterineburg; and as tallow is brought from Siberia and the Kirghis Steppe in enormous quantities, it is the intention of the company to make stearine, and send it in casks into Europe; also to make sufficient candles to supply the whole of Siberia. This will, no doubt, prove a most profitable concern, if properly carried on.

Two enterprising young engineers have established machine works in Ekaterineburg; they are both practical men; one of them a very superior man. There is every hope that they will succeed. I do not wish it for their advantage alone, but for the general good they will confer on the Siberians, by introducing into that region machinery required for various useful purposes. The late chief of the Oural created many difficulties, and retarded their operations; a more enlightened man will pursue a different course, and benefit the people.

Verkne Issetzskoi Zavod, about three versts from Ekaterineburg, belongs to the Yakovlif family, and here resides the chief director of the whole of their vast mining property. These works have long been celebrated for the quality of sheet iron, which stands unrivaled. This Zavod has the appearance of a considerable town, with its large furnaces, churches, and other buildings. There is one enormous pile, in which are all the offices for the administration of this vast mining property; beneath are large warehouses for iron and other produce. Here are blast-furnaces for smelting the ore, forging mills, tilting mills, and rolling mills for bar and sheet iron, including every process until finished for the market, and each department is admirably managed.

The sheet iron made in this Zavod, and at some of the other works belonging to it, surpasses all other productions of the kind either in the Oural or elsewhere. It is rolled for various purposes—for covering the roofs of houses, for sheet-iron stoves, also for the manufacture of a great variety of utensils. The metal is of so excellent a quality that I have seen it rolled as thin as post paper, without either crack or blemish, and with a jet black polish. An enormous quantity of the various sorts of this manufacture is sent to America, where it is most extensively used.

The chief director, and the different officers under him, deserve the highest praise, every thing in these works being conducted with the greatest order. The public buildings have been erected in good taste, and are well suited for the purposes intended. The cottages for the artificers are of a superior class, the streets are kept clean and in good order, and the people look healthy and very comfortable in their dwellings.

CHAPTER VII.

IRON AND GOLD WORKS.

I MUST now pass to the South Oural, down the valley of the Issetz to Nijne Issetzskoi Zavod—iron-works belonging to the crown, where most of the castings required for the machine works in Ekaterineburg are made, from which it is only twelve versts distant.

On both sides of the valley low hills rise up, covered to the top with pine and larch trees, among which are seen the silvery birch waving its delicate foliage. In the valley a large lake has been formed by carrying a high embankment across the Issetz; and here stand the blast-furnaces, belching forth their smoke and flame.

When seen from the lake on a dark night, with their reflections cast on the water, and black figures dimly lighted by the red glare flitting past—sometimes in groups, at others singly, but soon lost in gloom—the scene has a touch of the infernal about it; still, it is highly picturesque and grand. After passing the Zavod the valley extends in width, and in many parts is very pretty; clumps of trees with grassy meadows, with the river winding along, sometimes lost in woods, then again breaking forth, shining like frosted silver as it rolls over its rocky bed. Twenty-two versts from Ekaterineburg is the village of Aramilskoï: at this place the road leaves the valley of the Issetz, passing over some low hills more toward the ridge of the Oural. After traveling about ten versts it descends into the valley of the River Syssert, in which stands Syssertskoï Zavod—iron-works belonging to the family of Salemerskoï, one of whom has taken up his abode here. The situation is pretty, and well sheltered among wooded hills. On approaching the Zavod, the church, hospitals, furnaces, and warehouses have a very imposing appearance; the streets are well laid out, and the cottages built in a much better style than is usually adopted in the Oural. Altogether, the town was clean, and evidently kept under the eye of the master.

Mr. Salemerskoï is undoubtedly a man of good taste, and possesses some valuable works of art. He is a good musician as well as a horticulturist, and his garden, green-houses, and hot-houses are on an extensive scale. He has a large orangery, well stocked with lemon and orange trees, some in full fruit, others in blossom, giving out a delicious perfume. There is also a very large house in which cherries, plums, and peaches are grown in great perfection. It was, indeed, a pleasure to see these trees in full blossom; they reminded me of home and my childhood, bringing to my recollection scenes that can never return. As such trees can not stand this climate, it is only under glass that the fruit can be produced. His flowers and tropical plants are splendid, and well arranged in several different houses to suit their proper temperature: in one there was a collection of more than 200 sorts of calceolaria, and almost every plant in flower; I never saw any thing more gorgeous: the colors were perfectly dazzling, and were in all shades, from the deepest purple, crimson, scarlet, and orange, to a pale yellow; these, with the beautiful green of their foliage, produced an enchanting effect. Mr. Salemerskoï is also devoting his attention to the breeding of English horses, and possesses some very fine animals.

Having spent two days in this Zavod, sketching a view of the works, on I traveled over a wooded, undulating country. In some parts extensive tracts of rye were growing most luxuriantly, in others fine pastures for cattle extended far among the trees: the verdure and foliage indicated that I was going in a southerly direction. The country for about thirty-five versts after leaving Syssertskoï has not one single point either of interest or beauty, but on approaching Lake Silätch the scenery improves; to the west of the lake pine-clad hills rise up until overtopped by Mount Sugomac and the crest of the Oural. From this point the road passes into a fine woodland country, sometimes through rich pasture-land, with large clumps of birch and poplars. Occasionally the path was close on the shore of the lake, which was exceedingly shallow and rocky; again the road turned into the woods, winding along some park-like scenery, until at length Kaslinskoï was seen standing close upon the margin of the lake, with its Zavod sending up a dense black smoke; its churches and other large buildings, with their green domes and golden crosses sparkling in the sun, gave it a grand and imposing appearance.

These iron-works are famed throughout the Oural for the superior quality of castings they produce. On going through the warehouse, I was astonished by the sharpness and beauty of the different articles manufactured, consisting of tables, perforated in tracery and foliage, most delicately executed; chairs of a similar pattern, small boxes, baskets, and dishes for cards, in beautiful open-work; animals, paper-weights, and various other articles, cast equal to any thing produced in Berlin. With a good designer and carver in these works, they could cast any thing, as the metal used possesses much fluidity.

From this Zavod the road runs along the shore of the Irtiash Lake, which is near twenty versts in length, and in places ten broad, extending nearly up to the foot of Mount Sugomac. Some parts of the eastern shores are rocky, but of no great elevation; here and there very large masses have been detached from the rocks, and are now lying at a considerable distance. It is somewhat difficult to account for their removal; small blocks would be forced out into the lake by the recoil of the waves, but masses weighing from sixty to one hundred tons are not so easily moved. They may have been lifted out with the ice during a gale of wind, as sometimes the storm tumbles the water about in the lakes fearfully. A short distance to the east there is another lake, Kizil-tash; this is also of considerable dimensions. In fact, the country abounds in lakes, interspersed among fine woodland scenery and rich pastures.

After passing the Kizil-tash the road crosses some thickly-wooded hills for about five or six versts; then we looked down into the valley beneath, and saw at a short distance Kishtymsky Zavod, with its large mansion called the castle. It is, indeed, an enormous edifice, forming three sides of a quadrangle, with its out-buildings, and inclosed on the fourth with a wall and iron railing; in the centre are massive brick gate-piers and iron gates. This dwelling of a miner in the Oural would make some of our best baronial mansions look insignificant if placed in contrast with it. The building is of brick, now become black from the smoke of the iron-works, which stand at a short distance to the west. Nor has it been finished externally; only a very small part has been plastered with cement, just sufficient to show the design and details, which are exceedingly bold. The interior has been completed; in the centre, on the ground floor, there is a large entrance-hall, with a beautiful groined ceiling in brick-work; beyond this is a large room, also groined and made fire-proof, the ceiling well finished with ribs and tracery; the centre window opens to the floor, leading to a large circular portico, from which two circular flights of stone steps descend into the garden. The whole of this floor is used by the director for his residence. At each end of the building are two magnificent stone staircases leading to the upper story, which contains the principal rooms: they are most spacious and lofty. Here, again, we see the hand of Demidoff, this place having also been built by him. Every plan that has been made either by him or under his direction possesses something characteristic of the man. In mines, and all connected therewith, he has shown a mind as great as his patron's; and so long as a mine is worked or a furnace smelts ore in the Oural, his name will descend to each succeeding generation as one of the most distinguished of his era.

The situation for this mansion has been well chosen, near the head of the lake; the views from the principal rooms take in the finest points in this part of the Oural, and some are particularly beautiful. Mount Sugomac is seen rising high above the lake, forming the last watch-tower looking over Siberia. Here I also observed the sun go down. When just below the horizon, a splendid yellow and orange color spread over the sky, with deep crimson clouds stretching along in feathery and wavy lines; higher up rolled billowy masses, tinged on their lower edges with a deep red shading into gray. Against this golden sky Sugomac reared his dark purple crest, which, with his misty ravines and dense forests, were distinctly reflected in Nature's mirror at his feet. Then the glorious colors of the sky were shed upon this lake, lighting it up like liquid fire, and it was rendered still more brilliant by the deep shade of evening spread over the dark woods which surround it. Truth obliges me to add that during the summer months no one occupies these rooms, and this magnificent scenery, therefore, excites no admiration.

The garden, which extends along the shore of the lake, has some fine avenues of lime-trees, now in full bloom, forming a most delightful shade in summer. These, and the great variety of flowers and shrubs in bloom, gave forth a most delicious fragrance; in addition, from the midst of the shrubbery the nightingale warbled forth his delightful song. Such enjoyments, with the gentle ripple of the lake, and the calm and beautiful sunset, which diffused over every thing a heavenly radiance, made me forget that I was on the border of that much-dreaded and often-abused Siberia.

Having remained several days at this Zavod, sketching the scenery, visiting Mount Sugomac with its caverns, one of which is said to be three hundred feet in length, and other interesting objects, I took leave of my hospitable host and passed on to other scenes. My road was along the eastern flank of the chain to Soimanofsky gold mines; there the scenery becomes more wild: masses of rock are seen among the pine and birch trees, and not far to the eastward is Lake Uvaldi, with its small islands. In this region lakes are very numerous: I have been told that more than one hundred can be seen from the summit of Mount Sugomac.

After crossing the River Kialim, I followed its course to Lake Argasi, in the Ilman-tou, which was worth sketching. My route was now up the valley of the River Maïas, in which there are several gold mines: some have been very rich; they are the property of the crown. This valley is beautifully studded with birch, poplar, and willows; several kinds of flowering shrubs are also growing along the banks of the river; and, being well sheltered from the cold winds, the herbage, flowers, and foliage were most luxuriant. In the open glades a splendid crop of grass was growing, in some places nearly up to my shoulders; of this I had abundant proof, having walked through it, and shot many double snipes while crossing to one of the gold mines. In a few days the whole of this grass will be cut down and made into hay, affording to the hardy peasants of the district abundance of winter food for their cattle. Every family in this region possesses horses, cows, pigs, and often poultry; good milk and cream they always have, but few of them understand how to make good butter. Their gardens will produce almost every kind of vegetable. On the hills is found plenty of wild fruit—strawberries, red and black currants, bilberries, a wild cherry growing on a small plant not more than two feet high, and raspberries, all having a most delicious flavor. In the mountains there is plenty of game, not protected by game-laws. Each peasant walks off with his rifle, kills either birds or deer, and then returns to his cottage to feast on his spoil. In most of the mountain streams grayling are found in great numbers, and very large pike are caught in the lakes.

Leaving this lovely valley, the road crosses the Oural-tou to the westward, skirting round the rocky summits called Alexander-sopka, named after the present emperor, who visited it when in the Oural. This forms the watershed between Europe and Asia, and into the latter the Maïas, along whose banks I had been traveling, runs. Having crossed the ridge, the road descends rapidly into the valley of the River Aï, which finds its way through many a winding gorge into Europe. At a short distance below the summit of the ridge I had a beautiful view looking down into the valley, where I observed a large lake, and a small part of Zlataoust, its white buildings shining brightly in the sun at the foot of the Urengà.

The descent was rather abrupt in some places, and afforded, at the different turnings of the road, several fine views of the higher peaks of the South Oural; and at about ten versts distant to the northeast is Taganaï, signifying, in the Bashkir language, "Tripod of the Moon," which rises boldly above the surrounding mountains. Its bold rocky peaks are seen from a great distance; and the best aventurine found in the Oural has been obtained from some rocks near the summit. To the southwest are seen Iremel and Iaman-tou: these three are the highest points in the South Oural. After a gallop of about seven versts down this steep descent (a speed the yemstchick considers absolutely necessary), we reached the valley, where the road turns sharp round toward the north; and here stands a small chapel, at which the passing peasant always offers up his prayers. From this point there is a fine view of Taganaï.

The road now runs at a short distance from the shore of the lake, affording a good view of Zlataoust, nestled between the mountains, with the Urengà rising far above it. After crossing the small river Tisma on a rough wooden bridge, the road turns to the west, under the high rocks at the head of the lake, along which we bounded, and in about ten minutes were galloping at full speed into Zlataoust. There was a great festival; the people were all going about in their holiday attire; the women and girls dressed, as usual, in very gay colors, and playing in groups; and the bright sunny day made the Zavod look absolutely charming.

Zlataoust is the Birmingham and Sheffield of the Oural, and stands on the banks of the River Aï, in a very narrow part of the valley. A high embankment has been carried across, which has formed a lake six or seven versts long, and about two versts broad. Here are erected all the different works required for this great manufactory of arms, to which this body of water gives the moving power.

There is a large blast furnace where the ores are smelted; also forging mills, in which the pig iron is hammered into bars; in fact, every process is carried on, until the raw material becomes steel. Up to the year 1847 these works were under the administration of General Anossoff, one of the most skillful and ingenious metallurgists of the age.

Here is also an enormous fire-proof building, consisting of three stories. In the ground floor, sabres, swords, daggers, cuirasses, and helmets are forged, while in the upper stories every other process is carried on (except grinding, which is done in another large building near at hand) until the weapons are completed. The etching and ornamenting on some of the swords are most exquisitely executed. These workshops were designed by, and built under the direction of General Anossoff. I have not seen either in Birmingham or Sheffield any establishment that can compare with them; indeed, this is one of the most extensive and best-arranged fabrics of arms in Europe.

There is also an excellent museum, built by order of the Emperor Alexander the First, containing a fine collection of arms, cuirasses, and similar curiosities, with specimens of every variety of sabre, sword, or other arms manufactured in these works since the commencement of the establishment, beautifully disposed in columns and pyramids; several of the rooms are splendidly decorated with arms and implements of war. There is also a library, and a well-arranged collection of minerals.

These works had been under the care and management of Colonel Anossoff for many years previous to 1847, in the spring of which I first made his acquaintance. During this long period the colonel had turned his attention to the ancient art of damascening arms, which had long been lost in Europe; and he, by indefatigable zeal, with much skill succeeded in rescuing this long-lost art from oblivion. Being placed on the confines of Asia, where damask blades are still held in high estimation, he had opportunities of seeing sabres, ataghans, and daggers of great value, which some of the Asiatic chiefs still possess; also of procuring specimens through the aid of the caravans from Khiva, Bokhara, and even India. Added to this, General Perroffsky, the governor of Orenburg, and commander-in-chief of the army in this region, had one of the rarest private collections of ancient and modern arms in the world, and with a liberality which so truly characterizes a great mind, placed it at the disposal of Anossoff. Select examples were taken to Zlataoust, their material and fabrication studied with untiring assiduity, and chemical experiments resorted to, until, step by step, and after years of toil, damascene sabres and arms were produced, perhaps unequaled even in ancient, certainly never approached in modern times.

In the summer of 1847 General Anossoff was made Governor of Tomsk, and Chief of the Mines in the Altai. He soon removed to his new appointment, which prevented our meeting again until the following winter. On my return to Barnaoul after my first ramble in the Altai, with true hospitable kindness he invited me to his house, and, feeling much interest in his discoveries, I often made them the subject of our conversation. Although removed to other regions, far from the spot on which he had through many a sleepless night wrought out his path to fame, besides having other important functions to discharge, he found time to pursue his favorite study, and actually began making steel, or, as he named it, *Boulat*, the material which he used for making damascene arms. In May, 1848, I accompanied him to some of the Zavods in the Altai, at one of which he said, "I will make arms here even superior to those I have made at Zlataoust, and this shall be the Birmingham of the Altai."

Here we separated, and I wandered far over Asia before we met again in March, 1850: he was still occupied with his researches, and showed me some dagger-blades made in the Altai, which he considered peculiarly fine. I often urged the general to complete his treatise on this subject, one in an abridged form having been published several years before, since which time important and valuable results have proceeded from his investigations. I was assured that every process had been carefully noted down, and that he was in possession of much invaluable information, which at some future time would be given to the world.

In 1851, while I was sketching among the mountains and plains on which more than six hundred years before Genghis Khan marshaled his vast hosts, my friend died at Omsk: not one member of his family was near to soothe his last moments or receive his parting blessing, they being in St. Petersburg, near two thousand miles distant.*

* Captain James Abbott, of the Honorable East India Company's Artillery, has paid a just tribute to the genius of Anossoff in his narrative of "A Journey from Heraut to St. Petersburg." I may also add that his visit to the "Siberian home" of this amiable family has never been forgotten. I am also in a position to add that the shawl in which he was wounded in the night attack of the Huzzauks has been united, and is still preserved as a treasure by his Ouralian friends. "So far Colonel Anossoff [he was made a general in 1843], a man whose researches in this department of science have enabled him to revive the natural damask in a degree of perfection which I have never observed in the workmanship even of the ancients, and which certainly can not be approached by fabrics of any Eastern nation at present existing. The Russian damask, on the contrary, discovered by my friend Colonel Anossoff, is natural. It is a peculiar modification of cast steel, by which it is im-

When Anossoff left Zlataoust its glory departed as far as regards damascening arms. The works were placed under the superintendence of a mind infinitely inferior; and in the summer of 1853, on my visit to Zlataoust, I found that a damask blade could not be manufactured. On my return from Asia I brought with me a few of these blades, and one I presented to a friend who has sought glory at the cannon's mouth. At present he fills a most honorable post in his country's service. Should he at any future time be called upon to lead her sons to battle, I trust he will do it with this brand; it is one that will never fail him: he will find it true as his own courage.

After sketching in Zlataoust and the neighborhood, I visited the mines where garnets and some other rare minerals are obtained. I also sketched a few scenes on the River Aï. I left the place with regret, and, as I ascended from the valley, looked back on the spot where my friend had successfully labored, convinced that I should never see it again. My road was now up the Ou-

pressed with a peculiar character in its crystallization, which character betrays itself when the corrosion of acids, by acting more violently between the interstices of the structure than elsewhere, traces out the arrangement of the crystals. This property is communicated to the damask of Zlataoust by a process tending to perfect the quality of the steel, and to impress upon cast steel the elastic properties of a softer material. The general fault of European blades is, that, being forged of shear steel for the sake of elasticity, they are scarcely perceptible of the keen edge that cast steel will assume. The genius of Anossoff has triumphed over this objection, not in hardening the soft steel, but in giving elasticity to the hard; and it may be doubted whether any fabric in the world can compete with that of Zlataoust in the production of weapons combining an equal degree of edge and elasticity. The water of this variety of damask resembles most that of No. 5, of my list above. It is a succession of small bundles of almost parallel lines, occupying the whole breadth of the blade, the ends of the bundles crossing and mingling at the point of junction; I have called them nearly parallel lines, because such they are to superficial observation. They are, however, a series of minute curves, forming together lines, disposed in bundles articulated together, and dividing the length of the weapon into many sections. They have not the regular articulation of the articulated Khorussaunie blade; their lines are infinitely finer. I have seen several, which were condemned for insufficient temper, submitted to the action of the engine by which they are broken. The blades were bent double, and back again, several times ere they could be divided. The red hue observed upon damask blades I have seen only on those of Zlataoust."

In another part of his narrative the captain expresses a hope that the man who is "building to himself and his country a name in the world of science" may not, like too many of the illustrious, wear his laurels over his tomb. Alas! his country has not added one stone to his simple monument, or a line to his epitaph. He lies forgotten by all except his family, and a few friends who knew his worth.

ral-tou, over which I must cross to the gold-mines in the south. The peaks of the Oural-tou are on the line dividing Asia and Europe: they are rugged and picturesque. The highest of these rocks has been named Alexander-sopka, and an inscription near the summit records the date of the Grand-Duke Alexander's ascent. These peaks are about 2500 feet above the level of the sea, and are seen at a great distance when approaching the Oural from the steppes of Asia.

Not far from this summit, in one of the valleys of the Taganaï, a singular incident happened to an old woman. Her cow had strayed, and was nowhere to be found in her usual pastures. This gave the good dame considerable anxiety. At last she determined to search for her in the higher valleys. Leaving her cottage early one morning, she rambled on for several hours, and at length found herself far up on the Taganaï without coming upon any traces of the fugitive. This was very disheartening; still, she would not give up her search. The valley she had entered upon was thickly wooded with pines in many parts; in others there were fine open glades, with clumps of bushes and shrubs, and among these she wended her way from one little plot of grass to another. At last she spied the well-known dark brown hide through some bushes. The old woman thought of the many hours she had been searching for the truant, and, stealing softly on, determined to give her sufficient chastisement. When within reach of her birchen staff, the blows fell fast. Up sprang the animal and turned sharp round, when, to the dame's horror, she saw a large brown bear. The two stood staring at each other, apparently with equal astonishment and apprehension, when Bruin, seized with a sudden panic, turned tail and bolted.

Near the scene of this heroine's adventure, two children, one four and the other six years old, rambled away from their friends, who were hay-making. They had gone from one thicket to another gathering fruit, laughing and enjoying the fun. At last they came near a bear lying on the grass, and, without the slightest apprehension, went up to him. He looked at them steadily without moving; at length they began playing with him, and mounted upon his back, which he submitted to with perfect good-humor. In short, both seemed inclined to be pleased with each other; indeed, the children were delighted with their new play-fellow. The

H

parents, missing the truants, became alarmed, and followed on their track. They were not long in searching out the spot, when, to their dismay, they beheld one child sitting on the bear's back, and the other feeding him with fruit! They called quickly, when the youngsters ran to their friends, and Bruin, apparently not liking the interruption, went away into the forest.

I shall frequently have occasion to speak of Cossack and Kalmuck hunters, also of the daring of the Siberian peasant in his combats with the bear, but shall now introduce to my readers one of my acquaintance of the softer sex, who was not surpassed in courage and daring by either Kalmuck or Cossack. In one of my rambles after leaving Pavdinska, which led me to the east of Verkoturia and as far as the River Tavda, I came upon a party of peasants in the forest cutting wood, and among them were several women. It was here that I first made the acquaintance of Anna Petrovnaia, the bear-hunter. Her fame has spread far from the scenes of her conflicts with Bruin, who has not in the wide range of Siberia a more intrepid or dangerous enemy. At this time she was about thirty-two years of age, neither tall nor stout, but her step was firm, and she was strong and active. Her countenance was soft and pleasing; indeed, there was nothing in her appearance that indicated her extraordinary intrepidity. It is true she came of a good stock, her father and brothers being famous hunters. I was informed that very early in life she had displayed a love for the chase; and having been taught how to use the rifle, many wolves and other animals had fallen by her hand. Each time that bear-skins were brought home by the different members of her family, her desire increased to add one to her other spoils. Without breathing a word to any one, and with this object in view, she set out on a sporting ramble, the conversations of her family having afforded sufficient intimation of the course she ought to take.

One day a large black bear had been seen by one of her brothers when ranging through the forest with his pea-rifle in quest of smaller game. This was spoken of in her presence, and the plan of a campaign arranged, to be carried into effect in a day or two. The next morning, long before any member of the household had left their beds, she had put on her hunting-gear, saddled a horse, slung her rifle over her shoulder, and rode away. Anna was so erratic in her movements that her absence caused no uneasiness, and before day dawned she was many versts from the cottage. Early in the morning she reached the forest and secured her horse, so that he might feed while she penetrated the thick and tangled wood before her.

There was a heavy dew on the grass in the open glades, and she observed that Bruin was taking his morning ramble, his track being quite fresh. Looking to the priming of her rifle, and adding powder from her flask, she went on with a firm step. The bear had made many turnings on his march, but she followed him with all the sagacity of a bloodhound, and never once lost his trail. Hour after hour passed, however, and she had not caught a glimpse of him. As it threatened to be a long chase, Anna had recourse to her little bag, sat down by a small stream and made her breakfast on a piece of rye bread, washed down with a draught from the pure liquid flowing at her feet. Having ended her frugal meal, she shouldered her rifle and again pushed on. She had another long and fruitless walk. Satisfied, however, that she was on his track, she pursued it till she arrived at a bed of high plants, that included the giant fennel, of the flowers of which the bears are very fond. While proceeding along the edge of this bed, a fresh indication, well known to hunters, assured her that the long-sought-for game was at hand. As she was creeping cautiously forward, out rushed the bear, with a loud growl, about twenty yards in front. Quickly she threw forward the prongs of her rifle, dropped on one knee and got a good sight, the animal staring at her almost motionless. She now touched the trigger, there followed a flash, a savage growl succeeded, then a struggle for a minute or two, and her wish was accomplished: the bear lay dead!

After taking off his skin, she started in search of her horse, which she found at no great distance, for she had been brought back nearly to the spot where she commenced the chase. She was shortly on her way home, and astonished her family, on her entrance to the cottage, by throwing the skin on the floor. Since this time Anna Petrovnaia has engaged with and killed *sixteen bears.*

Our horses were turned once more toward the south, and by a winding track we descended to the Tchornia, passing from this into a longitudinal valley thickly wooded with birch, aspen, and poplar. We were now entering into the golden regions; and after passing one small chain of hills, should soon reach Zarevo-Alexandroffsky, lying in a broad valley, with several conical hills rising up of no great elevation. Formerly this tract was exceedingly rich in gold alluvium, very many lumps of solid gold having been found here varying from one pound to fifteen, *then* considered enormous masses of the precious metal.

In the year 1824 the Emperor Alexander the First visited the Oural and the different Zavods belonging to the crown and to private persons. The gold mines also received some of his majesty's attention, this region in particular, as large pieces had not been found in any other place. Lumps of fifteen pounds weight are unquestionably worth digging for, and perhaps this induced the emperor to excavate for gold in a part of the mine with his own hands. After digging and delving for somewhat more than an hour, his imperial majesty's arms intimated that wielding the pickaxe and shovel was physically more laborious than holding the sceptre. He gave up, having thrown out a quantity of sand from which some gold was washed in small grains. A workman continued the excavation, and at the depth of two feet below where his majesty left off digging, found a lump weighing twenty-four pounds sixty-eight zolotniks. To commemorate the event, and point out the exact spot on which his imperial majesty labored as a gold-digger, a small pyramid was erected.

These mines continued to be worked with great success for many years. In 1843 another large piece, weighing two poods four pounds, was found at no great depth under one of the old buildings. Years before, they had excavated all round it, little dreaming of the treasure over which the workmen trampled daily. The peasant who discovered this large mass was made free by the late Emperor Nicholas, and a pension granted him for life. It is only in this valley, near a small stream named Tash-kuturgun, and immediately around the work of Zarevo-Alexandroffsky, that the large pieces have been found. In 1853 these mines were still being worked successfully. I was greatly surprised to find the gold alluvium covering the small hills; in some places there were not more than twelve inches in depth of this earthy matter above the rocks, and in many places these elevations were covered with bushes. The workmen were stripping the rocks, and sending their gold-bestudded garments to the washing-machine.

This quiet little valley, less than half a century ago, was smiling in verdant beauty, and covered with a rich green turfy carpet, bespangled with many a blossom, while various flowering and other shrubs were dotted about in masses, among which the wild deer wandered with her fawn, cropping the young shoots, and sporting on every glade, divested of fear. But man's thirst for gold led him hither, and he is rooting up the earth from every crevice, absolutely sweeping the rocks bare, and leaving them bleaching in the sun.

But man and his works have their appointed time: the mighty sovereign who here dug up the dust has returned to his mother earth, and the small pyramid built little more than thirty years ago has fallen into decay, and no relic of it remains. A subscription was raised among the mining engineers in the Oural to erect a more lasting monument on the place. A granite basement has been built, with an arched recess on one side, closed in by a pair of iron doors, wherein a table is placed, on which stands a small box containing some of the grains of gold dug out by his imperial majesty; the shovel and pickaxe used on the occasion rest beside the box; above them hangs a picture of a saint. These relics are carefully guarded.

On the top of this granite basement, which is diminished by four steps, a cast iron pedestal is placed, having panels on the sides; on one is an inscription, and on the others military trophies. It would have been more in character to have filled the compartments with bas-reliefs, showing the digging, washing, and other processes used in collecting gold. At each angle, on the corner of the pedestal, sits the double-headed eagle. Above the pedestal rises up a Corinthian column, with a wreath of oak-leaves twisted round it, very well executed, both in the modeling and casting. On the top of the capital stands a bust of his imperial majesty Alexander the First—an excellent likeness. This monument will last for ages, unless hurled down by an earthquake. About two hundred yards from the column a wooden post marks the place where the large piece was found in 1843: both are deposited in the museum of the Imperial School of Mines.

I spent three days visiting the gold mines, and sketching several views in this valley, once so rich in the precious ore. Even now it is interesting, as all the lower hills of the Oural are well wooded and picturesque; and farther down in the valley are several small lakes, in which are found great numbers of water-fowl.

CHAPTER VIII.

ENGLISHMEN IN THE OURAL.

ENGLISH mechanics have been employed in the Oural from a very early period in its mining operations. More than one of them have become celebrated for their eccentricity, whose names will be handed down through many generations in connection with the works. In the reign of the Emperor Paul, a young mechanic, named Major, was engaged by the Russian government, and sent to Ekaterineburg to superintend a small mechanical establishment. In this town Major spent a long life, and constructed many machines, which, rude as they were, proved of essential value in the mining districts. Peasants were sent to him from the different villages, who had never in their lives seen any mechanical tools except an axe and a saw; indeed, they were supremely ignorant. In making a cog-wheel, when the cogs and spaces had been divided for them, they never supposed it of the slightest moment if the cog happened to be an inch thicker than was required, the space less, or *vice versâ*, if it suited their humor.

Major entered upon his duties scarcely knowing a word of the Russian language, which, of course, added much to his difficulties. However, as years rolled on he acquired some knowledge of it. German he also learned by coming in contact with the miners, many of whom were from the Hartz Mountains. French was spoken by the superior officers in the Oural, and he contrived to add a little of this to his stock. His pay was liberal, and living cheap, which enabled him to maintain a good establishment. He was kind and good-natured to the workmen, and gained their esteem, as well as that of the officers who served under him, while his eccentricity afforded a fund of amusement for all. After conducting the machine works for some ten or twelve years, a better understanding prevailed. He established a sort of jargon peculiarly his own. In giving his instructions he would begin in Russ, add a few words of German, then a scrap of French, glide into an English sentence, and conclude with a thundering oath.

He was peculiar in his habits, and particular about the machinery under his charge being kept in good order. When dressing in the morning he invariably put on three pairs of stockings, and a pair of wide Russian boots over them. Thus prepared, he would sally forth on a tour of inspection, and the first soil he discovered, he would call for the engineer and rate him in a polyglot of an exceedingly impressive character; then would sit down, pull off his boot, and draw off a stocking, with which he would personally remove the dirt or stain. On he went, repeating the operation as often as necessary, leaving a stocking at each place where it had been used, and returning home in the evening sometimes with one stocking on, and very often with bare legs. Woe betide the delinquent who failed to bring home the stocking left at his machine, for the birch would be sure to refresh his memory the next morning: he never forgave this neglect.

When the Emperor Alexander the First visited the Oural, his imperial majesty was greatly pleased with the works Major had established, and, as a token of his satisfaction, presented him with a piece of land containing about twenty English acres, with all the minerals it contained, and gold was known to be deposited there. Though several versts distant from Ekaterineburg, Major built for himself a house here, still holding his situation of principal engineer to the Oural mines. A few years later he began to excavate and wash the gold sand, usually obtaining more than two poods of gold a year at a very small cost of labor. This was worth about £3500. He had gone on in this way for several years, living at his country house with very few people about him, often having no domestic except an old woman. The gold-washing ceased about the middle of September, and the workmen employed were paid their wages and returned to their homes. The quantity of precious metal obtained during the summer was accurately known to these men, each day's produce being weighed, entered in a book, and delivered to Major every evening. He deposited it in an iron box which stood in his cabinet, and carried the key in his pocket. This year had been more than usually productive, and there were more than three poods of gold in the box. It was also well known that within a very short period of the works closing the engineer would send this box and its contents to the smelting works in Ekaterineburg to be cast into bars, after which it would be forwarded to the Mint in St. Petersburg.

One Sunday evening Major and his old housekeeper were alone in the house, he occupied in his cabinet, and she sitting in her own room not far from the entrance-door. Suddenly her attention was drawn to a noise in the outward lobby, which induced her to leave the room. The moment she got into the entrance, she was seized and thrown down a staircase leading to some apartments below. Her screams and the noise reached Major in his cabinet, who rushed out with a candle in his hand, when a blow from an axe fell upon his head, and he never breathed again. After this the murderers possessed themselves of the box and gold, ransacked the place in search of other treasure, and then departed, closing the doors after them. All this time the old woman was lying at the foot of the stairs in a state of insensibility, quite unconscious of the tragedy which had been enacted in the rooms above. It was not until the morning of the third day after that one of the officers from the machine works went to consult Major on some matter of importance.

On reaching the house no smoke was rising from the chimney, the windows were closed, and a solemn stillness reigned over the place, which oppressed him with unpleasant forebodings. After securing his horse in the usual place, he ascended the steps and entered the house, where lay the ghastly and mutilated body of his friend still grasping the candlestick. Rushing from the house, he sprang into his saddle and galloped furiously to announce the terrible discovery. Presently other officers and the police were seen hurrying toward the spot, the news spreading rapidly, and causing a great sensation. Search was made, and the old woman found at the bottom of the stairs, still living, but insensible. Every means were adopted to restore consciousness, which in time was effected. It was only then that she learned what had befallen her master, but she could give no description of the villains.

A strict investigation commenced, when it was ascertained that the gold had been carried off, though the papers and letters he had been writing remained on his table untouched. Suspicion fell on the workmen, who were seized and examined, but it was clearly proved that they were innocent. The housekeeper remained in a very critical state, so great had been the injuries she had received by the fall and the effect which the murder had produced on her mind: she relapsed into a state of unconsciousness, and so remained for many weeks, medical aid being useless. At last she began to revive; gradually improving in strength, her mind became calm, and her reason perfectly restored. Great hopes were now entertained that she would be able to give evidence by which this mystery might be unraveled.

It was a well-known fact that Major was in the habit of sitting up till a very late hour, and the woman proved beyond all doubt that the murder had been committed about a quarter before two o'clock in the morning. She had been seized so suddenly that she could not tell how many men were in the lobby, but she thought only three. This was all the evidence that could be obtained; a strict watch, however, was kept over the actions of several men, in the expectation of their trying to dispose of the gold. One of them was a small merchant, whose dealings in gold the police had some reason to suspect. He was taken and examined, but he clearly proved to the satisfaction of the police that he was ninety versts distant shortly after six o'clock on the morning of the murder, at Kamenskoï Zavod with the director, and was set at liberty.

Years passed over; the murder was often the theme of conversation in Ekaterineburg, but all hopes of penetrating the mystery with which it was invested were given up. At this time the quantity of gold stolen from the mines and sent into Tartary and Bokhara had become so enormous, that the Russian government determined to discover how it was effected. An officer of gend'arme was dispatched to Ekaterineburg, where he in due time arrived disguised as a peasant. His passport was in order, and so well was his object kept secret, that even the police and other authorities believed him to be what he seemed. He soon ingratiated himself among his class, living and drinking with them at the *kabacks*, and hearing all that passed, and gradually acquired from his unsuspicious associates the knowledge of which he was in search. He discovered that there were persons engaged in these gold robberies far away from Ekaterineburg, through whom the precious metal was got out of the country. During his stay among the peasants in this town and at the mines he provided himself with gold, and now changed the locality of his operations. Without exciting any suspicion among his companions, he departed for Omsk to dispose of his stolen treasure; he was even intrusted by some of his new friends with small parcels to sell for them.

Shortly after his arrival in the capital of Western Siberia he began to associate with the Tartars, and very cautiously intimated that he had a little gold to dispose of. This was done in so professional a manner that he was soon introduced to the great gold dealer, whose influence was so great that the Tartars dared not buy gold unless it had passed through his hands. This was getting to the fountain-head. Several anxious days passed, when early one morning a Tartar acquaintance called, and said the police had been making inquiries about his visit to Omsk which might lead to unpleasant consequences; he therefore advised that the gold should be disposed of without delay, and proposed to accompany him to the dealer. Nothing loth, he was ready with his parcels in a few minutes. The Tartar told him to be under no apprehension when he saw the buyer, as it was all right and safe. On they went, and after a long walk his guide led him through a yard into a large house, taking him at once into a room in which stood a table with a multitude of papers. He then went out, returning in a few minutes, saying that the gentleman would come to them shortly. It was not long before a man came in with a long Bokharian kalat on, tied round his waist with a shawl. Taking his seat at the table, he asked the assumed peasant, in a very rude manner, how much gold he had stolen, where he came from, and a variety of other questions calculated to frighten him. All these were answered in a very submissive tone. The gold was then ordered to be produced, which was done, and the weight of each packet marked thereon. The Tartar was told to pour all the gold into a scale; but to this the peasant objected. He was, however, instantly informed by the dealer that it all belonged to thieves, and that they must settle it among themselves. It was found to weigh much less than the seller knew it to be, when he quietly suggested that the scales might not be correct. The other turned upon him with a scowl, crying out in an angry tone, "What, thief! thou art not content with robbing thy employers, but thou wishest to cheat me. I shall soon hear of thee in the mines of Siberia. What is the price?" The man named the sum, and was offered half. So small an amount he declined to take, intimating that he would try some other dealer. This roused the rage of the receiver: "I give thee," said he, "five minutes to consider whether thou wilt take the money I offer, or be handed over to the police." The assumed peasant now professed great penitence, and promised that in all future dealings with his excellency he would never offend again. After this he received his money, and a reprimand enjoining him to be diligent in his calling. He was then dismissed with an admonition to be discreet, or the mines of Siberia awaited him. The Tartar also gave him advice as to his future proceedings, as well as introduced him to others of the fraternity.

The following morning the scene was changed: a gend'arme officer was seen driving through the streets of Omsk, followed by two mounted Cossacks. He drove straight to the house of the "Gorodnetche," or chief of the police, who received him with great politeness, not recognizing his visitor; and when the Cossacks were called in to take him to prison, he appeared as if struck dumb. The smaller agents were left to other hands to secure, and many of the Tartars made their escape into the Kirghis Steppe.

The gend'arme, having accomplished his mission in Omsk, now started for Ekaterineburg to complete what he had so well begun. The first man arrested was the merchant who had been examined and acquitted of Major's murder. He was again accused of this crime, and two other men were shortly in safe custody on the same charge. The wife of the first now revealed where the gold was buried; and on searching for it, they found the axe with which the murder had been committed.

This man had long been engaged in gold-smuggling, associated with those who stole it from the mines. For this purpose he required good horses, and possessed one of extraordinary power and speed. Immediately the gold had been secured after Major's murder, he mounted his horse, and in about four hours rode ninety versts, presenting himself to the director at Kamenskoï. The murder was now proved against all who had been engaged in it; they were sentenced to "run the gauntlet" (that is, to walk between the lines formed by a regiment of soldiers, consisting of 3000 men, each man striking him with a rod), and died immediately after the punishment. The bands of gold-stealers were broken up; some were sent to the mines of Siberia, and the gend'arme returned to

St. Petersburg to receive a reward for his arduous and really dangerous labor.

I have another sad story to tell of a countryman, who also lost his life in this region. Some years ago, a young engineer, a Mr. Patrick, of Manchester, was engaged as a mechanical engineer in the iron-works of the Generals Sevelofsky. These works are on the west side of the Oural, at a distance of three or four hundred versts from Perm. He remained there several years, and was highly respected by his employers. They had gold mines also on the eastern side of the Oural, which at that time were the farthest north in the chain. Patrick's mechanical duties called him to these mines in company with some other officers from the Zavod. The time of their visit was rather late in the season for this northerly region. When their duties were finished, it was proposed by one of the officers that they should devote a day or two to the chase, as there was plenty of game in the neighboring mountains; and Patrick, accompanied by his friend and a large number of peasants, started in that direction. As their hunting-ground was some fifteen or twenty versts from the mine, it was arranged that they should remain the night, and continue their sport on the following day. They arrived at the place early, and commenced their sport, but were not very successful. Some time after midday they dined in the forest, after which Patrick proposed to try one of the mountains near them, and on his companion declining, he started alone. Several hours passed, and nothing was heard of the absent hunter; at length a party of peasants were sent to seek him. They returned, stating that they had used every effort to find him, but in vain. Some suggested the probability of his having fallen in with a herd of deer, the pursuit of which had detained him.

Night passed over and morning dawned, still Patrick did not appear. Another party were sent up into the mountain: they shouted and fired their guns without any response. They had gone over the ground in every direction, feeling quite sure that if any accident had happened to him by a bear, his gun, parts of his clothing, or his dog would have been found. The officer who had accompanied him now stated that it was of no use seeking further, and ordered all to return to the mine. The next day snow fell, and he made no other effort to find his friend, satisfying himself by reporting to his employers that Patrick had ascended the mountain alone, where he had probably been killed by a bear, adding that he had searched for him in every direction without effect. Winter arrived, and nothing more was attempted; but before summer came, dark surmises were in circulation, and suspicions arose that Patrick had met with foul play.

In consequence, the Sevelofskys ordered a most rigid search to be made in the region where the event had happened, but this also ended without any discovery; not a trace of arms or clothing could be met with. Suspicion now settled into conviction that Patrick and his dog had been killed and buried, and his gun concealed. Little more than three years passed over, when one day a peasant went into a watchmaker's shop in Ekaterineburg and offered a watch for sale. It proved to be an English one. An officer who was standing in the shop examined it, and discovered Patrick's name on the inside. He instantly ordered the man to be detained, and the latter was very shortly in the hands of the police. When brought before the authorities, he was questioned as to his possession of the watch, but no information could be elicited from him. He was whipped and otherwise punished, but nothing could be extorted, though there could scarcely be a doubt that he was cognizant of Patrick's fate. He was kept in prison some time, and afterward sent into Siberia. Suspicion now pointed to the officer who had accompanied Patrick to the hunt as the man who had planned, if not actually engaged in his murder, and jealousy was supposed to be the cause.

While traveling in the North Oural I slept one night in a peasant's cottage near Pavdinskoï, and found there a couple of volumes on mechanics, with Patrick's name written by himself. Having obtained these, I carried them with me to Ekaterineburg, where I handed them to a friend; I, however, do not anticipate that they will lead to any elucidation of this terrible mystery.

Having related these tragical events, I will add one of a totally different character, illustrating the career of another of my countrymen. I must premise that the individual who will figure in it is fond of a good dinner, which with him is a serious matter of business. He is very stout; indeed, is well qualified to play the hero of Gad's Hill without stuffing. It was his duty for many years to visit the works and inspect the machinery at the different Zavods belonging to the government in the Oural. Some of these journeys were made in summer, when the temperature is usually very hot, especially in the southern part of the chain. He was always luxurious; and his carriage had a compartment for provisions, wine, &c., which was sure to be well stocked. It was also so arranged that it could be turned into a bed, over which was placed what he called "a tufeck"—a leather bed filled with soft hair. Whenever he traveled through the night, this was prepared by his man with the greatest care.

About the middle of July, on one of the hottest days of summer, my friend was traveling in the South Oural on his tour of inspection. He had dined sumptuously at one of the Zavods, and started onward in the evening to enjoy the cool breeze of the night. But there are some nights which will not cool (I have often found such), and this was one of them. His carriage had been standing in the burning sun, and had become so thoroughly heated that the inside was like an oven. When his servant made his bed for the night, my friend found that it was impossible to sleep in his clothing; he consequently undressed, and was covered over with a sheet. In this way the night was passed pretty well; at last daylight appeared, and the sun shed his rays over the mountain tops, leaving the deep valleys in shade. They had now arrived at a station in the mountains, and the horses were changed while he slept. The servant and the yemstchick, seeing the master sleeping comfortably, saw no reason why they should not drink tea. Into the house they went, and were soon enjoying a quiet glass, forgetting both steeds and carriage. Whether it was the snoring of the inmate which frightened the horses, or something else, I can not tell, but off they started, and rapidly got into full speed.

The carriage began to bound over the rough road, tossing its occupant from side to side; this soon roused him, when, to his horror, he discovered that he was alone, and at the mercy of four horses abreast, tearing along like wild steeds of the Steppe for the first time yoked to a vehicle! To jump out was impossible, so he clutched the sides of the tarantass, trembling with fear. On they went like furies till they reached a steep hill, which made them gradually slacken their speed. He knew the road, and that a still deeper descent awaited him on the other side of some three or four versts in length. His fears, consequently, were so terrible that he stood watching for the moment when he could leap out. At last, observing that he was near the top, he could endure his position no longer; so out he sprung, fortunately without accident. The sight of his strange figure frightened the horses, and on they went again at full gallop. He declares that he thanked God for his safety, and quietly sat down on a fallen tree to reflect on his situation. Shoes or stockings he had none; in short, only one linen garment, and that somewhat scanty; and he was in the middle of a forest, surrounded by hosts of musquitoes humming about him evidently ravenous for his blood. He had not sat long in this plight, when he discovered a peasant woman on horseback coming toward him. She had approached very near, when, suddenly getting sight of the singular apparition on the fallen tree, she pulled up her horse and looked aghast. He addressed her in a very tender tone, saying, "Matushka moi pady suda" (Come here, my mother). She mustered courage to ask what he wanted. "Your petticoat," was the reply. "I have but one; take it, and spare me!" she murmured almost inaudibly, dismounting and handing him the garment. He lost no time in putting it on, and then marched along the road. Shortly afterward his servant and the driver came up at full gallop, and were much relieved when they beheld him safe, but could scarcely maintain their gravity at sight of his extraordinary costume. The horses continued their furious pace to the station, whence two men were instantly sent back with the carriage, and in about an hour my friend was enabled to resume his proper habiliments.

CHAPTER IX.

ADVENTURES AMONG THE MOUNTAINS.

After leaving Alexandroffsky a few versts, the road crossed a range of wooded hills and ran along the side of a beautiful valley, in which a lake of no great size lay calmly in the bottom, with clumps of birch and aspen growing on the shores. The ground in many places was covered with *cloubnika*, or wild strawberries of a large size and delicious flavor, which might be gathered in enormous quantities. On advancing farther the country became less wooded, with wide grassy plains stretching away between the mountains, which now appeared more rocky, pointed, and picturesque. At length, after crossing some hills, we reached a broad, undulating valley of rich pasture-land, where in some parts fields of rye were growing; to the northwest rose up the rocky crest of the Oural-tou, blue and misty, the lower mountains strongly defined in deep purple; at their feet lay a brown sloping steppe.

Aoush-kool, Ah-oosh, or Holy Lake, is about twelve versts distant from a gold mine, near the foot of the Ilman-tou, where I had taken up my abode; the track leading to it was along the valley for a few versts, to a point where some low hills close it to the west. Here I found another gold mine in a small ravine running up into the mountains. After crossing the low hills at the head of the valley and descending a short distance, we beheld the Holy Lake spread out in another valley, opening into a very extensive plain, which stretches far away to the southwest toward Ui-tash. This plain was almost destitute of wood; in some parts a few bushes were growing amid most luxuriant pastures, to which the Bashkirs would return at the end of summer, with their herds of horses.

This Holy Lake of the Bashkirs is beautifully situated, and of an elliptical form; the length is about seven or eight versts, and it is probably four versts broad. On its northwest side rises a conical hill to the height of 800 feet above the level of the water, named Aoush-tou, or Holy Mount; near the foot of this, to the northeast, stands a Bashkir village, their winter dwellings—in other words, a heap of log huts. These are about twelve feet square and eight feet high, the roofs flat, and covered with earth and turf. They have a doorway three feet wide and four feet six inches high; a small opening to admit light, about twelve inches square, with a hole in the roof for the escape of smoke: such is a Bashkir's winter home. A fire is made on the ground in the middle of the room, the smoke soon rendering the interior black as coal; round the room are benches close to the logs, and on these they sleep. It is no uncommon thing to find six or eight people packed away in these little dens, surrounded with filth and covered with vermin.

At a short distance from the back of this village a thick belt of timber extends far up the mountain, consisting of birch-trees and mountain ash, some of large size. On ascending, we passed through this wood, and found in many places large masses of beautiful serpentine and porphyry jutting out, which compelled us to seek another track. A walk of an hour brought us to the summit. Here rest three Bashkir chiefs, each covered up in a pile of stones that forms his tomb.

Here they sleep in peace, mountain flowers blooming and fresh breezes wafting the sweet perfumes around. Their ashes will neither be scattered to the winds nor removed to make room for the dwellings of other races. Could their spirits visit this spot, they would look down on those beautiful plains over which, almost from their childhood, they freely galloped, but would see that their descendants have degenerated. Half-civilization is generally worse than what is usually termed barbarism. The Bashkir, in his genuine state, wild as his steed, possesses the feelings of a gentleman. To be sure, he may have a slight tendency to plunder, but he does it openly, and meets his victim in fair fight, while the semi-civilized Bashkir will skulk and cut your throat, if you allow him a chance. He has all the evil of both races, without a particle of the good of either.

The view from the summit is very fine; it takes in the Oural-tou, Ilman-tou, and the Ui-tash, with their intervening plains, on some of which people are seen rooting out gold, which is found on all the little streams in this region. On the south, toward the lake, this mount is the most abrupt; there are some parts on this side which would be extremely difficult to climb, where the porphyry is broken into cliffs. To the northwest it is also very steep, descending in parts abruptly into the valley; there I found another small lake extending along the valley toward Ilman-tou. I made sketches from three different points of the Holy Lake, and of other places on the plain.

Now for another gallop over these Bashkir plains, on which there is neither tree nor shed under which to take shelter, though a thunder-storm is growling in the distance, and a three hours' hard ride is in prospect. The Oural-tou is shrouded in deep black clouds, rolling on in great commotion, against which the stony crest ot the Ui-tash stands out in its light tint. Soon the storm will be here; it comes on like a race-horse, rushing straight toward us. Hark! here comes the blast, twisting the reeds and grass, and laying them flat; on it speeds with great fury, almost tearing up the bushes. Now the flash makes our horses start, throw out their fore legs, and tremble as they see the electric stream strike the ground a few hundred feet before us, tinging all around with red; then the crashing thunder echoes from every hill, and rolls off into the distant mountains. There is enough in all this to excite most men into a gallop; but when the rain comes streaming down, it urges us on furiously, and nothing is thought of but to reach the shelter of some friendly roof. This we found at Bal-bouch gold mine, where the kind-hearted director treated us most hospitably.

The gold mines at Bal-bouch extend over a large space; they are not the property of the crown, but belong to a family in St. Petersburg, and are under the direction of a very superior man. The gold-washing machines have been constructed from his own plans, under his own direction, and are decidedly the best I have seen in the Oural. Every thing is conducted here with the greatest regularity and most perfect order, producing a considerable profit to the proprietor, notwithstanding that the gold deposit is found deep below the surface. To obtain it, all the upper strata have to be removed; in some instances these consist of earth and stones from twenty-five to thirty feet thick, adding greatly to the cost of working. This superincumbent mass tells us of the ages that have rolled on since the gold was washed down from the mountains and deposited in these valleys. Here they never seek the precious ore in its original rock in the mountains; many even doubt its ever being found in any of the upper strata at present exposed to view in this region.

I made an excursion with the director of the works to the Kara-ghi-kool, a picturesque lake in the Ehren-dick Mountains; on our way we had to ride over several ridges. When on the first range of hills he said, "It is from these rocks, which once were much higher, that the gold has been washed into the valleys; in every little ravine we find the ore; but beyond this ridge, in the upper ravines, we find no gold: a proof that it has never existed in the higher chain."

While at the Kara-ghi-kool, quietly preparing my sketching traps, my eye caught sight of something in motion close to my side, on a piece of rock most conveniently elevated for my seat, and, looking more intently, I beheld a large serpent just lifting his head out of his coil. Starting back a few steps to get my whip, he began to hiss, was uncoiled in a moment, and, bending his long body into curves, showed a disposition to strike, when my short and heavy lash fell upon him and changed his intentions. He now tried to escape, and got into a deep cavity before I could repeat the blow. In this den there were others, as I judged by the sounds which greeted my ears: no doubt a nest had been disturbed. After this I changed my position, and finished my sketch without molestation. On mentioning this circumstance to the director, he told me that serpents were numerous in this locality, and some of them venomous.

From many points of view near Bal-bouch the prospect was exceedingly fine, and I made several sketches, some of the gold-washings, others of the country around. These mines are on a beautiful undulating plain, running far up between the mountains. On one side rises Ui-tash, with its picturesque peaks; farther to the north are the Ehren-dick Mountains, with many conical hills rising from the plain; there are also several small lakes giving great variety to the scenery. This has made a lasting impression on my mind, particularly by its romantic mountains and beautiful plains, covered with rich pastures, in which were growing a great variety of flowers, many quite new to me, affording employment for both artist and botanist. For the sportsman there was much amusement on these plains, snipes and double snipes existing in swarms; woodcocks were very numerous in the woods, with plenty of wild duck on every lake. On some of the mountains the wild goats feed in large herds, and deer are found on the lower hills in abundance. Although my great object was in sketching the scenery, my gun was not always idle. I could have spent a few months in this region most agreeably; but mine was a wandering life, and, like a certain legendary celebrity, on I was obliged to go.

During a very hot day, at about two o'clock in the afternoon, our horses' heads were turned toward the south. We crossed the plain, and, after riding about two hours, passed through a narrow valley in the Kuma-tash, coming out upon the old frontier of the Kirghis Steppe. We followed the old Cossack road for a short distance, then turned into the steppe. On our right rose up Kuma-tash, rugged in many parts, and its summit crowned with bare rocks.

This region is quite destitute of timber. In some of the ravines there are a few small birches and other bushes, but the ground was covered with wild strawberries. After traveling about fifteen versts, we turned to the west, up a small valley, and soon reached Iltabanaffsky gold mine. Here, as usual, though completely a stranger, I received a most hospitable welcome from the director and his family; they were preparing for a festival (his daughter's name's-day), and several of their friends had already arrived.

This gold mine is situated on a small ravine at the foot of some hills, which rise to a considerable elevation on the north, and is worked at a great cost, on account of the depth at which the gold-sand is found, and because the washing-machines are turned by horses, as no water-power can be obtained here. Farther up in the valley another small mine has just been opened, and it is expected will turn out valuable. Immediately around Iltabanaffsky there is no particularly fine scenery; but the director informed me that there are some large caverns in one of the mountains, about fifteen versts distant, and proposed to make up a party to go there. In the mean time we were to visit a lake about ten versts distant in another direction, which would afford me an opportunity of seeing the country. On the shore of this lake he had a farm, where his horses and cattle were kept in winter. I found here a good view, with bold jasper rocks rising from the water on one side, and larch, birch, poplar, and aspen growing above. Farther down, a narrow ledge of rocks, elevated a few feet above the water, ran quite across the lake, the top being well wooded; beyond these rocks the lakes extended several versts.

The following morning I rode along the plain for some distance, and then turned up one of the ravines to the northward. Having crossed several ridges, I stopped on the summit of the last, and had a fine view of the Oural-tou, Ui-tash, and Ehren-dick Mountains; Iremel I could not see. At length I reached the marshy valley, in the bottom of which lay a small lake. I rode to the head of it, but with great difficulty, and then beheld the summit of Iremel above the other ridges. There was nothing particularly striking or interesting in this view: it was not worth one hour's ride, yet I had been six hours on the road, and a sixth part of that time struggling through a morass, often up to the saddle-flaps. I found a dry green mound at the head of the lake, where the horses were let loose to feed, while I and my guide refreshed ourselves from the contents of a small bag which had been packed for my use.

My man proposed that we should return by another route, as he said, to avoid the morass. After riding in this direction about an hour, we were congratulating ourselves on having escaped the swampy ground which might swallow us up, when, having crossed one high ridge and descended into a valley, to our surprise we found ourselves caught, in spite of all our precautions; before we had proceeded many steps our horses sunk so deep that we had great difficulty in getting out. This compelled us to ride along the side of the mountain for a long distance, and then make another trial. At last we crossed, but only to get into a difficulty worse than the last. At length, after floundering about for some time, we extricated ourselves, unfortunately, on the wrong side; nor could we get over to the other, therefore were again compelled to take to the ridge. We rode along till we came to the very point whence we had descended to the lake. From this to the lake was one hour's ride, and we had been more than three returning. It was now near five o'clock; and we had still a five hours' ride before us; there was, however, one great advantage: we knew the track, and could retrace our footsteps; therefore, though both wet and weary, we rode on, crossing ridge after ridge, until at last we reached the plain, with good solid ground, when our horses pricked up their ears, and carried us at a canter into Iltabanaffsky.

A bright sunny morning induced my host to prepare for our trip to the caverns. We dined at the gold mine at twelve o'clock, and started immediately after. Our party consisted of two daughters of my host, three ladies from Maïas, and six of my own sex, nearly all delighted with the idea of sleeping a night on the mountain. We traveled in telagas to within half a verst of the precipices in which the caverns were situated; beyond this we must go on foot. The road was rough, but that has little effect on these Siberian vehicles, which are made without either nail or bolt. Indeed, there is not one scrap of iron about them, they being put together with wooden pins and withes: this permits them to twist about in every way, and to suit any road, rough or smooth, but not the traveler, who is almost shaken to pieces by the jolting. In about two hours we reached the place where we had to quit these machines and ascend; this, however, was not difficult. A walk of half an hour brought us to the foot of a very high precipice of granite rocks, which at once dispelled my illusion about the much-talked-of caverns. I had anticipated being able to penetrate almost to the centre of the mountain, and pry into nature's secrets. Large apertures had also been described, looking like portals opening into some mighty subterranean hall. We found the balagans prepared, and placed with their fronts looking down into the valley. A fire was burning brightly; the tea-traps and other things were spread on the ground, giving the place the appearance of a most luxurious encampment; but the rocky chambers had more charms for me at this moment.

The cliffs rose up nearly perpendicular for two hundred and fifty or three hundred feet, and then set back a little, forming a terrace: here were the supposed caverns. From this point the rocks rose again several hundred feet higher. I began to ascend, and three of my companions followed; after climbing from ledge to ledge, we got within about forty feet of the terrace, whence it was almost a perpendicular wall. We sat down for a few minutes to rest, when two of my friends, having looked up at the rocks, turned back. This did not deter me. I began to climb with the aid of bushes and crevices, and mounted, followed by my only companion. After two or three attempts, we succeeded in reaching the top, when the discovery was made that the supposed caverns were only inconsiderable recesses in the rocks. When seen from a distance they looked dark and deep: thus many people had been deceived. From this place we had a fine view of the Oural chain, with the valleys, and several small lakes between the mountains. Having climbed so far, I determined to go to the summit; my companion followed a short distance, when we found a place very easy to descend; higher he would not go; I left him to find his way down, and scrambled upward among huge masses of rock tumbled about in great confusion. When near the summit I was startled by hearing something rush from beneath some large fallen blocks, and the next moment a fine wild goat went bounding from rock to rock. I gave a shrill whistle, at which he stood for a minute to gaze at me, and then bounded on again; fortunately for him, my rifle was below, or this had been his last leap. When I gained the summit I was rewarded by a most splendid view over the steppe as far as the eye could reach. I beheld many lakes, some very large, with low hills stretching away to the south. After sitting a short time I began to retrace my steps, descending very rapidly, when I came upon a track made by the goats; this guided me down, and I was soon at the bottom of the precipice, at only a few hundred paces from our encampment. In the society of my friends, while enjoying the refreshment that had been provided, I soon forgot the fatigue I had experienced during my adventurous scramble.

The sun was now sinking fast, all the valleys had been deprived of his rays, and white vapors were rising up and covering the lower hills. As the shades of evening began to draw around us, the desire for a night's lodging at the foot of these rocks began to evaporate. This was not alone the case with the ladies; the gentlemen seemed quite as little to relish the situation—indeed, were evidently anxious to beat a retreat. The musquitoes had found us, and commenced their attacks in swarms, keeping every one occupied in brushing them off. To eat under such circumstances was no easy matter, without peppering our food with these insects every time it was raised to the mouth. This was not to be endured. We therefore made small fires all around our encampment, and threw on them long grass, which made a great smoke, and drove the hungry tribe to the other side of our intrenchments.

At about ten o'clock, however, it was decided to abandon the works to our enemies and descend to the telagas, though these, as it was now quite dark, it was no easy matter to find. Any thing, however, was considered better than being either eaten up by musquitoes or poisoned with smoke. So we started, but shortly found it very difficult to proceed, as we were constantly stumbling about among the fallen rocks and getting separated. I had the care of a stout lady, who held on like a leech, and we had several tumbles, fortunately without any serious consequences. At one moment there was a shriek and a tumble in one direction, then the same in another; some were calling out, "This is the way," and others shouting, "The telagas are down here!" In fact, ours was not a retreat; it was a regular rout, and the squadrons we were flying from pursued us with the utmost ferocity.

After walking more than an hour, by which time we ought to have reached the telagas, they were not to be seen. We had now got into long grass, where I was joined by another lady, who had lost her guardian. This long grass convinced me we had been going in the wrong direction. While standing still for a few minutes we could hear shouts on both sides, but on one side they came from a distance, and were evidently from our drivers. I hallooed to our friends to return, and then went off toward the sound, which at first was very feeble; however, after proceeding for some time in one direction, it became more distinct, though still a long way off. Presently the shouting proved that we were all moving toward the same point, and gradually drawing together. At length we discovered the horses at a short distance before us, and several of our friends already in the telagas; three, however, were missing. We could hear shouts in answer to ours, and in a short time two came up. Only one was now absent: we all hallooed, but obtained no answer. We waited some time, then three men started back in search. In about half an hour they received an answer to their call, though from a great distance; on they went in that direction, and soon came up with our friend, who was sitting down. It appeared that he had fallen, and been precipitated into a deep place, where he lay, completely stupefied and unconscious; fortunately, he stumbled down a grassy steep, with long grass at the bottom, otherwise he would have been much hurt.

Day was now beginning to dawn, which enabled us to ascertain our position and see our way; the telagas were put in motion, and, following the track of our friends, we soon reached them. The gentleman who had met with the accident was made as comfortable as possible, but he had evidently been very much shaken by his fall. A little before four o'clock we reached the gold mine, when the doctor was called in, and his patient at once put to bed.

My next move was toward Iremel, calling on our way at Preobrajenskoï gold mine. The road to it is over a most uninteresting country. Late in the evening we reached the mine. It is small, and, I believe, produces very little; indeed, every thing about it indicates that even gold can be bought too dear. We passed the night here, and returned to Iltabanaffsky the next morning by another route, which made the distance about fifty versts. I wished to start early next morning, but this they would not permit until we had again enjoyed their hospitality. I left in a light carriage, drawn by five horses; three, yoked to the vehicle, were driven by a Kirghis, and one of the two leaders was ridden by a boy of eighteen. My route was across the steppe—a fine flat country, and it was soon quite evident our Kirghis coachman intended showing how his cattle would go; our speed for the first two or three versts was a sharp trot, after this the horses were put into a gallop, and then driven at full speed. The whip was not once used, the whole being effected by the driver talking to his horses, they apparently understanding every word. At times he used a shrill call, when the animals would bend to their work like greyhounds; and by speaking to them in another tone, he would bring them up into a canter. In about an hour the outrider was quite done up; the Kirghis stopped after a few minutes, ordered the man up behind, and then mounted his box again, without any reins to the leaders, which rather startled me at first. We were on a fine level country, crossing a steppe extending far into Asia, without either fence or tree. The horses were put into a trot for a short distance. I now noticed our Jehu regulate the reins of his three horses, seat himself firmly on the box and give a whoop, when we went off at a fearful speed. It was a splendid sight. Our Kirghis was in ecstasies, talking to his horses as if they were human beings. The man looked round to see what effect this had upon us, and was delighted on noticing that we enjoyed the race. From full speed a word brought these fiery steeds into a trot; after going at this pace for a short time, he would put them upon their mettle, and continue talking till they went along like race-horses; again would stop—in fact, he did just what he pleased with them; and when we dashed up to the station, the Cossacks were greatly astonished at not seeing a man on one of the leaders. I have never seen horses in a circus under better control; but our position was widely different: the former can not get out of the ring, while we were on a steppe, and had nothing to check them had they chosen to bolt. If I had required a coachman I would have given this man any wages, not exclusively for his good driving, but for the care he took of his horses, which are never touched with a whip. We parted from him with regret; and, although years have passed since, I have never forgotten the excitement of this ride over the steppe.

From this Cossack station to Maïas it was about twenty-five versts. What a change in both cattle and man! The first few hundred yards showed the difference—the whip was constantly going; our Cossack Jehu used very irreverent language, calling his horses "chort," and a few other elegant names, which I dare not repeat, evidently, from the fullness with which he rolled them off his tongue, intensely expressive. After the two hours' ride with our Kirghis, this was really painful; but there was no help for it. Having passed through a pretty country, we arrived at Maïas just as the evening was drawing in, and drove straight to the director's house, to which both he and his amiable wife gave us a most hearty welcome.

Maïas is the centre of the gold region in the South Oural; an officer is specially appointed for this branch of mining, and resides in the Zavod. There is a large edifice for all the offices for the administration of the gold mines; buildings in which gold is washed both in winter and summer; warehouses and other structures, with many good houses, which give this place an imposing appearance. A lake, about ten versts long, runs up among the hills, which has a picturesque effect when approaching the Zavod from the south. The Ilman-tou rises close to the town, on the east bank of the Maïas River, and is in some parts very beautiful.

The Lake Chirtanish is a few versts from Maïas, to the north-west; the road leading to it is charming in many parts. It is situated in a rocky valley, beautifully wooded. The director of Maïas accompanied me to this lake, which he said had some peculiarities besides its picturesqueness. He has ascertained, beyond doubt, that it is a lake above a lake; the upper one is eight to ten feet deep, the bottom of this is four or five feet thick, and underneath is another much deeper. The director supposes that this floating bottom of the upper lake has been formed by vegetation, here very thick and matted, which has decayed, and become like peat, thus, after a series of ages, forming the solid mass now floating under the water.

Our next visit was to Ilmenskoï Lake, in a picturesque region at the foot of the Ilmen hills. After sketching the scenery I had a ramble over the rocks, which are highly interesting to the geologist and mineralogist. Some years ago the Duke of Leuchtenberg, when visiting this region, ordered excavations to be made in the rocks in search of zircon, and some fine crystals were found. I also made a search among the *débris* thrown out, and found several crystals, but none were pure and transparent. These rocks had to be blown asunder by gunpowder, when, no doubt, many crystals were destroyed. The following stones are also found in these mountains—beryl, tourmaline, garnet, topaz, and sodalite; also fine masses of pure quartz. Specimens of all these stones are cut into gems and ornaments in Ekaterineburg.

With Maïas my journey in the South Oural finishes. I can not depart from this region without thanking all my friends for the kindness, hospitality, and assistance afforded me on my journey. I met with but one exception, a pig-headed fellow from Ekaterineburg, whom I found at a gold mine near Iremel, whose ignorance was only equaled by his self-importance.

CHAPTER X.

BORDER LANDS OF ASIATIC RUSSIA.

By the advice of my friends in Ekaterineburg I was induced to hire a servant. When this was first proposed I decidedly objected. "You are starting on a journey of many thousand versts," they said, "into a country thinly inhabited, into which all the criminals from Russia are marching weekly, and you scarcely speak a word of the language; accidents may happen on such roads, and then you will be in the hands of people who can not understand a word you say. Although you might defend yourself against robbers, you could not against sickness; if this should seize you in a village far from any assistance, your journey may be ended almost before you begin it." These, and many other arguments used, it was impossible to resist; so at last I consented. A young man was sent to me, about twenty-four years old, who spoke German fluently; a great advantage, as I, knowing a little German, should be able to give him directions, which he would translate into Russian. This youth had been brought up in the University of Kazan, and was intended for the medical profession. Unfortunately for himself, his studies had been neglected, no warning from the professors having been attended to, and when the examination came on he was "plucked." He was a natural son of the highest medical officer in the Oural, and his disgrace so enraged his father that he cast him off. The authorities most cheerfully gave the necessary papers for his accompanying me, and, having bade adieu to my friends, I stepped into the carriage, and away galloped the horses. After I had proceeded about three versts, I found that the road ascended a high hill, which gave me a view of the Oural chain both to the north and south, with the town of Ekaterineburg lying in the valley.

In spite of every effort, a feeling of deep sadness crept over me when I took my last look at the high crest forming the boundary of Europe; nor could I for a moment help thinking of the hundreds of chances against me on the long journey I had undertaken, each one of which might make this really my last look on either European rock or sky. But the die was cast; I gave the word "Forward!" and sat down; the horses dashed off, and we were galloping onward into Asia. Wooded valleys and pine-clad hills are passed on this road—the last elevation of this chain before reaching the steppes of Asia—quite similar in their features to the scenery all along the south of the Oural. After traveling ninety-one versts, we arrived at Kamenskoï Zavod a little after twelve o'clock, and drove to the house of the director. I entered the gate of this gentleman, a perfect stranger to me, but in the full conviction that I should be received as a friend; nor was I mistaken. A Cossack, who let me into the house, at once announced my arrival. The director, who was in bed, got up immediately, came to me, and gave me a most hearty welcome. In an incredibly short time the customary beverage was brought in, and during the tea-drinking I perceived other preparations were being made. In a short time I was taken into the adjoining room, and there I found supper laid out, and the lady waiting to welcome the intruder to her table. All this is done with so much good-will, without either ceremony or formality, that a man feels at home at once.

In Kamenskoï Zavod very heavy guns have been made for many years past, and some splendid pieces of ordnance have been sent from here both to Cronstadt and the Crimea: the works are on the River Kaman, and not far from the River Issetz. Having expressed a wish to make some sketches, the director, when we met at breakfast, ordered a boat to be got ready to take me down the river in the afternoon, and a young officer was appointed to attend me. We got into the carriage and drove over a flat country covered with birch bushes, the plain extending a long distance. My companion had recently returned from England, where he had been sent to examine the coal mines, and was now engaged in sinking shafts to obtain this useful mineral. We visited some of the places where coal had been discovered; the seams were very thin, and not far below the surface, but he expected to find them thicker and better lower down. After riding six or seven versts, we came all at once upon the Issetz, running in a deep gorge between limestone rocks, some three hundred feet below us. The carriage was sent back with orders to meet us at another point, and we descended the rocks to the river, where the boat was waiting. We were soon floating very gently and very agreeably down the stream, between high cliffs of limestone, and beheld several exceedingly beautiful scenes. We passed what are called "The Gates," a prodigious mass of limestone, perforated with a capacious opening.

Farther down we came to a very high cliff, with some caverns near the summit; three apertures are broken through from the face of the rocks, and this bears the name of "Adam's Head." After descending the river a few versts lower, we found the carriage waiting, and drove back to the Zavod, much pleased with what I had seen. In the evening all the officers and their families assembled at the house of the director: this occurs every Sunday, and on many other holidays during the year. They drink tea, play cards, eat bonbons, dried fruit, and toward eleven o'clock sit down to a good supper. Thus they spend their time very agreeably, to them, for a few hours, when they return to their homes perfectly satisfied and happy. These little friendly reunions pleasantly while away the time, and often include men of great intelligence. Every one felt great interest in my progress through the regions I was about to enter. This is the last mining Zavod before reaching the mining region of the Altai, a journey of 2000 versts: to me, quitting it was like leaving a friendly shore and plunging into an unknown sea.

On a splendid morning I commenced my artistic labors, and spent the day most industriously, as my portfolio can prove. The rocks on this river are very picturesque, the coloring most beautiful. The director insisted on sending for me to dinner, after which a party was invited to drink tea in his garden on the Issetz, several versts from his house. The next morning I was early on the Issetz, and by one o'clock had finished a sketch of "Adam's Head."

This being the name's-day of the doctor of the Zavod, to have neglected paying a visit and dining with him would have been considered an offense. Having spent some agreeable hours among my friends, and received their parting blessing, I once more got into my carriage and departed from Kamenskoï Zavod, but not till I had been made to promise a visit of some days to these amiable people on my return. It was exceedingly dark when we left, and there is a very steep descent to a bridge which crosses the Kamen; but we got over it safely, and ascended the opposite hill without difficulty. The yemstchick gave his horses a breathing, and then went off at full gallop. He had received orders to drive quickly, and fulfilled them to the letter, for we traveled to the station (nineteen versts) in fifty-five minutes. In a short time fresh horses were yoked, and away we went again at full speed. Though the night was still dark, either the horses or the men knew the road well, as the former bounded on without accident. At first it was not a very agreeable sensation, being carried along at such a speed through the gloom, ignorant of what obstacles might be in the way; the ringing of the bells, however, would warn other passengers of our approach, and make them draw quickly on one side. In some teams we had a bell fastened to each horse; with others, three bells were fastened to the bow which passes over the shaft-horse. These keep up a most tremendous clangor; sometimes they have a most melancholy sound when heard in the dark forests of Siberia. About midway on this stage several men called to the driver to stop, saying they wanted to beg; he thought otherwise, and pushed on. It was certainly a strange time to be on the road begging. We traveled this stage (twenty-five versts) in one hour and a half. In a quarter of an hour we had fresh horses, and galloped away. About three o'clock the day began to dawn. I could now observe that we were running along a level plateau, considerably above, and at no great distance from the River Issetz, which I could trace by a white misty line twisting about in the valley. About half past three the sun rose in all his splendor; he appeared as when rising from the sea, for all to the east was one unbounded plain, and that plain SIBERIA.

The valley of the Issetz is several versts broad, with a high bank on each side; between them the river winds about in many a turn, sometimes crossing the valley to one side, then sweeping off to the other in a most tortuous course. In the spring, when the snow is melting in the Oural, the whole of this valley is under water. About an hour after the sun rose I beheld at a considerable distance the domes and towers of the great Monastery of St. Dolomete. Not having been apprised that such an establishment was here to be met with, it was a great surprise, and I watched our approach with much interest. In the distance the different objects grouped well; but I was not prepared to find such an architectural composition so far away, as I had always been led to suppose, from civilized life. It stands on a little eminence on the left bank of the Issetz, near its junction with the River Tetcha, which comes in from the south—in fact, has its source in the South Oural. On approaching the town, the walls which surround the monastery give the latter the effect of a Kremlin; and on coming closer, I found the same style of architecture had been adopted, with towers at the angles, beautiful in form and proportion. Near the eastern end of the inclosure stands the great church, an elegant edifice: its outline is grand, while the detail gives a fairy-like lightness to its parts, and renders it one of those works which a man of great genius may imagine, but rarely finds opportunity to realize. In fact, this monastery contains so much that is good, combining true architectural feeling with fine effect, that it deserves to elevate the designer far, very far above the crowd of professors of the present age. I might almost say that I envied him; less, however, for what he has done, than for the opportunity afforded him to achieve distinction. Most sincerely did I offer up my humble tribute of respect to his genius and memory.

Dolmatou was once a town of considerable importance; it has fallen into decay, and is now only a village. While the *somervar* was preparing, I strolled out to examine the monastery. Having walked round the walls, I entered through the large portal, a monk very kindly escorting me round. Could I have spared the time, I should have found plenty of occupation for a day; but to delay was impossible, and I left the old monk with regret. On reaching the post-house the *somervar* was steaming; I brewed my tea, and sat down to breakfast. My friends at Ekaterineburg and Kamenskoï had provisioned me for ten or twelve days, knowing full well that every traveler who intends to eat on the road in this country must carry his food with him. As this was the first station in Siberia at which I had stopped for refreshment, I began to contrast it with those on the European side of the Oural. The *smatrical*, or officer appointed by the post-house authorities, appeared in his full uniform, and was exceedingly attentive, and the house at this post-station was perfectly clean. Even the wooden walls and ceiling of the rooms had been scrubbed; the benches round the room and tables were white and without a spot, and the floor equally so. The clothing of the inmates, though both short and scanty, partook of the same character—a marked contrast to the stations and people on the European road, where I found squalid misery and filth in almost every post-house.

The horses were yoked, and the yemtschick seated on the tarantass before I left the room. The moment I had taken my seat the officer gave orders to drive fast; I moved my cap to him, and away we went with four horses abreast. I found the Siberian horses and drivers as superior to the European as were the stations. Our road was still along the high bank of the Issetz, and when clear of the town the yemtschick shook his whip, gave a shrill whoop, and away went his team at full gallop. The road was good and slightly on the descent; his horses not large, but sturdy, well-fed little animals, with long flowing manes and tails: they snorted, tossed up their heads, and bounded along at a great speed. The morning breeze was fresh and invigorating, and the sun shone brightly, making every thing look charming, while in the valley the haymakers were tossing the grass about and singing gayly. The plain over which we traveled was well wooded, but with many large tracts of country covered with rye and wheat, that promised heavy crops. There are no fences to the fields in this country: every village has a ring-fence of posts and rails round it, inclosing a large tract of land, often seven or eight versts in diameter, with gates on the road, and a watchman stationed to open and shut them. Within this ring-fence all the cattle of the village are turned out to feed—there is not a peasant who has not several cows and horses—while pigs, geese, ducks, and fowls are also very numerous on these common pastures. Where corn is grown each peasant has his plot, and cultivates as much as he pleases. Near the corn-land feathered game is in great abundance, which the peasants kill and trap in large quantities in winter.

Our fine little team was still galloping along when the next station was pointed out to me. Having approached within about half a verst, the yemtschick gave a shrill cry, the horses bounded off at a furious speed, and in a few minutes we dashed up to the post-house like racers. The tinkling of our bells and rattling of the wheels, however, had brought the men out, our steeds stopped, and in a moment several hands were at work unyoking. My papers were given to the officer, who read them, and ordered fresh horses immediately. I now looked at my watch, and found we had been one hour and twenty minutes driving from station to station, a distance of twenty-two versts: again the lash had never touched a single horse. This station was at a small village, beautifully situated on the bank of the Issetz, backed by fine woods to the north. The valley of the Issetz here expands considerably, and appeared covered with rich crops of grass, in many places cut down, some already made into hay, and in other parts the haymakers were spreading the new-mown grass: they were all actively engaged, and the village almost deserted.

The wheels of the tarantass having been greased, the horses harnessed, and the yemtschick on his seat, the words "Pashol carashinka" were given by the officer, and away we trundled through the village. At a short distance beyond we left the bank of the Issetz and turned into the forest, still over a good road. The sun had now become intensely hot; the deep shade of the trees was therefore very agreeable to both man and beast. Here pine, larch, birch, and poplar were growing, some of the first of very large size, and in many parts we found thick bushy underwood. After traveling through this forest about twenty versts we once more came upon the bank of the Issetz, the river shining brightly in the deep valley, while in front I could see the domes and spires of Shadrinskoï some eight versts distant. The country about here is very pretty, in many parts beautiful. As we drew nearer the town had a very pleasing effect, the white churches and other large buildings, with their green domes and gilded crosses sparkling in the sun, contrasting agreeably against the dark forests beyond. I had scarcely time to take in a general view of the objects before we were rattling along the broad street at a furious speed, having traveled this station, twenty-eight versts and a half, in one hour and forty minutes. We stopped at the post-house, where I saw a post marking 2591 versts from St. Petersburg—a moderately long drive. I handed my papers to the *smatrical*, and walked back a short distance to look at a fine church and a large *gastinoi-dvor*, or market. Here are very large warehouses, and several establishments for the conveyance of merchandise. Russian brandy is made here, and much commerce is carried on with other parts of Siberia. There are also many large and fine houses, proving the wealth of some of the inhabitants. Altogether it appears to be a town enjoying considerable prosperity.

I returned to the post-station in about twenty minutes; the horses were ready, my papers were handed to me, and I took my seat in the tarantass, when the whip and reins were shaken, and we once more bounded along. At a short distance from Shadrinsk we entered upon a beautiful country — fine pasture-lands, with woods which appeared as if planted by man. We now left the Issetz at some distance to the south, and continued our drive through this woodland scenery. The next station was a mere village, standing on this woodland plain; here we again changed horses. After driving a few versts we came to the bank of the Issetz, pursued our route along the side of the valley about fifteen versts, then turned into a forest which surrounds the station. Here I drank tea, which I made dinner and supper, to lose as little time as possible. Two meals a day are ample for travelers in this region, and both should consist of tea, with meat or eggs. Spirits are very bad either in hot or cold weather.

After leaving the post-house and crossing a small river, I found that the road again turned toward the Issetz, running for some distance close to the river, now a broad stream gliding smoothly along between willowy banks and through rich pastures. About the middle of the station we crossed the boundary between the governments of Perm and Tobolsk, where I hoped to find greater variety in the scenery; but night came on fast, rendering every object indistinct and gloomy, during which we traveled over one hundred and thirty versts, crossing the Issetz in the dusk, and the Tobol just as day was breaking.

Leaving Iloutrovsky about twenty versts to the north, as the morning advanced we were on the Steppes of Ischim, a very uninteresting tract of country lying between the rivers Tobol and Ischim. There are many lakes in this district, and in some places pine woods on the small sandy elevations, which can scarcely be called hills; in other parts good pasturage is found for the cattle.

About two o'clock this morning we came up to a large party of convicts marching into Eastern Siberia: these unfortunates have a long journey before them. There were ninety-seven in the gang; seventeen men and three women in chains led the van, destined for Nertchinsk, and have yet to march more than four thousand versts. It will take eight months before they reach their place of banishment: they were a most desperate-looking set. The others followed in pairs, on their way to the government of Irkoutsk: they have a journey of three thousand versts to go, and theirs will be a march of six months. Behind them followed telagas with baggage, and there were eleven women riding: some of these poor creatures were following their husbands into exile. In front and on each side were mounted Cossacks, who kept a strict guard over their prisoners.

Barracks are built at each station, usually outside the village. The front buildings are occupied by the officers, guards, and other persons employed: from each end extends a high stockade to the distance of about forty to fifty feet, which returns at right angles, and extends about sixty feet; it is then carried along the back, and thus incloses an area of two hundred feet by sixty; in the middle of this space are the buildings for the prisoners. The stockade is formed of trunks of trees twelve inches in diameter, standing fifteen feet above the ground, and cut to a sharp point on the top; placed close together, they form a barrier which the prisoners can not scale. Besides this, they are well guarded. They march two days and rest one; the distance varies: on some days they make twenty versts, on others twenty-five, and a few stations twenty-eight. A gang leaves Ekaterineburg every Monday morning. That there are among these convicts many dreadfully bad men no one can doubt, but there are also not a few who have been driven by cruel treatment to rebel against their brutal masters, some of whom use them worse than dogs. A word, or a blow in return for the lashes they have endured, may have been the cause of their exile. This is not mere speculation, for it has often happened.

Having gone over a most monotonous country for many stations, we arrived at Bezroukova: the road passes within about twelve versts of Ischim, and then turns to the eastward. As we traveled along I could see the church and some other large buildings rising above the plain, which is named the Steppe of Ischim, a continuation of the Kirghis Steppe. In some parts it is sandy and sterile, with a number of salt-lakes extending far toward the south. We were now only about one hundred and sixty versts from Petropavlovsky, the great mart for Asiatic produce and Kirghis cattle: it is visited by several caravans from Tashkend in the summer to exchange such merchandise as they carry for Russian produce. This town is on *the present* frontier of the Kirghis Steppe, which is guarded by a line of forts and Cossack posts. We now wended our way along sandy roads to the bank of the River Ischim, which runs in a very deep bed, and crossed the stream near Abatzkoï by a ferry. At Kroutoia we passed near a large lake; indeed, the whole of this country around has a particularly aguish aspect, and is deemed very unhealthy. Forty versts farther we passed through Toukalinsk, a small town containing many good houses. Some of the people are said to be wealthy, which they ought to be if they do much business, for I found it necessary to get some small change for silver ruble notes, and was obliged to pay twenty per cent to procure it. At the post-stations you can seldom induce the yemtschicks to give such money, and, to avoid being imposed upon, it is absolutely necessary to carry a bag of small silver coin.

After leaving Toukalinsk and reaching Beokichevo station, we turned to the northeast, toward the valley of the Irtisch. On approaching this river the country improves, the sandy plain having given place to good pastures amid woods of birch and poplar. My first view of the Irtisch was from some high ground a little after daybreak, when I beheld the river winding its course through the valley. Near this place are many large tumuli covering up the ashes of ancient heroes who have passed over these scenes ages ago. Whether these indicate battle-fields, or the burial-places of a tribe or a nation, it is impossible to say. They are almost invariably placed on high land near the great rivers, and command views over the whole country.

About ten o'clock we reached the station "Tchernoï Ozernaia," or black lake, and then crossed the broad valley of the Irtisch, where the river runs at the foot of the high bank, which on the eastern side at this point rises more than 100 feet above the water. All these rivers have cut a broad and deep channel into the great plains, in some places ten, twelve, and as much as fifteen versts in width, leading to the belief that in former ages a mighty flood swept along, filling this valley from bank to bank. If so, its sources are dried up, and in comparison it has now become a very insignificant stream, although at this place more than three times the width of the Thames at London. This broad valley is covered with fine pastures, where hundreds of cattle feed near to the villages on its banks. There are large wooded patches in many parts; and in May, June, and July, when the water comes from the mountains, it spreads over the entire width, making these clumps of trees appear like islands dotted over a lake. I have crossed this river when it was ten versts broad.

We are now at Serebrenaia, safely across the Irtisch. The station is clean and comfortable. From hence the route is along the eastern bank of the Irtisch for a distance of forty versts, which afforded me several fine views of the twisting and winding of the broad river as it flows on its course.

At Ponstink station the road leaves the river, turning to the east. Here appears a plain, extending farther than the eye can reach, apparently covered with timber. Just at nightfall we passed two obelisks, marking the boundary of the governments of Tobolsk and Tomsk.

CHAPTER XI.

APPROACH TO THE ALTAI RANGE.

THE sun set, leaving a stormy twilight, which ended in drizzling rain; later in the evening we had several heavy claps of thunder; after this the rain poured down, and the night became very dark. This checked our speed, and made the driver cautious, as we frequently had deep morasses on the sides of the road. The lightning continued to flash, lighting up the lakes near us, and the thunder rolled till its echoes were lost in the plain. Even a rainy night must terminate, and a little before daybreak the last crash of thunder rolled heavily, the clouds gradually cleared off, and I saw signs of a bright morning. So soon as the storm ceased I slept, and only awoke when the horses stopped at Touroumova station. It was not yet daylight, and I was detained some time before the horses were yoked; this induced me to jump out and hasten the proceedings. I perceived, before stepping into the tarantass, that there was something the matter with my servant: he looked unusually pale. At last he informed me that we had three stations to travel over on which robberies were constantly being committed, adding his opinion that it would be better to wait at the station till daylight, as many convicts had escaped and were now in the woods. Two or three days before, he assured me, they had robbed a carriage during daylight in a woody part of the steppe, a few versts farther on. I called to the yemtschick to stop, when the face of my man brightened up. I was certain, by the tone of his voice, that he thought we were going back; but when he heard me order the head of the tarantass to be let down, there was a very perceptible change in his aspect. I laid hold of the spring on one side, and made him push at the other, when down went the top; the moment this was done, I called out to the yemtschick, "Pashol carashinka" (Drive on fast), and away he went. We were sitting with our heads high above the carriage, which enabled me to keep a good look-out on all sides; I drew my pistols from the holsters, examined the caps, and laid them on my lap, determined neither to be stopped nor robbed with impunity.

Before leaving Ekaterineburg, I had, at his own request, bought my man a double-barreled pistol, with eleven-inch rifle barrels—a deadly weapon if well used. I now put fresh caps on the nipples, and told him to take good aim at any rascal who should attempt to stop us on his side; I, however, discovered that he had no nerve for any such encounter; indeed, I believe at the sight of a stray pedestrian he would have been ready to drop his weapon, and gladly surrender the carriage and its contents to secure his own safety. The yemtschick kept his horses at full gallop all through the wood: this he thought the best course, as it would be very difficult for robbers to stop us unless they could strike down or shoot one of the horses as we passed, in which case we should have to fight for it. We emerged from the wood without having seen either man or beast, and were on a large open space on the steppe, where the yemtschick pulled up his horses and drove slowly on. About a verst distant appeared another thick wood, just before reaching which the man looked at me, and then put his horses into a gallop, intimating the necessity of keeping a sharp look-out; but we again drove through without molestation. We passed several other woods in the same manner, and reached the station, having made the seventeen versts in one hour and five minutes.

While fresh horses were being harnessed, many questions were asked of the yemtschick and my servant, and an opinion confidently expressed that, as we had not seen the robbers on the last station, we should be sure to find them on this; however, fortunately both for them and for us, we did not meet. Before we had gone half the station it was daylight. The two next villages were much dreaded, being convict colonies. Now that we could see, I found that this was a wretched country, having a great deal of brushwood and swamp. The very air I breathed appeared to taste of ague, which made me determine to drink tea at the station, if hot water could be got, notwithstanding the bad character of the people. In due time we reached the village, and fortunately found a *somervar*, but in a most miserable place. A sickly squalor was stamped on all the inmates, and the furniture as well as the room appeared masses of filth. From this station there were two stages more to Kiansk, the road still over a swampy country, which might very properly be called the place of Torment, as these morasses breed millions of musquitoes, apparently more bloodthirsty than any I had before encountered.

Kiansk is a moderately large town, consisting mostly of wooden houses, inhabited by many hundreds of Polish Jews, a race whose nearer acquaintance I have no desire to cultivate. Instead of the yemtschick driving to the post-station, he took me straight to the house of the man who had the contract with the post-office authorities to supply horses. He too was a Jew, and strove to delay me by asserting that he had no horses; subsequently he offered to provide them if I would pay double price; had I consented, I should have been subjected to the same extortion at every station beyond, as the fellow would have sent forward to inform his gang. I proceeded to the police-master, who, the moment I had stated my case, called in one of his people, and gave some orders which I did not understand; then told my servant, who acted as interpreter, to say that the matter would soon be settled, and desired me to remain. In a few minutes I observed two mounted Cossacks ride out of the gate, and in a very short time return, bringing the culprit with them. The police-master ordered him to give me horses immediately. The fellow swore "*Ye Bhoga!*" (by God) he had none, and unless I would pay double his friend would not give them. No further argument with him was attempted: the police-master gave orders to the Cossacks; the Jew was hustled into an adjoining room, and two other Cossacks having joined them, he was laid on the floor, and stripped of his clothing from the back downward. The birch was just going to be applied, when he bellowed out that he would give the horses. The police-master then declared that he should have twenty-five blows for causing the delay, but I begged that he should be set free, when orders were given to release him. At this moment, however, the Cossack raised his birch, and it fell on the target beneath, the men let go their hold, and the old sinner sprang to his feet with a frightful howl.

In less than twenty minutes the tarantass was at the door. I drank a glass of tea with the police-master, thanked him for his kindness, stepped into the vehicle, and away we went at full gallop. The fellow who supplied the horses had given me six, four yoked to the tarantass and two leaders. I was delighted to leave this town, it being the worst in all Siberia. Whenever Prince Gertchikoff, the General-Governor of Western Siberia, traveled this road, horses were always sent outside the town to meet him, and with these he galloped through, without stopping in this nest of thieves.

After leaving Kiansk I traveled directly south, having determined to visit the Lakes Sartian and Tchany, the remains of a great inland sea; from Lake Tchany there are a series of lakes extending to the southwest for nearly two hundred and fifty versts, in some parts fifty or sixty versts broad. The country in this direction was still swampy, occasionally rising into very slight undulations, covered with long coarse grass, and frequently having extensive clumps of birch-trees and aspens, or a thick underwood of bushes. Such was the general aspect of the country between

Kiansk and the lakes, which last are so surrounded by a broad belt of reeds that there were but few places where I could obtain even a view of the water, when I observed wild-fowl by thousands. After passing the lakes the country improves, many parts are thickly wooded, with extensive tracts of cultivated land between the forests, on which fine crops of rye and wheat were just beginning to take their yellow color. Large herds of cattle were grazing in the pastures near the villages, and the people looked healthy and comfortable; their cottages were better built and clean, and the women and children were no longer clothed in rags. What a change a few hundred versts had made both in the aspect of the country and the inhabitants!

Proceeding onward, I found it somewhat difficult to believe that this was a part of the Barabinsky Steppe; there were gently-sloping hills crowned with large timber, encircling extensive plains, which appeared like the boundaries of some immense park; and to aid the illusion, I saw several groups of wild deer bounding over the glades. The plain was dotted over in parts with plantations of large timber, in other places belts of young trees stretched along in the very places a landscape gardener would have selected to give effect to the scene. Good Dame Nature has been the decorator, and has made, by the judicious distribution of wood and water, a fine woodland country out of a most dreary steppe. The ground was covered with a great variety of flowers, among which were geraniums, two varieties of delphinium—one a pale blue, the other a beautiful deep blue—a white, and also a deep crimson dianthus growing in large clumps, a deep red single peony, and purple crocus, with many others unknown to me. White and yellow nymphæa were growing in the lakes, along the shores of which the road winds for several versts, affording many fine views. I frequently amused myself by picturing a noble mansion on one of these sites, the architectural features being simple and vast, in keeping with the immense sweeping plains around. These day-dreams aided greatly in ridding me of the weariness brought on by ten days and nights' confinement in a tarantass. Indeed, so worn out had I become, that I should have been glad of another robber-excitement by way of a change. Game I often shot, having marked down the broods of tetery which we disturbed in crossing the steppe. They seldom flew far away; I have often strolled through the long grass into the very centre of the brood before they moved —in fact, have trodden on them. In two instances I got three birds with two shots; I trod upon one, and killed one with each barrel; with a dog any quantity may be shot here.

During the evening we reached the shores of a lake named "Gorkoï Ozera," or bitter lake, having thousands of ducks and divers swimming over its surface. Not far off stood a scathed and shattered pine-tree, and on one of its bare branches a large eagle was sitting; the tarantass was instantly stopped, and I tried to get within rifle range, but before I could succeed he expanded his wings and soared majestically away. This was a great disappointment; still, as I had seen one, I knew that there must be others in this region. The people of the next station were very anxious that I should remain all night, representing that my next thirty-eight versts would be over a horrible road. To this, however, I would not consent. They gave me seven horses and three men, a certain sign of what was in store for me. Some long ropes were placed beside the driver, and then we started. The first three versts were across the inclosed pastures round the village, over a hard and very good road. After passing the gate we almost immediately entered a thick wood, and here the ground became swampy. Farther on bushes and reeds had been cut down and laid across our path, by which at once our speed was brought to a walk. I could see that the road had become wavy, like a chain bridge. On each side of us were high reeds and fine bulrushes, which showed me that we were crossing a deep morass. We had gone over about a verst of this when we reached hard ground again, but even now our progress was very slow in comparison with what it had been. The night came on with heavy dark clouds rolling up from the horizon—a bad prospect; still we proceeded, and soon reached another bush and reeded path, across another morass. Before driving on to this frail road the driver got down and went on some distance to examine it; on his return he exclaimed, "Otchin khooda" (very bad), mounted his seat, and drove gently on. The horses pressed the branches and reeds under water, and when the tarantass got upon them it sunk into the water up to the axles. It was frightful to be thus dragged along, but stop we dare not; we must keep in motion or be stuck fast. The flogging of the horses and shouting of the men added to the horror of this stagnant lake, which on either side was deep, although thick with reeds, affording no pleasant reflections. At length we were again on hard ground, when the yemtschick crossed himself, and pulled up to give his horses breathing-time. During my anxiety while crossing the morass I had not noticed that the rain was falling fast; it soon poured down and became very dark. Our pace was now a walk, the tarantass being jolted from side to side frightfully, and I almost began to regret having left the station, as the men could hardly see before them; certainly they could not observe the bad holes in the road. Sometimes we were actually brought to a stand-still. Hour after hour passed in this way, and, as the yemtschick had informed me, we had still the worst place to cross. However, there is nothing like patience on a bad road in a dark and rainy night. At length I saw a narrow line of light on the horizon; at first I thought it was a fire very far off; as it extended, I observed to my great satisfaction that it was day breaking, and the gray morning light began gradually to creep over wood and steppe: I now ascertained that we were on a perfectly flat country.

In about half an hour we came up to a very high bed of reeds, within which lay our last difficulty on this station. Again we stopped, and two men went forward to examine the place; when they returned they held a long council, and the man who had driven the middle pair now mounted the leaders, and we went slowly on. After going about one hundred paces, the leaders began to flounder about very much; still, we got on; and on standing up, I saw we were nearly through. A few paces farther, and the tarantass stopped, nor could the horses, with all their efforts, move it an inch; indeed, they could not hold their feet in the mud and reeds. The man on the middle horse dismounted, when I observed that he was far above his knees in water; he unloosed the traces; the yemtschick threw him the long ropes, one end of which he fastened to the carriage, and the other to the traces of his own horses; when this was done he mounted, and the four steeds went on, the ropes reaching to the hard ground.

The tarantass and wheelers had remained quite still; harness was now looked to, ropes tied afresh, the men mounted, the yemtschick gave a shout, the horses pulled, and we got on a few yards. After resting a short time we got on another few yards, and with a few more efforts hoped to be out of this frightful place. At last, after more than an hour spent in the morass, we stood on hard ground, and a little after five o'clock in the morning reached the station, having been the whole night traveling thirty-eight versts.

Again I had seven horses, this being also a bad station, but only a short one of fifteen versts. Ropes were again required, indicating a morass in prospect; we should, however, have it in daylight, and thus be able to see our difficulties. The country around was very flat; still, we passed through some cultivated land, on which the rye appeared almost ripe. After driving at a slow trot for about an hour, we reached the swamp, where several men and horses had been sent on before us. They were evidently afraid that we should not get over this place, though it was not more than fifty yards in width. After a long consultation, the spare horses were sent to the opposite side. I watched them pass; for about thirty yards they proceeded well, then all at once sunk deep in water. It was now our turn, and we drove very gently along till the leaders got into deep water and mud. The four horses were now loosed from the carriage, and several long ropes secured to it, the ends of which these horses dragged over to hard ground. The men then began to fasten the animals to these cords, four abreast; this done, four other horses were harnessed in front. After many consultations and directions given by the driver, the men again mounted, the yemtschick gave his usual shriek, and on they went. Our horses were in the deep pool in a minute, then in plunged the carriage, the fore wheels going under water: the shouting was now temendous. Presently our steeds were dragged to the solid earth, then the wheels touched it, and we were out in a minute. With fewer horses and men we should have stuck fast, and the tarantass would have sunk down deep into the morass, when all my things must have been spoiled. To my great relief, I was told that this was the last bad place on the whole road to Barnaoul. I rewarded and thanked the men, and in half an hour reached the station.

We were now only twenty versts from Krontikha, on the Ob. At this station we returned to our usual team, as the road was said to be good. Immediately on leaving the village the country improved, swelling into rounded hills, and affording rich pastures to large herds of horses and cattle which I saw grazing. We were also approaching a thickly-wooded region, and should now be traveling near or along the banks of the great Siberian river Ob, whose source is among the mountains toward which we were hastening. While commencing the ascent of a steep hill, I observed a fine eagle perched on a tree, about two hundred paces in our front. Determined to get a shot at him if possible, I made the driver pull up his horses and walk them along. I then seized my rifle, which unfortunately had got damp, and I feared useless; at least, I did not like to risk it; only one barrel of my gun was loaded, but with this I intended to try my luck. Getting out of the tarantass on the opposite side to where the noble bird was perched, I walked stealthily along under its shelter, telling the man to go on slowly. When within about fifty yards, the eagle raised his head and prepared to take flight. I stood still, the head of the tarantass passed me, and I sent the contents of the barrel after him as he soared off the branch. Down he fell, but was not dead, as he proved by springing upon his feet before I could get near him. He could not fly, but made off at a good speed by springing up with his feet, and by the aid of one wing, the other being broken. After running about two hundred yards, I in quick pursuit, he stopped, and turned upon his back, with his legs drawn up to strike. I now found it required much caution to secure my prize, as his talons looked formidable, and I knew them to be dangerous at close quarters. After looking at him for two or three minutes, I tried to place the butt of my gun on his legs. He struck out, driving his talons into the stock; simultaneously I caught his neck with my right hand, and while he was holding fast to the butt of the gun with his claws, let the barrel drop against my right arm, and seized his legs. The gun was thrown down in the scuffle, and he struck with his wing fearfully. At this moment my man came up, we got his wing secured under my arm, and I carried off my prize. The yemtschick fastened his legs with a leathern thong, and then killed him; when we reached the station, his head, wings, and legs were cut off, and I carried them along with me. He was a very large and powerful bird.

From Krontikha we had a fine view looking down the valley of the River Ob.

At this station the valley is twelve or fifteen versts wide from one high bank to the other, between which the Ob winds along, crossing and twining first toward one side and then to the other. The river is divided into several streams, and forms islands, sometimes very large, at other parts of the river small and numerous. Standing on the elevated bank and looking down the valley, there is a magnificent view. To the northeast, and about 150 versts distant, is Kolyvan, formerly the chief town of the government, which has been transferred to Tomsk, 150 versts farther in the same direction. Looking either north or east, there appears one level plain, densely covered with dark pine forests as far as the eye can reach. When traveling across these regions, which look vast interminable forests, large tracts of open country are found in a very good state of cultivation.

Having crossed the Ob, our road was up the valley, among rich pastures not long since under water. The yemtschick galloped over this flat country at a good speed, and I perceived that we were approaching the mining regions by the quantity of charcoal wagons we passed. In the evening we reached Sousounskoï Zavod, copper smelting works belonging to the crown: here is also a mint for coining copper money. I shall not attempt any description of these works, my stay having been only long enough to partake of the hospitality of the director. We traveled on through the night, but not very fast, as at times it was exceedingly dark, and the road difficult to find.

We were still traveling up the valley of the Ob, but eight or ten versts from the river, and through a thick forest of dark pine. Early in the morning I found myself at Pavlovsky Zavod—large silver smelting works belonging to the Altai mines—but no ore is found here. The director was exceedingly amiable, and induced me to remain to luncheon. I then started, having only fifty versts to Barnaoul. After leaving this Zavod I entered upon a sandy country, with thick pine forests stretching out to the west; to the south there were small straggling woods, and the country looked bare and barren. The road is carried along the high land on the west side of the Ob, ten or twelve versts from the river, in some parts even more, and there is nothing to vary the monotony of the scene.

The last station was passed, and we had reached some high ground, which gave me a peep across the Ob to the south—the direction in which lay the Altai—but no mountains were visible; nothing but black pine forest. At five o'clock we drove into Barnaoul, tired and weary for want of rest during a journey of twelve days and nights. The Chief of the Mines had prepared rooms for me, and a Cossack led me to the house. My traps were soon unloaded, and I prepared to take a night's rest that should recompense me for my journey of 4527 versts from St. Petersburg. I am at last in Barnaoul, the chief town in the mining district of the Altai. The "*Gornie Pravlania*," or Board for the Administration of the Mines, is here, and all the officers connected with it reside in the town. I slept nearly twelve hours, and wishing to take advantage of every day, as the summer was gliding fast, at ten o'clock called upon the Chief of the Mines, who received me with great kindness. I handed my papers to him, when he stated that he had received instructions concerning me from the minister in St. Petersburg, and was ready to afford me every assistance I could possibly require. He gave me most valuable information about the region I was going to visit; also a marche route, by which I could travel to many interesting places; and invited me to dine with him. He spoke a little English, which was exceedingly agreeable to me; equally so was my introduction to his wife, whom I found a most amiable woman. On my first acquaintance with this gentleman and his family, it was quite clear to me that civilization of a very high character had reached these regions, united with great kindness and genuine hospitality. In the evening I called upon the officer whose acquaintance I had made at a station on the Oural, he having given me his address in Barnaoul. I was quite delighted to see a face I had met so far away, and he appeared equally pleased. He invited me to dine with him the following day, when I passed two or three most pleasant hours in company with two of his friends. Before I left I called upon the director, who gave me letters to some of his officers at the mines in the Altai; he had also ordered a Cossack to accompany me, who was well acquainted with the region to which I was going. He went with me through the silver smelting works, and to the furnaces in which the gold is smelted, but these were not in operation.

Our direction was nearly south, over low hills, which extend for some distance on that side of the town; from the top of one of these there is a beautiful view, looking over the Ob toward Tomsk.

We traveled over deep soft sand, very heavy for the horses; this continued for many versts till we reached other hills, and then the road was good. The country in some parts was prettily wooded with pines; there were also many small valleys or deep sandy ravines running down toward the Ob. During our ride over the second station I perceived a change. We had left the woods behind us, and the country was still undulating, but it was evident that we were approaching the steppes extending westward to the banks of the Irtisch. These were formerly inhabited by Kirghis, before they were driven back across the river, and a line of forts built extending from Omsk along the Irtisch to the River Bouchtarma. These form the frontier to the Kirghis Steppe, which is guarded by Cossacks, the whole length of the line, perhaps not less than 2500 versts, extending far up into the Altai and along the Chinese frontier.

We passed over several stations, all equally monotonous—dreary level plains stretching out in every direction, with trees only along the water-courses. The country at a distance from the river has a most sterile aspect, the principal product on most parts being wormwood. About three o'clock on the second day I first distinctly saw the Altai Mountains, very little elevated above the plain, and watched the misty forms as we rolled on with intense interest. After galloping for about an hour, much more of the chain was visible when looking across a small lake, on the banks of which several birches were growing near the dead trunks of two old willows, now shattered by the storms, which often blow with great fury across these steppes.

Having sketched the above scene, I pushed on again, and each ten versts brought other parts of the chain into view. I now noticed a storm gathering over the mountains, which were shortly completely obscured. We were near the post-house, at which I proposed drinking tea, and, if the weather became bad, remaining for the night, being anxious to see the Altai as we gradually approached the chain. This was explained to the Cossack, who objected to my stopping, the station being small and dirty. He proposed to take me to a village some twenty versts nearer the mountains, where I could stop and be more comfortable, and then we should pass over a hilly country the next day. To this arrangement I consented; and the horses having been yoked, we left the road, and traveled across the steppe more to the eastward. The land gradually rose toward the chain we were approaching. In about an hour we saw that the storm was rolling on fast, covering up every thing with its black mass of vapor. Presently it changed its course, and came directly toward us; but no village appeared near in which we could ask for shelter. The Cossack urged the yemtschick to drive on, though it was evident that by doing so we should only meet the storm the sooner, and get a thorough drenching.

After riding a few versts farther, we looked down into a valley, in which I discerned a moderately large river running, which they said was the Tchurish. The storm was following the course of this river, and was now not far from us. The thunder, which had hitherto been growling in the distance, bellowed forth in magnificent peals every two or three minutes, bringing the dark mass of vapor nearer.

We had reached the edge of the valley, and beheld the village five or six versts distant, just being obscured in the falling rain. Not a drop had yet reached us, but we saw that our turn was coming. After descending into the valley, we were going over some very rough ground, when a terrific stream of lightning and a tremendous crash of thunder burst over us; at the same moment the clouds divided, and rolled off in opposite directions. It was like opening the curtains to some mighty and fearful scene as the heavy dark masses were carried up and off at either side, leaving a thin vapor between them hanging like a veil. The sun was setting, casting a pale and red tinge on the vapory curtain, which produced a wonderful effect. I stopped the carriage to watch the changes, and observed the opening gradually extend into a larger space, which became a deeper and deeper red as the vapory curtain expanded more and more. The hills were now dimly seen through it, much magnified, and resembling mountains glowing with fire; not bright, but more like red-hot metals losing their white heat, and changing into a dark red.

The vapor gradually rolled off and separated. At length a dull red tinge spread over all the under parts of the clouds, extending high up into the heavens, giving the entire scene a supernatural appearance. The sun was now sinking fast. Gradually the clouds lost their colors, and in a short time all had passed away, leaving me bewildered and fascinated by the grandeur and sublimity of the fleeting vision. This was a scene never to be forgotten. Unfortunately, it was one my pencil could not paint or my pen describe; I only profess to be able to shadow it forth dimly. Before we reached the village the dark gray of evening was spread over the whole country, and all was calm and quiet.

This morning the sun was obscured by a thick fog, which soon acted like a Scotch mist, wetting us completely. About nine o'clock the weather cleared up, when I beheld the offshoots from the Altai extended far into the plain. We were crossing these hills to the westward, and came out upon the steppe. A few versts farther we discerned Kolyvan Lake shining beneath some dark mountains with broken and rugged tops. It had been mentioned to me in Barnaoul as possessing some beautiful scenery. On approaching nearer I observed many curious objects standing on its shores, having the appearance of a ruined city: masses of rock, and pillars of various forms, standing quite isolated, backed by picturesque mountains, give to the place a very singular effect. This was merely a flying visit; nevertheless, I made a few sketches, since which time I have become thoroughly acquainted with its scenes, and have explored on foot its rocky shores and ravines. It is a most curious region; the granite has assumed most extraordinary forms; in some parts it appears to have been forced up in a soft or liquid state, and has flowed over and cooled, after which it has been forced up again, thus forming thin beds with rounded edges, exactly like liquefied metallic substances after flowing a short distance and cooling.

About five versts from the lake stands the village of Saouchkina; almost immediately after passing it the road begins to ascend the granite mountains, which are very steep. This induced me to walk up; so, quitting the road, I followed a track which led to some high crags; on reaching the summit of these, they afforded me a view over all the country I had passed through after leaving Barnaoul, and the steppe to the northwest, with its numerous lakes. To the south still higher craggy masses rose, interrupting the prospect in that direction. After going a little farther I observed that this spur of the Altai, which I was crossing, terminated in the plain about sixty versts distant. There are some exceedingly picturesque rocks on these mountains—some like ruined castles, with circular apertures perforating the huge towers; others have taken the form of human heads of a gigantic size, beside which the Great Sphinx of Egypt would appear an infant.

The tarantass having come up, I sat down, and away we went at a speed that would soon give me a peep at the other side of these rocks. After riding about half an hour we descended into a valley, on the opposite side of which were other hills of greater elevation, and a little to the eastward of the road were some rocks of a great height. I stopped the carriage and ascended to the summit, whence I had a fine view, looking over the plains toward the Irtisch, that separates Siberia from the Kirghis Steppe; while to the south and east rose up some of the higher offshoots of the Altai chain, the mere sight of which made me doubly anxious to begin my rambles among their rugged passes. At every half verst there was evidence that we were approaching the silver mines, by the charcoal wagons we passed on their way down into the valley. We also met several hundred small wagons containing silver ore going to Barnaoul. A little farther on we ascended another hill, from which we saw at a short distance the smoke from the smelting furnaces. They stand in the bottom of the valley, on the bank of a small river which falls into the Alei. We passed near to the works, and ascended a steep hill into Zmeinogorsk, the richest silver mine in his imperial majesty's dominions. We drove to the house of the director, who received me most kindly, acknowledging that he had received instructions to afford me every assistance on my journey into the Altai.

Although I had felt very unwell for the last two or three days, I determined to shake off this indisposition and start on a journey into the Altai, to visit a part of the chain considered highly interesting; but, after traveling about seventy versts, I was compelled to return, glad to reach the hospitable dwelling of the director in Zmeinogorsk, and he immediately called in the doctor. I was carefully nursed—indeed, treated with the greatest consideration; but, what with bleeding, physic, and starvation, a great change was soon produced, and I was rendered thin enough for any mountain journey. This illness was a great disappointment at the time, and worried me much during my eight days' detention. I was determined, however, sooner or later, to visit the region I had thus been obliged to leave unexplored.

CHAPTER XII.

ASCENT OF THE ALTAI.

I LEFT the Zavod and proceeded to Oubinskoï, where I arrived the following morning. From this point I began to ascend the valley, which is closed in by rounded hills of no great elevation, destitute of wood, giving it a sterile and monotonous aspect. Having passed Oubinskoï, I found the River Ouba, a broad and deep stream, with islands in several parts, most of them covered with willows. It runs moderately fast, over a stony bottom, and contains plenty of fish, the grayling being found here in great abundance, and of excellent quality. Having decided to dine at one of the villages, my Cossack sent two men to the river with a net, and in about half an hour they returned, with from fifty to sixty of these fish, varying from half a pound to a pound and a half in weight.

Continuing our journey up the valley, on the right side were seen the tops of the Oubinskoï Mountains, and in the extreme distance the high summits of the Oulbinskoï chain. A few versts beyond the village where we dined we left the valley of the Ouba, crossed the mountains, and descended into the valley of the Oulba, where I found the scenery much finer. It is wooded with birch, poplars, and willows, among which the river runs, leaping over rocks, and sparkling in the sun. Pine-clad hills extend along each side of the valley, overtopped by rocky-crested mountains rising from three to four thousand feet above it. This indicated that we were approaching a more grand and picturesque region.

Our road was up the valley, at a short distance from the river, sometimes through woods of pine and birch, affording frequent views of the higher mountains, some of which I transferred to my sketch-book. At length, after traveling about fifteen versts, my road passed along the bank of the river, in some parts on rocks overhanging the stream, where it has been necessary to guard against accident by placing strong wooden railings. Here the rocks rise from the road to a great height, in rugged and picturesque masses. On the opposite side of the river is a thick wood of pines and poplars; farther up the valley it is thickly fringed with weeping willows, birches, and small pines. Above these, and in the distance, rises Ivanoffsky Belock, partly covered with snow.

A little beyond this point we forded the river, ascended the valley a few versts farther, and then crossed to Sokolnic Roodnick, or "silver mine," a short distance beyond which is the mine of Riddersk. Some rich veins of silver ore have been found in the low hills thrown up in this valley, which is nearly surrounded by high mountains. It is a singular fact, that wherever the silver ore is found the country is almost destitute of wood. As there are no smelting works at Riddersk, the ore is broken up and sent to the smelting works in Zmeinogorsk, Barnaoul, and Pavlovsky; to the two latter works it is conveyed not less than six or seven hundred versts.

About fifteen versts from Riddersk is Ivanoffsky Belock, a mountain on which snow lies all the year, and a bold mass it appears when seen from the valley. There is the source of the Gromotooka, one of the wildest rivers in the Altai; and, as its name Grom (thunder) implies, it is truly a thundering stream. Its roar is heard at a great distance; and when near, it is impossible to hear any person speak. At times it sweeps huge masses of rock down, tearing up every thing in its course; and even when the water is low it is exceedingly dangerous to cross. Some years ago a mounted mining officer was crossing, when both horse and rider were swept away in a moment, and carried down the roaring torrent. Fortunately, the latter was driven against some rocks on the bank, where he was caught up by one of his own men; but it was long before he recovered: the horse was lost.

Beyond Riddersk the journey must be made on horseback, as no wheeled carriage could travel in these valleys. Twenty horses were engaged to accompany me, and fifteen men; and as five of the latter carried rifles, and the other ten axes, I must own we had rather a bandit-like appearance. We left Riddersk at eleven o'clock in the morning, having to ride only twenty versts to the last village in this part of the Altai. Our track was along a valley at the foot of Ivanoffsky Belock, affording me several views of the chain, and at four o'clock we arrived at Poperetchnaia, where we were to pass the night. The kind-hearted villagers gave us a most hearty welcome, and brought me fresh honey in the comb, deliciously flavored, like the perfume of the wild flowers on which the bees feed.

This place stands in a lovely valley, apparently closed on all sides with high mountains; and when standing near, there appears to be no outlet for the water which is running rapidly past. While I was sketching a view of the village looking to the westward, the sun descended below the mountains, spreading a glorious light upon this quiet little spot, occupied by only eighteen families, who live here undisturbed by events that shake empires to their centre. Each family have their horses and cows; there is pasture around the village sufficient for large herds, while in some of the valleys they can make abundance of hay for their winter fodder. They have also free access to the stags on the mountains and the deer on the hills, and find a great variety of fish in the rivers. Every peasant possesses numerous hives of bees, which produce great quantities of delicious honey; wild fruit is also very plentiful. Fashion and finery have not yet intruded into this quiet valley, and every one is contented. They have all the necessaries and many of the luxuries of life, which only a man with a good income could procure in Europe. One thing, however, they do not possess—"freedom." Even in this far-distant spot their number and age are known. The sons are ordered to the mines, perhaps a thousand versts away, where they must work and toil for less than threepence a day, probably without seeing home or parents for years; their lot may even be much worse—they may be made soldiers, and then it is almost certain they will never see either their friends or this peaceful spot again.

An incident happened here the summer before my visit which will be a subject of conversation for a generation or two to come. The little rivulet Poperetchnaia has its source in the Ivanoffsky Belock, from which it flows very rapidly, especially in the early part of the summer, when the snow is melting in the mountains. About half a verst above the village there was a slight depression in the little valley, and here the villagers decided on building their mill. A small embankment was carried across, that raised the water sufficiently to get a fall for their water-wheel, and the building was soon erected with logs. The whole of the rude machinery was constructed by the peasants, and put together in the mill; the water-wheel turned, the mill-stones ground the corn, and all went on well, till one day in the summer a frightful thunder-storm occurred over Ivanoffsky Belock, and the rain poured down, as the villagers said, in streams. At length a very unusual sound was heard in the mountain, even above the rolling of the thunder. The men left their cottages alarmed; some of them ran toward the mill; the man employed in it was also frightened, and joined his neighbors. The roaring came nearer, when one of them exclaimed, "It is water coming down!" While some ran back to the village to give warning to their families, the others stood watching on the elevated ground. At last down came the torrent, driving before it trees and stones, and tearing up every thing in its course. On it rushed, rolling the stones with terrific fury, till all at once it reached the mill-pond, when the embankment and mill were swept away in a mass; nor were the mill-stones ever found. Fortunately, the houses remained intact; the only structure that suffered was the mill.

Having sketched the scene of this disaster, with the gorge and Ivanoffsky Belock in the distance, I started on foot toward the wood which skirts the foot of the mountains. Here I found evidence enough of the power of the flood: immense blocks of stone had been brought down and thrown on to the bank, and others were piled up against them. I measured some, and found them from twenty-five to thirty tons in weight; one contained 470 cubic feet.

I was the guest of the patriarch of this little community—a fine old man, with a head and countenance that might have served as a model for one of the Evangelists. His gray beard was set off by the ruddy glow of his face, which bespoke health and happiness. His dress was a simple white shirt hanging over blue linen trowsers, and tied round his waist with a red sash; his trowsers were tucked into a pair of boots which reached nearly to his knees: this was his summer dress. In winter he would add a wolf or sheep skin coat, that then completed his costume. One of his sons, a fine young man, had been ordered to join my party; and his wife, a respectable and clean-looking woman, had every thing in perfect order in her cottage. The walls, benches, tables, and floors were very clean, being often scrubbed with birch bark and coarse sand, which makes the wood look new. Her dress was a white linen chemise, a pink striped sarafan, with a bright red handkerchief, formed into a cap, on her head; shoes, but no stockings. Every thing around this family indicated ease and comfort.

The following morning I was out very early sketching, and at ten o'clock all were ready to start. The whole of the population turned out to see us. I thanked the old couple for their kindness, said good-by to the villagers, and rode away along the valley at the foot of Ivanoffsky Belock, whose high, snowy peaks and rugged precipices formed a striking contrast to the wooded valley beneath, now smiling in all its summer glory of luxuriant foliage and flowers. The ride was most delightful, through a country having fine clumps of birch and pine trees spread about, forming beautiful groups.

A Forest Ride by Moonlight.

Among these park-like scenes, every few versts afforded something new for my pencil. Indeed, so much had I been interested with the scenery, that I had taken no note of time till night began to draw in, and caught us in a part of the valley destitute of water. We were now compelled to continue our ride, and ascended a ravine. Late in the evening we reached a clump of fine cedars, near which a small stream was dashing and leaping among the rocks. At a hundred paces distant we found grass for the horses; this decided me to encamp, and my bed-room was prepared under a large cedar. Each man was busy at his duties; some unloading the horses, and stowing the baggage under the trees; others cutting wood and making fires, which were soon burning brightly. The Cossack and my man were getting the tea apparatus ready, and very soon the smoking beverage was placed before me. Having taken a liberal portion I strolled to a little distance. In front of me were large blocks of granite, which had been rolled down by water, and lay tumbled about in marvelous confusion, having large plants and bushes growing among them. The fires were burning fiercely, tinging the rocks and trees with a red glare, while the dark figures of the men flitting to and fro, the arms hanging from the branches, and the baggage piled up under the trees, gave to the scene the character of robbers feasting after a successful expedition.

After studying our night's quarters and our unprepossessing appearance, I returned, rolled myself up in my cloak, and was soon lulled to sleep by the dashing of the water and the sighing of the wind through the branches. When I awoke in the morning I found every thing covered with a white frost, which indicated that we had ascended considerably above the valley.

Almost immediately on leaving our resting-place we entered a dense forest of cedars, apparently covering the mountain over which we had to ride, and were soon in a thick underwood, which rendered our progress slow. Large trunks of trees were lying almost covered with moss and plants—some so much decayed that they crumbled into dust when a horse placed his foot on them; others, more sound, caused many a stumble. We had a very steep ascent for a couple of hours, after which we emerged from the underwood into a magnificent cedar forest, where the ground was covered with grass and plants, and free from bushes. It was a splendid forest scene, with gigantic trees on every side, their gnarled and twisted branches forming a canopy through which the sun could scarcely penetrate. I had before seen cedars in the Oural, but in comparison with these they were very small. Here I found them in a southerly region, high in the mountains, and in their native woods, where the tree grows in all its grandeur and beauty. There was one spot where we stopped to breathe our horses which I think was the most lovely I ever saw. I sketched the scene; we then mounted, continuing to ascend, and in half an hour reached the summit. We rode two or three versts along this ridge, and then began to descend on the south side of the mountain. A striking change was visible. At first there were a few straggling trees in the ravines, and then they disappeared altogether. This had a strange effect, but I afterward found it was almost universal, as no forests grow on the south declivities of the chain. After descending for about an hour, and crossing another ridge, we had a fine view into the valley of the Koksa, with the Kaier Koomin Mountains in the distance.

It was now past three o'clock, and the River Karaguy, on which we were to encamp, was still a long way in front. This induced me to take two men and descend into the valley of the Koksa, and send the party forward the nearest way to our destination. Their direction was southeast, ours nearly due north. In less than an hour I reached the Koksa Lake, which is near the source of the River Koksa. It is now small, but has been extensive at some very distant period, before the river broke through a mass of rocks at the lower end of the valley. There are several beautiful varieties of jasper and porphyry in the mountains, but they are too far away to be used. After sketching a view of the lake, we crossed the country to follow our companions. We had a small mountain to cross, and on gaining the summit I saw that evening was covering the valleys with her dark mantle, while the high peaks around were still glowing with light. But these had become gray and indistinct before we reached the valley, nor could we see any signs of our people. We now put our horses to a sharp trot, following a track we found leading down the valley. In about an hour we turned round some rocks, and beheld a fire blazing brightly at the distance of a few versts. We lost no time in reaching the spot, where I refreshed myself with my favorite beverage, and very shortly afterward, wrapped up in my cloak, was fast asleep.

I had a dip in the River Karaguy before the sun rose, though the ground was again covered with white frost, which rendered the grass crisp under my feet, and made the morning air rather chilly. Soon the mountain tops were tipped with the sun's rays: this had a cheering effect; the light gradually crept lower into the valley, the crystals which sparkled on the grass so brilliantly melted away, and the scene changed.

On looking round I discovered the skeletons of some Kalmuck winter dwellings; the birch bark had been stripped off these conical houses, and only the bare poles were standing.

At this time of the year the inhabitants are up in the mountains, where they find plenty of grass for their cattle, and where they are free from those torments, the musquitoes.

In autumn they will return to this place, cover their *yourts* with new bark, and in a few days their winter dwellings will be completed. I was informed by the natives that in some of these upper valleys of the Altai the winters are peculiarly mild, heavy falls of snow seldom occurring. Here the cattle and wild animals easily find their food throughout this dreary season. At the end of October, or by the first week in November, the three families who occupy this spot are made prisoners for the winter, as it is impossible to cross the mountains when once the snow is deep.

With two companions I rode toward the River Arakym, having arranged that the other men should remain, pack up the things, load the horses, and follow our track. I forded the river, turned up a narrow valley to the southward, and rode along the bank of a small stream for about an hour, after which I crossed the valley, and began to ascend the mountains to the eastward. These form a small chain which separates the valleys of the Karaguy and Arakym. Our way was through woods of birch, pine, and larch, but not growing thickly or with underwood; in many places I almost fancied that the trees had been planted and the grounds laid out, with little glades between the plantations, along which we rode, wending our way upward. Having reached an open space, I observed that we were on a low ridge, between mountains which rose to a great height on both sides, terminating in lofty crags, with cedars growing out of their riven sides. We had now a fine level grassy turf, with a few scattered rocks, which had rolled from the mountains above.

While riding along this beautiful place, I saw, for the first time, many black squirrels skipping about in the branches; they enlivened the scene, and looked very knowing and pretty, sitting among the foliage. Their fur is a dark gray in winter, at which season only the Kalmucks kill them, for it is not good in the summer. For the last half hour I had ridden slowly on, watching the gambols of these little creatures in the grass, and their scampering up the trees. When we came near them they would run along the boughs, and leap from tree to tree, sometimes two or three on different branches evidently racing. While I was staring up at the squirrels my horse suddenly stopped on the edge of some rocks overlooking the valley of the Arakym.

This valley is a celebrated hunting-ground for the Kalmucks, and, as they state, the great battle-field of the bucks in the rutting season. Stags are numerous in the mountains around, and great numbers are shot when they come to drink at the lake. As we descended I found a pair of large horns which had been shed by one of these noble and graceful animals. One of my men, an old hunter, said we should not find any stags here now, as they were all in the higher regions near the snow, where the musquitoes and flies can not follow them. Even the bears, with their rough shaggy coats, can not remain in the valleys in summer, where these insects are extremely numerous. Two frosty nights have already effected a wonderful change; it is only in the warm sun, and in a sheltered situation, that the musquitoes are troublesome: three or four more cold nights, and their annoyance is over for this year.

On reaching the bottom of the valley, I found it thickly covered with small picta-trees and long grass; in spring much of this part is under water. After riding about ten versts, we came to a branch of the River Arakym, running from the south, where the valley extends up toward the Cholsoun chain. It was necessary to wait here till the other men arrived, otherwise we might get separated, as several ravines branched off into the mountains, and the river divides into two branches near the head of the valley. We therefore stopped at the foot of some high rocks, near which was plenty of grass, and our horses were turned loose to feed.

Very soon we had a large fire burning and refreshments prepared. The men arrived in about half an hour.

We recommenced our ride up the bank of the little river, and followed its windings two or three versts, when we came upon some rocks which crossed the valley, and formed it into a lake. The water has cut a channel fifty or sixty feet deep, through which it rushes with great force; although small, it is exceedingly picturesque. Birch and picta-trees are growing out of the crevices, and the river forms several beautiful cascades. After sketching, I rode on into a much broader valley, and crossed toward a fine belt of timber, on reaching which I found myself on the bank of the Arakym. The river was wide and rapid, rolling and dashing over large stones with a great noise. I wanted to cross to the opposite bank; but here it was impossible, as no horse could stand in the stream. We turned up the bank, and rode fast toward a great ravine in the mountain, through which I supposed the river entered the valley. Although it appeared quite near, we were two hours riding sharply before we reached it. Here I observed that the river was divided by a great mass of rocks, piled up picturesquely, having been washed down during a series of ages, and trees and bushes now grow upon them most luxuriantly. The rocks on both sides of this gorge rise to a great elevation, and are broken into very rugged crags, with dwarf cedars springing out of the clefts; on the summit there is scarcely any vegetation, a proof that we are getting far up in the Altai.

Even now, when the water is very low, it is impossible to hear any one speak when near the river. What will it be when the floods come down during a storm? then, indeed, the rushing water must be sublime, and the roar terrific. Before I had finished my sketch the evening was drawing in fast; one of my men ascended some high rocks to look out for the smoke at our encampment, but none could be seen. I was determined to ride up into the gorge and see what it was like before returning, as well as to ascertain if we could pass through it, because otherwise we must seek another route and cross the mountains to the westward. We mounted our horses and rode up the valley for about a verst, when we reached the mouth of the gorge, and came upon a track leading into it, rapidly ascending high above the river. After riding along this ledge for some distance, we saw that it would be possible to pass through the gorge. It was fearful to look down into the chasm, and see the water rushing past at so great a depth beneath our feet.

The rocks were almost perpendicular: bushes, plants, and flowers were growing on the small ledges and from the crevices, adding great beauty to the rugged spot. While gazing on this scene, one of the men asked me what o'clock it was, probably supposing that I did not notice how fast night was coming on. As I took my watch out of my waistcoat pocket it dropped from the chain, falling over the edge of the rocks, and, being stopped in its descent, hung on the thick branches of a small bush several yards below the ledge. I looked at the chain, and observed that the pin had been shaken out of the swivel while riding, which explained the accident. We all dismounted, and the horses having been secured, we peeped over the precipice. It was impossible to reach the watch. To recover it by any means at our disposal seemed equally hopeless. Knowing, however, that each man possessed a long rein to secure his horse with, of considerable strength, I had the three tied together, and with one end fastened under my arms, and with the two men grasping the other, I hastily undertook the descent; for the trinket being an old friend, as well as of some value, I did not feel disposed to abandon it without making an effort for its recovery. All being ready, I found that it was necessary to go a few paces up the path; then I got down, holding on as well as I could by the crevices, and the men keeping the leather thong tight. I was not long in reaching the narrow ledge, but I could only move along by their holding me up. At last I got close to the bush. The difficulty now was to reach the watch without touching the branches, otherwise it might drop through into the roaring torrent below. The men above were sustaining me with a tight grasp, watching my proceedings with anxious faces, not venturing to say a word, hardly venturing to breathe. Firmly fixing my foot in a crevice, I cried to them to let me lean over considerably; carefully they followed my directions, and I was enabled to reach the watch without disturbing a leaf; a minute sufficed to transfer it to my pocket in safety, which being done, the men, at a signal, joyfully pulled, and I scrambled to the top, where I landed without accident, much to the satisfaction of my companions. It was only while riding quietly down the valley seeking our encampment that I thought of the risk I had run, and then it made me shudder. My men seemed powerfully impressed by the incident: it was a subject of conversation during the evening, and evidently excited no slight interest.

Our camp was all in motion as the day was breaking—even before the mountain peaks were touched with light, and when all was gray and gloomy. My ablutions were made in a large granite bowl, some ten feet in diameter, and about five feet deep, scooped out of the rock, in which some small fishes were playing, the water being constantly changed, and so cold that it made me shiver.

When the sun had risen high enough to send his rays into the valley, my two men and our horses were ready to retrace our steps toward the pass, leaving the others to pack up and follow. We rode slowly on by a new track, and ascended a spur of the mountain which juts out into the valley. This enabled me to obtain a peep into a ravine on the opposite side of the river, which it was utterly impossible to reach, as the rushing torrent formed a barrier no man could cross. Having sketched the view, I rode on, and was soon at the place of our last night's adventure. We stopped, and I looked down with feelings of gratitude upon the friendly bush that had intercepted my faithful time-keeper. One of the men fixed a branch to point out the place to the rest of our party when they passed.

As we ascended farther into the pass, the track became more difficult and the scene more rugged. On the opposite side of the torrent the crags rose up in the wildest grandeur. Time had chiseled them with his unsparing hand into varied forms—some like turreted battlements and mighty towers; others into enormous buttresses propping up the mountain. After riding about half a verst we emerged from these rocky masses into a small valley that must have been a very deep lake before the gorge was rent open in the mountain. I have crossed this region twice, and have brought back with me some beautiful specimens of porphyry and jasper from these mountains. Having sketched the little valley, through which the river runs sluggishly, I turned and rode on. I soon observed a great change in the aspect of the country, the trees diminishing in number as well as in size, and there was as sensible a falling off in the vegetation. Short mossy grass had taken the place of a more luxuriant herbage, sprinkled over with loose masses of rock, round some of which the dwarf juniper was twining its branches.

Hearing the sound of falling water from the opposite side of the valley, I rode in the direction, and discovered it in a small rocky ravine to which it was impossible to ride. Leaving one man with the horses, I started with the other, following up the little stream through a thick mass of cedars and fallen rocks, covered with dark green and yellow moss, which rendered them exceedingly slippery and difficult to walk over. I had several tumbles before I reached the object of my search; at length I stood before a beautiful waterfall, that came bounding down in three leaps, the whole height being about sixty feet. The water looked white and sparkling as it fell over the dark purple precipice; the lower fall spread out wider, and appeared like a piece of gauze hanging over the rocks.

I was determined to ascend to the top of the precipice forming this ravine, and succeeded in doing so. I then followed up the stream for about three hundred paces, and found that it issued from a small lake or mountain tarn, apparently very deep. The water was of a dark green color, but as clear as crystal, and the rocks surrounding it were quite perpendicular. We returned to our horses over high masses of jasper, and saw three stags far up in the mountain, looking down upon us apparently with much astonishment, but there was no getting within shot of them. After riding a short distance we observed our friends ascending a mountain to the south, about a verst distant. We tried to make them hear by shouting, but this was fruitless; at last I fired both barrels of my gun, which they heard, and immediately halted.

Our horses being fresh, having rested several times during my sketching, enabled us soon to form a junction, and, after enjoying sufficient rest and refreshment, I prepared to ascend the summit of the Cholsoun. The last stunted cedars were soon passed, when, with two companions, I gained a small depression on the mountain that was rich in plants and flowers. Our horses trampled on a beautiful bed of *Aquilegia:* the plants, reaching up to our saddle-flaps, were in full bloom; the flowers were varied, blue and white; some a deep purple, and others purple edged with white. Fortunately, I obtained plenty of ripe seed. Near this place I also met with *Cypripedium guttatum*, with its white and pink flowers. (This I had found in the Oural.) There were also many fine *Primulæ*, of a deep red color, flowering in large bunches. These and the short turf rendered this spot quite a little garden among the rugged precipices towering far above it. Immediately after quitting it we turned the point of some rocks, and looked down into the lake; it was lying in a deep bowl-shaped depression, quiet and calm, within its grassy banks. I rode down on to its shore; it was shallow for a few paces, and then appeared to descend perpendicularly, most probably to a great depth, as the water looked very dark. We were compelled to retrace our steps, the other sides of this bowl being exceedingly steep.

The ascent of the Cholsoun from the north side is not abrupt, though the last half verst is steep and rocky: nevertheless, we rode our horses to the summit, or rather to the foot of the large rocky peaks that shoot far above the rounded mountain top. These are bare granite, without a blade of grass upon them, and do not form a continuous ridge or crest on the mountain, but stand up in isolated masses, often at a considerable distance from each other. Having ascended with some difficulty to the top of one of these peaks, I saw our little caravan, composed of the men I had left to proceed by another route, skirting the mountain lower down. I knew that they would cross the summit seven or eight versts to the east, go straight to the Cholsoun pass, and descend into a valley on the south, which I had arranged should be our place of rest for the night.

The views from this part of the chain (which is not the highest) are very grand. On one side Nature exhibits her most rugged forms, peaks and crags of all shapes rising up far into the clear blue vault of heaven; while on the other, mountain rises above mountain, vanishing into distance, until they melt into forms like thin gray clouds on the horizon. It was impossible to spare much time going from place to place, looking to the north, south, or west, to decide which view I should sketch first. The chains to the north happened to be beautifully lighted up, some in sunshine, others in shade, producing a wonderful effect of distance and space. This induced me to sit down to work in right good earnest, and I was soon so absorbed in my occupation that I neither thought of time, distance, nor the country we had to ride over. Our horses had been secured and left to feed, and my men were much interested in my work, until at last, as I supposed, they grew weary.

First one would leave, and go to the south side of the rocks under which I was sketching. Soon after he returned the other went; yet they said nothing. I had now been at work more than two hours, and this going to and fro had occurred several times. At length I was certain that they wished to speak to me. I looked at them, and waited for the communication. Then one of them said, "*Grom scora boodit*" (It will thunder soon), and made a sign for me to go with him. I put down my sketch, and hurried to the other side of the peak, when I beheld the cause of their alarm: evidently a frightful storm was coming toward us, for the high peaks to the west were just being wrapped in a terrible black mantle. There was not a moment to lose; the men ran to bring the horses, and I hastened to pack up my sketching materials. This was but the work of a few minutes. We then mounted and rode past the rocks to see if the storm was approaching. Several of the peaks were already obscured, and now the clouds were wheeling round a very high summit, which I supposed to be eight, or, at most, ten versts distant, across a deep valley. To be caught on this summit in such a storm was something fearful, and the men were really alarmed. There was only one place on the south side by which we could descend: it was the Cholsoun pass, and that was perhaps more than eight versts distant. Having watched the storm two or three minutes, we heard the distant thunder, and then knew that the conflict of the elements had begun.

Without speaking a word, we turned our horses, and started off at a gallop. It was a race for the pass, as it was only in this ravine that we could hope for shelter. Every few minutes the thunder rolled nearer and nearer, and on we galloped; the horses, with an instinctive dread of what was following, putting forth their full powers without either whip or spur. Road or track there was none; only some high rocky peaks pointed out to my companions the head of the pass. Our course was straight toward these; sometimes over fine mossy turf, then over ground rough and stony, which would, under any other circumstances, have caused both horse and rider to hesitate before dashing onward at the speed at which we were going. The storm was still behind us, for as yet we had only seen the flash, but not the streams of lightning that were descending every two or three minutes in our rear, followed by claps of thunder, which resounded among the mountains until the distant echo was lost in another loud roar. At a short distance in front of us I beheld huge pillars of rock rising up fifty or sixty feet, which reminded me of Stonehenge, but on a most gigantic scale. My men turned a little to the left to avoid this labyrinth of rocks. I looked at the place with intense interest, determined to visit it, if possible, on the morrow. We were within a couple of versts of the head of the pass when we heard a great rushing sound behind us. Instantly our heads were turned to see what was coming, when we beheld branches of cedar torn up from the valley, carried over the rocky peaks, and whirled high into the air: this was the blast before the storm, which now swept on with terrific force. Fortunately for us, the rocky pillars broke the fury of the gust, or we should have been hurled down to a certainty; for at a short distance on each side of us, the dwarf cedars which creep over the rocks were torn up, and carried along by the hurricane. We found it difficult to sit our horses, as they swerved and bounded on when the fearful squall rushed past.

The storm was now near, but for the last few minutes there had not been a flash. This was even more appalling than the loud thunder. I turned my head, and saw a thick red stream strike among the rocks we had just passed; at the same instant there were three reports like the firing of a heavily-loaded musket over our heads, and then came a crash which made our horses shudder, although in a gallop. Now came hailstones so thick that for a moment they almost blinded us; the lightning flashed in quick succession, and the thunder was incessant.

We reached the pass, and turned into its rugged jaws with a delight known only to a mariner when he runs his sinking craft into a safe haven. In about ten minutes we were quietly standing under the shelter of some friendly rocks, our tired horses trembling with fear. The men crossed themselves; nor did I forget to offer up my thanks for our preservation. The storm still raged above us with terrific fury and awful grandeur; but the overhanging masses under which we crouched afforded us complete protection, and I listened to the dreadful tempest with mingled feelings of awe and pleasure. In a very few minutes the ground was covered with a thick coating of hail, giving a wintry aspect to the scene which had been so calm and beautiful two short hours before. The storm rolled on: in about an hour we could only hear its murmurings in the distance. Presently the clouds were dispersed; the sun shone out in all his splendor, rendered still more brilliant by the intensely black masses of vapor which enveloped the distant crags. My companions now discovered that we were not in the Cholsoun pass, but in a small ravine down which it was impossible to proceed even on foot, for at a very short distance below our sheltering place the precipices were perpendicular to the depth of at least three hundred feet, over which a little stream was leaping, to be dispersed in vapor before reaching the bottom. It was the dashing of the water which drew my attention to it; from below, no doubt, it must have appeared exceedingly pretty.

It was now quite time to descend, as our people were encamped somewhere in the valley beneath. One of my men found that we had missed the pass, and had gone considerably beyond it during the storm. We therefore rode back and turned into a ravine, which he said would lead us to the right track lower down. This proved correct; and in about two hours we were quietly seated by our camp-fire, under some magnificent cedars, on the bank of a roaring torrent greatly swollen by the storm. Our companions had heard the thunder in the distance, and there had been a few drops of rain, but not even enough to wet the ground. The forest was so thick around our camp that they could not see the mountains; it was only the rising and thundering of the torrent that told them what had happened there.

After taking sufficient refreshment, and writing up my journal by the light of a blazing fire, I turned down at the root of a magnificent cedar, wrapped myself in my cloak, and slept soundly until morning.

It was delightful to see the sunbeams struggling through the branches, and hear the birds singing their matin songs. All this betokened a fine day for my return to the Cholsoun. Knowing it would take at least four hours to ride to the rocky pillars which we passed in the storm, I hastened our departure, and at six o'clock we started, having arranged that our little caravan should follow the stream toward the valley of the Kaier Koomin, and encamp after traveling three, or, at most, four hours, to enable me and my two comrades to join them in the evening. Our ride through the forest was not agreeable, for the branches and rank herbage, which in many places were far above our horses' heads, were covered with large dew-drops, sparkling like diamonds, and giving us a shower-bath every few steps. Before we got half way through the forest we were completely drenched, which was rather unpleasant, as we should soon have the sharp mountain air chilling us to the bone. On emerging from the forest I observed that all the upper part of the Cholsoun was wrapped in a dense cloud, extending far down its rugged sides. A little lower in the pass the fog was being carried up in curling eddies: this was a good sign, and I anticipated a fine day. We rode on shivering in our wet clothing: sometimes a cold, cutting breeze rushing down the ravines made my teeth chatter, but did not in the slightest degree affect my sense of the picturesque; for on reaching a part of the pass presenting peculiarly striking features, I sat down on a large block of granite, and sketched a view looking down toward the Kaier Koomin, and the mountains to the south.

While at my work I often looked toward the summit of the Cholsoun, hoping to see the fog clear off. At last I perceived it slowly rising, which gave me hopes of a fine day. We immediately mounted and rode on, but had not ascended far when the sun broke through the rolling vapor, and cheered us with his genial warmth. In an hour we were at the top of the pass, riding in splendid sunshine, the fog, however, still hanging on the summits. Although the huge rocky pillars were enveloped in mist, I knew the direction in which to find them, and turned that way. Presently we came up to some fallen rocks, and threaded our way among them. The fog was now rolling over us; still, we rode on slowly; but, after somewhat less than an hour, it became so thick that we were obliged to stop at the foot of some precipices. Here we dismounted, and sat down with a full conviction that we must remain so long as the fog continued. One hour passed without any change for the better; the second was fleeting fast, which gave us great anxiety. If the fog did not clear off soon, we should undoubtedly be detained here for the night, when hunger would be added to cold. At length the clouds began to drive past us from the westward, with a very gentle breeze. Suddenly one of the men, after listening very attentively, exclaimed in Russian, "There is a waterfall!" I took out my compass, and found the sound came from the southwest. This induced me to think we had been riding straight toward some frightful precipices which I had seen the day before; if so, we must be very near the brink, to hear the rushing of the water in the valley below, and any attempt to move now would be madness. The second hour was nearly gone, when, to our infinite joy, we began to see indistinctly forms in front of us; in a few minutes we beheld more clearly a colossal mass rising up, its summits lost in driving clouds; farther on were the dim outlines of broken crags below us. At last the mass of vapor passed off, and a deep gulf, with the rocks and mountains beyond it, was laid before us, as if by enchantment. It was evident that we had ridden along for four or five hundred paces parallel with these precipices, and not more than twenty yards from their fearful brink. The clouds now rolled up, like some vast curtain uncovering these mighty mountain chains; and, after sitting so long wet, cold, and shivering, it is impossible to express the delight with which I watched the sun burst forth, lighting up peak and valley with his radiance.

To the southeast stands Bielouka, proudly rearing his lofty double head, adorned with eternal snows and glaciers, and far overtopping all the other chains, although many mountains around him are covered with the same everlasting garment of snow. Beneath these were many other summits tipped with white, showing that they have also passed the line of congelation. Still lower was one vast sea of mountain crests, surrounding these giants of the Altai—some so distant that they looked like ethereal vapor dissolving on the horizon; others, with their peaks and crags a little more distinct, sparkled brightly in the sun. Nearer was a lower range, extending far, with many a dark purple peak and ridge, inclosing valleys and ravines, into which the precious metal has been washed ages ago. Still nearer are the brown, gray, and green ridges of the Cholsoun, with their jagged rocks, and cascades streaming down their rugged sides; these, with a foreground of gigantic granite peaks heaved far up toward heaven, rich in many a mossy color, with dwarf cedars creeping over their curious forms, with mossy turf around their bases, and small clumps of a deep red *Primula* scattered among the grass, form the principal features of one of the grandest panoramas in nature. Such scenes, and many others through which I have passed, offer most glorious studies to the lover of Nature, possessed of sufficient courage to woo her in these sublime regions when bedecked in her wild and gorgeous attire.

About half an hour's ride from the place where I sat and sketched stood the labyrinth of rocky pillars which we passed in the thunder-storm. They are granite, worn into pillars of various forms, curiously grouped around a large mass in the centre. When seen from a distance they had reminded me of Stonehenge, but on approaching them I found that they were prodigious masses; it was, however, only by riding through this curious place that I could judge of their magnitude. Not far from them, to the west, are some enormous precipices; perhaps these rocks have once formed part of some higher cliffs, which have overlooked the dark valley below. It is somewhat difficult to comprehend how these isolated masses should have been left here, unless the intermediate parts should have decayed and crumbled into small particles, and in this state have been washed into the valley: fallen blocks are not found in this neighborhood of any considerable size or quantity.

Having delineated this extraordinary landscape, I observed that it was time to descend toward the valley and seek our encampment. After examining the country for a few minutes, I thought we could save a considerable distance by crossing a lower range. Our only difficulty was the rocky precipices to the west: could we descend these, or find some way to the river in the valley, we should soon reach our destination. We turned our steps westward till we came upon a ravine, which we succeeded in descending on foot, leading our horses, for riding down was impossible. After several difficulties had been overcome, we reached the valley, and skirted along the side of the steep ground above the river; this led us into a pass infinitely more grand than the Cholsoun. Down this wild scene we found our way; in one part it was a narrow chasm, with rocks on each side of enormous height. Looking back, a very high conical mountain was seen, with broken and almost perpendicular crags, forming a beautiful picture seen through a natural frame.

Hunger now began to intimate that, however fine the scenery, the cravings of the inner man would not be satisfied without something more substantial. We therefore hastened on, and reached our old encampment at six o'clock, having saved at least a two hours' ride. A bright fire was burning; from this we supposed our friends had not long left, which induced us to hope we should soon find them, and we pushed on as fast as possible, following their track. After riding another hour, and fording the river, from one bank to the other, several times, night began to creep over this narrow valley, rendering it difficult to find our way. Again we had to ford the river, which became deep and rapid, nor could we discover the path, or any thing to guide us. My men now objected to fording it again in the dark; it had become too dangerous. Under these circumstances, there was no alternative but to go supperless to bed, and the sooner the better. It was therefore decided to sleep here, if sleep were possible in such a place; and with this intention, we forced our way into the wood to some thick picta-trees, where we found a small space of open ground; a light was struck, and some birch bark stripped off a tree and piled up, which, being ignited, made a strong light. While the men fastened and unsaddled the horses, I made the fire, which was shortly burning famously. Our saddle-cloths were spread, and the saddles arranged for pillows; plenty of wood was piled on, making a large fire sufficient to roast a sheep, had one been ready for us. Unpleasant as the circumstances were, we were in warm and comfortable quarters in comparison with our detention among the rocks on the Cholsoun, where we must have remained had the fog continued; and though we were hungry, we felt that we might have been much worse off. Our horses fared better: they had dined, and found something even here for supper. My comrades were soon fast asleep. I lay for a time thinking over the scenes on the mountains until tired nature could stand it no longer, when I followed their example.

About three o'clock in the morning, one of the men awoke me by throwing wood on the fire, more fuel being required, as it was then very chilly. Soon as the fire had been replenished, I stretched myself out again, and slept until daylight. When we awoke our horses were quickly saddled. We crossed the river, discovered the track, and in about two hours found our companions fast asleep; they were roused up, tea made with the utmost dispatch, and liberal libations prepared us for new adventures. But a very sharp frost this morning was a sure prognostic of approaching winter, that would put a stop to mountain traveling; new snow had already fallen on some of the higher parts of the Cholsoun, and these unmistakable signs induced me to hasten onward.

CHAPTER XIII.

FRONTIER OF THE CHINESE EMPIRE.

I ORDERED another man to join my party this morning, as we might find some difficulty in fording the river, should I think it necessary to do so. We rode down the valley of Kaier Koomin, leaving the rest to follow. The country was now losing its sterile appearance; indeed, the valley is beautifully wooded, and covered with fine grass. The river, which winds about very much, is a rapid stream running between thickly-wooded banks, in which we beheld as we rode along grayling and other fish sporting in shoals; among them several large *talmane*, not less than three feet six to four feet long. They appeared to consider themselves free from any attack, as they swam slowly about close to the bank, at our horses' feet. On my dismounting to try the effect of a bullet, they gave a splash with their tails, and sculled away in a minute. Shortly after this we had to swim our horses over the river, which we found rapid and deep.

The sun now broke through the mists which had obscured him, and the clouds were dispersed from the upper mountains. We also began to feel the effects of his cheering influence and warmth; the men greeted his appearance with Russian songs, that made the valley ring again as we rode along; most of their music, though rather melancholy, has a pleasing effect. In one part of the valley there is a charming echo; we stopped opposite to the rocks from which it proceeded, and the men made the place resound with their voices.

Russian peasants are excellent fellows; those with me thought nothing of their hardships of yesterday; when we were sitting hungry and shivering on the Cholsoun, not a murmur was breathed.

After riding for about two hours I observed a ravine running into the mountains to the north; this I determined to explore for a short distance. We therefore turned into it, and it afforded a fine subject for my pencil. My work accomplished, we returned,

Swimming a deep Stream.

and galloped off down the valley, as we found by the track that our caravan had passed; we overtook them a few versts ahead, preparing the midday meal. They had seen our track up in the ravine, which induced them to stop sooner.

The mountains were much lower, and we were evidently approaching a warmer region. Our ride was exceedingly agreeable, for we traveled over a fine grassy turf, often winding through woods and among clumps of trees. At four o'clock we reached the north bank of the Bouchtarma, a very broad and deep stream; and on the men shouting loudly, two small boats put off from the opposite shore. In the mean time the horses were being unsaddled, as they must swim the river. When the ferryman had reached the bank, I observed that their boats were cut out of a single tree, without any attempt at boat-building. My sketching and shooting materials having been placed in one of these canoes, three of us sat down; the man rowed us across the river, then returned to aid in swimming the horses over, six of which were brought at one time by each canoe, two men holding the reins. In a little more than an hour, all our party, horses and baggage, were safely landed. From this ferry there is a splendid view of the northern part of the Cholsoun chain, over which we had passed: the southern portion was enveloped in a mass of dark clouds, most probably another edition of the storm we had had a few days before.

We rode off at a sharp trot toward Zirianovsky, along a good road, but over a very uninteresting steppe, with low mountains on each side. In a little more than an hour we turned to the west, and stopped at a point which afforded me a view of Zirianovsky, and the Eagle Mountain beyond. The sun had set behind this picturesque mountain about half an hour before, and now the effect was most gorgeous. A deep yellow was spread over the lower part of the sky, shading upward into a silvery gray: thin fleecy clouds of a crimson color were beautifully scattered over the horizon, rendered still more brilliant by their contrast with the purple tones of the Eagle Mountains. A great depth of shade extended over the steppe from the foot of the mountains, covering the Zavod with its sombre hue. The foreground was a rich reddish-brown and dark gray, inclosing a small pond reflecting the sky in all its brilliancy.

It was just dark as our large party rode into the Zavod. My Cossack had gone on before to ascertain where we should be quartered, and had sent a man to conduct us to the house, while he got every thing prepared for our meal. Our progress through the street was marked by the barking of a numerous tribe of dogs, apparently much put out of temper by our intrusion, as they tried to avenge themselves on the heels of our horses. Some of them felt the effects of our heavy whips, which sent them howling, and raised a concert of canine music, enough to rouse the whole population to arms. A house at the very top of the street had been appointed for our reception, in which I found a decent room; my baggage was brought in, and I was soon installed in my new abode. After paying due attention to the refreshments, I lay down on some fresh hay, wrapped my cloak round me, and was soon in the land of dreams.

While sitting at breakfast the next morning, the Director of the Mines, a young mining-engineer officer, came into the room; he said the Chief of the Altai had informed him of my intended visit, and had desired *that* every attention and aid should be given to me. After a one o'clock dinner, to which he gave me an invitation, he proposed taking me to several places from which I could obtain good views of Zirianovsky and the country around. Consequently, at the conclusion of the meal, we rode first up the valley along the road toward Narym for six or seven versts, and then returned by the same path. Approaching Zirianovsky from this side, there are many fine views looking toward the village. On the right hand Revnevaya Gora rises about eight hundred feet above the plain, while the rugged crests of the Cholsoun chain are seen in the distance, shining brightly in the sun, for to-day there is not a cloud hanging over them. Farther to the west are some high mountains, near the Bouchtarma River, while to the left rises the Eagle Mountain, with others in the distance, among which the Irtisch winds its course. A great plain extends up to the foot of the mountains to the west, and as far as the ferry on the Bouchtarma; there are a few birch-trees and some flowering shrubs on this plain; but, on the whole, it has a sterile appearance, and the mountains are entirely destitute of wood.

Zirianovsky stands on some rising ground at the northwestern side of the plain, almost surrounded by mountains to the west, and about six or seven versts distant the Eagle Mountain rises up rocky and picturesque. The whole space from the village to the foot of this mountain is covered with a deep morass, which renders the place extremely unhealthy; added to this, the water is very bad. At the time of my visit great numbers were sick in the hospital, and many people die here, who are continually being replaced from other villages in the Altai.

The silver mines at Zirianovsky are the most valuable (at the present time) in the Altai. Some of the ores, which are exceedingly rich, are got at the depth of two hundred and eighty feet, and in some places they have been followed to the depth of four hundred and ninety feet. The greatest difficulty the miners have to encounter is the vast quantity of water almost inundating the mines: at the period of my visit it was drawn out by pumps worked by water-power, the wheels placed at a distance of more than seven hundred yards from the shaft. This, with the great friction caused by the long series of wooden rods extending from the water-wheels to the shaft, and the rude machinery constructed to work the pumps, renders their efforts almost useless.

A steam-engine of one hundred or one hundred and fifty horse power would keep these mines perfectly dry, and the men could work in comfort; besides which, the health of the miners and the economy of human life are surely objects worthy of consideration in a country like Siberia. His imperial majesty has in Ekaterineburg a machine manufactory almost equal to any establishment in Europe, in which a steam-engine could be made at a comparatively small cost, and transported by the River Irtisch to within one hundred versts of Zirianovsky, which, if employed here, would not only effect a great saving in working the mines, but would preserve the lives of hundreds of his people. This is only one instance in which his imperial majesty's machine works might have been turned to a profitable account; there are many other places in the mining districts where the same advantages could be obtained. A manufactory so conducted would soon ruin any firm less wealthy than his majesty, for it produces comparatively nothing—indeed, I might say less than nothing. Could he count the cost which enables one of his generals of artillery to parade through these works two or three times in a month, covered with decorations, the men drawn up in lines on each side, cap in hand, and shouting as he passes "*Drai-jelyu*," I apprehend his imperial majesty would indignantly dispense with the show, which produces nothing else.

There are more than two thousand horses employed in transporting the ore from these mines to the smelting works. First it is taken in small carts, with one horse in each, to Werchnayan Pristan on the Irtisch, a distance of more than one hundred versts; from here it is sent down the river in boats to Oust-Kamenogorsk Pristan; thence it is again conveyed in carts to Barnaoul, Pavlovsky, and other Zavods, making a distance of nine hundred versts from the mines to the smelting works.

The first day after my arrival was devoted to the mines and the neighborhood of Zirianovsky; the following day I proposed to devote to sketching. My disappointment, therefore, was very great when I heard the rain pouring down, and on going out in the morning I observed that all the mountains were covered with snow. The director told me that the snow would now remain on all the higher elevations throughout the winter, and continue to descend lower every time we had rain in the valleys. Still, he considered the 4th of September very early for the mountains to put on their winter garb. Later in the day it came on a thoroughly pelting rain, with a strong wind whistling through the broken squares in my windows, which made me think even this room a palace in comparison with my rocky shelter on the Cholsoun.

Next morning the weather was better; the rain had ceased, but the clouds were still rolling over the mountain tops. I watched their movements with intense interest, and at last observed that they began gradually to ascend. I now hurried my men to get the horses ready, which was quickly done, when we started to the ferry on the Bouchtarma. On arriving there I found that the mountains to the west were free from clouds, while those over the Cholsoun were evidently rolling away. I lost no time in taking the view looking down the river, and before my sketch was finished the northern part of the chain was clear. Here I had a grand landscape, and set to work at it with a right good will. Day was fast drawing to a close by the time I had finished, and the southern part of the mountain was still a mystery.

Before we reached Zirianovsky the sky became suddenly clouded, and a keen cutting wind was sweeping down from the snowy summits of the mountains; presently it poured with rain. Riding through the street on my return, we were greeted with the same canine concert that had welcomed our arrival. When the shutters were closed over my broken windows, I felt quite comfortable and happy as I heard the wind roar past. During the evening my Cossack came in, and told me it was snowing fast. This made me anxious, as I had now good reason to fear that my artistic labors would soon be ended, if they were not already, for this year, and this before I had reached the Irtisch. On turning out this morning I found the ground frozen quite hard, and the wind bitterly cold, with a clear sky and a prospect of a warm sun. As this was the last day I could devote to sketching, I lost no time in riding out on the road toward Narym, to the point from which I purposed sketching Zirianovsky. Sitting down under the shelter of some rocks, I began my occupation. It was at first very cold, but as the sun rose it became warm and agreeable, and I succeeded in bringing back a vivid representation of his imperial majesty's silver mines close to the Chinese frontier. In the afternoon I rode to the westward ten or twelve versts, which afforded me a fine view of the beautiful scenery on and beyond the Bouchtarma River. The effect of this scene was magnificent; as the sun was sinking immediately behind one of the high conical mountains, I beheld the great fiery orb descend nearly over the centre of this mighty cone, presenting a singular appearance. Presently its long deep shadow crept over the lower hills, and soon extended far into the plain, till at length the place on which I stood received its cold gray tone. The mountains to the right and left were still shining in his golden light, the snowy peaks of the Cholsoun appearing like frosted silver cut out against the deep blue sky. Gradually the shades of evening crept up the mountain sides; one bright spot after another vanished, until at length all was in shadowy gray except the snowy peaks. As the sun sunk lower, a pale rose tint spread over their snowy mantles, deepening to a light crimson, and then a darker tone, when the highest shone out, as sparkling as a ruby; and at last, for only a few moments, it appeared like a crimson star.

When the excitement of these magic changes was over, a cold shiver came over me; I jumped on to my horse, and started at a gallop. My Cossack said the cold had frozen him; but an hour's hard ride put our blood into circulation till we reached our quarters, when sundry glasses of hot tea made me feel quite comfortable. Late in the evening we had more rain; but my sketching was finished in this neighborhood, and I was now only anxious about my future progress. The two following days were very bad—all rain and sleet. The director urged me to remain, assuring me that some part of the country over which I had to pass was very elevated, and that sketching in such weather was impossible.

The morning of the third day being clear and sunny, with a hard frost, at six o'clock we were on the road traveling in telagas. The first eighty versts is over a very uninteresting country, chiefly low hills destitute of timber. After passing through several villages, the inhabitants of which appeared poor and miserable, we reached a larger one—Moorzinsky—where I was assured that it would be impossible to cross the mountains, as snow would be then three or four feet deep. This did not prevent us making the attempt, as we might have more snow in the night, and then be stopped altogether. A few versts beyond this village we began to ascend; the mountains to the right rose up into a high ridge covered with new snow, which descended far down toward the valleys; on our left were also snow-capped summits; and now the track turned over some high hills between these two. After traveling little more than an hour we began to ascend rapidly, and soon reached the snow. It was not deep enough to stop us. By four o'clock we were on the summit, and not far from a much higher ridge called Mount Chesnooka (garlic). Beyond this, to the eastward, were seen the high snowy peaks of the Cholsoun, and directly south rose up the Kourt-Chume Mountains, which form the Chinese frontier. I had been told that they appear like a wall, and found them one continuous chain extending down to the valley of the Irtisch, where they turn to the south, and run toward Nor-Zaisan, with very few passes into the country beyond. These mountains seem destined by Nature to be the boundary between the two empires. They were covered with snow, and at this time formed a complete barrier to our farther progress in that direction.

Having spent a short time examining the country, we continued our journey, and descended rapidly toward the south, reaching in two hours Little Narym, a small outpost of Cossacks stationed on a plain, and within a few versts of the Chinese frontier. We were now on the military road, which extends only about twenty versts farther to the east, to the last outpost from Western Siberia. A few versts, and our route would be to the westward, looking toward the land of my birth. A fine old Cossack provided us with horses, two telagas, and Cossack drivers, who galloped off at full speed. We were now traveling parallel with the Kourt-Chume Mountains, and within five versts of their base. They are not thrown up into high peaks; the outline is scarcely broken; but many offshoots project from the chain, falling very abruptly into the valley, like buttresses propping up the higher mass.

The River Narym flows down this valley, and falls into the Irtisch about sixty versts distant. Our Cossack drivers galloped along at a tremendous pace. The sun had set some time; his yellow tints had faded from the sky, and were succeeded by a deep gray, on which the stars shone forth with great brilliancy. It was a beautiful calm night, which made us feel we were in another climate as we drove into Great Narym. They quartered me in the house of the Cossack officer, and he told me that I could not pass the frontier without an order from his superior, who lived sixty versts distant. This was a great disappointment, as it involved another long ride. I drank my tea in a clean warm room, and determined to take things quietly, as it was utterly impossible to proceed in the dark. I very soon tumbled down on a wooden sofa, and slept as a tired man ought until five o'clock the next morning.

At six o'clock I left Narym, and rode up the valley about ten versts, where I sketched two beautiful views—one of the Chinese frontier and the valley of Narym, the other of the mountains to the north, which are rugged and picturesque: they are granite without any vegetation. To the north of Narym there are some remarkable granite rocks rising out of the plain, without one blade of grass growing upon them. These have once been held in great veneration. Figures have been cut upon them by a race of men of whom we have no record, or even a trace by which we can ascertain either who they were or at what period they lived. This is a most singular place. In one of the small valleys there are many pillars or blocks which have been forced up, and are now standing in a mass of granite, which seems once to have been liquid, that has flowed round their bases like lava.

Having examined the rocks and finished my sketches, I returned and sketched another view of part of Great Narym, with some Kirghis *yourts* in the foreground.

While I was engaged on this view, the officer sent a Cossack to tell me that the colonel commanding the district would be at Narym at twelve o'clock to inspect the men. I hastened to finish my sketch, and returned, when I found the colonel inspecting the Cossacks. As the officer had already informed him of my wish to cross the frontier, I handed him my passport, after reading which he said I could pass the frontier and sketch wherever I wished, but that it was utterly impossible to go to Nor-Zaisan by the route I proposed across the Kourt-Chume chain, as the snow was so deep on the mountains that we should undoubtedly be lost or frozen to death. He advised me to go through the Kirghis Steppe, and proposed to forward me from one Cossack post to another till I reached the fortress at Kochbouchta. I accepted his offer, and arranged to meet him in Oust-Kamenogorsk. We dined together; after dinner, he left on his journey of inspection, and I returned to my sketching. All being settled to my satisfaction, I determined to hasten as fast as possible to Werchnayan Pristan on the Irtisch, where orders had been sent to provide me with a boat and men to descend the river, stopping when and where I required.

Great Narym is a fort; the inhabitants of the village are all Cossacks, and a fine body of men they are. I saw a number of chubby little fellows, who are destined to be the future guardians of his imperial majesty's frontier, most probably far to the south of this region. The country around this place is very pretty; the valley of the Narym supplies them with hay for their cattle and horses; there are also abundant summer pastures, where their herds feed in plenty. They grow wheat and rye on some of the lower hills; the rivers supply them with abundance of fish, and game is plentiful on the mountains; vegetables, cucumbers, melons, and watermelons of a superior quality are grown in large quantities, and the bees produce plenty of excellent honey. The Cossacks have the exclusive right to all fisheries in Nor-Zaisan, the Irtisch, and other streams falling into it; besides which, they can trade. Thus they are in good circumstances, possessing comforts and various luxuries. Their dwellings are clean and comfortable, and many of the men are wealthy. I have known Cossacks who possessed five hundred horses. There are a few Kirghis living in their *yourts* near Narym: they feed their flocks and herds on the plains, and winter here.

We left Great Narym in the afternoon, going down the valley, which is very pretty. After traveling about an hour we saw the Irtisch winding its course within the Chinese empire, at the foot of the Kourt-Chume chain, which here returns directly south toward Nor-Zaisan. In the evening we entered the valley of the Irtisch near the point where the Narym falls into it. The scenery at this point is so exceedingly fine that I could not resist sketching the view. The mountains on the opposite side of the Irtisch are also very picturesque and beautiful in color, varying from deep orange, yellow, and red, to gray and the deepest purple. This variety in tone is not caused by vegetation alone: red, gray, and purple are the colors of the rocks; and the orange, yellow, and green are produced by mosses growing upon them. The steppe at the foot of the mountains is burnt by the sun into a deep brown, and the banks of the river are a bright green. Many islands are dotted about in the Irtisch, most of them covered with willows; but trees there are none. The river once formed the boundary of the Russian empire: the opposite bank is the Kirghis Steppe, which is gradually being absorbed.

CHAPTER XIV.

DESCENT OF THE IRTISCH.

I ARRIVED at Tschinimschanka a little before dusk, and, after consulting the Cossacks, decided on descending the river in canoes, as by this arrangement I should reach Werchnayan Pristan before daylight. Having drunk our tea, and feasted on rye bread and honey, we started on our voyage down the Irtisch in two canoes, which I was assured would take us to Werchnayan Pristan in five hours. I sat watching the daylight fade from the snowy peaks of the Altai, and night envelop the hills and valleys beneath, waiting with anxiety the rising of the moon, which was to light me on my watery way. Long before she penetrated the deep valley that shrouded me in gloom, I marked her approach by the cold, silvery light shed on the snow-clad summits far above me. At length a pale light was seen beyond the rocky peaks rising high above the steppe, and presently the moon rose majestically over these lofty crags, which cast their shadows far across the steppe. Soon her rays shone forth on rock and flood with a soft and dreamy effect. This was the signal for our departure; we seated ourselves in the canoes, the Cossacks plied their oars, and we glided smoothly down the stream. It was a calm and beautiful night, without even a breeze to ruffle the water; there was not a sound save the plashing of the oars: all nature seemed asleep.

Our course had hitherto been along the middle of the river, passing on our way several small islands which divided it into different streams. The Cossacks were resting on their oars; not a sound was heard, when we glided into a narrow channel between a long island and a thick bed of reeds. Our canoes had not floated more than fifty yards, when one of the Cossacks struck the reeds with his oar, and simultaneously they all gave a loud shout. In a moment there came a shriek as if a legion of fiends had been cast loose, which was followed by a rushing sound and a flapping of wings on every side, rising high into mid air; then the wild concert was taken up and repeated far above us. We had come suddenly on the covert of thousands of water-fowl. After this uproar the Cossacks pulled out into the middle of the stream, and passed quickly along through some beautiful scenery.

It was impossible for me to sleep in the midst of such scenes; they had a charm, or I ought to call it a fascination, which I could not resist, and my eyes were continually strained, trying to penetrate the deep gloom in the shade of the mountains.

A little after two o'clock we reached Werchnayan Pristan, when our Cossacks roused up the officer, who ordered the *somervar* to be prepared, and tea, as usual, was soon ready. I felt a deep regret that our moonlight voyage was over—indeed, should have been glad to have floated on until day dawned; my companions, however, were not artists, and were delighted when we landed. Presently I lay down on a wooden bench, and soon became equally oblivious of enchanting moonlight scenes and monster concerts of the feathered tribe.

A beautiful and bright sunny morning followed our moonlight voyage on the Irtisch. After breakfast the officer said he had received instructions about me, and that every thing I required should be done.

Horses and men having been provided, I rode along the bank of the river. After going a short distance in this direction we crossed the steppe, cutting off a great bend in the Irtisch, and this brought me to a part where I found much to interest me and to occupy my pencil; I therefore spent several hours here, after which I returned to the pristan and sketched another view.

Wishing to proceed on my journey, I went to examine the "bark" (so it was named) that had been prepared to take my party, now amounting to nine persons, including the boatman, down the Irtisch. My surprise was great when I found that, in place of a good sound boat, two small canoes had been lashed together, five feet apart, with bearers placed across, the whole boarded over, giving a platform of fifteen feet by ten—plenty of space certainly, and it looked well enough when lying on the wharf, but I most decidedly objected to such a machine. At this moment dinner was announced, and my host assured me that all the necessary alterations would be completed by the time I had dined. This is the place to which the silver ore is carted from Zirianovsky, and here it is loaded into boats, and sent down the Irtisch about two hundred and twenty versts to Oust-Kamenogorsk. The river runs very rapidly through narrow valleys and deep gorges in the Altai till it reaches the Kirghis Steppe below Oust-Kamenogorsk, where it spreads out into a large river, studded with numerous islands great and small. A boat has gone this distance in eleven hours, for on some parts of the river the current runs at a fearful speed.

The baggage having been placed on board, and every thing made secure, my host accompanied me to the bark, which I found nearly in the same state I had left it; the only alteration that had been attempted was the placing some broken boards on the platform, both this officer and the workmen insisting that it was perfectly safe. Making no farther objection, I stepped on board, but war far from satisfied. I had no fault to find with the deck—there was room enough and to spare—my fear was for the hulls of our craft; but, seeing that nothing was to be gained by delay, good-by was said, a cheer given, and the bark cast loose. A man sat in the head and stern of each canoe—four strong, sturdy fellows they were, thoroughly acquainted with the river, and each had a small paddle, a little larger than a child's garden spade; their only duties were to guide the craft; the stream would carry us quickly enough. They received instructions before starting to stop whenever I wished, and do every thing I might require. The bark was soon paddled into the middle of the river, which at this place is more than a thousand yards broad; and once in the current, we floated rapidly along. I was watching the changes in the scene as one mountain peak after another came in view, when suddenly, and without any previous intimation, two of the men called out that their canoe was filling fast, and that they must make for the shore without a minute's delay! Before we got half way to the bank she was nearly full of water, and when within about a hundred yards the men cried out that she was sinking;

this brought our broad deck down to the water on one side, and helped to float her. The men paddled with all their might, and at last we reached a thick bed of reeds, which assisted in keeping us afloat till we succeeded in getting near enough to the bank to throw our luggage ashore, and then we landed.

I now ordered my servant to follow me back to the pristan, where, after some trouble, I obtained a good boat, in which ore is conveyed, with four men, although the director wished to convince me that three were sufficient. Just as I was leaving him, a boy came to inform us that two of the men were taken very ill from being so long in the cold water, all four having got a thorough ducking; and two of them were changed. I returned to the unfortunate canoes, and on my way met people bringing the two boatmen back in a telaga. Knowing it would be some time before the boat arrived, I took my sketching traps, and ascended the bank to some magnificent rocks, from which I got an excellent view looking up the valley, taking in part of the steppe and the Kourt-Chume chain. In about two hours I saw the boat floating down the river; it reached the place of our misfortune before me; and on my arrival the men had got all the baggage on board, and were ready to go. The Cossack told me one of the boatmen had run away immediately the baggage had been placed in the boat, and could not be found: this vexed me much. Several people had followed from the village to see the wreck of our craft, and were standing around enjoying our disappointment. I called the Cossack ashore, having previously made my selection from the group looking on, who, I had learned, had favored the fugitive's escape. So soon as the Cossack came up to me, I laid hold of the man; the matter was understood in an instant; the Cossack seized him, and before he recovered from his surprise we had him in the boat, and pushed off into deep water. He now bellowed out to his friends to aid him; they ran down the bank, but we were beyond their reach; they, however, called out furiously to have him put ashore. Finding that we could not be intimidated, two of them went a short distance into the reeds, and brought out the missing man, offering him in exchange. To this I immediately consented, taking good care, however, to secure one before giving up the other. This arrangement satisfied all parties except the deserter, whom my Cossack promised a sound drubbing if he made another attempt at escape.

We had been much delayed by these proceedings; the sun had sunk below the distant hills, and there was no place in which to put our heads for many versts, nor wood for a fire. The upper mountains were covered with snow, and now a keen, cutting wind began to blow up the river, which made us all shiver. As we floated on, the shades of night began creeping fast over the valley, gradually ascending up the mountain sides. There were no signs of any resting-place, and the scenery was becoming more and more gloomy. We now turned a high, rocky point, and beheld at a great distance a light glimmering; but whether this was a fire on the bank of the river, or in a dwelling, it was impossible to determine. Our boatmen plied their oars with a right good will, which sent us on fast, and as we came nearer we observed that the fire was in some covered place, which we very soon reached. It proved to be a wretched station for a few Cossacks, and on entering it I found the poor fellows cooking their suppers in a most filthy room. My Cossack quickly arranged with them, and they turned out into a shed.

Asia is the land for tea; it is there a man learns to appreciate the herb at its full and proper value. After drinking mine, I took a long walk alone on the bank of the Irtisch. The scenery on this part of the river is very beautiful, and was here seen with a peculiar effect under the influence of a splendid moonlight, which cast the lower mountains into deep shade, while the higher snowy summits were tipped with silvery light, giving a more intense gloom to the deep valleys. How infinitely small the sight of these mighty masses made me feel, as I wandered on in my solitary ramble! Excepting myself, I could not see one living thing; all was silent as the grave. I had passed some high rocks that shut out the Cossack post from my view, and had entered a valley, running up into the mountains, which lay shrouded in dusky shadow. Two white peaks rose far into the cold gray sky, the full light of the moon shining upon one of them, and aiding much in giving a most solemn grandeur to the gloomy scene. Fancy began to people this place with phantoms, ghosts, and goblins of horrible aspect. It required but the howling of the wolves, and the shrieks I had heard last night, to give a seeming reality to the creations of the imagination.

I found on my return that the Cossacks had spread some dried fern for my bed, which looked quite inviting, notwithstanding that there were hundreds of *Prussacks* (a small kind of cockroach) creeping on the walls and roof. I had scarcely lain down when I fell fast asleep, nor did I once wake until morning. Soon as I left my leafy couch, I went out and saw the sun rise in splendor; but, with all the glory shed over the scenes around me, there was a certain indication which convinced me that we should have wet coats before midday. I lost no time in sketching the views that had so much interested me at this place. On both sides of the river the mountains are very picturesque, with rugged crags of granite, crowned by high snowy peaks, and a steppe at their base, through which the river runs between low banks thickly fringed with reeds and bulrushes, having a considerable breadth, with three small islands overgrown with willows. Among these reeds there were hundreds of wild ducks and other water-fowl; some of a delicious flavor, as I afterward found when they were served up at dinner.

In the forenoon we left these generous Cossacks and their miserable dwelling. They assured me that I should have very bad weather, and wished me to remain; but I was obliged to go on. The boat was pushed out into the current, that floated us along at great speed, and soon carried us beyond some bold rocky masses, which shut out of sight the smoke at the Cossack post, and opened a view into new scenes. As we expected, the change in the weather was near; the wind rushed down from the mountains in gusts; dark clouds began collecting on their summits, and every thing indicated a furious storm. Our boatmen watched these signs with some anxiety, as they knew what was coming, and plied their oars vigorously, hoping to reach a more sheltered part of the river.

Every few minutes the clouds gathered blacker, covering up the white summits, and descended the mountain sides, affording me a fine study of a mountain storm. Broken masses were driven rapidly along; and now a dense body of surging vapor spread over the valley. Presently we heard the howling of the wind as it rushed through the mountain gorges, and soon it swept up the river, chilling us with its cold and icy blast. The wind was dead against us, and it required all the power of the boatmen to force the little craft through the water. Already snow was falling fast in the mountains, which soon reached us in rain and sleet, and in a very short time penetrated through our clothing to the skin, giving us a most unpleasant shower-bath. Unfortunately, we had reached a part of the river where it ran through a broad valley, in which there was not the least shelter for us. On the Kirghis side of the stream we beheld several *yourts* about a mile away, and near them twelve camels were feeding. I thought this rather strange, not expecting to find these animals in so cold a region; but they would soon move into the warmer valleys of the south: winter had come very early upon them.

It was long past midday when we arrived at the mouth of the River Bouchtarma, now a broad and rapid stream, greatly increased by the numerous small rivers which fall into it between this place and the ferry near Zirianovsky. The town and fortress, which take their name from the Bouchtarma, stand on the banks of the river, about three versts above its confluence with the Irtisch. Formerly the place was of much more importance than at present. The town has several large buildings, which give it rather an imposing appearance in this wild region. The mountain chains to the north are very high, and some of the lower ranges are well wooded. The steppe or valley around Bouchtarma is of considerable extent, and affords good pasture for large herds of horses and cattle. On the northwest side of the town there is a conical mount, quite peculiar in its form, and exceedingly picturesque, and in the neighborhood are many ancient tumuli: some have been opened, when gold and warlike implements were found in them. I have in my possession part of a copper knife or dagger dug out of one of these mounds. When it was discovered the Cossacks thought it was gold, and cut it in two. This instrument must have been made at a very early period.

I wished to ascend the River Bouchtarma to the town, but my men declared that it was utterly impossible to take the boat up, the water being too high. Under these circumstances, we were compelled to continue the voyage down the Irtisch, much against our wish in such weather. A little below the mouth of the Bouchtarma commences the finest scenery on the Irtisch. One of the first objects seen is a fine, bold mass of black rock, which we had some difficulty in passing, as the wind and current drove us toward it with fearful rapidity, placing us in a dangerous position.

Had we succeeded in bringing the frail bark to this place, nothing could have saved us, the water rushing against these rocks with terrible rapidity, and the gale rendering it tenfold more dangerous: the bark would have gone to pieces the moment it touched the rocks; nor do I think any man could swim out of such a boiling flood. The rain and sleet still poured down, shutting out of view the mountains on both sides. At length smoke was seen in the distance, and the men strained every nerve to row us on against the furious blast. In a short time we got under a high shore, which gave us some little shelter, and enabled the rowers to pull more rapidly. About three o'clock we reached Bouloshnia, the first winter station on the Irtisch, where the caravans rest when conveying the ore on the ice from Zirianovsky to Oust-Kamenogorsk. Rapid as this river is, it is entirely frozen in the winter from November till March.

Our boat was stopped at the foot of a steep bank, when we jumped ashore, delighted with the sight of smoke. On gaining the top I observed a very small wooden hut, with a shed at the back, a most unpromising place for a night's lodging. We determined, however, to remain; for even a shed with a little straw would be better than an open boat, or the shore where no wood could be got to kindle a fire on such a night. There was not a man among us who was not completely saturated. Without going to the hut to make any inquiry, the Cossack ordered all the baggage up. We then entered the little building, and a most miserable place I found it. There was a room about fifteen feet by twelve, in which were sitting five men, two women, and three children. The two small windows were closed in with calico, rendering the place particularly gloomy; the water was dripping in from the flat roof, and there was scarcely a dry spot on the floor. It is only those who have been in such an apartment full of people, with their wet clothing steaming from the heat of a Russian stove, that can fully appreciate the odor which greeted the olfactory nerves on entering. Even my Cossack turned his head to the door for a moment. He then spoke with one of the women, who instantly opened a small low door, and led the way into another room, we following. This little chamber was twelve feet by five, with a Russian stove taking up more than one third of the space. At the other end there was a small window covered with calico; here also the rain was dropping fast. A wooden bench was secured along the side, and made wider at one end, evidently intended as a couch. Had there been a forest near, we could soon have rigged up a balagan, which would have kept the wet off, and a large fire would have made us comfortable. The Cossack ordered wood to be brought, and the stove was soon lighted. This made the little den look cheerful when compared with the one adjoining, which now, in addition to its own inmates, contained all our people.

The roaring of the wind as it raged in the deep valley, and the pattering of the rain, had a great tendency to reconcile me to every discomfort. Every ten minutes or quarter of an hour I went out, first to take in fresh air, and then to see if the storm was clearing off. All was black above, the rain pouring down, and the wind roaring with increased fury; and the people said it would be worse in the night. I now ordered the stove to be opened in the larger room, and a fire lighted. This would at least ventilate the place; and I shortly perceived the benefit it produced. Had the stove continued closed, the place would soon have been as bad as the Black Hole in Calcutta. The men seemed strong, hardy fellows; their occupation was out of doors, where they had plenty of exercise and pure air; but the women were indeed miserable beings: one had scarcely a rag to her back; what little covering she could boast of was tied round her waist with a piece of twisted hemp. The other had a similar costume, with the addition of a very ragged sarafan. Each had a blue handkerchief tied on the head, but shoes and stockings they had none. Their faces were dingy and careworn, with squalid misery stamped on every feature. The two children had a few dirty rags fastened on them somehow or other. One was about four years old, thin and emaciated; its little face already bore the marks of ill usage and sorrow. The other was rather more than two years old, somewhat chubby, very dirty, and exceedingly sallow. The sight of these poor creatures made an impression on my mind that I have not to this day forgotten. That we may have many scenes of destitution and misery in our own land I am well aware, but the worst den in the vilest lodging-house that may be seen among us could not equal this. They were peasants employed in conveying the ores from which so large a revenue to the Russian empire is obtained. I recommend their condition to the authorities in the Altai.

The people were quite right in their opinions about the weather, for the storm raged with unabated fury, at times making the little hut shake to its foundations; nevertheless, it must have stood many a heavy blast, as they are frequent in this region, more especially so at this season. This hovel was built with trees, halved together at each end, with moss put in between to keep out the wind, having a flat roof of squared timber, with about six inches of earth spread over, on which grass and plants soon grow, usually sufficient security against wet, but this day the rain was tremendous. In winter the roof has a deep covering of snow, which makes it very warm. A few stones had been piled up for a chimney, and an old cask placed on the top, secured to the stones with twisted willows. There was a little shed at the back, and a wicker fence round the small yard, in which the cattle are secured in the night to protect them from the wolves, that are numerous here in the winter.

Such were my quarters on the Irtisch during part of a frightful day and night; but, bad as they were, every man of the party, I believe, felt thankful for even this shelter when he heard the wind howling up the valley. Night came on dark and dismal; it was impossible to keep a candle burning, for either a large drop would fall upon it, or a strong puff through one of the many chinks put it out in a moment. After many vain efforts and much sputtering of the candle, I gave in and lay down on the wooden bench, wrapped in a coat and cloak. I had already driven two sticks into a joint between the timbers about two feet six inches apart, and had hung a towel over them to keep the heavy drops off my face. In this position, hour after hour passed in listening to the shrieking of the tempest music. At length Morpheus got the better of me: I slept, and that most soundly, till daylight next morning, when I went out and found it snowing fast, but with very little wind. During the morning the snow ceased falling and the clouds cleared off; this induced me to wander up the valley, accompanied by two men. A walk of about three quarters of an hour brought me to the point from which I intended to sketch a view looking down the valley toward some fine mountain peaks, that rise up majestically above the river.

The scenery on this part of the Irtisch is particularly fine; some of the ravines running up into the mountains have an exceedingly savage character. Tremendous precipices rent by deep chasms, and huge masses of rock hurled down from some of the higher peaks, prove that water has not been the agent that has caused these terrible disruptions. In one place I found the mountain rent asunder: the chasm is not more than thirty feet wide, and not less than eight hundred feet in height; some parts are even higher, the sides being almost perpendicular, and would fit into each other could they be brought together. Time has toppled many of the crag-built peaks into this abyss.

A little farther up the valley there is a curious conical mount, broken into precipices, with small cedars and young picta-trees growing on every terrace—some also on its summit. To the north it is exceedingly abrupt, and around this cone the mountains are riven into rugged peaks, with enormous precipices. In one of these ravines I found some beautiful specimens of jasper, and deeply regret that the weather prevented my exploring more of these mighty gorges.

While making a drawing the men called my attention to a storm coming over the mountains to the westward, which they said would be very bad, advising me to return and take shelter in the hut as quickly as possible. I had determined to finish this sketch, or, at all events, work until the rain or snow should drive me back to the little den. I occasionally took a glance toward the clouds, apparently advancing fast, and looking dreadfully black and angry. After sketching somewhat more than an hour, and congratulating myself with the hope that ten minutes more would finish all I required—the interest I took in my labor having prevented me casting a look up the valley for some time past—my cap was torn from my head, and my sketch-book blown ten or fifteen paces away. The blast was so sudden that I felt quite confused; this feeling, however, was of short duration, for the snow and rain came down so thickly that it roused me into action. I sprang after and secured my sketch-book, while the men were running for my cap, which I expected would reach the Irtisch before them: I succeeded in placing my drawing materials in their leathern case as the men returned with my cap. One of them strapped my bag on his shoulders, and, while doing so, assured me that the storm would soon be worse. Our position was a very bad one—high up in the hills, without any thing to afford the smallest shelter. The two men thought example would do better than precept, so started off, running as fast as possible down into the valley. I followed, but our race was short. The snow and rain fell so thick it almost blinded us, besides which we could not run against the tempest: it was even difficult to force ourselves on edgeways. I now found, to my cost, that the men knew very well what was in store when they first advised a retreat—I had got a wet jacket as well as my sketch. This was certainly a disagreeable walk, for we did not reach the hut till past midday. In about an hour the storm cleared off, the baggage was packed into the boat, and we left this wretched spot.

The river here runs through a deep channel along the foot of very abrupt mountains, in some parts rising to an enormous height above the water, and are so nearly perpendicular that nothing could climb them. There are many parts where it is impossible to land on either side, and the water rushes on between the rocks at a great speed. Some of those we passed are jasper of a dark reddish-brown, others are of a deep purple, contrasting beautifully with the yellow and green moss growing among them. The summit of one mountain was of a rich pink color, which had a fine effect. Lower down the rocks were gray and mossy, while beneath were some fine bold masses of red granite, rising perpendicular from the water. In this part of the valley there is no timber; near some of the summits a few diminutive picta-trees only are growing from the cliffs; nor has it yet been found to possess any mineral wealth. The scenery of the Rhine, however, is very small and tame compared with that of the Irtisch. Had the race who inhabited these regions, like the Rhenish barons, built castles on the precipices, they might have added much to the interest of the landscape, but without improving its grandeur.

This was a day of sunshine and squalls; nevertheless, I succeeded in making several sketches; but it was not till long after dark that we saw the light of Tulovskoï Simoveë, the second winter station on the Irtisch. As we approached we discerned lights streaming from two little windows, which guided us into the mouth of a small river falling into the Irtisch. A cold blast had been rushing down the ravines as we rowed along, and heavy black clouds were rolling over the sky, making it so dark that we could scarcely see to land. The moment we got ashore, the Cossack

Barks on the Irtisch.

ordered the baggage up to the house, which we could see by the lights stood at a little distance on a high bank above us. Our men had shouted very loud, in the hope of bringing some person to aid us with a light; but we were obliged to grope our way up in the dark without assistance. After stumbling about among blocks of stone, we at length found the door, and entered a room about fifteen feet square, where a large fire was blazing in the stove, throwing a strong light on the inmates and the dirt. In a few minutes my eyes got accustomed to the light, and then I began to examine the group standing before me. This consisted of four women, three children, and eight men—fifteen persons in all—much too many for the space; but when my party of nine entered, the chamber was literally filled. To remain the night in such a room was out of the question; come rain, come wind, I determined to seek my rest in our open boat.

While my evening meal was preparing I had time to examine each individual and the room in which we were located. The stove stood in one corner, with a bright blazing fire, to which, since we entered, logs of wood had been added to give warmth and ventilation. It would require a far abler pen than mine to describe this scene of filth and misery. The floor was thickly covered with wet grass, that had been trodden for weeks, and from which came an effluvium mixed up with various noxious exhalations, rendering the place almost unbearable, even with such a wind as was now blowing. To make me more comfortable, and the floor clean about me, one of the women brought in a large armful of wet grass, and spread it under my feet. A bench ran round the room, on which the inmates sat and slept; some had their beds on the top of the stove; and the berth was offered to me, being dry and warm; but I was obliged to decline this act of kindness. The walls and ceiling were black from the smoke of the stove, that was constantly sending a puff into the room whenever a gust of wind rushed down the chimney. Two of the women were strong, sturdy jades, who had just reached this miserable abode; the other two were poor, emaciated creatures, sallow and sickly, and looking old, although, in reality, quite young. One of the children, a little girl of about five years of age, was almost a skeleton: her countenance bore the marks both of pain and sorrow; the other two were younger, with scarcely a rag to cover their squalidness. Two of the men appeared ill, half starved, and borne down with sickness and care. The others were boatmen in ruddy health, whose stay here was only temporary. They had not yet suffered from the foul air of the room; and their occupation, and the fresh breezes on the Irtisch, keep them in health.

Having got thoroughly warm, I went down to the boat; some wet grass had been spread at the bottom, over which a "*voilock*" (felt made of camel's hair) was laid for my bed. I pulled on a pair of fur boots and a warm cap, wrapped my cloak around me, and lay down to sleep. The wind was cold, but it was now clear and starlight. The Cossack slept in the boat, and the other men remained in the hut. Fatigue will make a man sleep any where; and I was soon in the land of dreams, being quietly rocked in the boat by the surging waters of the Irtisch. I was awakened long before daylight with cold; the moon was shining brightly, and all around me was covered with white frost. I rolled myself up again, and slept till morning, when I got up, jumped ashore, and moved about rapidly till I became warm. Shortly after this the boatmen turned out, and, coming down to the shore, made a fire and prepared their breakfast. It was now time to look after my people. I repaired to the hut, and found the Cossack preparing the *somervar*. On opening the door of the room, all seemed fast asleep; and so in fact they were, bad as was the place, and difficult as it was to breathe in. I closed the door, for I felt quite sick. After breakfasting on shore near the boatmen, I sketched the place, then stepped into the boat and departed.

The aspect of the country below Tulovskoï Simoveë, through which the river runs, is greatly changed from the district we passed yesterday. In place of magnificent mountains, rounded hills appear of no great elevation; neither trees, nor even a shrub, grow on them, but they are covered with a short mossy turf. The rocks forming the banks of the river are often varied, even in the space of a few hundred yards, and great disruptions have taken place all along this valley. The strata have been broken and twisted about in singular contortions, affording a splendid study for the geologist. During this day's voyage there was little to interest an artist, especially after the grand scenery higher up the river. The Irtisch has extended very much in width; it has worked out a much broader channel as it approaches the steppe, and runs more sluggishly; this and a dead wind against us, often blowing with great fury, delayed us, and it was not till evening we landed at Oust-Kamenogorsk, when we went straight to the house of the director of the pristan. The silver ore from Zirianovsky is landed here, and then forwarded in small carts to Barnaoul, and other smelting Zavods six hundred versts distant. What with unloading the ore from the boats, weighing, and loading the carts for their distant journey, this is a very busy scene. The men in charge of the caravans are held responsible for every pood of ore they take; and it is carefully weighed on their arrival at the Zavods. There are near three thousand horses employed in transporting the ore. Instructions about me had been sent to the director here, and, as usual, I was received with kindness, and treated with great hospitality. A clean and comfortable room added much to my comfort. By the time I had changed my wet clothing, a good dinner was placed on the table, to which I did ample justice. Then I heard that, two days before, the colonel commanding the Cossacks in this region had called upon the director to inquire for me, and desired to be informed the moment I arrived.

The following morning I waited upon the colonel, who received me with great cordiality, and said, if I still wished to continue my journey into the steppe, I could do so, for the Cossacks would escort me from station to station; but he greatly feared the season was too far advanced for me to sketch much before the winter set in. He was also apprehensive that I should find some difficulty, as all the Kirghis would be gone southward.

CHAPTER XV.

THE KIRGHIS STEPPE.

At two o'clock the next day the colonel sent two Cossacks to inform me that the escort was ready, and they had instructions to take me across the Irtisch. On arriving at the opposite bank, I found two sturdy-looking Cossacks mounted, and armed with sabre, musket, pistol, and a long lance, presenting a formidable appearance. There was also a Cossack driver without arms, and three horses in a small light telaga. These, with my own Cossack from Barnaoul, and my own arms, were quite sufficient for our defense against ten times the number of Kirghis, should they venture to attack us to keep up their reputation for plundering. A level plain extends from the Irtisch about eight versts to the first range of hills, which we ascended, and then a new scene was presented to our view: high granite rocks, broken into curious and picturesque forms; in many parts mounds, or, rather, they might be called hills of quartz, sparkling like snow in the sun. There were also a great number of Kirghis' tombs, apparently very ancient, as the present race only sink a shallow grave, cover up the body with earth, and throw a few small blocks of stone over it.

These tombs are all built of rough stone, consisting of a basement sometimes ten or twelve feet square, and eight feet high, on the top of which rises a small pyramid. There are many others around them much less in dimensions, which induced me to suppose that a chief and part of his tribe had been buried within each group of sepulchres. Beyond them to the westward the Monastery Mountain was seen looming over the steppe at a distance of thirty or forty versts. The track along which we traveled was very bad, and the telaga constantly bounded over rough blocks of granite. In about two hours we reached a Cossack picket; in ten minutes a new escort was mounted, and the telaga at the door, our baggage packed in, and away we went at full gallop over a smooth steppe. We were now ascending a high ridge, and shortly entered a pass in a granite mountain quite destitute of herbage, scarcely a blade of grass being to be seen among the rocks. The road ascended considerably during the last three or four versts, after which we began to descend into a most singular place. Our track was along what appeared to have been the margin of a crater, the granite blocks and fissures all radiating from the centre. A little farther on we passed over a part which had every appearance of having been forced out of the crater in a liquid state, flowing down a slight declivity, and cooling before it reached the bottom. There are numerous waves or beds of this, each stopping several yards from the edge of the one beneath, leaving scarcely a doubt on my mind that this granite had once run down like lava or molten metal. Our way was up a ravine for some distance, and then we began a difficult descent to the steppe.

As we proceeded farther to the south the country became less interesting, made up of rounded hills and undulating sterile country. After traveling a little more than two hours we arrived at a *priesk* (gold mine) close to our track, and stopped to look at the works; I accepted the invitation of the director to stay the night; a *yourt* was placed in front of his little dwelling, and dinner almost immediately placed on the table. On mentioning my wish to visit Nor-Zaisan, he proposed to give me horses and Kirghis guides to cross the mountains, as it was only a two days' journey by this route. After dinner he sent to an encampment not far distant for two Kirghis to act as my guides, and on their arrival the matter was explained to them, when both exclaimed that it was impossible to proceed by the mountains, the snow at this season being so deep. The only way I could go, I was told, was round by the steppe, which would be a five days' journey on horseback.

Nothing my host could say would induce the two Kirghis to attempt the journey over the mountains. By their appearance I should think fear was not one of their failings, for they had thorough bandit countenances, which spoke intelligibly what they would do on the first favorable opportunity. My host was a well-informed man, and a perfect gentleman, who had been banished into Siberia from his native land; he had spent some years in the University at Kief, and, like many others of his countrymen, was

Discussing the Journey to Nor-Zaisan.

more devoted to the sword than the pen. I sincerely hope, before this, he has been permitted to return to his native Poland. We walked along the course of the little brook, where excavations were being made, in the expectation of finding a rich bed of the precious ore; but, like hundreds of others, it proved delusive. The discoverer of this mine arrived in St. Petersburg, carrying in his pocket samples of gold declared to have been found on this spot, and produced a statement showing how many zalotnicks of the precious metal could be got from a hundred poods of sand; also describing the extent over which this valuable deposit was spread. The bait was too tempting to be resisted, numbers being anxious to possess shares in a mine that was to produce so much wealth. The subscriptions were paid willingly, and the man returned to Siberia with more than one hundred thousand rubles in his pocket, to be divided among his accomplices. The poor exile was offered the directorship of these mines, and for a mere existence was induced to banish himself still farther from men. It was to obtain bread, which his own exhausted funds would barely provide. He had been sent to this place, where gold was said to be lying in such quantities, more than eighteen months before my visit, up to which time not a single pound of the ore had been found. Shortly after I left, legal proceedings were commenced against him by merchants in Siberia, who had supplied goods for this company by his order. It redounds to the credit of two of the highest authorities of Siberia that, when these circumstances became known to them, a stop was put to proceedings which would soon have deprived him of his liberty even in his exile. Since then we have met far from this pretended gold mine, in Oriental Siberia, where I fortunately was able to return his kindness.

I spent the afternoon and night with this gentleman, who leads a most solitary life here, his only neighbor living at another gold mine thirty-five versts distant. The Cossack picket is within three versts of his house, but there is no officer—only eight men. He related to me accounts of several great "barantas" which had taken place in his neighborhood, such bands of robbers being very numerous, and they carry on their depredations with most daring audacity.

About two months before my arrival a tribe of Kirghis were living in one of the valleys to the eastward, near Irtisch; and one day, while watching the horses at a considerable distance from the *aoul*, some of them perceived several horsemen reconnoitring the country from one of the high ridges. This roused their suspicions, and induced them to drive their horses toward the encampment earlier in the evening, and communicate to the tribe what they had seen. A council was held by the chief, when it was decided that a vigilant watch should be kept up through the night, and that proper arrangements should be prepared to defend their dwellings. Scouts were sent out in the direction where the men had been seen, but they returned without perceiving any one. The night was dark, and the watch was set; each man, having something to lose, kept a strict guard over the property. Some time after midnight the dogs became uneasy, and were frequently heard to bark, but this was attributed to the wolves, as the men could not hear a sound even by laying their ears to the ground. The barking of the dogs became more frequent, and consequently the men more watchful; soon a distant tramp of horses was heard approaching slowly, but nothing could be seen through the gloom. At length the barking of the dogs became so furious that all in the *aoul* were roused up and made aware of the danger.

Presently indistinct objects could be seen approaching; the Kirghis sprang on their horses, with battle-axes in hand, to defend their homes and their property. They were scarcely prepared when the bandits made a charge into the encampment; both parties fought with desperation, and several were struck down on each side. While this was going on, shrieks were heard among the women and children, another party having rushed in from the opposite side, and were driving off both horses and camels. Day broke, and saw this little community despoiled by the plunderer, and four of its inhabitants murdered; two women and three children had been carried off by the robbers, with near three hundred horses and forty-two camels, while several of the men and two women were wounded. But the plunderers had not escaped; five of their number were left on the field, three dead, and two dangerously wounded; these also died in the course of the following day. It was supposed the *aoul* had been attacked by a party of about fifty. These people are in continual warfare, and their robberies are often on a much greater scale. During the evening a gale of wind sprang up, which shook the little dwelling to its foundation, and sounded vastly like winter, which, I feared, was coming apace.

At seven o'clock this morning I left my kind host. The road for more than forty versts is of the same uninteresting description —rounded hills with short grass; in some of the ravines a few stunted birches were growing. After this we ascended a small chain of mountains which runs toward Nor-Zaisan; one summit has a very peculiar form, like a monk's head, with his shaven crown, the rocks bristling out on the sides forming his hoary locks. It rises far above all other parts of the chain, is seen from a long distance across the steppe, and is named Kolmack-Tologuy. The Kirghis have a curious tradition about this mount. Having reached the top of the crest, over which the road passes, we had the vast extent of steppe spread out before us. The view was magnificent. A small chain of high granite rocks runs to the westward; to the south appeared one interminable plain: there was neither town nor any other object by which one could measure its magnitude. I sketched this scene while the sun was sinking fast below the western chain, covering the sky with a most vivid golden yellow. The mountains were purple and misty, casting their shadows far over the plain. A streak of deep purple passed across the steppe, in which a small lake was sparkling like burnished gold, while nearer and beneath the steppe was undefined in gloom. The stony locks and shaven crown of Tologuy were lighted up with a golden hue, and the foreground on which I stood, with its broken rocks of reddish porphyry, and the browned and burned-up grass, were tinged with a deep orange, making a splendid picture. Having finished my sketch, we descended rapidly into the plain, over which we galloped at a furious speed, and arrived at Koch-bouchta about an hour after dark.

It is said by the Kirghis that the steppes about Nor-Zaisan were occupied ages ago by a very great and ancient people, about whom they give the following tradition. At this extremely remote period—which I may perhaps be allowed to call the mythological period—two mountains, the one called Kolmack-Tologuy and the other Sarte-Tologuy, stood in the Tarbogatai chain; and two heroes or giants, father and son, engaged to carry Kolmack-Tologuy to the rocky shores of the Irtisch, and place it on the plain where the town and fortress of Oust-Kamenogorsk are built, for the purpose of damming up the river. At a certain distance from the Karagol Mountains the heroes were to pass the night. Having put down their load, the son asked the father permission to go and visit his bride, who dwelt on the broad steppes extending along the shores of Nor-Zaisan. "Remember," said the father, "that the *kalim* is not paid, and that you can not stay with her in the right of a husband." The son proceeded to the *aoul* of his bride, but was so charmed with her beauty that he forgot his father's strict injunctions, and remained till sunrise, when the stern old man, growing impatient of his son's delay, had already raised his side of the mountain. On resuming his labor, the young giant found, notwithstanding all his efforts, that he was utterly unable to move his portion of the load. Enraged by this proof that his injunctions had been disobeyed, the old man ordered him to place himself under the mountain, when he remorselessly let go his hold, and the enormous mass fell, crushing both.

The mother anxiously awaited the return of her husband and son. At length, tormented by painful uncertainty about their fate, and feeling a presentiment that some misfortune had befallen them, she determined to follow on their track. She at last recognized the mountain, now the monument under which her husband and son lay buried. The bereaved widow and mother sobbed bitterly, absolutely, according to the best authorities, shedding tears of blood. She mourned her loss for a long while and would not be comforted. Finally the blood-drops ran dry, and when she wept again her tears were pure and transparent as a spring. The rocks were the silent witnesses of her misery, and have preserved the proofs of her sorrow and devotion, the tears of blood and drops of crystal having become petrified and transformed into layers of argil and quartz, which can be distinguished from a great distance by the color of red and white. This mountain of quartz is about five versts south from Kolmack-Tologuy. It is named by the Kirghis Ac-Tas, or white stone, and is held by them in great veneration.

Kolmack-Tologuy is seen from a great distance, and is easily known from all other mountains by its peculiar craggy sides and arched summit. On its smooth dome figures of men and of different animals have been sculptured by the Kalmucks ages ago. Solitary or Sarte-Tologuy stands in its original position on the northwest slope of the Tarbogatai, within the frontiers of China. This tradition is most faithfully believed by the Kirghis; indeed, it would be dangerous in some places to express any doubt about its truth, or attempt to ridicule the narrator.

I was up at dawn of day, and went to a new fort, which is not yet completed. Sitting down on a plank, I looked toward the east, and in a very few minutes the sun rose majestically, as if from the sea. My ride to-day would be directly toward the point whence I saw the sun rise. Having returned to my quarters to breakfast, my host, who has the charge of the Kirghis, told me the horses were already arrived to take me to Nor-Zaisan. At twelve o'clock all was prepared, and we started with six Cossacks besides the Siberian Cossack, and twelve horses. There was a fine turf on the steppe, which enabled us to go on rapidly. We soon passed the low hills to the south of Koch-bouchta, and then entered on the great steppe, which extends down to Nor-Zaisan on the east, and to the Tarbogatai Mountains on the south. There are many undulations on this vast plain, which in summer affords pasturage for immense herds of horses. We frequently passed places where *aouls* had stood, the inhabitants of which were gone toward the Tarbogatai.

About half past three o'clock we stopped on the bank of a large river, now dry, with the exception of a few deep holes. In April and May, when the snow is melting on the mountains, it is a majestic stream, more than a verst broad, washing out holes in the steppe in some places twenty and thirty feet deep, and sweeping every thing away in its course. Here we ate our dinner, during which I pointed out to our guide a small column of white smoke, evidently a very great distance off, which I supposed to be at a Kirghis *aoul;* but he assured me that there were no encampments in that direction, and that the smoke proceeded from the reeds burning on the shores of Nor-Zaisan. Our dinner was soon finished, and we traveled straight toward the smoke, sometimes over rich pastures, at others over gravel and stones, on which there was little vegetation. After riding two hours, we were near enough to see that the steppe was on fire, and not the reeds. Our route had been along the foot of some low grassy hills for many versts, where our guide expected to find an encampment. We discovered the place, but the Kirghis had left some days before. One of the Cossacks dashed off up the hill, riding along the summit a short distance, and then returned, saying that he had seen a single *yourt*, and that we should not find another for thirty or forty versts. Our horses were turned up the hill, and we soon gained the summit, near a fine old tomb: the crests of these hills are studded with them, and some are of great antiquity. From this elevated position I observed that the fire was spreading fast over the steppe. Just at dark we reached the *yourt*, and found it a poor miserable place, in which were a dirty Kirghis woman and four young children, three of whom were very ill. She added fuel to her fire, and made our kettle boil; in return, I made tea for herself and the children: the latter were lying on a *voilock*, covered up with skins. When the woman gave them the tea, I saw that they had not a rag of clothing to cover their little bodies. No one can conceive the wretchedness of some of these people, and more especially the females. The only part of this woman's garments which indicated her sex was a piece of dirty cotton thrown over her head, forming a cap. She had on a pair of old leathern *tchimbar* (wide trowsers), boots with very high heels, and an old sheepskin coat, with many rents in it, proving beyond all question that she had not a rag of under-clothing. This poor creature and a man had been left with the sick children, the *aoul* having been moved to fresh pastures many versts distant.

While sitting drinking my tea, I could see on the steppe the reflection of the fire, which was advancing very fast; and as we were not more than half an hour's walk from the old tomb on the hill, I determined to go there, whence the whole extent of the conflagration could be seen. Three of my people accompanied me, and when we reached our destination, what a scene was presented to us! The fire was still about ten versts to the east, but it was traveling directly west and along our track, extending in breadth across the steppe probably twenty-five or thirty versts. The flames ran along the ground, licking up the long grass with their forked tongues with great rapidity, and making a tremendous glare. We remained more than an hour looking upon this sublime and awful scene, and then returned to our lodging. I sat up in the *yourt* a long time, watching the woman feed the fire with dwarf bushes and camel's dung: she might have been taken for a witch blowing up a fire for some unholy rite. Strange and dirty as this place was, I wrapped myself up in my cloak and slept soundly.

Early this morning we were ready for the road: the woman was also preparing for departure. I gave her tea and sugar, and saw the children drink it with great delight. They were to be packed up in *voilocks*, and carried on the back of a camel. We left them, and traveled to the south over some low hills, and from the top of one obtained a view extending over the steppe as far as the eye could reach. The fire had advanced some fifteen or twenty versts, and was still raging fearfully. We had a thick short turf to ride over for several hours, which must have made fine pasturage for the horses and cattle during part of the summer. A little before noon we arrived at a large *aoul* just as the men were drawing water from a well about ten feet deep to water their herds and flocks. First came the goats and sheep in very large numbers. It was quite interesting to see them march up, fifty or sixty together, pushing each other to get to the long wooden trough, some twenty of them drinking at a time, and then march off in the opposite direction. One division after another came up, drank, and trotted away without creating any confusion. When the sheep had finished, then came the horses, snorting and kicking; but the men would at once drive out any refractory individual, and punish him by not allowing him to drink till the last. I saw several undergoing this discipline. The camels are watered at some distance: they did not come to this well. The men were stripped, having only their *tchimbar* and boots on, and fine athletic fellows they were.

Almost immediately we arrived at the *aoul* a sheep was killed; two Kirghis set about dressing it, and in an incredibly short time it was cut to pieces, put into a large iron caldron covered with a wooden lid, and placed over a fire made in the ground; a boy was constantly employed putting small quantities of wood under the iron vessel to keep up a blaze. The men who had dressed the sheep took their stand beside the seething pot, each having a wooden ladle, and occasionally lifting up the lid to skim the boiling mess. The Cossacks dined with the Kirghis; I did not, having seen the entrails put into the pan after undergoing but a very slight purification. This induced me to order tea, which I knew would be clean. I did not even enter the *yourt* during dinner. Directly this meal was over we started for Nor-Zaisan, and soon came up to beds of reeds higher than our heads, growing on the sandy plain; still, no water was visible. No doubt there are times when the whole is under water, for an easterly wind will extend the lake ten or fifteen miles in this direction. On we went over a sandy plain, through and between beds of reeds, without one single point of interest. At last, a little before night, we arrived at another *aoul*, and on going up to the *yourts* I saw the lake through a small opening in the reeds. Fifty paces brought me to the shore, and great was my disappointment. I could see nothing but reeds forming the boundary of the lake—not so much as one foot of sandy shore. Nor was there a canoe in which to go out into the open water. I rode along the shore, through these beds of grass, for five or six versts, and frequently forced my horse into the water above the saddle-flaps, but without being able to get a single peep into the lake.

During my ride I found many places where the wild boars had been rooting and lying, but I did not see one of them; nevertheless, they are very numerous here, more particularly so on the western shore. After this I returned to the *aoul* greatly disappointed. My lodging was in the chief's *yourt;* carpets were spread, tea handed round in Chinese bowls, with "*kishmish*" (small dried raisins) and dried apricots—a most delicious evening meal. The Kirghis at this *aoul* were wealthy; the chief had more than three thousand horses, and nearly three hundred camels, with oxen and sheep in great numbers. My host was rather short in stature, but a very gentlemanly little man, dressed in a black velvet kalat, a crimson shawl round his waist, a beautifully embroidered cap on his head, and a pair of small high-heeled red leather boots on his feet. His wife was dressed in a silk kalat, striped with yellow, red, and green, giving her a very gay appearance. She had a cap formed of white calico hanging over her shoulders, a green shawl round her waist, and red boots. They had four children, and these were running about naked. There were eighteen *yourts* or dwellings in this *aoul*, making a large population when they all came out to see the strangers. During the evening a sheep was killed and cooked as before, but as the Cossacks broiled some of the mutton for me, I got it clean. When the meat was cooked, the whole of the *aoul* attended the feast, men, women, and children—dogs included. For some cause, the sheep was not eaten in the chief's *yourt;* they all assembled in another some little distance off, leaving me the sole occupant of his dwelling. Thinking they might have some scruples about my being of the party, I would not intrude upon them, but remained and ate my supper in quiet.

My host informed me that it was only a two hours' ride from his *aoul* to the Irtisch; and thinking I might obtain better views of the lake from that part, I decided on going there. We started immediately after breakfast, riding through the reeds for more than an hour in the hope of finding a wild boar, but without success. We continued our ride over the steppe, having in some parts fine grass, in others sand and gravel. The ground being little above the level of the water, a south wind will cause it to be inundated for many miles. In about two hours and a half we reached Kara-tas, or black stone, the Cossack fishing-station on Nor-Zaisan, close to the Irtisch. A low island extends from the mouth of the Irtisch to a considerable distance into the lake, covered with very high reeds and bulrushes, and closing up the view in that direction. In front of the fishing-huts there are about four hundred yards of shingle and sand extending along the shore. The sand has been blown into heaps by the wind, and forms many small mounds reaching far into the steppe.

Although disappointed with this visit, I felt a great desire to explore the country to the east of Nor-Zaisan. I could see the misty outlines of mountains, but at a very great distance, besides which I was determined to follow the Irtisch to its source. This river is the principal supply and only outlet of Nor-Zaisan. It was far too late to think of visiting the Tchornie-Irtisch this year, nor could it possibly be done from this place. Under these circumstances, desiring to retrace my steps to Koch-bouchta without delay, we rode back to Kliee, the *aoul* of my host, and started on our return after drinking tea. He sent eleven of his own Kirghis to accompany me to the next *aoul*, supposed to be about thirty versts to the westward. We were undoubtedly a wild-looking band, consisting of nineteen men and twenty-seven horses. As night was drawing in fast, and the *aoul* very distant, my new escort went off at a gallop, which we kept up over steppe and rough ground for an hour, when it became quite dark. After this our speed was slower, nor was there any certainty when or where we should find an encampment. Two or three Kirghis rode off to some distance on each side of our route to look out for either a light, or some other indication which might guide us to a *yourt*. Having ridden more than an hour in this way, the party who had been out on our right came in, and said there was an *aoul* in that direction not far off. A Kirghis was sent to recall the other men, when we turned toward the encampment, crossing some rising ground, and shortly were greeted by the barking and growling of many dogs as we rode up to the *yourts*. It was now about nine o'clock; and a Kirghis *yourt* is never lighted up at night excepting by a small fire in the middle, which makes only a reddish glare, as the camel's dung does not blaze. A few minutes sufficed to spread the carpets and roll ourselves up for the night.

We left this encampment soon after daylight in the morning, and in little more than an hour came upon our old track, followed it, and just at dark rode into Koch-bouchta, my host delighted to see me return safe and well. Tea and various good things were soon placed on the table, which, after so long a ride, were most acceptable, and several of the Cossack officers came in to spend the evening. *Wodky* and other drinkables were produced. My Cossack friends sang Russian songs, and I made an attempt at some English ones. Thus we passed a very agreeable evening on the frontiers of his celestial majesty's empire.

A little after dark on the evening of the seventh day after leaving my friend at his gold mine, his dogs gave notice of my return. I was hailed with delight, and we spent several hours very pleasantly in his little room. He presented me with one of his beautiful dogs, long afterward a faithful companion and an excellent guardian during my sojourn in Chinese Tartary.

CHAPTER XVI.

AMONG THE KIRGHIS.

TO-DAY, Saturday, the 9th of October, New Style, there was a beautiful eclipse of the sun, commencing at eight minutes to twelve, and ending at six minutes past four. I watched this with much interest as we rode over the steppe, knowing it would be visible in Europe. The country over which we passed was not particularly interesting—low hills running down into the steppe, with numerous small valleys, in all of which my companions told me there was gold. We passed large flocks of wild turkeys; but they are very difficult of approach, even to within rifle-range. Night had now come on, and we were still far from the mine. It was not till two hours after dark that we saw the light, and shortly after entered the little dwelling. The lady of my host received me kindly, and I found her a very pleasant companion. Both host and hostess did every thing they could to make me feel at home, and it was exceedingly agreeable to me that I could now converse with them in German without an interpreter. We supped most sumptuously; then I slept in a comfortable and warm room.

Sunday morning broke with a fog so dense that it was impossible to see any object ten paces distant; nothing could be done outside; even the gold-washing was stopped. I spent the forenoon very pleasantly with the baron and his doctor, an intelligent man, from whom I collected much information about the country. He had been the medical officer at one of the Cossack fortresses in the little horde of Kirghis, and a conversation I had with these gentlemen decided me to travel through the different hordes in the steppe.

The baron informed me that the Kirghis inhabiting the steppe around here and to the westward are great robbers, continually making *barantas;* that only eight days since they had robbed two Cossacks, who carried his bags with all the letters, and seven hundred rubles in gold and silver—a little more than a hundred pounds—stripping the men of their arms and every thing they possessed. This was done in the daytime, in a mountain pass not far distant. The Cossacks were surrounded in a moment by fifteen Kirghis: one fired his pistols, but without effect, and they were instantly secured, the two men having no chance against this gang of banditti. While we were sitting at dinner, five Cossacks arrived, bringing with them one of the gang whom they had taken: he was a strong, hardy-looking scoundrel, not likely to stand upon trifles when out on a plundering expedition. Having been told that a man had recognized him, he replied that he would not do so next time: his meaning was fully understood by those who saw and heard him.

Again it was wet, with a cold, cutting wind blowing direct from the northeast and across the snowy summits of the Altai: this was likely to be another day spent in-doors; but the weather having cleared up in the afternoon, I sketched the gold mine. Another Kirghis dog was presented to me by my host, belonging to one of the best breeds in the steppe; two horses had been given in exchange for him: his name in Kirghis is "Mitaban" (elastic sole); my other dog's name is "Iattier" (one that can catch). They are a beautiful pair. I was assured that Mitaban had run down and killed not less than thirteen foxes this summer.

The ground was hard-bound with a strong frost this morning, a proof that winter was near. After breakfast I made a sketch of the valley about two versts from the mine. This was a very busy scene: the gold-washing was finished for the year, and the men paid off, great numbers of whom are Kirghis. Their *yourts* were placed in the valley, wherever fancy dictated; some in snug, warm corners under the rocks, others in the grassy slopes, and some even on the hills. Horses and camels were standing in small groups, the men were busy packing up their goods and chattels, and the women had begun dismantling their *voilock* dwellings. In less than two hours the camels were loaded with all the wealth of this people, and the women had mounted, and were leading off their patient hump-backed companions. The men had secured their hard-earned money in sashes tied fast round their waists; the keen edges of their battle-axes were examined; the thongs tried, to see if they fitted their wrists, and then they mounted and rode away. A few put their horses into a gallop, uttered loud shouts, and brandished their battle-axes in defiance of the banditti they supposed to be lying in ambush to plunder them of all they possess. Most of these men succeeded in carrying off a small quantity of gold besides their pay. Their precautions were, on this occasion, quite necessary, for it was well known that a large band of plunderers were on the look-out for them. They mustered eighty-three men; still, they might be met by three times that number of spoilers.

This evening we had a fearful gale, with rain and sleet, rendering it impossible to see twenty paces.

A fine calm morning followed the stormy night, which induced me to start on a sketching expedition. The valley of the Isilksou had been mentioned as very beautiful; I proposed going, when the baron ordered two good horses to be saddled, and a Kirghis to guide me across the country about two hours' ride. We left the gold mine before nine o'clock, riding in a northwesterly direction over low hills, and frequently passing large masses of quartz. At about a verst distant to the west some rocky peaks rose up; my man turned in this direction, and pointed out a herd of wild goats feeding among the crags. We rode on toward some rocks, under the shelter of which I hoped to approach near enough for a shot. I dismounted, and scrambled from rock to rock for some time, and then had the satisfaction of seeing them look out for me from the crags half a verst away, the valley of the Isilksou being immediately beneath. These rocks form its rugged sides; in many parts are precipices five or six hundred feet high; in other places ravines ran up into the mountain on which we were standing. The valley was about two versts broad, with the River Isilksou winding through the middle, twisting and writhing about like the folds of some huge serpent.

On the opposite side the rocks rose in dark masses, higher and more picturesque. I mounted my horse, and rode toward the west, to seek out a ravine by which we could descend to the river. At last we found a track made by the goats and other animals on their descent for water. I turned to go down the ravine, but to this the Kirghis made many objections, and stopped his horse. Thinking he supposed it impossible to reach the valley this way, though the track seemed good, I continued to descend without any great difficulty, calling loudly to the man as I went on. At last I came to a part down which it was impossible to ride; I dismounted: this obliged me to lead my horse along a very stony path and across the ravine. Just at this moment the Kirghis appeared, calling out—I supposed wishing me to return. I could see no farther difficulties, and went on. When I reached the bottom of the ravine, on looking round, I observed the Kirghis slowly descending from this place. The valley was beautiful, but it was much more so from the opposite side; this decided my movements, and I rode off over a fine grassy turf, crossing the plain toward the river. The man came up to me at a gallop, still talking in Kirghis, which I did not understand. I put my horse into a sharp trot, and soon reached the river, which was flowing fast over a rocky bed; but it was not deep, nor more than fifty yards wide. We crossed, and presently reached the precipices, which were split and riven into exceedingly picturesque crags, with scarcely any herbage upon them. They were of a dark purple color, almost black; some were basaltic; in other places there were thick veins of quartz intersecting them.

I turned to the eastward, and rode to some Kirghis tombs, from which I got an excellent view of the valley, which I sketched. This was a most romantic and beautiful spot, and I deeply regretted that the lateness of the season prevented my spending several days among these picturesque scenes. Whatever had been the object the Kirghis had in view, he was now quiet, and watched my proceedings with evident interest. It was only when I began to ride farther down the river that he again objected, and pointed to the other side of the valley, apparently to tell me the scenery was better there. Not far to the east I saw some grand groups of rock, and rode on toward them, when I came upon a magnificent scene. A huge mass of dark basalt rose near a thousand feet above the valley. I dismounted, and climbed up great rocks of red jasper, rising fifty or sixty feet above. On reaching the top I looked down into a deep place, having the appearance of a crater, in the middle of which this immense mass of basalt was elevated; the whole scene had a black and hideous aspect, quite in character with the terrible power which must have produced this fearful locality.

While I was sitting sketching this view, the Kirghis approached and pointed out two men on horseback, riding fast up the valley, not half a verst distant, as if intending to cross the river two or three versts above us, as they went straight toward a great bend in its course. Our position was so elevated, with our horses standing near, that they must have seen us. The man began talking again, pointing across the valley lower down, evidently wishing to be off. I now caught the word "*baranta*," and the whole was explained to me in a moment. He had been all the time objecting to descend into the valley, fearing we might meet the freebooters known to be in the neighborhood.

I now cast a look after the two men in the valley, who were going at full speed toward the river; then leaving the Kirghis to watch them, I continued my sketch. In about a quarter of an hour he touched my shoulder and pointed up the valley: they were at this moment crossing the river; then, after ascending the opposite bank, they turned their horses round to look at us. Having stood a few minutes, they went off again at a gallop, and soon disappeared beyond the rocks. My sketch was finished, and my things being packed up, when we were greatly surprised by the low growl of what we supposed to be thunder at a very great distance; but, from our position, we could see nothing of the storm, all being clear and bright. The Kirghis led our horses down, but before reaching the bottom of the hills stopped, and pointed out a man standing on some rocks near the place we had last seen the two horsemen. There could be no doubt that he was watching our movements. The girths of our saddles were looked to, and we started, the Kirghis leading the way across the valley to the south, toward a great ravine I could see on the opposite side.

There was evidently something mysterious about these people, and my man kept a sharp look-out up the valley. I fancied he expected to see a party crossing to cut us off before we could reach the gold mine; but this was conjecture. We had to ride some distance down the river before we could descend the bank, and find a place to ford it. At length, after going nearly a verst, we came to a point where many horses had passed this morning. As the footprints were quite fresh, we were certain that they had been made since the rain, which proved beyond doubt that there were many people in the valley somewhere, and my man seemed a little perplexed as to which course to take. He followed the track until we discovered that they had gone up the valley straight to where we had seen the two men disappear.

After proceeding a short distance, we came upon the track of the two men who had come from the pass we were riding to; the Kirghis stopped suddenly, looking intently along the valley, and pointing to a place up the river, perhaps four or five versts distant, where we distinctly saw three men driving a number of horses toward the high precipices which bounded the valley. We also caught sight of the man who was still on the rocks watching us. All this had a suspicious appearance, and the horses we had seen were quite as near our friends at the gold mine as ourselves.

We now started at a gallop toward the pass, not knowing whether we could ascend through it or not. I had no fear of its being occupied, as the gang were most certainly farther up in the valley. It was exceedingly fortunate that I turned downward to sketch; had I gone up we should have ridden into their den, and been caught without a chance of escape. I had my rifle, and the Kirghis his knife, but these would have availed us little with great odds against us. Before reaching the pass we stopped on some rising ground to look up and examine the valley, when we saw seven men, four crossing the river, and three following down the bank. The Kirghis said something and spat toward them, and I saw that we should have a ride for it. I examined my rifle, placed a new cap on the nipple, and then made the discovery that my powder-flask had been left on my table at the gold mine. The charge in the rifle was all I had to depend on, and this I determined to keep for the leader of the band.

We saw our suspicious acquaintances ride up the bank, when they all stood still, looking toward us. No doubt we were observed, for, as soon as we moved, they did. Ten minutes carried us up into the ravine, where we found a track, in some parts extremely steep; we jumped off our horses, and led them as fast as they could walk. In a little more than half an hour we were near the summit, with our horses quite fresh. We mounted, and rode on a trot for a short distance, when the Kirghis put his horse to a gallop; I followed, and away we went toward the gold mine. We were very soon on the ridge of the first hill, whence we could see a long way beyond the place from which we had descended into the valley: not a man was to be seen. To wait for these robbers would have been folly, so we pushed over the undulating steppe to the second ridge, from which point we could ride to the gold mine in less than an hour.

We now pulled up to look over the country, when we observed two men ride up one of the ridges, evidently looking out for us, but they were at least three versts behind; presently three others joined them. At this moment we rode over a high mound, giving them a full view of us as we stood on the top. Our horses were not blown, and I felt a great desire to have the leader of this band within rifle-range. We stood looking at each other for a few minutes, and then turned our horses down the hill, putting them into a gallop, and reached our friends at the gold mine without seeing any thing more of the gang, who, no doubt, had expected to catch us.

I told my host where we had been, and he was horrified, exclaiming, "Had I known that you had descended into the valley of the Isilksou, I should have given you up for lost, for it was in one of these ravines that the Cossacks were robbed." I then related to him all that had passed between the Kirghis and myself before going down the pass. My friend said the poor fellow knew it was a bad place, and the risk we should run, besides which he had received instructions to be careful. I acknowledged the fault had been my own, as I had forced him to go by riding on into the valley, and he had honorably maintained his place beside me. The man was sent for, when he gave a perfectly true account of the whole affair, and said he had done all he could to keep me back. He gave the baron other information, which I saw made him uneasy. In the evening this was explained to me; the fact is, we were to leave the gold mine the next morning, and were to carry with us the whole of the gold which had been got during summer. Our route was across the valley of the Isilksou, a little farther down, and the Kirghis had suggested that these men were probably waiting to pounce upon the treasure.

During the evening the doctor was occupied in cleaning his own and the baron's arms, consisting of two double-barreled guns and two pistols: the former he loaded with twenty small rifle-balls in each barrel. As it was probable that my stay here might prove of some value to my kind host, having seven barrels at his service, I followed the doctor's example—set to work, cleaned up all my armory, and put them in good fighting condition. Altogether we mustered fifteen barrels; possessed of which, with the doctor's prescribed dose in six of them, we should prove rather formidable; the more so, as the attack must be made in daylight, if done on the road. It was thought by both my friends that these plunderers might pay us a visit during the night, so the dogs were all turned loose as a security. These Kirghis dogs are exceedingly watchful, and would be certain to give notice of their approach. We supped and sat up talking until a late hour, the baron and the doctor relating many accounts of the plundering expeditions of these wild Kirghis.

Long before daylight there was a storm, which made the little wooden building shake, and when I got up I saw that we were doomed to be detained another day, for the wind was roaring, and the rain and sleet falling so thick that no one could travel: this weather continued nearly the whole day, and kept us in-doors. During the night it was bad again, but the following morning there was a considerable improvement, and all were now actively preparing for the journey. The arrangements were, that the baron, his wife, and daughter, with the gold, should be in one telaga, two children and two servant-women in another, the doctor and myself in a third, with three horses to each. We had six men on horseback, and the three drivers. Our order of march was two men on horseback a little in advance, then the doctor and myself; the baron and his family followed; the children and women were last, with the four men in attendance.

We started at a good speed toward the dreaded valley, and in about an hour and a half were at the head of the pass, down which we must descend: here it was narrow and rocky—a capital place for an attack. The carpet, which had been thrown over us and our arms, was turned down; my pistols lay on my lap, and the gun on my right side. The doctor had his pistols on his lap, and his gun in his hand; my rifle I held ready. The men were obliged to drive very slowly down the pass; but we arrived in the valley without seeing either man or animal. We were now on good ground, and could not be taken by surprise. The valley was crossed, the river forded, and we commenced the ascent of the very pass in which the robbery had been so recently committed.

The ladies and their female attendants began to get frightened as we entered between the dark basaltic crags, among which hundreds of men could lie concealed, and the baron became also alarmed on account of his gold. The doctor had some valuables with him; I, however, had little beyond myself, but had no inclination to be made a slave. The ravine was steep and rugged, making our progress very slow, and at every turning we expected to see the caps of these fellows among the rocks; but not one appeared, and we reached the top in safety. We were now traveling over a hilly, open country, with neither tree nor bush to be seen. Veins of quartz ran across the mountains in perfectly straight lines, extending several versts in length, some two feet broad, others more than three feet thick. In every little ravine or small valley gold can be found, but in many it is in such small quantities that it would not pay for working.

The granite chain over which we passed is in some parts a mass of bare rock, with no vegetation excepting mosses. In some places the rocks were singular deep bowls—some filled with water, others quite dry, and some I saw were filled with rounded stones, exactly like the boulders found in a mountain torrent. As we approached near the summit, their crests became rugged and broken into numerous crags, often taking the forms of fine old ruins, with battlements and turrets of gigantic dimensions. Descending toward the north, we crossed what appeared to be the dry bed of a mighty river, covered with large and small blocks, all undoubtedly rounded by the action of water. In its present position no quantity of water can ever be collected; it must have been the bed of a river heaved up when this chain was elevated above the steppe. On one side of this channel granite precipices rise six and eight hundred feet, quite perpendicular. Going still lower toward the steppe the scene changes; grassy slopes extend up among the rocks, and little torrents come tumbling and fretting down their rugged and deeply-cut channels. At one time the water appears like vapor waving in the breeze, and all the forms are seen through it; then it goes rolling on like foam as it leaps from rock to rock; at other places the rocks inclose it altogether, and then it is seen rushing out of an aperture into a large granite basin fifty or sixty feet below. From this it boils over, and is lost under masses of fallen granite, which fill up part of the little gorge.

Hitherto the mountains on the Irtisch and the more distant Altai had been enveloped in clouds, but just as we reached the foot of the granite chain the fog began gradually to rise from the steppe, first revealing a lake in the valley some six versts distant. As it rolled up higher, a small granite chain, like the one we had just crossed, appeared with quaint and curious forms. There was one mass of granite on the opposite shores of the lake which at this distance appeared like a vast Sphinx not less than three hundred feet high. As the vapory curtain ascended other mountain forms came into view, those on the Irtisch and the lower ranges beyond. Still higher the clouds rolled up, till at last the snowy ridges and high summits of the Altai stood out in all their grandeur. From this place most unquestionably the finest general view of the Altai is obtained. There is a vast steppe studded with several lakes, small picturesque granite ridges rising abruptly from the plain, bold in form and bright in color, assuming the most beautiful and aerial tones as they recede, almost lost in bluish vapor, while above are seen the snow-capped summits and glaciers of the Altai glittering in the sun.

We had now reached the steppe, where it was proposed that our party should remain, while I proceeded with three or four men to the Monastery Mountains, about ten versts distant. But the baron fearing these roving bands of robbers known to be hovering about the steppe, it was deemed prudent that we should push forward as fast as possible with the gold. Fresh horses were waiting to take us on, carpets were spread under the shelter of some rocks, the provisions were unpacked, wine and Russian brandy circulated freely, and the *somervar* soon gave us tea, which completed our repast in the far-off steppe—a repast thousands might have envied—the sauce having been given by a long ride in these shaky telagas and the keen mountain air.

Our dinner being ended, away we went at a rattling speed over the level and grassy steppe, the object being to cross a small chain of mountains before dark. Night caught us, however, before we reached them, and rendered our progress both slow and tedious. It was shortly so exceedingly dark that we could not see ten paces before us. At length we passed the summit, and as we began to descend, discerned the lights at Oust-Kamenogorsk, more than an hour's ride distant. When we arrived on the banks of the Irtisch the boatmen objected to cross, the night being very dark and windy. Fortunately for us, we had passed a small Kirghis *aoul* half an hour before reaching the Irtisch. We therefore drove back to it, and took up our quarters in their temporary *yourts*, which were neither warm, clean, nor comfortable. We, however, made the best of the accommodation, and slept the night.

Soon after daylight one of the men rode with me to the river to get the boats ready, the wind still blowing a gale, which rendered it exceedingly difficult to cross. The rest of the party arrived in the telagas, when the ladies and the baron were put in a large canoe; I took charge of the children in another, and the doctor brought over the two women. We crossed the river in safety, and in due time arrived in a comfortable dwelling, all very cold and excessively hungry. Shortly after the gale increased, and the rain poured down in torrents incessantly for two successive days, keeping me shut up a prisoner. Sunday was a clear day, with every appearance of fine weather. The colonel commanding here ordered me an escort of three Cossacks. These, with my Cossack from Siberia, my servant, and myself, made a party of six well-armed men, and at one o'clock I bade adieu to the baron and his family, who wished me a safe return from this region of banditti.

There was a strong wind blowing, which caused us to take exactly an hour in crossing the Irtisch. We landed on the Kirghis side, where I found my escort and three horses, which had been sent over before, also a man to bring the animals back from the first *aoul*. The three Cossacks were soldier-like fellows—men who I felt sure would never flinch under any circumstances. After a short delay we mounted and rode across the steppe toward the mountains to the west. When we reached the ridge the sun was sinking fast. We examined the steppe in front, hoping to find some indication of an *aoul* where we could stay the night, but nothing could be seen indicating that there were living beings on this vast plain. The Cossacks were now at a loss which route to take, consequently we were obliged to ride slowly down the steep mountain, frequently examining the steppe, when one of the men saw a smoke a considerable distance to the southeast. Although this would take us a long way out of our road, as nothing else could be seen, it was decided that we should sleep there.

The sun had set before we reached the plain, and night was fast approaching, yet the smoke was still visible, and I took the bearing with my compass. We were now going to ride without track or mark of any kind; there was not a tree to guide us, and in less than an hour it would be quite dark. One of the Cossacks said we must ride fast, or we should have great difficulty in finding the *aoul*, as no lights are shown after dark to mark the spot. We went off at a gallop, and after riding hard about half an hour we could scarcely see the smoke; I took the bearing again, and away we went at a gallop over the turfy steppe. We had not ridden long before my servant began to lag behind, and called out to me, begging some one to wait for him; at length he was so far in the rear that we were obliged to pull up and wait, or we might lose him. Nothing could be observed to guide us, and it was difficult to see my compass. The laggard was assured that he would be left on the steppe if he did not keep up with us, and certainly fall into the hands of some of the gangs known to be plundering: this frightened him greatly. It was now quite dark, and still we galloped on for more than half an hour, when a Cossack expressed a wish for us to halt and stand still. We did so, and listened, hoping to hear the dogs barking.

One of the men dismounted, walked a little in advance, lay down on the ground and listened, but could hear nothing. We rode on slowly again, listening to every sound, when a Cossack called out to stop, and then we distinctly heard dogs at a very long distance, more to our left. This was some satisfaction, for we were at least getting nearer. Turning to the proper direction, we rode toward them, occasionally hearing their cheerful voices. It is only the tired traveler wandering for hours over the steppes on a dark night who can appreciate these canine voices: they are sweeter than the song of the nightingale.

At last they ceased barking altogether. We had ridden some time without hearing any thing to guide us, when one of the Cossacks stopped, and sent two of his comrades forward, all the others remaining quite still. In about a quarter of an hour they returned, having come upon the shore of a lake, but without hearing any thing; this was bad, and we now agreed to turn more to the right. We had ridden but a short distance in that direction when we heard the dogs again, more distinctly, and apparently right before us. Two men rode off toward the sound, and presently they were heard shouting; we pushed on, and in a short time reached a large *aoul*. The Cossacks rooted out the chief, and established me in his *yourt*. In a very few minutes brick-tea was prepared for my companions, and smoked horseflesh handed to me; this I declined, at the risk of being thought a barbarian, and contented myself with tea, which I drank with great zest after our cold and hard ride.

We had caused a great commotion by riding into the *aoul* at this late hour, all being asleep except the watchman. When they awoke they heard the dogs barking so furiously, and the men shouting so vociferously, that they thought the banditti had come. The *yourt* was soon filled with Kirghis, anxious to look at the people who had caused them so much alarm. I gave the old chief tea with loaf-sugar, to his infinite delight, and insisted on his sitting with me on the carpet which had been spread opposite the door—the place of honor in his *yourt*.

It was bitter cold, with a strong wind blowing over the steppe from the northeast, which penetrated into the *yourt*, and made my teeth chatter.

My host was a fine old man, with a scanty gray beard and a deep scar on his left cheek, received on one of his plundering expeditions many years ago. He had on a coat of brown horseskin, with the mane extending half way down the centre of his back, tied round the waist with a scarlet shawl, while a foxskin cap on his head fell over his ears, rising into a cone on the top, and lined inside with crimson: a pair of high-heeled madder-colored boots completed his costume. His wife looked old and dirty. She had on a black velvet kalat, reaching to her feet, tied round the waist with a white scarf. A white calico head-dress was formed into a sort of turban, and a part of it fell over her shoulders, covering up her neck. She had boots like those of her husband. The children, dressed in brown lambskin coats, sat near the fire, intently watching all my movements.

The Cossacks thought it was time to take some sleep, and soon

ARKAT MOUNTAINS AND SALT LAKES, KIRGHIS STEPPE.

cleared the *yourt* of all but the chief and his family. *Voilocks* had been spread for me where I had been sitting, on which I lay down, wrapped up in a fur, and was soon snug and warm. The *yourt* was about twenty-five feet in diameter, and ten feet high in the centre. Close to where I slept were several rich carpets rolled up, and four or five boxes containing all the old man's wealth. On the other side of these valuables my host and his wife slept, and near them three children. My Cossack from Siberia, and the one who had command of my escort, spread *voilocks* and slept in this *yourt.* I do not know whether this was matter of precaution on my account, but it was always done.

Horses were brought to the *yourt* at daybreak. After a bathe in the lake I sat down to breakfast, when the Cossack brought me some broiled lamb, one having already been killed and nearly cooked in the iron caldron for the morning meal. My servant came into the *yourt*, looking miserable; I fancied the idea of a day's hard riding was the cause, but it was not. He had heard the Kirghis relating stories of the robbers on the previous night, which the Cossacks translated into Russian, and this had frightened him. When I said that he should return to Oust-Kamenogorsk with the horses, and wait for me there, the effect was wonderful; in ten minutes he was actively engaged in packing my things, and telling the Cossack what he would have to do for me. My delight at sending him back almost equaled his own, seeing how much he dreaded going among the Kirghis.

On the opposite page is a view of the Arkat Mountains—an inconsiderable chain, which stretches across the steppe: these peaks are bare granite, and exceedingly picturesque. Near them are many salt lakes fringed with the *salsola*, with its deep crimson color, which produces a splendid effect. There are Kirghis *yourts* in the foreground, and the small earth pyramids mark the road to the Cossack pickets.

CHAPTER XVII.

ADVENTURES IN THE STEPPE.

The old chief ordered two of his Kirghis to accompany me and bring back the horses. It was necessary to be fully prepared for a hard gallop, which induced the Cossacks to pack my small quantity of baggage into leathern bags, always used by the Kirghis, and to take two extra horses to carry them. They would then have very light loads, and be able to travel at a gallop when necessary. This being accomplished, we left the old chief and rode away, directing our course to the southwest. The morning was calm and beautiful, more like a summer's day than one so late in the autumn; but there was nothing to interest me on this vast steppe, the herbage having been eaten up, and flowers there were none. After riding several hours, we came upon a part almost destitute of vegetation, the whole surface a coarse reddish gravel, with a few rounded blocks of stone of small dimensions. A little to the left of our route, and apparently about ten versts distant, we saw an encampment. The two Kirghis said we must go there, as we should not find another before reaching the Monastery Mountains. Our horses were turned toward it, and we galloped on, as I was anxious to reach this *aoul* as early as possible, and get nearer the mountains. Before noon the horses were changed, and while this was being done I made a sketch, looking toward the Chinese frontier on the Irtisch, the scenery in this region being extremely pretty. Having finished, we started on again with two Kirghis, and horses for the baggage. Riding fast over the steppe for an hour and a half, we arrived at a place which afforded me a capital view of the Monastery Mountains; having finished a drawing of this, we rode on again, seeking the *aoul* of Mahomed, a celebrated chief, reputed very wealthy. The Kirghis said we should find him near the Mantilla Rocks, which they pointed out far away to the south. Judging by the misty tone of their color, I was certain that they were thirty versts distant at least; but it requires considerable experience before the eye can measure with any degree of accuracy the distances on these boundless steppes. Unless we pushed on very fast, there was every probability of our

Group of Kirghis, with Koumis Bottle and Bowl.

being obliged to sleep on the steppe without shelter. We had good horses, and the Kirghis were equally anxious with ourselves to reach the *aoul;* they therefore secured the bags on the horses to prevent their shaking, and then away we went, galloping over the smooth plain straight toward the misty mass.

For more than an hour we had gone on looking to the right and left, but not one living object had been seen, nor was there any great change in the appearance of the Mantilla Rocks to indicate that we were much nearer. Having reached the edge of a slight depression or a very broad undulation, we stopped to examine the country over which we had to ride, but neither camels, horses, nor *yourts* could be seen. The sun was sinking fast; in an hour he would be below the ridges to the west; there was no time to be lost, as a starlight ride in this region was somewhat dangerous—at least our Kirghis thought so, and they did not spare their horses. After crossing the depression in the steppe we were once again on the elevated ground, and stood some minutes gazing over the country, when the Cossacks and Kirghis declared no cattle or *yourts* could be seen. I thought otherwise, and pointed to a dark mass descending the slightly elevated plain toward the Mantilla Rocks; but not one of them could see it; nevertheless, I was certain it was a herd of horses being driven toward the *aoul*. This was not the first time I had discovered objects far beyond the range of vision of many other persons. The Cossacks and Kirghis had no hope; however, half an hour's hard riding convinced them I was right; they could now see that such an object was there, and that the mass was moving toward us. The Kirghis understood the matter at once, and turned to the southeast.

We had not ridden more than five or six versts when we reached another of these broad depressions. From this bank of four or five versts we saw a large *aoul* on the shore of a small lake, with great herds of horses and camels going slowly toward it. This was a delightful sight to us, as we rode our horses down the bank, and were very soon passing through an immense herd of camels, being driven in from several different points; great numbers of sheep we could see already around the encampment. As we rode along the Kirghis eyed us keenly, no doubt wondering who and what we were. A Cossack had been sent on to announce our coming to the chief. Approaching nearer, the dogs began to greet us with a very loud barking; they were a pack of savage-looking rascals, who would bite as well as bark when the opportunity served. They kept close in attendance with their music till we nearly reached the *aoul*, and were only induced to retreat by the whips of the Kirghis, who had ridden out to meet us. They led me up to a large *yourt*, at the door of which a long spear, with a tuft of black horsehair on it, was standing. A fine old man took hold of the reins of my bridle, and gave me his hand to dismount; to refuse his assistance would have been an insult. He then conducted me into his *yourt*, a beautiful Bokharian carpet was spread, on which he placed me, seating himself on the *voilock* near. I invited him to a seat on his own carpet, which afforded evident satisfaction to all those assembled in the *yourt*.

This was Mahomed, and the three Kirghis who had met us were his sons; they were seated near to us. My arms were matter of great interest to them when a Cossack brought my saddle into the *yourt* and took the pistols out of the holsters. The old man and his sons being anxious to examine them, I removed the caps to prevent any accident, and they were scrutinized with intense interest. They could not understand why I had taken the caps off, and seemingly thought there was some secret in these which I did not wish them to comprehend. To satisfy them, I drew the shot from both barrels of my gun: this was equally a curiosity; I then put a cap on one nipple and wiped the other; cocked both locks, and went out of the *yourt*, followed by all. I pulled the trigger and let the hammer strike the nipple without a cap; they looked at it, and wished me to pull the trigger again. I now pulled the other trigger, when they were all startled by the report. I then put a cap on the first nipple, cocked the lock, and handed the gun to one of the sons, who held it to his shoulder, touched the trigger, and was much astounded when the report rang in his ears. With this exhibition they were highly delighted. When we returned into the *yourt* my tea was ready; I poured it out, handed a tumbler of the beverage and a piece of sugar to the old chief, also one to his wife, who seemed perfectly astonished—I could not understand why at the time, but I was wiser in a day or two.

Having taken a liberal quantity, my Cossack added water to the pot and made tea for the sons, giving them sugar from the box, to their infinite satisfaction. It was now quite dark, and the fire gave very little light to the *yourt*. Presently a Kirghis came in with a large bundle of small bushes, put them on the floor, sat down by the fire, took a handful, placed it on the ashes, and blew the embers into a flame. These twigs burned brightly for some time; as soon as the flame began to die away he added another small portion, and thus he kept up a continual blaze, which gave me an opportunity of examining the chief, his family, and their dwelling.

He was upward of sixty years old, stout and square-built, with broad features, a fine flowing gray beard, a pair of small piercing eyes, and a countenance not disagreeable. He wore on his head a closely-fitting silk cap beautifully embroidered in silver; his dress being a long robe, or kalat of pink and yellow striped silk, tied round the waist with a white shawl; his boots were of reddish-brown leather, small, with very high heels, causing him, I thought, some difficulty in walking. His wife was much younger—I supposed not more than thirty, or, at most, thirty-five years of age. She wore a black *kanfa* (Chinese satin) kalat, with a red shawl tied round the waist, boots of the same color and make as her husband's, a white muslin cap, rather pointed, with lappets hanging down at the sides nearly as low as her waist, beautifully worked on the edge with red silk. Her face was broad, with high cheek-bones, little black twinkling eyes, a small nose, and a wide mouth; nor was there any thing either prepossessing or pretty in her appearance. While examining her features, I could not help thinking how much a Russian bath would improve the tints of her yellow skin and complexion. There were three young children—one boy about five years old, dressed in a yellow and red striped kalat, his only garment; the other two little sturdy urchins were younger: they were rolling about on the *voilocks* perfectly naked, and playing with a young goat, who every now and then stepped back, made a spring forward, and sent one of them sprawling.

Near the door a fine hawk was chained to a perch stuck into the ground. The *yourt* was formed of willow trellis-work, put together with untanned strips of skin, made into compartments which fold up. It was a circle of thirty-four feet in diameter, five feet high to the springing of the dome, and twelve feet in the centre. This dome is formed of bent rods of willow, one and a quarter inch diameter, put into the mortice-holes of a ring about four feet across, which secures the top of the dome, admits light, and lets out the smoke. The lower ends of the willow rods are tied with leathern thongs to the top of the trellis-work at the sides, which renders it quite strong and secure. The whole is then covered with large sheets of *voilock*, made of wool and camel's hair, fitting close, making it water-tight and warm. A small aperture in the trellis-work forms a doorway, over which a piece of *voilock* hangs down and closes it; but in the daytime this is rolled up and secured on the top of the *yourt*. Such is the dwelling of a great and wealthy chief in the steppe.

The furniture and fittings of these dwellings are exceedingly simple: the fire being made on the ground in the centre of the *yourt*, directly opposite to the door *voilocks* are spread; on these stand sundry boxes, which contain the different articles of clothing, pieces of Chinese silk, tea, dried fruits, *ambas* of silver (small squares about two and a half inches long, one inch and a half wide, and about three tenths of an inch thick). Some of the Kirghis possess large quantities of these *ambas*, which are carefully hoarded up. Above these boxes are bales of Bokharian and Persian carpets, some of great beauty and value. In another part of the *yourt* is the large leathern *koumis* sack, completely covered up with *voilock* to keep it warm and aid the fermentation. This is a most important piece of furniture in a Kirghis domestic establishment. I have seen one five feet eight inches long, and four feet five inches wide, with a leathern tube at one corner about four inches in diameter, through which they pour the milk into the bag, and draw the *koumis* out. A wooden instrument is introduced into the bag, the handle passing through the tube, not unlike a churning-staff; with this the *koumis* is frequently agitated. This bag is never washed out: it would be spoiled by doing so.

Near the *koumis* bag stands a large leathern bottle, sometimes holding four gallons, often much ornamented; so are the small bottles made to carry on the saddle. In another place stands the large iron caldron, and the trivet on which it is placed when used for cooking in the *yourt*. There are usually half a dozen Chinese wooden bowls, often beautifully painted and japanned. These are used to drink the *koumis* from: some of them hold three pints, others more. On entering a Kirghis *yourt* in summer, one of the Chinese bowls full of *koumis* is presented to each guest. It is considered impolite to return the vessel before emptying it, and a good Kirghis is never guilty of this impropriety.

The Kirghis begin making *koumis* in April. The mares are milked at five o'clock in the morning, and at the same hour in the evening, into large leathern pails, which are taken immediately to the *yourt*, and the milk poured into the *koumis* bag. The first fourteen days after they begin making this beverage very little of it is drunk; but with fermentation and agitation it is considered by this time in perfection, when it is drunk in great quantities by the wealthy Kirghis, as a man must have a large stud of brood-mares to afford a corresponding consumption of this beverage. Almost every Kirghis has a *koumis* bottle slung to his saddle in summer, which he loses no opportunity of replenishing at every *aoul* he visits.

The saddles are placed on the bales of carpets. Rich horse-trappings being highly prized by the wealthy Kirghis, many of their saddles are beautiful and costly. If of Kirghis workmanship, they are decorated with silver inlaid on iron, in chaste ornamental designs, and have velvet cushions; the bridles and other trappings covered with small iron plates inlaid in the same manner. I saw one set of this decorated harness which cost the owner fifty horses. The battle-axe is also richly inlaid with silver, and the iron rings round the handle are ornamented in a similar style. This is really a formidable weapon. The head of the axe is moderately heavy, and sharp, a handle about four feet six inches long being secured by a leathern thong round the wrist. The Kirghis is very expert with the use of this weapon, which he wields with terrible effect.

Leathern thongs and ropes made of camel's hair are hung up on the trellis-work, common saddles, saddle-cloths, and leathern *tchimbar*. This part of a Kirghis costume is frequently made of black velvet, splendidly embroidered with silk, more especially the back elevation. They are made so large that a Kirghis can tuck the laps of his three or four kalats into them when he rides, and are tied round his waist with a leathern strap, thus giving to the centre part of his person a globe-like form, out of which a very diminutive head and legs protrude, and to the whole figure a most unwieldy appearance.

Having described the Kirghis and his dwelling, I must give an account of my first evening with the old chief. When we arrived at his *aoul* he instantly ordered a sheep to be killed and a feast to be prepared. While this was being done we spent the time in drinking tea and examining the arms. Then one of his sons came to say that all was ready: my Cossack had told them I should not eat again after my tea. The old chief ordered that something should be kept for me, and the Cossacks having assured him that a part of the sheep should be cooked for my breakfast, he was satisfied, and all went off to the feast, even the youngest children. Carpets had been spread for me to sleep upon, and the Cossack had placed my fur ready, when I wished to turn in. I sat some time watching the fading light of the little fire, which I frequently replenished, until at length the bushes were finished; this induced me to prepare for the night by putting caps on my pistols and placing them under the articles which formed my pillow. I then rolled myself up in my fur. In about an hour they all returned; a light was blown up which lasted about ten minutes; the children were packed in their *voilocks*, the old chief lay down in his fur coat, and his wife wrapped herself up, and took her berth near the children. The two Cossacks made their beds and placed their arms near, then they turned down, a Kirghis dropped the *voilock* over the doorway, and we were made up for the night.

All were out with the dawn, and then commenced a scene in pastoral life highly interesting to me. I had left the *yourt* and looked around in every direction, but beheld only a mass of living animals. The whole of the herds are brought to the *aoul* at night, where they are most carefully guarded by watchmen and dogs placed in every direction, rendering it almost impossible to enter any *aoul* without detection. In my childhood I lived in localities where there were many horses and cattle, and used to think a flock of five or six hundred sheep a large one, but was now astonished by the numbers before and around me. The noise at first was almost intolerable: there was the sharp cry of the camels, the neighing of the horses, the bellowing of the bulls, the bleating of the sheep and goats, the barking of the dogs, and the shouting of the men—a very Babel. I counted one hundred and six camels, including their young; there were more than two thousand horses, one thousand oxen and cows, and six thousand sheep and goats. Even these, large as the number may appear, were far short of the total number of animals belonging to the patriarch chief; he had two other *aouls*, at each of which there were one thousand horses and other cattle. Women were busy milking the cows, and the men were preparing to drive these vast herds to their pastures. The horses and camels are driven to the greatest distance—as much as ten and fifteen versts; the oxen come next, and the sheep remain nearest the *aoul*, but these ramble five or six versts away. It was, indeed, a wonderful sight when they were marched off in different directions, spreading themselves out in living streams as they moved slowly along the steppe.

With tea and broiled mutton I made a capital breakfast; and this was quite necessary, as I had a long ride before me. The horses were already at the *yourt;* my sketching traps were handed to a Kirghis, who was to accompany me, and my gun to another; I slung on my rifle, and we rode off toward the Monastery Mountains.

Distances are very difficult to estimate on these vast steppes, with their clear atmosphere. We had ridden more than an hour, when I found a point from which I got a good view, and yet we seemed but little nearer the mountains than when at the *aoul.* Having finished my sketch, we rode on again over undulating ground; a few versts farther we came upon numerous blocks of granite piled up, and forming the top of rocky masses, broken into singular shapes, and often quite perpendicular toward the west, where the ground sunk into deep hollows. Hitherto we had been riding straight toward the southern end of the Monastery Mountains, and had reached a more elevated steppe. Seven or eight versts to the south of us rose a splendid group of granite, which I deemed it best to visit first, as this would prevent me going over the ground again. We turned our horses and rode toward those ridges; but, when nearer, I found that what had appeared a rocky mountain in the distance was in reality a great number of isolated masses, some of the most singular and picturesque shapes, from this place appearing like ruined castles, churches, fortresses, and other buildings of a vast city.

On a closer approach they appear still more curious; indeed, it was difficult to believe that some were not the works of an ancient race, who had built up these huge edifices with wonderful solidity and picturesque effect. In several places large masses of rock were standing on very small bases, considerably elevated; in others, pedestals supported what might well be taken for the ruined shafts of columns of gigantic dimensions.

Farther on were ruined towers and mighty battlements, with turrets rising high above, on which I almost expected to see grim watchmen peering over the vast plains. Had these been the days of genii, surely on this spot they might have been found. I felt somewhat reluctant to enter among such strange and gigantic forms, knowing that a closer examination would dispel the illusions fancy had been calling up while transferring the scene to my paper; but, having finished my drawing, I determined on a closer inspection, and rode into what in the distance appeared streets, but were deep ravines cut in the granite—rugged, and in many places forming steps twenty and thirty feet high. I dismounted, and, accompanied by a Cossack and a Kirghis, began scrambling over rocks and through places which these children of the steppe consider the residence of "Shaitan." Few, if any, of the tribe would be hardy enough to remain with a herd near this place till nightfall.

After climbing among the labyrinth for nearly two hours, we descended on to the steppe at a considerable distance from where we entered. I fired my gun as a signal, and in a short time my other two companions galloped toward us. The day was too far advanced to permit of our proceeding farther westward; I therefore decided to continue our ride along the foot of this little chain. We had not ridden far when I was induced to make another sketch, looking through a wide chasm to some high peaks beyond.

Before my drawing was finished the sun was sinking fast, and we turned our horses toward home. The snowy summits of the Kourt-Chume Mountains were seen extending far to the southward, while the higher summits of the Altai shone out like burnished gold, changing into red as the sun sank down. A most beautiful effect was produced by a contrast of the deep blue and purple shades of the lower range with the rich brown on the steppe. I watched the changes as we rode on until night came creeping over the rocks and plains, which induced us to put our horses into a gallop, and in a little more than an hour we reached the *aoul.*

Since leaving the *yourt* this morning I had ridden many hours, walked and climbed much, and made several sketches, without tasting either food or water (the men always carried something to eat with them); therefore now I was fully prepared for my evening meal, which the Cossack soon placed before me; it consisted exclusively of broiled mutton with tea. The old chief and all his family were assembled to see me eat, and many other Kirghis were sitting round the *yourt* equally interested in my operations. As the baron had sent a bottle of rum along with other good things, I ordered the Cossack to hand it to me. I drew the cork, intending to take a little in my tea; before doing so, however, I poured some into a small silver cup and handed it to my host, expecting that it would afford him great pleasure. He looked at it a moment, and then gave me the cup back without tasting a drop; nor could he be induced to put it to his lips. I gave it to the Cossack who had been my companion, and he drank the liquor with much gusto; I tried a little of it myself, and did not find it bad. My audience looked aghast, apparently expecting "Shaitan" to appear in person and claim me as his own. I drank a second and a third tumbler of tea, with a little of the spirit, to their increased horror. It had now become quite dark, and my evening meal having ended, all had left the *yourt* except the old chief and his wife, who was wrapping up her children and preparing for the night. Mahomed dismissed our fireman, and then made signs to see the cup. I gave it to him, and he wanted to taste the rum. I instantly got the bottle and filled the small cup. He looked round the *yourt* to see that all were gone, then drank it off. While his sons and the people were present, he would not touch the cup with his lips; now he asked for a second taste; I gave him a small quantity with a little water, but this he did not relish. The Cossack had prepared my bed of *voilock*, placed my pistols under my pillow, then covered me up in my fur, and made me snug for the night. Very soon all was still in the *yourt*, and I fast asleep.

We were on our way before the herds left the *aoul*, going to the north of our yesterday's track for a considerable distance among masses of rock projecting up above the steppe. They were not blocks that had rolled down from an elevated site: these stones were lying on their natural beds. I found several fine seams of quartz running in perfectly straight lines toward the mountains. After this the ground rose into mounds or small hills, with stony crests, each rising higher as we approached the foot of the abrupt mountains above us. We now turned to the south, riding along about a verst from the foot of the high rocks, and had not gone far when we came upon a large inclosure surrounded by a thick wall built of very large blocks, with smaller stones fitted in between them. This wall incloses a space of almost a verst in length and half a verst in width, extending up to the foot of some perpendicular rocks. It has been a work of great labor, and must have been built by a different race from the present, who look upon it with wonder. In some parts it is six feet high, in others a little less, and seven feet thick. None of the blocks have been cut.

We turned and rode up toward the mountain, and discovered a part of the wall not more than two feet above the ground. I leaped my horse over this, and was followed by the two Cossacks, but nothing could induce the Kirghis to enter this inclosure; they immediately turned back, and rode round the wall to the opposite side. Continuing our ride toward the upper end, I saw near the centre a great heap of stones, with a large cluster of pillars rising out of them. In the distance this had all the appearance of a ruin. On coming close up I dismounted, and climbed over the fallen blocks to the pillars, when I ascertained that they were basalt, forming a precipice toward the mountain of more than one hundred feet high. I visited some other large masses of rock, but observed no indication of building within these walls. After examining another mass of basalt, we rode toward the Kirghis, who were standing in front of a gateway in the south wall. It is probable that these walls were built to inclose the site for a temple, and that war, or some other cause, stopped the project before the foundations were laid—at least before the superstructure could be raised.

We rode on to the southwest, ascending a high ridge covered in parts with mossy turf; the other was bare rock. Having gained the summit, we had a very extensive view of the steppe stretching away forty or fifty versts toward another small chain rising abruptly from the plain. Riding for about an hour, we descended to the steppe on the western side of the Monastery Mountain, and then turned to the north. This was to be my sketching-ground to-day; nor was I long in finding a subject; and it so much resembled an old castle, that I rode up to it before I could believe it to be one of Nature's edifices.

Our ride was continued to some high ground running down into the steppe, when we came upon a splendid scene. In this region Dame Nature has evidently been in one of her most frolicsome moods, having assembled together a most singular variety of forms. On one side she has erected the ruins of a fine old Norman castle, jutting on to the steppe, as if to guard her other treasures. About three versts from this she has raised a pyramid of red and gray porphyry more than seven hundred feet high. In the distance are abrupt precipices rising from the plain, crowned by mountains and picturesque peaks. A brown grassy steppe extends around the pyramid, completely isolating it from all other large objects, giving full effect to the grandeur of its fine proportions, while numerous small mounds of red porphyry rise up near its base. At some distance from these is a small salt lake bordered with orange and crimson plants, forming a beautiful frame to the sparkling incrustations on its surface. The Cossacks and myself tried to ascend the pyramid both on the south and east sides, but discovered, after many efforts, that it was impossible. On the south side I succeeded in ascending about two thirds of the height, but found it a far more difficult task to descend.

We then went to the west side, which is more abrupt, and continued our ride to the north: this side appears less difficult; still, I doubt if it would be possible to accomplish the ascent without the aid of a strong line. On the south and west there is scarcely a blade of grass growing; on the north and east there is a little vegetation in the clefts. About six versts from here there was an enormous gap or cleft in the mountain, toward which we bent our course. Riding along the steppe near the high precipices, I could not help remarking how much they resembled the cliffs near a sea-shore. The fallen rocks and gravel only required the sea-weed to give this place the appearance of a sea-beach at low water. As we rode on we passed headlands and small bays, some running deep into the high ridge over which we had ridden in the morning. We had now reached some very high precipices, immediately beyond which I expected to gain access to the great cleft, but ascertained that there was no possibility of approaching the place from here, not even on foot, as the cliffs rose up almost perpendicular nearly two hundred feet.

Our horses were put into a gallop, in the hope of finding a ravine or some other place by which we could reach the top. After riding a short distance I stopped and made another sketch of this curious region, during which time the Kirghis and Cossacks were holding a council as to our farther progress. When I had completed the view, and was preparing to proceed onward, the Cossacks said, "*Seevodny nilza*" (To-day it is impossible); I was informed that the country beyond this place had a bad reputation, and that, should we continue our journey in this direction, it would be dark before we could find a pass by which to cross the Monastery Mountains. Our only plan was to return and try to cross the western end of the ridge; if this could be done, we might reach the *aoul* in three hours; if not, it would take us five. The horses were good and fresh, we had not ridden them hard, and they had rested every time I sketched. It was now four o'clock, the evening would soon be drawing in, and no time was to be lost. We therefore rode along the steppe quickly, and one of the Kirghis guided us toward a cove running into the mountains, bounded by very high cliffs. I could see no means of escape from this place; still he rode on, followed by our little party, and after going about two versts, turned past some high rocks, and found ourselves at the mouth of a very rugged ravine.

Our guide dismounted, and we all followed his example, when he took the reins of my bridle and began to ascend, leading the two horses after him. I pushed on in front, and soon discovered that the path was not easy for a biped, much less for a quadruped. None but Kirghis horses would have faced this broken and rugred track, and no horse could have descended. We mounted slowly, and at last reached the top without accident. I was much afraid some of the horses might slip and break their legs between the rocks. We let them breathe about ten minutes and then sprang into our saddles, and away we went over a thick mossy grass growing on the mountain slope. In less than half an hour we came upon our track of the morning; then, for about three versts, we had to descend over loose stones, and this rendered our progress slow. Night was coming on fast when we reached the steppe; but here we had good ground to ride over, and our horses were not spared, to the great joy of one of our Kirghis, who flourished his whip and shouted with delight as we bounded over the plain.

It was quite dark before we reached the *aoul*, where camels, horses, and all the stock were at home resting. When the rum-bottle was brought out I could see the twinkle in the old man's eye. Again I handed him some in the cup, which I felt sure would be rejected—I was right—it passed to less scrupulous lips; but the moment the sons and other Kirghis left the *yourt*, he made signs to me for his portion. The first cup was not enough; it was drunk, and immediately held out for a second. Fancying this might lead to mischief, I took a piece of stearine candle out of my box, lighted it, and put it beside me. I then poured a small quantity of rum into the cup, leaving it standing on my tea-box, which I had placed before him. He looked into the cup and was greatly dissatisfied with the quantity, asking for more; I poured a little into a teaspoon, and held it over the candle without letting him see what I was doing. When the spirit caught fire I took the cup, poured the burning fluid into the rum, and placed it before him. As the blue flames curled up he looked perfectly aghast, muttering something about Shaitan. After the flame had burnt out I offered him another cup, but nothing could induce him to touch it, even with his finger. I spent two more nights at this *aoul* without even having induced him to taste rum in tea.

About two o'clock in the morning the whole *aoul* became a scene of intense alarm and confusion. When lying on the ground every thing is more distinctly heard than when sleeping even a little above it, and I was awoke by a great noise, which appeared to come from some subterranean cavern. At first I thought it was the rumbling of an earthquake, and instantly sat upright; the sound rolled on, approaching nearer and nearer; presently it passed, and the earth shook: it was the whole herd of horses dashing past at full gallop. Now came shrieks and the shouting of men, from which I at once knew that robbers had invaded the *aoul*. It was but the work of a moment to seize the rifle standing close to my head and rush out of the *yourt*, when I beheld the Kirghis, with their battle-axes in their hands, spring upon their horses, and dash off toward the place where we heard the shouting. The herds were galloping furiously round the *aoul*, and the Cossacks were out with their muskets in their hands; in short, it was a scene of terrible confusion. Old Mahomed was shouting with all his might; the women and children were shrieking and running from *yourt* to *yourt;* nor could we see what was going on in the distance. Presently we heard the sound of horses galloping toward us, but whether friends or foes we knew not; in less than two minutes a dark mass rushed past at full gallop, about twenty paces distant, yelling forth shouts of defiance. I could distinguish for an instant the heads of men through the gloom, and the women shrieked out "the robbers;" in a moment five balls whistled after them; there was a scream from a horse, but we could hear that they galloped on. Presently our Kirghis went past in pursuit, by which time two Cossacks were mounted, and off also.

There were not less than twenty men on the track of these robbers, who were somewhat encumbered by the horses they had caught, and others they were driving off. After riding about a

NIGHT ATTACK ON THE AOUL OF MAHOMED.

verst the Kirghis came up to them, when they discovered that the banditti were three times their number, and prepared to defend their booty. Our friends were now obliged to beat a retreat, having no chance against such odds. It was our arms that frightened these villains, or they would no doubt have returned, and made another attack on the *aoul.* I deeply regretted it was not daylight; had it been so, some of these desperate fellows would have bit the dust, as they passed in one thick mass within pistol-shot, and the rifles would have brought them down at a long distance. There was no more sleeping after this; all were on the alert, and the women and children much frightened. It was supposed that the rascals had got more than a hundred horses; but at daylight several were observed feeding on the steppe, six or seven versts distant, which had escaped in the dark, or when the Kirghis rode up. Two of the tribe were sent to seek for any other animals that might have been left, and in about two hours returned, bringing back seventeen: the robbers had got off with a hundred.

The dogs and a boy on watch first detected them: a party had got among, and were trying to divide the herd, intending to kill the watchmen, and then sweep off a vast number in the confusion which would ensue. This band of villains had undoubtedly been lurking among some of the mountains to the west—most probably had been watching our movements when sketching the day before. We had not been near enough for them to seize us, and if they had failed in the attempt it would have put Mahomed on his guard. It was quite certain that they had driven their plunder off in this direction.

Notwithstanding this affair, I was still determined to follow up my researches after the curious and picturesque in nature, which I expected to find in the region beyond my ride of yesterday, and three Cossacks and two Kirghis accompanied me. Our arms had been examined to see that all was right. My pistols were not carried in the holsters to-day; I had them in my belt; not that there was any fear of our coming up with the large band who had visited us in the night; they would be far away with the horses; but it was thought that we might meet with a gang of ten or fifteen remaining behind to pick up any horses that had escaped or were left; also to watch the movements of any party attempting a pursuit, and lead them off the track.

We left the *aoul* about eight o'clock, taking our course in a straight line toward the point in the mountain we had crossed last night: this would shorten our ride materially. As we rode on, the Kirghis pointed out the route the robbers had taken, and after we had passed the most distant point where the horses feed, we had no difficulty in tracing the bandit track by the many indications left on the steppe. Having reached the mountain, one of the Kirghis said he could guide us to the great chasm I had tried to reach yesterday, and afterward take us down to the steppe. We turned toward the north, along the slope of the western side of the mountain, and rode some two versts or more, when our leader turned up a very abrupt part, to avoid a deep ravine it was impossible to cross. We were soon among large blocks of granite, tumbled about and lying in extraordinary confusion. A little farther on we came upon pillars of basalt, forced up in curves to a great height, and other rocks with horizontal strata butting against them.

A little beyond this place our track was along the side of a mountain of bare rock, so fearfully steep that the guide, dismounting, led his horse along, and we all followed his example. A stumble would have been fatal to man and horse; nothing could have saved either; both must have been torn to pieces by rolling over the granite surface. There were about five hundred paces of this fearful path to pass over. After this we reached a part less steep, up which we ascended in an oblique direction, and gained the summit. We crossed the ridge, and found the opposite side, also very steep, scooped out like an enormous crescent. Down this we began to descend in a zigzag direction, but even here had to use great care. In rather less than half an hour we accomplished this last dangerous descent, and stood at the foot of the mighty chasm—a mountain rent asunder by some terrific power. I sat down and sketched this wonderful scene, with its gigantic pillars of basalt.

From this place we descended toward the cliffs, and as we rode along had a splendid view over the steppe toward the northwest, which was uninterrupted for fifty or sixty versts. Small steppes were seen running in among the hills, but in no part could we see any signs of the robbers with their booty. They were most probably concealed in some of the narrow steppes until evening, when they would continue their march, or perhaps try their fortune at some other *aoul.* Our ride was parallel with the cliffs for more than three versts to the ravine, down which the Kirghis intended to guide us to the steppe. When we reached the place it was found impossible to descend. We stood on the top of a precipice nearly perpendicular; in some places it was even overhanging, and not less than five hundred feet high; there was a complete barrier; still the Kirghis persisted in saying we could get down. He turned his horse and rode toward the mountains, while I examined the wonderful scene beneath, with the brown steppe and purple mountains in the distance. For a few weeks in the spring these steppes are covered with rich grass, and a great variety of flowers; large herds of horses, camels, oxen, and sheep are then feeding and wandering over what now appears a solitary waste, as no living thing, save our little party, could be seen. It was not long before our Kirghis gave a shout; we rode up to him, and found the track by which we must descend into the fearful abyss. Looking down, it appeared impossible to descend, unless the men and horses were to hang on the rocks like flies. We dismounted, when it was agreed between the Kirghis and the Cossacks that the horses should remain above until we had proved if it were possible to take them down. Our guide, two Cossacks, and myself walked over the brink, the Kirghis leading the way down the bare rocks, which we found very difficult to scramble over in several places. At length we reached the bottom of the ravine, when the Kirghis immediately ascended to aid in bringing down the horses. In the mean time I proceeded up the ravine, and at a short distance discovered a warm spring bubbling up in a small rocky basin, the water flowing over, and running a short distance, when it was lost again among the masses of fallen rocks.

A little farther up I found a large vein of rose quartz, seven inches thick; it was of a beautiful color, some of it quite transparent, showing splendid prismatic tints when held in the sun. Without proper implements it was impossible to obtain a large solid piece; the specimens I gathered contained many fractures. Having spent nearly an hour examining the rocks, in some I observed small greenish crystals of olivine, none of which I could procure. By this time the horses had accomplished their hazardous descent, yet we had still some risks to run before reaching the steppe, as the bottom of the ravine was covered in many parts with fallen blocks, rendering our progress very slow. More than an hour was occupied in descending this rugged path, although not a verst in length. About two hundred yards before reaching the steppe we found positive proof that some persons had been attempting to ascend by this ravine not many hours before. They had returned back to the steppe, and continued their ride toward the south, most likely to the ravine by which we ascended last night. Our Kirghis said there were eight or nine in this party, and that probably there were some others among the hills not far away; had they gone up the ravine, we should undoubtedly have met somewhere among these rugged rocks, greatly to the astonishment of both parties.

We now rode off toward the north, intending to go to "Kessil-tas," or red stone, near the northern end of these high and rugged peaks. Our route was across the steppe, over which we rode for about three hours without finding any thing interesting, and then began to ascend a low ridge, which led us to the object of my search—"Kessil-tas." I had seen this from a long distance, and could not account for its brilliant red color. It is a mount of red and brown porphyry, with white veins and blotches, most beautifully varied in color, and rises high above a steppe, which has once been a large lake. At present there is an extensive sheet of water near the centre of this plain, and the part which forms the present steppe is little above the level of the water.

Having sketched these singular and beautifully-colored rocks, it was time to think of returning toward our home, as we had a long ride before us, part of it over a hilly country, and then across a fine level steppe. While I had been engaged sketching, a great change had taken place in the weather, and a cold wind was blowing, coming sometimes in sudden gusts. Clouds had long been gathering over the summits of the Altai, and now the chain and some of the nearer ridges were quite obscured. The Kirghis said we should soon have a storm, and proposed riding fast to the *aoul*. In rather more than an hour we had crossed the hills and were riding over the steppe, when the gusts became more frequent and stronger—a sure sign of an approaching tempest. We all cast looks of suspicion toward the Altai, and then observed that all the lower ridges rising from the steppe were obscured, while a dense mass of black clouds, extending a long distance from north to south, was rolling on toward us. We then looked wistfully toward the *aoul.* The Mantilla Rocks could be seen, but they were more than a three hours' ride away, and the storm was coming fast over the steppe. I called a halt, secured my pistols in their holsters, and had the rifle and gun put into their leathern cases—a drenching being inevitable, and there was not a tree or a rock under which we could receive the slightest shelter. We pushed on at a good speed, fearing what we saw, and knowing that night was fast approaching. The gusts of wind ceased, and for a short time it was a perfect calm. Looking toward the black mass, I saw that the clouds were in great commotion, while streams of vapor were rising out of the dark body and whirling rapidly round. Presently we heard a low murmuring sound, which gradually increased into a roar as the storm came over the steppe; our horses appeared to be greatly alarmed. In a few minutes we saw the grass and some low bushes twisted, torn up a few hundred paces in front of us, and whirled up into the air with fearful rapidity. The horses stopped suddenly; then we heard a rushing sound as the whirlwind passed. Fortunately for us, we escaped being caught in its terrible vortex. Presently the gust came again with redoubled fury; then rain and sleet, which almost blinded us. It was now nearly dark, which would shortly render it extremely difficult to find our way.

Already the Kirghis differed in opinion with regard to the right track. The Monastery Mountains and Mantilla Rocks were completely obscured, and we had no landmark to guide us. Still I felt convinced that we had kept too much to the west; perhaps the storm blowing with so much fury from the east had driven our horses out of the direct route. Every drop of rain, and the great flakes which struck us, seemed immediately to penetrate to the skin, and already we were as wet as if rising out of a river. At last our two Kirghis came to a dead stand, being at a loss which way to take. Although I had not taken the bearings of the Mantilla Rocks, I knew perfectly well by the compass that we ought to turn toward the east. Therefore, without farther consultation, I turned my horse in this direction, and rode on. We were now facing the storm, which made our position worse, and I had some trouble in keeping my horse to the proper point of the compass. No doubt it seems a strange idea to speak of riding one's horse to the different points of the compass; but those who travel on the great steppes of Central Asia will soon discover the advantage of remarking the bearings of different objects, with the view of finding a route either in the day or night. More than an hour had elapsed since I had taken the direction of our course. I knew that we had gone considerably to the east, and ought now to be at no great distance from the Mantilla Rocks; but nothing could be seen even looming in the distance. Our position had become critical; indeed, to remain all night on the steppe, exposed to such a storm, would be our destruction. We listened for the barking of a dog or the bellowing of a bull, but nothing could be heard except the roaring of the blast, and the plashing of the rain as the big drops struck us.

A Group of Mahomed's Kirghis.

After riding slowly a short distance farther, hoping to hear something that would guide us, one of the Kirghis recognized some rocks, by which he at once knew our position, and also the proper direction. He now led the way almost due east, and directly toward the storm, saying the *aoul* was not far away. We had not ridden long before we came upon a group of camels, and saw the light through the doorway of one of the *yourts*. Our horses were quite tired out, and we were almost done up; our joy, therefore, was indeed great when we dismounted at the doors of these *voilock* dwellings. Mahomed and the Cossack had begun to feel serious apprehensions for our safety. The *yourt* was cleared of its inmates in a few minutes while a dry shirt was put on, over which I wrapped my fur cloak, tied round the waist with a scarf. I pulled on a pair of dry boots, and then sat down to my tea; but, before drinking it, I gave a glass of rum to each of the men who had been my companions. Even the poor Kirghis drank it without showing any of the quackery the old chief had displayed.

The kind old man returned to his *yourt*, ordered in fuel, and a man to keep up a blazing fire. My clothing was hung up to dry. The Cossack examined, wiped, and dried the arms, and placed them secure from any chance drop which might find its way through the *voilock* on such a night. The wind was blowing a tremendous gale, and men and women were busy securing the *yourts* with ropes and poles. Notwithstanding the smoke was puffed about, and sleet driven in, I was snugly wrapped in my fur, and felt truly thankful for the shelter and comfort found in a Kirghis *yourt*. No robbers would disturb us on such a night; indeed, the howling of the storm was so fearful, I expected to see the *yourt* carried away. So long as the man kept up a blazing fire I listened to the roar. At last the old chief ordered the top of the *yourt* to be closed and secured for the night. After this, I was soon numbered among the sleeping.

CHAPTER XVIII.

RAMBLES AMONG THE KIRGHIS.

THE weather this morning was cold, wet, and windy, with clouds rolling over the mountain tops, making every thing look gloomy and miserable. I intended to leave my friend Mahomed this morning early, but the rain detained us. He assured me that after midday we should have fine weather, and was perfectly right: before twelve o'clock the fog and clouds cleared off, and the sun burst forth in all his splendor, giving the whole steppe a warm autumnal appearance. I said adieu to my host and his family, mounted my horse, and left with my escort and three Kirghis, whom the old chief had sent to conduct me to the next *aoul*. It was not known with any degree of certainty where we should meet with one, the Kirghis being so erratic in their movements, and seldom remaining more than eight or ten days on the same spot.

We expected to find the encampment at the foot of one of the small chains, about six hours' ride from my recent sojourn. Soon after twelve o'clock we were on our way, riding in a southeasterly direction, the Kirghis pointing toward a very distant mountain, and saying that the *aoul* was there. Our route was over a steppe, extending fifty or sixty versts, apparently unbroken either by elevations or depressions; there was nothing to relieve the monotony of this journey; hour after hour was traveled, and still we had the same scene around us. In about five hours we began to look out for the encampment, but nothing was to be seen. Nearly another hour had passed, when I saw a large herd of horses to the east; we turned toward them, and rode on for some time, when we met a Kirghis herdsman, who was driving his flocks home, and he pointed out the *aoul*, lying between two hills six or seven versts distant.

A Cossack and a Kirghis were sent on to announce our arrival, while we followed more leisurely and examined the country, which, as I observed, was broken into numerous low ridges, gradually rising toward the Altai. To the south the granite appears again, crowning the hills like old castles. We had arrived within a verst of our destination, when three Kirghis met us, and conducted me to a *yourt* prepared for my quarters, another close at hand being set apart for the Cossacks, and here we slept.

This *aoul* belongs to a wealthy Kirghis, who was at this time on a visit at another of his encampments about fifty versts distant to the southward, into which region this would be moved in the course of three days. It was a cold and raw morning, with heavy clouds hanging over the hills. Having still to cross part of the Altai on my way into Siberia, I did not deem it prudent to remain longer in the steppe. The Kirghis stated that there was another *aoul* eight or ten hours' ride distant to the northward, which would move away in a day or two; and as it would be on our way back to Oust-Kamenogorsk, it was determined that we should sleep there. This encampment had also been visited by the banditti, when seventy horses and five camels had been carried off the night before they had waited upon Mahomed.

A small band had been seen in the hills to the north by one of the herdsmen yesterday afternoon, which induced him to drive the horses homeward, and these people thought that we should most probably fall in with them. Possibly they wished it, and hoped that we should diminish their number, as they were keeping them in constant alarm. Our guides led us along the low hills for several hours, when we descended to the steppe, over which we rode for several hours. At last we reached a granite ridge, with many picturesque groups on the summit, but the day was too far gone to attempt sketching them. From the summit the Kirghis expected to see the *aoul*, but it was nowhere visible on the steppe; they then thought it might be among the hills, and wished us to ride fast, or we should have great difficulty in finding it after dark. As no one of us was desirous of spending a night on these hills without food or shelter, no farther arguments were required, nor did we spare the horses. Hill after hill had been passed, and still there was no sign of animal life. The Kirghis seemed greatly perplexed, and thought the encampment had been moved—a pleasant prospect for us, with a stormy night in store! We had already ridden more than seven hours, but onward we must go at all risks. Perhaps, from the summit of the next hill, we might see something to guide us to the remaining *yourts*, although the greater part of the *aoul* might be gone. We had not yet gained the summit when one of the Kirghis pointed to a herd of horses returning toward the encampment, which we were now certain could not be far off, and in the direction we were riding.

The man put his horse into a gallop, and presently reached the ridge, when we knew, by the signs he made, that there was a home for us in the valley. In less than half an hour we rode into the encampment, to the great astonishment of all there. The owner of this *aoul* was absent; still, the sheep was killed and the feast made, much to the satisfaction of both Kirghis and Cossacks. We had not been long in the *yourt* when the rain and sleet came down so thick that we could not see any object at ten paces off. A large quantity of small brushwood was brought in, and this time my fire was attended to by two women, as none of the men, most probably, could be induced to leave the smoking platters of mutton. I knew well that little, if any, would be left, and therefore determined that the women should also have a repast. The *somervar* was still boiling; I made tea, and gave them loaf-sugar and bread, when their countenances betrayed signs of genuine astonishment and pleasure. The first tumbler of tea being drunk, I handed them a second and a third, to their great delight. My fire was kept in a constant blaze, and the top of the *yourt* several times changed, to prevent the smoke remaining inside. By their excellent management it was kept free of this annoyance, notwithstanding that it was a terrible night.

As I sat writing up my journal, my companions were much interested, as no man among their tribes, excepting the Mulla, could either read or write. The book was a wonder to them, and they looked upon me as a very wealthy Mulla, being possessed of what they considered a large book full of amulets. The Mulla sells his amulets to them at a sheep for each scrap of paper, with a few characters traced upon it. My ring was examined, my knife also, and a piece of red sealing-wax made a wonderful effect. I got out a candle, made a seal on a piece of thick paper from my sketch-book, and presented it to one of them. When I put the wax away without making a second seal, the other woman looked quite miserable; observing her disappointment, I produced another seal, and she was happy. These will, I have no doubt, adorn their caps, and create a feeling of envy in the breast of many a Kirghis damsel. The opposite plate represents a group of Kirghis, with two brides in their marriage costume; the musician was the chief of a band of robbers.

When the feast was ended, several of both sexes came into the *yourt*, and sat round watching every thing I did. As I noticed that they were observing me wind up my watch, I held it to the ear of a woman sitting near; she evidently thought it was alive and talking, for she told her companion so, and they all wished to hear it speak. A Kirghis *yourt* is not the place in which any person would wish to keep late hours, and more particularly on such a night as this. So long as a fire is burning, the aperture at the

A GROUP OF KIRGHIS, WITH TWO BRIDES.

top of the *yourt* must be open to let out the smoke; at the same time, it lets the snow, wind, and rain in, which render the place any thing but comfortable. The Cossacks sent all our visitors to their own dwellings, and ordered the top to be secured; this made a wonderful difference; the apartment became snug and warm, feeling all the more so as we lay listening to the howling of the wind and the pattering of the rain against the *voilock*. In time, this music lulled me to sleep, from which nothing disturbed me until daylight the next morning; soon afterward I was again on my travels.

I had three Kirghis, and this time five spare horses, to enable us to change and ride fast. It was a cold, windy morning, with dark, murky clouds blowing across the sky, decidedly intimating that the day would be squally. Soon after leaving the *yourts* we descended toward the steppe, each of us, as we rode slowly down the hill, casting a suspicious glance at the black masses of vapor hanging over and covering the higher peaks of the Altai, these clouds looking blacker and more terrible by contrast with the pure white of the snow beneath. In less than an hour we were riding rapidly over what might almost be called a sea of dry grass. Track there was not; but our route was toward the northeast, and we were now leaving the hills and entering upon the vast plain. This is a most uninteresting season for a ride across these steppes, for the grass has all been eaten up, and the dwarf bushes cropped and spoiled of their foliage; there were no flowers, the sharp frosts having cut down leaves and blossoms.

Having ridden somewhat more than two hours, our horses were changed; we were thus able to keep up the speed, and give the other horses a rest: this mode is often adopted by the Kirghis when going a long journey. As the day advanced the wind became still more cold and piercing, with occasional snow-storms, giving to the country a most gloomy aspect. While riding along, one of the Kirghis pointed out five wolves not more than a verst from us, making their way along the steppe toward the south. The winter had driven them from the mountains; they were evidently out on a foraging excursion, and woe betide the poor horse they should fall in with, as they would run him down without a chance of escape. I have been told of the great cunning they display in the chase: if there be a morass near, they keep on the opposite side of their victim, heading him a little, and gradually forcing him toward it, till at length they drive him on to the soft and treacherous ground, when the first stumble or flounder he makes is his certain doom.

We had passed several little brooks that were much swollen by the rain in the mountains, and had come upon one twenty-five or thirty yards wide, running in a deep channel cut through the sand and gravel. It was difficult to find a practicable descent to the water, but at last we succeeded; still, we had to ride some distance up the stream, which was not deep, to a place on the opposite side, where there seemed a possibility of ascending the bank. A Kirghis led, I followed; but the moment my horse had got his hind feet out of the stream, the bank gave way, and plunged me into the water nearly overhead: this and his floundering splashed the water over me so much that I was completely saturated on a cold and wintry day in October, and that without a rag of dry clothing to put on, or any place in which to take shelter. The Cossacks instantly examined my rifle and pistols: they were found dry; the leathern case had protected one, and the holsters the other. My long shooting-boots were drawn off and the water poured out, but it was with great difficulty they were got on again. While this was being done the rum bottle was produced; fortunately, there was about half a tumbler of rum in it, a liberal portion of which I swallowed. We then mounted our horses and rode on fast, and this kept my blood in circulation.

For my especial consolation, one of the Cossacks said it would take us six or seven hours to ride to the Irtisch: there was no help for it, as our only chance was to push on for that river as fast as possible. After riding about four hours, we reached the foot of the hills which separated us from the valley in which the river runs. These were too abrupt for a rapid ride, therefore we ascended slowly; and now I began to feel the effects of my wetting. It had become dusk some time before we reached the top of the ridge; as we crossed it night fairly set in, and it became quite dark from the black clouds which were rolling rapidly over the sky. Presently we had sudden gusts of wind, which soon became a gale. Our descent in the dark was also slow, and as yet we had not seen a light at Oust-Kamenogorsk. However, the mystery was very soon solved: we were enveloped in a snow-storm so thick that we could see but a very short distance. Before we reached the plain the storm had passed, but the wind was terrific.

The Cossacks said that no person could cross the Irtisch on such a night; they therefore proposed seeking an *aoul*, which they knew was only a few versts distant along the foot of the mountain. We therefore rode on at a sharp trot, and were shortly greeted by the dogs. I believe we one and all thought these sounds had something celestial in them, as they were borne softly on the wind, apparently inviting us to shelter. We were not long in reaching the *yourts*, into several of which the Cossack went before I dismounted. At length my horse was led to the side of a large one, when I found it difficult to get off and enter. This place we found warm and comfortable. My wet clothing was at once stripped off, and I was wrapped in a fur; a good fire was kept up, and tea made, of which I drank a great quantity; but long before morning I felt that I was doomed for a spell of fever. As soon as it was daylight a man had been sent to call for the boats. We followed, but I could not mount my horse without assistance. The men placed me in the boat, and rowed over as quickly as possible, when I was conveyed to my kind friends, who sent instantly for the doctor, and again I passed through the ordeal of a Russian bath and bleeding.

On the eleventh day I was moving about again, and improving rapidly. During my illness there had been much rain in the valleys; on the mountains there had been snow, which I could see from my windows: no pleasant prospect, as I must cross those elevations before I could reach my winter quarters. The baron and his wife did every thing they could to improve my health, and if eating and drinking could have done it, they would soon have made me well and strong. They had accepted an invitation to a ball for me, and would take no excuse, as the doctor had given his consent to my going—to look on, but not to take a part in it. In Oust-Kamenogorsk they have not yet learned to keep late hours, for at seven o'clock all were assembled. The ball was given by a merchant, and the whole society of this little town mustered to do him honor. There were about fifty persons present, perhaps three or four more ladies than gentlemen; some gayly dressed in Chinese silks, splendid in color, although I can not say much for the taste in the selection. When standing together they looked like a bed of tulips. There was one lady sixty years old, who was dressed like a young girl of twenty. Her head was bedecked on one side with white cut-glass beads, on the other with green glass drops, most probably intended for chandeliers. On her neck she wore a chain, with a large square brooch suspended from it, also of green glass. She had bracelets on her arms studded with yellow glass, and round her waist a girdle with the same material. With her pink dress, gray gloves, yellow shoes, and decorations, she was one of the most curiously costumed ladies I ever met. She was the wife of the stadt-doctor—apparently a very respectable man, wearing several decorations, and has on more than one occasion entered the church, wearing his orders, on the greatest fêtes of the emperor, when every officer is obliged to attend in full uniform. Her fame has extended far. I once happened to speak in a society of persons, at least two thousand versts away from her abode, of her curious costume, when an officer present recognized the original. I asked if he knew the lady, and he exclaimed, "Not know her! Why, I should sooner think of going to Rome and return without seeing the Pope, than go to Oust-Kamenogorsk without making the acquaintance of Marie Ivanovna!"

Shortly after our arrival I remarked that the ladies took possession of one room, sitting round it without speaking a word. This was a most extraordinary scene—a social phenomenon never heard of. I mentioned it to my friend, and inquired if it was usual; he replied, "No, not when at home, as their husbands can testify." These gentlemen were in another room, preparing for the dance by frequent application either to wine or Siberian *nalifka*: *they* were noisy enough. The music struck up, when a lady and gentleman came forward and danced a Russian dance beautifully, representing the caprice of two lovers. After this came a quadrille, and then *Marie Ivanovna* and a Cossack officer performed a Cossack dance, in which both were inimitable. There are, indeed, few young girls who could in this accomplishment have excelled this old lady of sixty; I have never seen her equal. The ball continued; many persons danced well, but not one could make any approach to Marie Ivanovna. The evening ended with an excellent supper, in which our hostess displayed unbounded hospitality. Here was no stiffness or ceremony; the company had met together to enjoy themselves, and all appeared quite happy.

A few nights after, the baroness received all the good people at her house, dancing as usual a number of national and Cossack dances, and beautiful they were. We had the choir from the church, who sang many very fine Russian songs and choruses with great effect. The Cossack band had played some good music during the evening; after supper the commandant ordered them into the entrance-hall, when they sang some of their songs. More wild music I never heard. He led them, and sang well, giving great force and effect to their national music. Among the Cossacks, the officers and even the colonel will join the men in their songs. Their music is singularly effective, particularly while sitting round a camp-fire in a wild country.

It was not till after dinner that I was allowed to depart, and left in a light carriage with four horses, driven by a Cossack. Although snow had fallen, the roads were still soft, and it was easy to see that we were about to have a terrible journey. About four versts from Oust-Kamenogorsk, on a long wooden bridge, I crossed the River Ouba, which here is a large and rapid stream. I had been over it before on my way to Riddersk, where it was a small brook. A short distance from the bridge there is a fine view of the Cholsoun chain, which was now sparkling like a ruby under the setting sun. As we proceeded, the horses began to show symptoms of distress, frequently coming to a dead stand, and the road, for several stations, was horrible and uninteresting. I shall not soon forget the road between Praporschika and Krasnoiarska, a distance of about seventy-five versts. On descending the hill toward the latter village a splendid view opens, looking over the River Irtisch into the Kirghis Steppe. The river at this point is divided by small islands into several channels, in which it runs winding about on the plain; and far away in the distance a small and very picturesque mountain chain rises abruptly from the steppe.

Hitherto the road has been along the east bank of the Irtisch, over low hills, probably three and four hundred feet above the river, affording extensive views over the vast steppe to the south and westward. From this point my track leaves the Irtisch, and runs eastward, skirting the Altai chain. As we descended into the valley of the River Ouba the scenery became highly interesting, and from one point, a short distance from the village of Widricka, I sketched a beautiful view. The river winds up a narrow valley between high mountains, in some places running at the foot of lofty precipices, whence it enters a broad valley extending down to the Irtisch fifty or sixty versts to the westward.

We changed horses at Widricka, where the people strongly urged me to remain the night, on account of the bad roads, which would soon be rendered still more difficult by the snow-storm they saw approaching from the mountains.

When we reached the valley the men put on all their speed, and the wind and snow became fearful. It was dark before we reached the ferry. Here was another difficulty: with such a wind, the ferrymen declared it was impossible to cross.

Thus we appeared to be doomed to sit on the Ouba, perhaps more impatient than the spirits on another famed river; but our ferrymen were more amiable than Charon, for they kindly invited me to sleep in their *yourt* near a good fire. Just at this time a number of peasants came up, also wishing to cross. I desired the Cossack to say that I would give them some money if they would aid in taking us over the river. There was a consultation for some minutes among the whole party of ferrymen and peasants, and at length they decided upon running the risk of being drowned for two rubles, I taking my chance along with them. They set about it at once, and began hauling the ferry-boat up the stream far beyond the usual place for starting, to counteract the force of the wind, which would otherwise carry us past the point where we ought to land, and then we should be taken far away down the stream. Much argument was used among them; at last they reached a point, supposed to be far enough above the ferry, and pushed off into the stream. For two or three minutes we were sheltered under the bank; but, having got a little distance into the river, the wind caught us, the horses and carriage acted as a sail, and we were taken down the stream at a great speed. The men pulled and shouted loud enough to silence any ordinary hurricane; unfortunately, the one coming was of a stern and obstinate character, which would neither be frightened nor appeased. Down it drove us with all its malignant fury. When within about thirty yards of the landing-place, we all pulled, straining every nerve. To the great joy of all, we succeeded, but it took us more than an hour to cross. It was only a short distance to the station, and farther we could not proceed in the night.

The road turns off into the hills immediately on leaving this station, when we began a steep and long ascent. There was a strong cold wind blowing, and a little snow falling, and again the road was over rounded hills, without any remarkable scenery. This part of the country was better cultivated than any other region I had yet seen in the Altai. There are extensive tracts of corn-land here, from which very abundant crops are obtained. I saw hundreds of acres with the corn-shocks still standing and covered with snow. In some places they were taking the sheaves to the threshing-floor, where great numbers of the peasants were occupied threshing out the corn; others were dressing it: an operation best performed by a strong wind, and this was a splendid day for it. Men are constantly employed bringing the corn and chaff from the threshing-floor, which they throw upon one heap. On each side of this a man stands, having a small wooden shovel with a long handle; with these implements they throw up in moderately quick succession a small quantity to the height of twelve to fifteen feet, when the wind blows the chaff, sand, and seeds away, and the good grain falls on one heap. Even by this rude process the grain is moderately well cleaned. Although it was snowing fast, this did not interfere with their operations, which are all done in the open air.

On reaching the summit of one of these hills, I observed three wolves standing about five hundred paces from the road. I stepped out of the carriage, hoping to get a shot; but, before I was near enough to make sure of any one of them, they went off with a long swinging pace. A ball which I sent after them struck near one, who made a spring in advance of the others, when they all galloped away. Soon after we descended into a very broad valley, in which rise some remarkable rocks. When we reached the station, a man was pointed out to me said to be a hundred and two years old. He was in perfect health, possessed all his faculties, and had walked a considerable distance just before I saw him.

After leaving the station we shortly arrived at a far more interesting part of the road, which affords several beautiful views of the mountains about Riddersk, the Cholsoun chain, and the country near the Bouchtarma River. Cold as it was, I made a sketch, and regretted I had not time to make more. A few versts beyond the point whence this was taken, we made our last change of horses before reaching Zmeinogorsk. From this station the road continued to ascend over several high ridges destitute of wood. Altogether it was a very bleak country, rendered tenfold more so by the cold cutting wind and the snow driving in our face, my thermometer showing 15° Reaumur of frost. As we ascended higher the weather became much worse, and we met a tremendous wind, with small snow, which found its way through our clothing with extraordinary facility. Bad as this storm was, the drivers went on at a good speed, over a hard frozen road that gave us a terrible shaking, notwithstanding which they galloped down the hills at full speed.

Just at dark we arrived at Zmeinogorsk; in a few minutes I was installed in my comfortable room at the house of the director, who gave me a most cheering welcome. "You have had a taste of a 'Siberian *bouran*,'" he observed. I candidly owned the flavor was far from agreeable, and that I had no desire to dine upon it: my eyes, mouth, and ears had been filled with snow. He also thought it would be much worse through the night, and most probably prevent me continuing my journey to Barnaoul. Even now I could not cross the hills with the carriage, which accounted for the speed and anxiety of the drivers to reach the Zavod. I inquired if they would attempt to return during the *bouran*, and was told it was impossible; both men and horses would perish before they had proceeded one quarter of the distance.

I spent a very agreeable evening with my friend and his amiable wife, giving them a short account of my journey among the Kirghis, and hearing from them several anecdotes of these fearful storms. I mentioned the two claps of thunder I had heard yesterday, and was assured that such was not a rare occurrence, as it not unfrequently happens when the weather breaks up. As the director had anticipated, the *bouran* increased in its fury during the evening, making the window-shutters and doors rattle, and the house shake. No Zavod in the Altai is so exposed to the effects of these terrible storms as Zmeinogorsk, as it stands on very high ground, overlooking the vast steppe to the westward, from which point of the compass the great storms usually blow. They are also as sudden as they are furious, which often causes loss of life. My friend mentioned a circumstance that occurred to himself a few years ago. The church is erected on a wide open space on the summit of a hill; on one side stands the house of the director, and almost directly opposite are the dwellings of several officers. In front there is an open space extending three or four hundred yards to some buildings connected with the silver mines. From one corner of this a street extends for more than a verst toward the smelting-works in the valley, and at the east end of the church there is a large space, in which a market is held every Sunday morning, when the peasants from the villages bring in their produce for sale.

The distance from the door of the director's house to the door of the church does not exceed one hundred and fifty paces. One fine Sunday morning my friend went to the church, and remained during the service, which is usually over in less than two hours. While the congregation were solemnly engaged in their religious duties, some foul fiend in the storm department was not less actively occupied in blowing up a *bouran*, in which piece of mischief he was pre-eminently successful, for when the congregation left the church, they were met at the entrance by this terrible blast, with its clouds of snow almost as fine as flour. From the church gate my friend turned to the left direct for his own house, when he was whirled around, blinded, and twisted about to such a degree that he could not even find the building, which is not a small one. At last, after being blown by the wind first in one direction, then in another, he was driven up against a cottage, and succeeded in finding the door. On entering, he discovered that he had wandered nearly a verst from his home, but was compelled to remain till the wind moderated. This, I was told, was no uncommon event.

In the account of my journey down the Irtisch I have spoken of the Cossack pickets, and a road which runs along the frontier. This is traveled by the officers and men both in summer and winter, and my friend has frequently to visit the mines at both seasons of the year. On one occasion, he was on his way to Zirianovsky in the winter, and crossed the Altai Mountains in his sledge toward the Bouchtarma, traveling from one Cossack station to another, where he changed horses. One evening, a little before night set in, he was stopped at one of the stations by a *bouran*, and here remained the night, during which the storm raged with terrible fury. The following day it subsided, when he proceeded on his journey. A few versts from the next station he saw several Cossacks standing together a short distance from his track. Fearing something had happened, he stopped his sledge, got out, and went over to them, when a sad spectacle was presented to him: it was a Cossack and his horse frozen to death, whom they were digging out of the snow. The poor fellow had left the station before the *bouran* commenced, and it had caught him, most probably, when about half way, which induced him to drive on, hoping to reach his home. No doubt the horse had taken him on until probably after he was dead, as the Cossack was sitting perfectly upright in his sledge, with both hands holding the reins, his head erect, and looking straight toward the head of his horse. When he ceased speaking or moving the reins, the horse must have stopped, and was soon frozen stiff in his upright position. My friend said, when looking at them a few paces distant, it was difficult to believe that they were not living, and that he expected every moment to see the Cossack shake the reins and the horse spring forward.

Next morning the wind had moderated a little, when I started for Barnaoul, and had a terrible journey, only reaching the banks of the Ob on the third day in the afternoon. At a point where the view to the eastward is uninterrupted as far as the eye can see, appears one vast forest of dark pines.

While traveling I was suddenly much amazed by a bright crimson color spreading over the pine-trees; at first the distant pines were tipped with the tint, then the tops of the nearer trees, showing against the dark purple beyond like flames of fire. This was directly opposite to the sun, around which there was no crimson, but a deep yellow: I stopped the driver that I might watch this strange appearance. The color approached nearer and rested upon the trees, growing on the banks of the Ob, which seemed a town created by magic, beautifully reflected in the water. Even my men looked with surprise at this singular effect: it was plain they had never seen such a phenomenon before.

At six o'clock we reached Shadrina, the last station before Barnaoul; and not till half past twelve o'clock next day, in consequence of not finding horses ready, and owing to the badness of the road, did I find myself at my destination.

CHAPTER XIX.

BARNAOUL.

A FRIEND advised me to take a Siberian bath without delay, and stew out the effects of wet, frost, and thumps; for many a man has come out of an Irish row at Donnybrook with fewer bruises than I had to exhibit, the rocks of the Oural and Altai having stamped their seals upon me in strong and enduring characters.

Having adopted the steaming process, I turned out next morning fresh, in good health, freed from the pain of every kick or bruise, and with the full conviction that there is nothing in the world equal to a Siberian bath after such a journey.

This, the first day of November, was terribly stormy, with a fierce *bouran* driving the snow about like flour. It requires no small effort to close a man's jaws when a *bouran* has caught him in the teeth. I speak from experience, having more than once been nearly choked with the wind and snow before I could turn my head for shelter. This is not the season to see Barnaoul to advantage, though it is to enjoy its society and hospitality; for many of the officers, whose duties take them into the mountain regions, have returned to their comfortable and truly hospitable homes.

Passing by the long winter, I will speak of Barnaoul in the spring-time—I ought to call it early summer. Here the whole labor of spring is executed in three or four days at most, so rapid is the growth of vegetation when the snow is gone. This town is built on the banks of the small river Barnaulka, where it falls into the Ob; and until within the last thirty or forty years, nearly all its buildings were of wood; even now there are but few dwellings built of brick; the streets are wide, and laid out in parallel lines, and crossed at right angles by others; the soil on which they are built is a deep bed of fine sand, which renders the place rather disagreeable in summer. There are three brick churches, and not one has any architectural merit. A large hospital, simple in its style, contains spacious and well-ventilated wards for the sick workmen, where they receive every attention and comfort, but their wives and children are not admitted.

The silver smelting works are on a great scale: these operations are conducted in a very large building, under the care of most intelligent officers, who carry on the different processes in a thoroughly practical and scientific manner. It may be said with perfect safety that the Russian mining engineers, as a body, stand preeminent at the present day. No class of men in the empire can approach them in scientific knowledge and intelligence. Among them are many in these distant and supposed barbarous regions who could take their stand beside the first *savans* in Europe as geologists, mineralogists, and metallurgists.

In these works two hundred and fifty poods of silver are produced annually — about nine thousand pounds English weight. The whole produce of the silver mines in the Altai up to the year 1855 never exceeded one thousand poods, or thirty-six thousand pounds. To produce this quantity, fifty thousand poods of lead were evaporated. In 1850, twelve thousand poods of English lead were sent to Barnaoul to aid in this process. Since that period both silver and lead ore have been found in the Kirghis Steppe in large quantities. All the gold got in Siberia must be sent to Barnaoul to be smelted, excepting the portion which is obtained in the Yablonay Mountains, and that is smelted in Nertschinsk Zavod. Gold mines are worked on the Olekma and other rivers near Yakoutsk, in the Saian Mountains, and many in the government of Yenissey, where some of the richest mines of Siberia exist. The government of the Tomsk also supplies a large portion, but the crown is proprietor of most of the mines in the Altai. There are some in this region worked either by companies or private individuals, very few of whom have become rich.

In Eastern Siberia the gold-washing begins the first week in May, and ends on the tenth of September, when all the workmen must be paid off and sent to their homes: some have to walk as many as two thousand versts. The rich miner sends his gold away once a year, most of which arrives in Barnaoul in the beginning of October; but those who are not rich send it twice in the year—the first part in the beginning of July, and the second when the works are closed in September. When it is delivered to the authorities in Barnaoul it is considered the property of the crown, and the miner has no more control over it. Here the gold is smelted and cast into bars, ready to be forwarded to the capital; but, before the miner receives his share of the value, it has been in the possession of government five months. Six caravans leave Barnaoul with the precious metals every year—four in winter by the sledge roads, and two during the summer. The first winter caravan leaves early in December, and reaches St. Petersburg before the end of January; the others follow in succession. Two officers and a small guard of soldiers are sent with each caravan, and the gold and silver are delivered by them at the Mint. Although both metals have been assayed by the proper officer in Barnaoul, and the proofs sent to the Mint, it is again assayed to prevent the possibility of a bar being changed on the transit.

The silver obtained in the Altai contains a small portion of gold, with a minute quantity of copper. These metals are not separated in Siberia; they are sent in pieces, about fourteen inches square, by one and a half inch thick, and the gold is extracted at the Mint in St. Petersburg. About thirty poods of gold is extracted from a thousand poods of silver, the whole annual produce of the Altai silver mines. The greatest quantity of gold obtained in Siberia in any one year was about seventy-five thousand Russian pounds; this was considered enormous, but California and Australia have made it appear small in comparison. There is much of the gold regions yet unexplored, both in Northern and Eastern Siberia.

Barnaoul is the centre for the administration of the mines of the Altai. The Governor of Tomsk is at the head of this department, and in order that he may be fully qualified for such an important position, he is invariably chosen from the mining engineers. Once in two years he must visit every mine and smelting work in the Altai. Part of the year he resides in Tomsk, where his duties as governor require much time and attention; three or four months he resides in Barnaoul, where he must be in May, when a board of the principal officers meet daily, and arrange plans for working the mines until the next year. All arrangements are proposed at this board, which sits during the whole month of May, but they are subject to the governor's approval.

The Natchalnik, or chief Director of the Mines, resides in Barnaoul. This officer is responsible for the proper working of the mines, and every department is under his control. Once in the year he must visit every smelting work, iron work, gold mine, and silver mine; to accomplish this, he must travel more than six thousand versts annually, mostly in a mountainous country; sometimes in a carriage, often on horseback; also must descend the rivers on rafts, in boats, and in canoes, where he is often exposed to much risk and danger, to say nothing of the drenchings he receives from flood and rain. Every officer and man in the Altai is under him, and must obey his orders: this gives him immense power. Besides the officers, he has about sixty-four thousand people belonging to the mining districts under his charge. These are spread far and wide, both on the plains and on the mountains of Siberia, and such an assemblage requires much care to keep in proper order. Still, after visiting both Eastern and Western Siberia, and some parts of Russia, I must say that the mining population of the Altai are more wealthy, cleanly, and surrounded with more comforts than any other people in the empire. Convicts have not yet been sent to work in the mines of the Altai.

There are many very superior officers at the head of the different departments in Barnaoul; also as resident officers at the smelting works, copper works, iron works, and mines. Every summer eight or ten young officers are sent into the mountains, each with a party of from forty to sixty men, and the chief in Barnaoul assigns to him the valley or part to be examined by his company: in May they begin their operations. The region they are sent to must be thoroughly explored; they go properly provisioned, with dried black bread, sugar, tea, and *wodky;* their meat consists of such wild animals as they can procure, and as each party possesses good hunters, plenty of game is usually obtained.

A map is given to every officer of the valley his party are directed to search. Some of the men are employed digging holes about six feet square, which they sink to the bed of sand and gravel containing the gold; this is often found at from five to ten feet below the surface. After the upper earth and stones are removed, the sand is dug out, a sufficient quantity washed to test its value, and the officer notes down how many zolotnicks of gold could be obtained from one hundred poods of sand. Another hole is sunk fifty or sixty paces distant, and proved in the same manner; and they go on ascending the valley, digging out at such distances as may be deemed necessary to explore thoroughly the gold deposit. The specimens of gold got from each hole are numbered, corresponding to a number on the plan, and this enables the director in Barnaoul to decide if there is sufficient gold deposited in this valley to pay for working.

During the period that one party of the men are seeking for gold, the officer employs others in examining the rocks in search of silver ore; at the same time specimens of the rock are collected, and the different groups marked on the plan. These operations are usually concluded by the middle of October, when the officer and two or three of the miners return to Barnaoul, bringing with them the different specimens collected; the other men return to their different villages. On arriving at the Zavod, the officer and miners select and classify the different specimens of rock and minerals, arranging them in the order shown on the map. These are afterward examined by the Chief of the Mines, who has long been engaged in constructing a geological map of the Altai, which, when completed, will be one of the best ever laid down by any geologist, very few having had the same facilities for such a work.

There is a good laboratory, under the management of two officers, where the gold and silver are assayed, and all other chemical and mineralogical operations are carried on. There is also a magnetic observatory on the north side of the town, with proper officers to register the observations day and night: these are transmitted, at stated periods, to the proper authority in St. Petersburg.

For many years Doctor Gabler was the Inspector of the Hospitals in the Altai, which office he filled with great advantage to the peasantry and to all under his charge. He was also a distinguished naturalist, and possessed a choice collection of Siberian and other insects. His fame has reached Europe; there are some even of my own countrymen to whom he was known, by specimens he sent to different museums and to his correspondents. The doctor's collection consisted of more than seventeen thousand specimens. I spent many happy hours in his company during my first visit to Barnaoul. On his journey of inspection to the different mines he had visited many interesting places in the Altai, and from him I gathered much information relative to my journey in these regions. He died in 1850, after having lived more than thirty years in Siberia, and left three sons in service in different departments of the mines. His splendid collection of insects has since been sold.

There is a museum in Barnaoul containing a good collection of minerals, some of them very choice specimens; also a few Siberian antiquities, four tiger skins, stuffed, and a few Siberian animals and birds, also stuffed. The tigers were killed in Siberia at different places, some at a distance of about five hundred versts from Barnaoul; they had come from the Kirghis Steppe, and crossed the Irtisch into the Altai in the region around Bouchtarminsk. Their capture in two instances proved fatal to some of the peasants engaged in it, while others were seriously injured; for, unfortunately, the men had no idea of the powerful enemy they had to grapple with. Pea-rifles and hayforks are but poor weapons against the fangs and talons of these enormous brutes. They are rarely found in Siberia; it is only when they are driven from the steppe by hunger that they cross the Irtisch—most probably when following the track of their prey: many peasants do not even know them by name. The last was discovered early one morning lying on the top of a small hayrick near the village by a peasant going to fetch hay for his horses, who beheld with wonder and alarm the formidable beast crouching with glaring eyes; at the same moment his dog, catching sight of him, gave a loud bark, and dashed toward the rick. With a fearful growl the tiger sprung to the ground; the dog met him without fear, but was crushed in a moment. The man ran toward the village, where he gave the alarm, and presently returned with a group of friends—three armed with pea-rifles, others with hayforks and axes; and they were followed by several dogs. On approaching the rick, they were made acquainted with the position of the enemy by a furious growl; the dogs charged instantly; he, however, only crouched, and did not spring. One of the men then sent a small ball through his hide, which roused him, and at one bound he threw himself among the dogs, killing two in an instant by strokes from his terrible paws; the rest retreated toward their masters. Two other balls pierced his body, but only enraged him without stopping his bounds, and at the next spring he was in the midst of the group—struck down one man and held him in his grasp. The dogs again rushed at him, and the peasants stabbed him in the back and sides with their hayforks. This and the shouting caused him to leave his victim and retreat slowly toward a bank partly covered with some thick bushes, the dogs barking in his rear, followed by the men. On reaching the bank he faced round, gave some fearful growls, and crouched for a spring, which caused both dogs and men to halt. His position was such that he could not be assailed except in front. Other shots were now fired, but without effect, and the dogs kept up a furious barking at no great distance, yet he would not come out. As the man whom he had struck down was dead, his assailants kept at a respectful distance. However, after watching and consulting some time in what manner to make another attack, the dogs began to close in, when it was perceived that their antagonist did not move. One of the men then went nearer, and finally discovered that the beast was dead, a ball having pierced him in a vital part. He was accordingly dragged out, and proved to be a full-grown male tiger.

Barnaoul has a *gastinoi-dvor*, with some good shops, in which many European articles may be purchased at very extravagant prices. There are two or three who deal in all sorts of wares—jewelry, watches, plate, glass, French silks, muslins, bonnets, and other gear for ladies; sugar, tea, coffee, soap, and candles; sardines, cheese, sauces, English porter, Scotch ale, French wines, Port, Sherry, and Madeira—a most extraordinary assemblage of goods. I must add to the catalogue arms, swords, guns, and pistols.

The Chief of the Mines one day desired to see one of these general dealers on some important matter, and a Cossack was sent to desire his attendance. On reaching the establishment, he saw the man's wife, who told him that her husband was not at home. Having heard this, the Cossack returned and reported the answer, but was dispatched again with orders to find him and bring him forthwith. On reaching the house a second time, he told the lady that her husband must instantly be found, and return with him to the Natchalnik, therefore that she must declare at once where he was gone. This somewhat frightened her, when she acknowledged that he was in the cellar *making Port wine*, and had ordered that no one should disturb him during the operation.

All European articles are very dear, but there is a good market in Barnaoul, well supplied with provisions by the peasants from the neighboring villages. The following are some of the prices:

White flour per pood of 36 lbs. English, 3*s*. 4*d*.			
Black or rye flour	ditto	ditto	4*d*.
And sometimes	ditto	ditto	2½*d*.
Beef from 2*s*. to 3*s*. 2*d*. for 36 lbs.			
Nilma, or white salmon, 6*s*. for 36 lbs.			
Sterlett, 9*s*. for 36 lbs.			
Other fish, 2*s*. 6*d*. for 36 lbs.			
Grouse, 6*d*. a pair; repchicks or tree-partridge, 3*d*. to 4*d*. a pair.			
Fresh eggs, 1*s*. per hundred.			
Black currants, 2 gallons for 6*d*.			
Red currants,	ditto	5*d*.	
Raspberries	ditto	8*d*.	
Strawberries	ditto	8*d*.	
Bilberries	ditto	4*d*.	

It will be seen that living is very cheap in this part of Siberia; farther east the price of food is much higher.

Since my first winter in Barnaoul I have visited nearly every town in Siberia; have remained long enough to become acquainted with the inhabitants, and have entered into their recreations and pleasures, but in no town have I found the society so agreeable as in Barnaoul. They have an excellent band, trained by one of the under-officers, a very good musician and respectable performer on the violin, who received his musical education in St. Petersburg: under his direction they executed most of the operas beautifully, and with great effect. There are three ladies in Barnaoul who play the piano-forte well, and during the winter three or four amateur concerts are given which would not disgrace any European town. They have also several balls in December and January, when many young officers return from the mountains, where they have been banished from their friends for eight or nine months. There are a few wealthy merchants in Barnaoul who trade in furs and other produce of Siberia, which they send in February to the fair at Irbit, where all the furs procured in the vast forests of Siberia are forwarded. Merchants from Europe attend and purchase these goods in large quantities. Merchandise from Russia, Germany, England, and France is brought to this fair, which the Siberian merchants buy and distribute to every town in this vast region.

There are barracks in Barnaoul, and usually from six to eight hundred soldiers are stationed in the town. The population, including these, was in 1856 about ten thousand. The workmen live in small wooden cottages, most of which are clean and comfortable dwellings, and nearly all the peasants keep cows and horses. Those who are employed in the smelting furnaces work two weeks and then rest one; this is done instead of taking the holidays arranged in the calendar, as that would interfere with the operations in the Zavod.

Smelting the silver is a very unhealthy occupation, and the workmen suffer much from the fumes rising out of the furnaces, which give them the lead colic. Those who are engaged cutting wood, burning charcoal, carting these materials, and various other works which keep them constantly in the open air, enjoy excellent health; few, if any, men in Europe are more robust and hardy. They can, and often do, endure great fatigue; besides which, they are exposed to extraordinary changes of temperature without feeling any bad effects.

The River Ob is a magnificent stream, running in a valley twelve versts broad; and there are many small branches dividing this valley into islands, on which large trees are growing. In May, when the snow has melted on all the low land, this river becomes a mighty stream, laying much of the valley under water; but in June, when the snow is melting in the mountains, the water covers the whole width, from one high bank to the other, the tops of the trees alone standing up like islands, between which this vast flood is rolling on toward the Arctic Ocean. At this time there are many scenes along the valley of the Ob truly grand, especially when seen either with the rising or the setting sun. The crimson and golden tints of the sky are reflected on this vast flood of waters, bounded on each side by the deep purple forest, which stretch away for hundreds of versts till it is often difficult to distinguish the horizon from the golden hues of the sky.

This valley has great attractions for the sportsman from about the middle of June to the first of August. There are thousands of double snipes to be found frequenting the banks of the river, and the grass around the borders of the numerous lakes formed by the retiring flood. In 1848 the River Ob was unusually high, flooding the country, and covering land rarely overflowed; this kept me a prisoner, as it was impossible to travel while the waters were out.

About the first week in July I was invited by the director in Barnaoul to make one of a party of four to shoot double snipes in the valley of the Ob. We dined with him at one o'clock, and then started, having to drive sixteen versts to the place he had selected for our operations. When we arrived at the ground and were ready to begin shooting, it was near four o'clock. It was arranged that we should meet at the place where the carriage stood at seven o'clock, and drink tea. My three friends had each a good dog, I had none; we separated, and in a few minutes the work of destruction began. I was told to walk along near the edge of the water; I did so, and soon flushed some birds, several of which got away without a feather having been touched. After this I took the matter more coolly, and shot many, my friends keeping up a continued fusillade at no great distance. I now felt that a good dog would be most useful at this sport. Having continued shooting about an hour and a half, we all met not far from the carriage, when it was proposed that we should drink something and empty the game-bags. Mine was not half full, but the case was different with my friends; the wine was broached and drunk, and the birds thrown down in separate places. We then moved off along the ridges of grass lying between the large pools, and again shots were fired in rapid and continued succession. At seven o'clock we were recalled to the carriage, tea was prepared, and many other good things were spread on the grass. Before sitting down, each man counted the produce of his gun: mine was soon told: I had shot twenty-three double snipes; the director had killed forty-two; the apothecary counted out sixty-one; and my little friend of the Oural had slain seventy-two double snipes in something less than three hours and a half. After looking at his heap of game, I gave him the name of the "mighty hunter," and he is called Nimrod to this day. I doubt very much if any of my countrymen have ever done as much in the same time. Since then I have been out at this sport, and many times with the same party, but I never saw them kill more. "Nimrod" had shot on one occasion seventy-eight birds, and the greatest number I ever got at one time was thirty-eight, but mine were obtained without the assistance of dogs.

During the snipe-shooting season, when the water covers parts of the valley of the Ob, accidents occasionally occur.

One very fine day, at the latter end of June, the Chief of the Mines invited my friend "Nimrod" and another to go with him snipe-shooting. On this occasion their destination was up the valley of the Ob to a place about sixteen versts from Barnaoul. They dined with the director, and drove off immediately in his tarantass, traveling at a good speed to the point where they had to descend into the valley. The high banks were abrupt, but the man took them down slowly and safely. On arriving at the bottom of this steep bank it was found necessary to cross a broad sheet of water to some higher ground where the carriage would remain with the provisions; this would also land them at a good place to shoot over. The coachman was asked if he knew the track sufficiently well to keep out of deep water; he answered in the affirmative, and drove on. Having gone about a hundred paces, he got off the bank, and the wheels on one side sunk down, turning the trio over into deep water, in which they sunk overhead. Fortunately, their guns, ammunition, and provisions were safe in the boxes. After floundering about for a few minutes, they got out, the carriage was set right, and driven over to dry ground.

A council was held to decide what was best to be done. As the day was very hot and the snipes numerous, the idea of losing their sport could not be endured. The director proposed to send the coachman to Barnaoul on horseback for dry clothing, but that they should, in the mean time, strip off their wet garments, pour the water out of their long shooting-boots, draw them on again, and set to work dropping the snipes without delay, assuring his companions that the brandy each of them had taken, in conjunction with the exercise, would prevent any bad consequences. The suggestion was no sooner made than acted upon; the coachman mounted his horse, rode through the lake, and was soon ascending the steep bank, which having gained, he galloped off to Barnaoul, bearing the tidings of their misfortune; but three hours, at the least, must elapse before he could supply them with dry clothing.

The sportsmen at once prepared for the attack on the snipes; their wet clothes were pulled off and spread on the grass, their boots and their broad-brimmed hats completing their toilet. Thus, with only heads and legs covered, with game-bags slung over their shoulders, and the *patrone-tasches* strapped round their waists, they marched forth. The dogs, it is said, stared at this original outfit in mute wonder; they then stood firm, their heads up and tails stretched out, and proceeded on their vocation. In two or three minutes the snipes rose, but their efforts to escape availed them nothing; there were those on the watch whose quick eye and steady hand seldom failed. When once engaged in the sport, they forgot their mishap, their costume, time—every thing in the excitement; and when the man returned, they appeared astonished by his appearance. Not one of them suffered in the smallest degree from this exposure, and their adventure has already taken the position of a local legend.

In the autumn there is plenty of other game; in fact, tetery or blackcock may be shot in August; reptchicks, or the tree-partridge, in September; and this is continued into the winter. When the first snow has fallen, blackcock-shooting is splendid sport, and is conducted in this way: A common sledge, sometimes with one horse, at others with two, is prepared, and nearly filled with straw; upon this the sportsman sits down, and away the man drives into the forest, keeping a good look-out. When he sees the birds, he drives along till within rifle distance, and then stops. The sportsman must shoot the lowest bird; when this one drops, the others look down on their fallen mate, and remain quite still in the trees. I have more than once shot three out of the branches of the same tree before the brood have taken flight. When the birds are gone the man gathers up the game, throws it into the sledge, and drives on again. In these woods it is not difficult to shoot from fifteen to twenty brace of blackcock in a day. This can only be done with a pea-rifle, which makes a very small report, and is certain in its effect.

Wild deer are not found near Barnaoul; they must be sought at some sixty or a hundred versts distance. Hares are in great abundance in winter, and the wolves are more numerous than agreeable. I once came upon a party of seven. They were not more than sixty or seventy paces distant, and I had no gun—not even a stick. We stood looking at each other for three or four minutes; they then quietly filed away into a wood of small pines, where I lost sight of them: this was within half a verst of the town. Afterward I went many mornings to the same place, taking my double-barrel gun loaded with ball, and a rifle also, but I never met the brutes again.

CHAPTER XX.

SPORTING ADVENTURES.

My friend the director proposed that I should accompany him on his visit to the gold mines in the Altai. This was an opportunity not to be lost; it would take me into a new region, toward the sources of the River Tom. We left Barnaoul on the 15th of June, and descended the River Ob in a boat to Bieloiarskoï, where a carriage was waiting to convey us to a village on the Tom. For some distance after leaving the valley of the Ob the country is flat and uninteresting; but horses were ready at every station, the change was made in a few minutes, and they galloped over the road at a great speed. After proceeding on our course through the night, we reached a thick forest early in the morning, and traveled through it for many hours. About midday we stopped and took lunch on the banks of a little stream running quietly along in its rocky bed, where there were many grayling sporting in the pools, a sight that would have enchanted "Old Izaak." A few versts beyond this we came into a more open country, and in one of the little valleys were driven among plants higher than the carriage. I got out and found that they were the *ferula*, or giant fennel, some ten feet three inches high. My companion ascertained at the village near that the ground on which they were growing was covered with snow only five weeks ago. This may appear almost incredible, nevertheless it is a fact. I have frequently noticed the rapid growth of plants in Siberia when I have spent several hours making a sketch, where they were springing up around me.

About three o'clock we reached Tomsky Zavod—iron-works belonging to the crown, where both pig and bar iron are made. It was here that General Anossoff began to manufacture *boulat*, from which he intended to fabricate damask blades, and this is the place he proposed making the Birmingham of the Altai. Iron ore of a very superior quality is got at no great distance, but there is one great drawback—a small supply of water in dry seasons. I sketched this place, not on account of its beauty or grandeur, but as a recollection of the spot on which my friend would have effected a great change had he lived to carry out his plans. We dined here, and in the evening continued our journey, still through a woody country, which the shades of night soon rendered obscure. Just as day broke we passed through the town of Kouznetsk, which contains about two thousand eight hundred inhabitants; among them many Cossacks, a considerable number of Tartars occupied in hunting, and the rest Russians. Large quantities of skins are brought to this town by the Tartars and Kalmucks. It is here they pay the tribute to the government officers. The fact is notorious that each hunter, Tartar or Kalmuck, selects his best and most valuable skins for the emperor. I hope his majesty gets them.

After passing Kouznetsk we soon reached the River Tom, where the boats had been prepared for us. As we drove into the village I noticed a great number of peasants sleeping in the street: they were workmen on their way to the *priesk*, who would not proceed farther. An officer and a party of soldiers had them in charge to conduct them to the mines, and while tea was being prepared the former was sent for. In a few minutes he appeared, and reported that he had tried every means to induce the men to embark in the boats, but without effect. The director dismissed him with a sharp reprimand.

As we were taking our breakfast, about four hundred peasants assembled in front of the cottage, waiting to see the director. When our meal was finished he opened the window, and asked why they remained here instead of proceeding to the mines. A man immediately advanced from the crowd, and said that they would not go in boats up the River Mrassa, but had no objection to go by land. A number of Cossacks were standing near, ready to obey any orders, and the director told them to give the man twenty-five strokes with the birch rods. In a moment he was laid on the ground, two Cossacks held his legs, two others his arms and head, his clothing was turned down, and a Cossack was standing on each side with a birch equal to most rods used at Eton. The word was given, and down came a sharp blow, followed by one from the opposite side. After receiving half a dozen the victim bellowed out that he would go. The director stopped the operation, and in five minutes all the men were running to the boats. This matter being settled, we followed, and found our boats ready, each of us having one with two men to row, and a Cossack to take charge of our things. We were soon afloat on the Tom, which at this place is three times the width of the River Thames at Westminster. About midday we arrived opposite a Tartar village, beautifully situated at the foot of some fine hills, which rise into mountains more to the northeast.

After passing this village the valley became much wider, the hills recede far from the river on both sides, leaving a great breadth of rich pasture-land, but no large herds of cattle are seen grazing in these meadows. Most of the inhabitants of the villages on the Tom are hunters, and lead a very hard and solitary life, living much alone among the mountains. In the evening we arrived at a Russian village (*podobas*), where we remained the night, and supped on fine fresh fish just caught in the Tom by a Tartar. After rowing up the river in the morning for about two hours, we arrived at the mouth of the Mrassa, and turned into it. Our course was now nearly due south up this broad and rapid stream, which I perceived would soon lead us into fine mountain wilds. The oars were now laid aside, and the boatmen took up long poles, with which they pushed the boats along; but this was slow and difficult work. Every few versts carried us into finer scenes, where granite rocks rose to a great elevation, broken into singular and picturesque forms, often crowned by pines and drooping birches, that gave great variety to the views.

We stopped to dine under the shade of some magnificent rocks, on fresh grayling caught in a net shortly after we arrived: they were almost tossed out of the river into the pan, and very quickly placed before us. These rural dinners I enjoyed much better than I should a Lord-Mayor's feast, the locality and mountain breezes giving an amazing zest to the repast.

My men, who knew the country, were anxious to push on without delay, as the sky was black, and we had already heard thunder among the mountains in the direction we were going. I made a sketch of this place. While doing this, the clouds were gathering over the mountains higher up the river. The people said we should soon have a great storm, and wished me to remain, as we could not reach the next station in less than four hours. It was six o'clock when we sat down in the boat and pushed off;

and the men worked admirably, forcing the boat on faster than usual. The clouds now became blacker, the thunder louder, and after about an hour we found the storm was coming very near; the lightning shot down into the forests, and the thunder echoed from mountain to crag with sublime effect. It was not long before the storm reached us in all its grandeur, and the rain poured down in streams; still on we went, but with a strong wind and a rapid stream against us, which rendered our progress very slow. At last night cast her veil of thick darkness over mountain and flood, when the effect of the storm became truly sublime; it was darkness made visible, and then all was lighted up in a moment with a pink or reddish tint on rocks and trees. The lightning appeared to hang on the dead branches an instant, sparkling in the drops of water like globules of fire: this was wonderfully grand. Hour after hour passed away, and still the thunder rolled. When near the bank we disturbed some animal, which gave a deep growl; some one said it was a bear, but we could not see him. Shortly after this the men said that they could not get the boat farther, nor could they tell how far we were from the station. It was pushed to the bank, and we were consulting what should be done, when we heard the splash of oars not far from us. This proceeded from a boat with four men, sent by my friend, who feared that some accident had happened to us; two fresh men jumped into our boat, and our poor fellows into theirs. We now got on so much better that in less than an hour I had reached our little cabin, and, when I had changed my wet garments, found it was past twelve o'clock. We sat down to supper, partaking freely of the fine fresh fish placed before us after a six hours' voyage and the pelting of a thunder-storm. The next morning I discovered that we were at the foot of the great rapids on the Mrassa, the heavy rain in the mountains during the night having added much to the grandeur of this scene.

The river at this place comes rolling and tumbling with great fury over masses of granite, making a tremendous roar. Our boats had been drawn up the bank more than a verst to the head of this rapid. A wonderful scene was the boiling and surging water as it rushed down this rocky declivity, occasionally rolling huge masses of granite before it, and making a report like a piece of artillery each time the stone is turned over.

In the summer before my visit to this place a friend of mine had a very narrow escape. He was the officer who had charge of the gold mines in this region, and was conveying the gold to Barnaoul. The usual mode of descending this river is on a small raft constructed of trees; at the point where they embark it is guided by two oars, and by poles when necessary. The gold is secured in a strong wooden box bound with iron, and any other baggage the party may have is placed on the raft, forming seats, which, with a few branches and long grass, make the conveyance level and comfortable. On this occasion the officer was attended by seven or eight men; they descended the river without accident, and in due time approached the rapids, floating down the middle of the stream. It is necessary to stop in time and run the raft to the bank, land all the luggage, and carry it to the lower end of the boiling torrent, when it is placed on another raft, and the voyage continued to the Tom. In this instance either accident or mismanagement prevented their forcing the raft to the shore. Every effort was made, but the officer saw it was impossible. Ordering each man to leap into the river and save himself, he followed; and fortunately, after a terrible struggle, all landed safely on the bank, just in time to see the raft carried like a shot over the brink. Before it had gone two hundred paces it was shivered to pieces, and scattered in fragments on the surging flood.

The box containing the gold was heavy, and went to the bottom at once. The officer had some luggage, and a box containing paper money, which being light, were carried down, and found afterward some distance off, safe, but much damaged; also a bearskin *shube* or cloak, that floated down the river about sixty versts, was then caught in some bushes, and when the water subsided was left on the branches high and dry. One day a Kalmuck hunter was passing at some distance, and saw what he believed to be a bear. Creeping cautiously along till within rifle range, he carefully took aim and fired; but as he did not even see the fur fly, he thought the lead had missed its object. He was not long, therefore, in sending a second messenger on the same errand. Finding this did not arouse the beast, the Kalmuck marched up to the game, when he discovered that he had wasted powder and balls on a bearskin *shube*. Later in the summer, when the water was very low, many men were sent to search for the box containing the gold. After much difficulty they succeeded, and discovered it in a deep hole between some large rocks. Thus all the property was regained.

Having ascended the bank, and climbed over the rocks to obtain views of the great falls at different points, which amply repaid my labor, I joined my friend, who had gone on straight to the upper end of the rapids. We now sat down in our respective boats, the men once more commenced their hard labor of pushing us up the stream, which becomes more difficult and the scenery much finer as we ascend; indeed, I found some of the best scenery on this part of the river. Granite rocks rise to a great height, some of their summits bare, others fringed with birch and cedar trees, while shrubs and small trees grow in the clefts. The rocks are broken into pillars and pinnacles, some of them white, others yellow and gray, producing beautiful effects between the rich green and red foliage.

We had now reached the mouth of the River Orton, near its junction with the Mrassa, and turned into that river, following its course toward the east. We were among magnificent scenery; I sketched much of it, and deeply regretted that circumstances prevented my ascending the Orton to its source. It rises in a group of high mountains between the rivers Tom and Mrassa. The country in this region is very wild, and many rugged peaks rise to a great elevation; the navigation is also attended with increased difficulties. Taking my sketch-book and gun, I rambled on, frequently far ahead, and thus found time to sketch without delaying my party. A small but deep stream, flowing from the north, stopped my onward progress on foot, and compelled me to take to the boat again. In due time we reached a part of the river where it was exceedingly rapid, running among large rocks, some of them just covered, and others standing out of the water. Several times the torrent forced us back, but, nothing daunted, my men tried again, and by great exertion got through. Our difficulties were not yet over. We had not gone far when we came to a large block, against which the current dashed with great force. To pass round without being driven upon it required both care and strength. As we came near, the water dashed into our faces: it was, indeed, a hard struggle, and we got up inch by inch; indeed, had one of the poles broken, we should have been on the rocks in a moment, and then in the river. When the rock was nearly passed, one of the men slipped, and instantly our boat was half full of water; fortunately, they succeeded in getting to the bank, when the baggage was removed and the water bailed out. This place is the worst on the river, and passes by the name of the "Anossoff Kamen." On the first visit made by the general to the gold mines, when passing this rock his boat was dashed against it, filled, and went down; the party were carried out into the river in a moment, but other boats coming up, they were all rescued.

These, at first, appear unpleasant events, but a man here soon becomes accustomed to such little incidents, and they are in keeping with the wild nature around him. Passing several other rapids, we arrived at the place where men and horses were waiting to take us on to Petropavlosk gold mine. After leaving our boats we had a pleasant ride through a forest, where I shot some woodcocks, and late in the evening we arrived at the mines. Excepting the gold found here, there is nothing particularly interesting at this place. We slept the night at the mines, and started in the morning to ride over the mountains to another gold mine about thirty versts distant. It was arranged that two men who knew the country should accompany me wherever I chose to go, and this enabled me to visit some splendid mountain scenery. We left the track which leads from one gold mine to the other, and turned toward Petropavlosk Belock, where I sketched some beautiful views, the country being exceedingly wild and grand. Immense cedar forests extend through the valleys, in some parts so thick that it was almost impossible to force our way through. In other places we rode among most luxuriant vegetation, which rose far above our heads. Here I found the *ferula* more than twelve feet high, with its bunches of yellow-tinted flowers eighteen inches in diameter; of these I am told the bears are very fond. Also *delphinium*, with long spikes of dark blue blossoms, and others of a pale blue, as well as *aconitum* of two varieties, a blue and a pale yellow. Not far from these were growing red and pink roses, two sorts of geraniums, and several other flowers I had never seen before. To me it was indeed a beautiful garden, in the midst of wild and rugged scenery. Late in the evening I joined my friends at Tsaravo-Nicholiovsky gold mine.

This village stands on sloping ground in a small valley, the beauty and fertility of which have been destroyed by the gold-washing operations that have been carried on here for many years. At the period of my visit I was told that there were about six hundred men employed in excavating and washing for gold. I had seen the various processes and machines used in the Oural, but the machinery here I found of a totally different construction, and the whole moved by water-power.

These machines were designed and constructed by the officer whose *shube* took the hunter's two bullets. At the time of my visit the place was very unhealthy, and there were many patients in the hospital. Typhus fever was more than usually prevalent among the workmen this summer, and numbers had died from it. My old friend Doctor Gabler was here to inquire into the cause, and adopt such measures as would be most effectual in stopping its ravages. My ride in the mountains was over ground where bears are numerous; their tracks we followed, but without seeing even one. I passed places where fearful encounters with these animals have taken place. A very large one had been seen by the woodcutters about fifteen versts from the gold mine, and two men, one a hunter, held in great repute for his daring and skill, determined to make his acquaintance. After wandering about for some time they came upon his track, quite fresh in the long dewy grass. He was evidently near; this made them cautious, and they prepared for action. Presently a loud growl saluted their ears; then out he sprung from a thicket, about thirty-five paces distant, where he stood snuffing the breeze and eyeing the intruders.

The hunter fired, and the ball struck, but not in a vital part. In an instant the wounded animal charged; the other man, who was less experienced, reserved his shot until within twenty paces. The rifle missed fire; at once the brute raised himself on his hind legs, and, tearing the earth beneath him, rushed on his first assailant, striking him down with a blow that stripped his scalp and turned it over his face; then seizing his arm, he began to gnaw and crush it to the bone, gradually ascending to the shoulder. The man called to his companion to load and fire; but the fellow, when he saw his friend so fearfully mangled, ran away and left him to his fate.

Late in the evening he reached the gold mine and reported what had happened, but it was too late to make any effort in behalf of the mangled hunter. The officer ordered a large party out at daylight the next morning, with the coward for a guide. He took them through the forest to the spot where the encounter had taken place, of which there still remained ample evidence, but no remains of the victim were met with except some torn clothing and his rifle. By the state of the grass, it was evident that the man had been carried off into the thick forest. A most diligent pursuit was therefore made; sometimes the track was lost, but the pursuers of the bear were too well skilled in woodcraft to be foiled, and at length discovered his larder. He had dragged the hunter into a dense mass of wood and bushes, and, to render the place still more secure, had broken off a great quantity of branches and heaped them over his body. These were quickly stripped off, when, to their great surprise, they found the man, though frightfully mutilated and quite insensible, still living! Two long poles were immediately cut, to which saddle-cloths were secured in the middle. One horse was placed in front, another at the back, and the ends of the poles secured to the stirrups, thus forming a very easy conveyance. The sufferer was placed upon the saddle-cloths, and carefully propped up, and then began the painful march back as fast as possible.

On their arrival at the gold mine he was taken direct to the hospital; the doctor dressed his wounds, and administered all that medical skill and kindness prompted; his patient survived, but long remained unconscious of every thing around him. After more than two months had elapsed a slight improvement took place, and his reason appeared to be restored. His first question was about the bear, and then he referred to his own defeat. He spoke of nothing else, and was constantly asking for his rifle to go and kill "Michael Ivanitch" (the Bear). The medical men thought his mind seriously affected. As he gained strength, there arose in him so great a desire to have another combat with his powerful and ferocious enemy that it was considered necessary to place him under some restraint.

The summer had passed over and autumn had arrived; the frost had scorched the foliage, changing it into golden and crimson hues; and as it was now thought the poor lunatic had forgotten his adventure, less vigilance was exercised toward him. The opportunity was not lost, for he secretly left the hospital, and started off for his cottage. All the family being absent except some young children, he was enabled to secure his rifle and ammunition, and provide himself with an axe and a loaf of black bread, which he stowed in his wallet. Thus armed and provisioned, he left the village in the evening without being seen except by the children, and was soon lost to them in the forest.

When it was discovered that he had escaped, people were sent out in various directions to seek him, but they returned without success. More than a week passed over, during which nothing had been heard of him, when one day he walked into the hospital carrying the skin of a huge black bear on his shoulders, and throwing it down, exclaimed, "I told you I would have him." This man was a fine old hunter: it was not a spirit of revenge which prompted him to this daring act; the fact was, he could not brook the idea of a defeat. Now his reputation was re-established he was happy; his health was again restored; nor was this the last bear that fell before his deadly rifle.

From Tsaravo-Nicholiovsky our way was across the mountains toward the Tom, where a raft had been constructed to take us to Belasenskoï gold mine. The scenery is not particularly grand or wild—that is, in comparison with other portions of the Altai. In Europe it would be considered stupendous.

Our track led through a part of the forest where an incident occurred to a Cossack officer that I can not refrain from repeating. One afternoon he was quietly strolling through the forest, alone and unarmed, botanizing by the way, when, at a distance of about eight versts from the gold mine, he came out of the forest into an open glade on which stood some single trees. Almost immediately on entering this spot, he observed, at a distance of two hundred paces, a she-bear and her two cubs playing together. The moment she became aware of his presence she uttered a savage growl, drove her young ones into a tree for shelter, and mounted guard at the foot of it to defend them.

The Cossack retreated into the wood to provide himself with a weapon, having determined to carry off the cubs. The woodmen had been cutting timber, and from the stems of several young birch-trees lying on the ground he selected part of a strong one, near four feet in length, tried its quality against a tree in a succession of smart blows, and then, club in hand, retraced his steps.

As soon as the old bear observed his approach she began to growl furiously, moving to and fro with an uneasy motion at the foot of the tree. He slowly and steadily advanced. When within about a hundred paces her growl became more savage, and her actions showed that she intended mischief. Nevertheless, he quietly moved on, his keen eye steadfastly fixed upon her. The ground was a fine grassy turf, with no shrubs or bushes to impede his movements or entangle his feet. When within about fifty paces she made a savage rush that would have daunted most men; but he firmly stood his ground, waiting her nearer approach. At this moment the cubs began to whine, and she trotted back toward the tree again in increased fury; the Cossack followed, and when she turned round they were standing face to face, within twenty paces of each other. There was now no retreat; the brute eyed him keenly for two or three minutes, as if calculating his strength, he returning her gaze with as searching a scrutiny. Presently she made a second rush, her eyes glaring like balls of fire. At a few paces from her enemy she rose on her hind legs, intending to give him a settler with her powerful paws or to clasp him in her savage embrace; but on the instant he made a sweep with his club, and dealt a blow that toppled her over. She was up again in a second and ready for action, but another blow laid her prostrate. This added to her ferocity, and it at once became a close encounter of the most deadly and savage character. Many rounds were fought, her antagonist keeping clear of her paws. At last the blows began to tell on her courage. She endeavored to get behind him, but his cudgel met her at every turn, and was so well wielded that whenever within reach she received a stroke which drove her back step by step, till both came under the tree. Here the fight was renewed with increased fury, and every time the cubs whined she made her attack with redoubled violence. The battle continued to rage furiously, but the blows from the staff fell so fast, and were applied with so much force, that at last she began a retreat toward the forest, the skirts of which she entered; but the moment her brave assailant moved a step toward the tree, she would rush out, taking especial care, however, not to come within his reach.

The cubs remained in the branches, the sole spectators of this extraordinary scene; nor could the Cossack officer devise any plan by which he could get them down. At their respective posts the combatants stood, he guarding the cubs, and the mother growling at the edge of the forest. At this time a woodman returning to the gold mine rode into the glade. He was instantly hailed, and rode toward the tree; but when he heard the growls and beheld the bear, then in her most savage mood, his natural impulse to bolt was only checked by fear of a birching promised by his superior. He was ordered to dismount, and take from his saddle the *zumka* (large leathern bags) and open them, then to climb the tree and bring down the cubs. The man was soon up among the branches, secured a cub, brought it down, and then tied it safe in the bag; the other was also quickly placed beside it in the other bag.

During these operations the mother rushed at the Cossack, and was several times knocked down by his weapon. The peasant was now ordered to place the bags on his horse and lead the way to the gold mine, the Cossack covering the retreat, and beating off the enemy at every charge. After a walk of nearly two hours they reached the village, the bear keeping close up with them. As they went through the forest she made many charges, but each time was laid prostrate, and finally would not approach within striking distance. When they reached the village the Cossack officer hoped to secure the dam, but after following them to the cottages she returned to the forest, and was never seen again. The cubs were kept, and became great pets with the people. Even the hardy hunters of Siberia consider this a most daring feat, wondering at the power, and admiring the cool courage of the man who accomplished it.

From the scene of this conflict we ascended some high mountains, passing through fine forest scenery, and then descended to the Baliscou, which means "a river abounding in fish." There is a deep and extensive cavern in some limestone rocks here, but we could not explore it without a boat. We continued our ride down the bank for a short distance, and then crossed some low hills to the valley of the Tom, where we found a raft ready for us. After cooking some delicious fish, and eating our dinners in the wood, we embarked, and were soon floating down the rapid stream. The valley at this point has nothing particularly striking. To the northeast the mountains rise to a great elevation, some of them above the line of vegetation appearing nothing but masses of bare rock.

The afternoon became very wet, and the mountains covered with clouds rolling over them gave a most dreary aspect to the scene; still we floated rapidly along. About eight o'clock the raft was pulled to a small island in the centre of the river, where my companion intended that we should encamp for the night. The tent was soon pitched, and a large fire made. The net, having been cast into the stream, was dragged ashore, containing about fifty fine grayling; these were presently cooked, and made a splendid supper for the whole party. When dark, it was proposed to illuminate our little island. About a hundred paces from our tent there was a clump of fine picta-trees, which we intended should form the grand light; a small clump on each side of the island was also to be fired. All hands were soon at work collecting materials to place under the trees, and in about an hour every thing was ready; the piles of wood and birch bark were lighted. These burned slowly for a short time, until some pine branches caught fire, when they blazed furiously, communicating the flames to the trees. In a few minutes there was a general conflagration; the fire ran up and along the branches like gunpowder, making a tremendous roar. There is so much turpentine in these trees that it caused the flames to rise to a great height. After our illumination we slept soundly until day dawned, and then resumed our voyage. Here the river expands, becoming broad and shallow; indeed, we had not proceeded far when the raft began to drag on the stones at the bottom; presently we stuck fast. All hands were now compelled to step into the river, but the raft did not float. However, after much lifting and pulling, we succeeded in getting it into much deeper water, and on we went again, but only for a short distance, when we had the same process to go through. Happily, this was the last adventure of the kind, as we soon got over the rock, and floated along most delightfully through beautiful river and mountain scenery.

The small wooded islands and frowning cliffs fringed with dark cedars give to this part of the river a peculiar character, much aided by high mountain masses, some with scarcely a vestige of foliage, or even moss on their rocky summits. While in many of the gorges formed in their riven sides mountain torrents came rushing down, and were sometimes seen dashing in white foam as the water leaped from rock to rock, in other places they were lost under a thick canopy of trees growing in the bed of the ravine. I often found it very difficult to force my way into these rugged and picturesque spots. We floated down the Tom for seven or eight hours, passing mighty precipices and lofty towering crags, which seem almost toppling into the river at their base. Birch and cedar trees were growing out of the clefts, while flowering shrubs and flowers were clinging to their broken sides. Many of these scenes were singularly picturesque.

We had now reached a spot containing one of the most valuable of mineral treasures—thick beds of coal cropped out of the mountain side, dipping at an angle of about 22°. The faces of two of these seams, with the rocks lying between them, were broken off quite perpendicular, presenting the appearance of having been heaved up during some great convulsion. The upper bed of coal was twelve feet thick, resting on a stratum of gray and yellow rocks eight feet in thickness. Beneath these is another seam of coal ten feet thick, which rests on a bed of apparently similar rocks twelve feet deep; and below these I saw the upper edge of another bed of coal, but how thick could not be ascertained.

In this region there is a coal-field probably larger than any one in Europe. I found a bed of coal at another point of the river thirty-one feet thick above the surface of the water; the depth I can not say. What stores of wealth lie buried here—iron and coal in inexhaustible quantities! Gold is found and worked in some of the upper valleys, and jasper, porphyry, and a beautiful aventurine are among the rocky treasures of these mountains. There is also rich pasturage in many of the valleys, where great numbers of cattle might be fed. Both feathered and large game are abundant, and I can answer for the excellent quality of the venison. The keenest sportsman, whether of the rifle or the rod, will never lack employment here. If a sketch-book be added to his wallet, every rocky glen and mountain stream will afford him subjects of study equally novel and attractive.

Having descended the Tom to the mouth of the Bellousa, where we arrived early one fine morning, we found boats waiting to take us up this river to a gold mine in one of the small upper valleys. Here we breakfasted on grayling just drawn from the water and tossed into the pan. We had to ascend this rapid stream about thirty-five versts, two men in each boat forcing us on with poles, as on the Mrassa. There are many lovely scenes in this valley, several of which I transferred to my sketch-book. The vegetation was most luxuriant. I walked through beds of fern much higher than my head, and found the *ferula* thirteen feet high. It was no easy matter to force my way through some of these vegetable masses. Just at dusk we arrived at the mouth of the little valley through which runs the small river Ezras, where horses and men were waiting to take us to some gold mine about an hour's ride distant.

CHAPTER XXI.

ON THE LAKES OF THE ALTAI.

LEAVING the Bellousa, we entered a thick forest, now rendered more gloomy by the shades of night. Here arboreal giants reared their lofty heads, and intertwined their branches into a thick canopy of wood and foliage, their huge mossy trunks assuming a supernatural appearance in the deepening gloom. In some places lay masses of rock, heaped up in great confusion, that had tumbled from the high crags above. The small river was fretting and leaping along in numerous cascades, and occasionally we caught a glimpse of its white falling sheets, looking like ghosts flitting about on this wild spot. So supernaturally strange did the scene appear as we rode along, that I could not help exclaiming to my companion, "Surely this is the fearful glen in 'Der Freischutz.'" After riding about half an hour through this forest we came into a more open part of the valley, and reached the gold mine a little after dark. It belongs to the crown, and has only been opened about a year. The place on which the gold is found is not of great extent. Wooden houses were building for the workmen in most picturesque spots; but, like all newly opened mines, the locality was very unhealthy.

Immediately after breakfast, while my friend was engaged with the officers and people, I rode back to the Der Freischutz scene, and after some hours' occupation brought back a vivid recollection of a real Wolves' Glen, for these animals are numerous in this region. Indeed, it would have been quite in character had a herd of these brutes assembled to dispute our right of way, and brought on a conflict like the memorable one described by De Foe. Soon after midday we were floating along the Bellousa; in some parts we went down the rapids at terrible speed, the men managing the little craft with great dexterity. They had no slight difficulty in avoiding the rocks, which threatened every moment to shiver our little boats, and send us swimming down into some of the whirlpools, from which we should have found it no easy matter to escape.

Late in the afternoon we reached the Tom, and continued our course down the stream. It was a lovely evening, peculiarly Siberian. The sun had set behind some high mountain masses now steeped in a deep purple tone. Still farther in the distance, and stretching away to the south, were other parts of the Altai chain, tinted in colors of purple, blue, and misty gray as they receded till the farthest summits appeared melting into vapor. The sky was a deep orange toward the horizon, gradually changing, as it ascended upward, into a pale yellow, and then into a bluish silvery gray; bright crimson and gray clouds were spread over this in light fleecy masses. The forms were so varied that Nature seemed to have exercised her utmost power to produce this truly wonderful effect.

We were now floating on the broad bosom of the Tom, with scarcely a breath of air to cause even the smallest ripple. There are many thickly-wooded islands in this part of the river, which were reflected in their deep purple colors upon water that shone like molten gold, while all the mountains and valleys were covered with sober gray, indicating the gradual approach of night.

Later we beheld the Kalmuck paddle his little canoe into the stream, light a fire at the prow, and then stand with spear in hand, ready to transfix any of the finny tribe lured within the reach of his deadly weapon. I never saw one of these men miss his prey. He stands with a foot on each edge of the canoe, and balances himself with ease, a matter of no small difficulty to the uninitiated. I once saw a Cossack try this mode of spearing at the foot of a rapid, where the water was very deep, and fish in great numbers. The Kalmucks had brought out several *talmane*, some of them weighing thirty pounds each; one of my companions thought *he* would try; so, mounting the canoe, it was paddled up toward the foot of the fall. In a very few minutes the fish were gazing at the light, when he struck at a large one, failed in his aim, and went down among the fishes, to the great amusement of all present. We were under no apprehension for him, as he could swim like a duck.

About ten o'clock we reached a village at which we had slept on our way to the Mrassa, and here we remained the night. Our voyage was continued the next morning, and in the afternoon we arrived at a village where carriages were waiting to convey us to the silver mines at Salaier. The route was one we had traversed before, and presented nothing of interest. We passed over a country with low rounded hills, almost destitute of wood, and reached the iron-works at Goorieovsky, which belong to the crown; here they make pig and bar iron, but not in large quantities at present, as the new buildings are not yet completed. The officer who had charge of these works was an acquaintance I had made on Seene Gora, in the Oural, since when we have spent much profitable time together, for I found him a most worthy fellow. My companion having inspected the works, we traveled on to Salaier, and visited the silver mines. Large quantities of ore have been obtained in these mines for a long series of years. Some of it is procured from a great depth, and in other parts the ore is worked as in a stone quarry, at from twenty-five to fifty feet below the surface. It is not smelted on the spot, but transported in small carts to the smelting works at Barnaoul, Pavlovsky, and Goorieovsky.

Salaier is a pretty place on one of the spurs of the Altai, which runs down into the low country between Tomsk and Kolyvan. To the south there are pine-covered hills, extending over a considerable tract, while to the north there is very little wood. A few versts from the mines a bed of coal has been discovered, which is now being tried in the Zavod. Should this prove good, it will be of great value, as wood has to be brought from a distance of fifty and sixty versts to some of the smelting works. Formerly no care was taken in cutting down the timber, and much was wasted. Now, however, the forests are under the care of intelligent officers, educated in the Forest Corps in St. Petersburg.

As we had to ride across a country over which I had previously traveled, I shall merely state that, after a difficult and sometimes dangerous ride on horseback over a wild mountain region, we made our first night's lodging in a *balagan* on the Altin-Kool, or Golden Lake, under the trees shown in the opposite view.

This spot is near the outlet of the lake, not more than three versts from the point where it falls into the Bia. The lake is said to be about one hundred versts in length, varying from three to ten or twelve versts broad. In fact, it may be considered to lie in an enormous chasm formed in this vast mountain chain. It is entirely surrounded by high mountains, in many parts presenting precipices not less than two thousand feet in height, nearly perpendicular. I was informed by a Russian officer who had sounded it that one part was more than two thousand feet deep, while other places were still deeper, he being unable to sound them, not having sufficient line. It was my intention to have tested these measurements, and preparations were made, but I was prevented by storms that are frequent here, and exceedingly dangerous. There are many mountain peaks on the west side of the lake which rise to ten thousand five hundred feet, and several on the south even higher. On the east side they are somewhat less in elevation; still, they reach far above the line of vegetation into the region of eternal snow.

I have crossed one of the summits to the west ten thousand five hundred feet high, and one to the south somewhat higher, from which I could look down upon the lake. While contemplating the scene beneath, I could not refrain from speculating upon the geological secrets that lay undivulged in the mighty abyss almost at my feet, and which it would disclose were it not for the crystal fluid that, from this elevation, looked solid and black as ink.

After making the circuit, we found that, excepting the small plot on which we first encamped, there was not on any other part of the lake a single acre of flat land. Our party consisted of sixteen persons, eleven being Kalmucks to row the canoes. For the first ten versts along this shore the mountains do not rise very abruptly; they slope down to the north, and are covered with a dense forest of cedars to their summits, while the banks on the opposite side of the lake, facing the south, have scarcely a tree upon them. After passing a small headland the lake expands, and a splendid view burst upon us. To our right were frowning precipices of

ALTIN-KOOL, ALTAI MOUNTAINS, WESTERN SIBERIA.

great elevation, upon which dark cedars were growing. At the foot of these cliffs a huge mass of rock rose out of the water about five hundred feet, and from the inclination of the strata I was induced to think part of the mountain had fallen into the lake.

Beyond this, each few versts presented a new and beautiful scene; the lake stretched into a fine sheet of water, with picturesque mountains rising upon each shore. Several times I was pulled ashore and placed myself on jutting rocks, which afforded me good points to sketch from. Early in the evening we stopped near a torrent, which came rushing down a narrow gorge, and the Kalmucks proposed to remain here for the night. There was a nice bed of clean sand, about five paces wide, sloping gradually down into the water. Large cedars were growing between the upper edge of the sand and the rocks, and under these our *balagan* was made. Although it was but a few bare poles covered with birch bark, open in front, and the ends filled up with branches, we found it exceedingly comfortable, with a great fire in front, giving warmth and keeping off the musquitoes. I tried, accompanied by three Kalmucks, to penetrate the thick forest on the banks of the torrent, but, after forcing our way about one hundred paces, in half an hour we were compelled to give it up. Night soon spread her mantle over mountain and lake, when every thing was hushed in silence; scarcely a leaf was moved, nor was the lake ruffled by a ripple.

I awoke with the dawn, and found a fresh breeze blowing. We were completely sheltered by a high mass of rock; nevertheless, we could hear the roaring of the waves as they dashed against the rocks, telling us plainly that we were prisoners on this solitary strand. Beyond them we should enter on the broad parts of the lake, where I expected to find splendid scenery. This made me anxious to proceed; but, so long as the breeze lasted, the Kalmucks would not move, not even after it had moderated considerably. They examined the appearance both of sky and mountains carefully before they would attempt to pull us round the point. About ten o'clock they seemed to be relieved of their fears, when we pushed off, and in less than half an hour rounded the point of rocks, and entered into a large basin about fifteen versts long, and seven or eight broad.

The scene I now beheld was splendid; the mountains rose to a great height, some of them capped with everlasting snow. After the first burst of astonishment was past, I turned to examine the shore, not far from which we were rowing, when I found the rocks came sheer down for six or seven hundred feet without a ledge to which we could cling. There was, therefore, no place to effect a landing. Had we been caught in a storm on this part of the lake, nothing could have saved us in such frail craft. I was, therefore, fully convinced that the Kalmucks understood how and when to continue our voyage, and this determined me to submit to their arrangements. Having gone five or six versts, we reached an isolated mass, a little beyond which I was able to take a view looking down the lake.

The rocks at this point were a light blue slate, of a very compact grain, reminding me of the same material obtained at Ulverstone. From this point we pushed on again, crossing a part of the lake which formed a small bay in the mountain, and soon reached Tmek-tash, a rock forming the point where the lake turns directly south. This had been mentioned to me as the finest view on the lake, and it is truly grand. Our canoes were secured in a sheltered spot. We then climbed to the top of Tmek-tash, or Stone Chest, so named from its square form. I found these rocks slate of a similar kind, but in this instance great disruptions had taken place. In some parts the strata are lying in a horizontal position, while in others they are almost vertical. The top of Tmek-tash was covered with plants and flowers, several of which I secured. I also found some very beautiful ferns growing in deep shady clefts. The shores of this lake would be highly interesting to the botanist, as he would find here new and beautiful specimens, especially in rock plants. On the crags two thousand feet above me I saw moderately large trees, which, by their foliage, I supposed to be birch; but as they appeared to be hung with bunches of bright yellow and orange flowers, I thought they must be a new species, or, at least, a species unknown to me.

The view of the lake from this point is extensive, and embraces some bold scenery. Along the west shore the rocks dip to the east at a very sharp angle, while on the crest of these mountains crags rise up quite perpendicular. Overtopping these, a snow-capped summit appears shining like silver against the deep blue sky. On the east side of the lake the mountains are less abrupt, but there is one which rears his rounded and lofty head far into the clouds. At the time I was sketching billowy masses of white vapor floated across his rugged sides, leaving his crest, which had been decked for ages with snow, sparkling in the bright sun. The color and aërial perspective of these mountains are wonderful. I counted twenty-three distinct distances, each beautifully defined, and receding until they appeared like a thin transparent cloud on the horizon.

I had another object in ascending to the high crags above us—to look for some of the feathered race in the forest, and thus procure a dinner. Shouldering my rifle, I marched off, accompanied by four Kalmucks and our *Talmash* or interpreter, who also carried a gun. We scrambled up the rugged sides of the mountain and came upon some bear-tracks, which the Kalmucks said had been made only a few hours. We followed them toward the summit, but without any result. When near the top I found that my conjecture was correct; the trees with garlands of yellow and orange leaves, which, when seen at a distance, had exactly the appearance of long pendent bunches of flowers not unlike the laburnum, were birch. During this ramble a few birds were shot: they were black, and about the size of a jackdaw, but their food, being the cedar-nut, gives them a strong oily flavor. They were very wild, keeping out of the range of shot. I picked them off, however, with my pea-rifle, from the upper branches of the high trees.

Again we took to our canoes, passed Tmek-tash, and entered the large part of the lake. We had not gone far when I was pulled ashore, where I found the slate rocks dipping to the east at an angle of 41°; a little farther I found the dip was 46°; in both places the strata continued at this angle nearly to the ridge of the mountain, where they became broken and jagged. As we paddled along not far from the shore, and some twelve or fifteen versts from Tmek-tash, I heard the roaring of water, though it was hid from sight; pulling in toward the rocks, we found a narrow gorge down which the water tumbled with a great roar. From the lake nothing could be seen, but on climbing the rocks and ascending the ravine I observed a splendid view.

The rocks on both sides of the foreground are a dark red granite, those in the distance are slate. The plants and flowers growing with a tropical luxuriance upon and out of their crevices gave the scene quite an enchanting aspect. It was savage nature, adorned with some of her most lovely ornaments. The deep red on the granite, the gray, purple, and orange on the slate, with the bright yellow of the birches on the distant rocks, overtopped as they were by deep purple mountains, rendered this a study of inestimable value. Had Ruskin been here, he must have acknowledged that Dame Nature was as a colorist more Turneresque than Turner himself. After devoting several hours to this subject, I found it was time to seek a night's lodgings—no easy matter to accomplish on these rocky shores. Fortunately, after about an hour we came upon a spot covered with rough pebbles large enough for our encampment, close under some larch-trees. The canoes were drawn up to secure them against a gale, and we soon made ourselves snug for the night.

A discovery was made this evening of a startling character. The bread had been left at Sandip, about four hundred versts distant. All we had was a few pounds of black *sucarees*—small cubes of dried black bread.

The morning was fine, but a strong wind delayed our starting until near ten o'clock, when we once more got under way, passing some fine scenery, which gave me plenty of occupation. About noon we arrived opposite to a ravine in which was a beautiful waterfall, with a large body of water tumbling among rocks of very picturesque shapes.

The rocks around and in this fall are of every variety of color—some bright red, others purple, yellow, and green. I found several beautiful specimens of marble—one a white with purple spots; another, white with bluish-purple veins. These had been washed from the mountains above. There were masses of a deep plum-colored jasper, also tumbled down from their beds by the torrent. I made a great effort to ascend to the upper part of this fall, but, after many attempts in various directions, was most reluctantly compelled to depart without even a peep at the savage scene beyond. The scenery on this part of the lake is of a most wildly romantic character. Advancing farther, we came upon the slate formation, heaved up into a vertical position, in beds varying from one to three inches thick, that rose up from five hundred to seven hundred feet in many places—not perpendicular, but overhanging the lake considerably. Approaching these precipices, with a side-view they appear huge blocks broken into fantastic shapes, ready to topple over into these fearful depths. It was necessary to keep at a respectful distance, as we beheld during our voyage along this shore several pieces plunge in and cut the water with a great noise. When passing in front of these cliffs, I saw that the different beds projected out, leaving a deep cavity between. In some places a single bed three inches thick stands out four or five feet, rising forty or fifty feet above the water, like the leaf of some mighty doors: the effect is most peculiar. Such is the formation on this part of the lake for more than twenty versts, without one spot on which a man can place his foot. We were all delighted when these dangerous rocks were passed, and turned into a bay with a sandy beach, having large cedars growing to the water's edge, near the River Chealee. Here we encamped for the night; and very soon after our arrival a stiff breeze sprang up, dashing the waves far on to the sand. Had it come on an hour sooner, not one of us would have escaped.

Our *balagan* was put up in a spot sheltered from the wind by thick underwood; a bed of sparkling white sand lay in front, on which a huge fire rendered our lodging exceedingly comfortable. While the evening meal was being prepared, I rambled into the forest, hoping to procure food for to-morrow's dinner, but nothing could be found. At dark the night became stormy, heavy black clouds rolled over the lake, and thunder was heard in the distance, but the storm did not reach us.

On waking at daybreak I found we had a clear sky and a strong wind, which again delayed us until the middle of the forenoon. About two hours after we started one of the most wild and savage-looking scenes on the lake opened upon us. It is a deep circular recess into the Kara Korum Mountain, into which fall three streams. These are united near the top of the mighty precipice, and then come tumbling down in a succession of falls until they reach a mass of rocks, snow, and ice, under which the water passes, and at last rushes out through a natural arch and falls into the lake, where at this point it runs in among the precipices. From the level of the lake to the top of the cliff, over which the water takes its first leap, is not less than two thousand feet. Avalanches must at times sweep over this place, and large trees are bent down and stripped of their branches. Huge rocks are torn up and hurled along, crushing and grinding every thing in their course as they rush on into the lake. No man can conceive the chaotic confusion into which the mass of ice and rock has been heaped. One enormous stone, weighing not less than one hundred and fifty tons, had been placed on its end, on the edge of the rock, in an overhanging position toward the lake. While engaged sketching this view, I observed the Kalmucks bringing the strong trunks of some fallen trees, of which they made levers, hoping to tumble the mass into the lake. All their efforts were fruitless, for which I was not sorry. The mass was left standing—an enduring monument of the mighty power which had placed it on its pedestal.

Having spent several hours on this wild but interesting spot, we once more embarked and proceeded onward. The cliffs still retained their rugged appearance and perpendicular form, over which numerous little rills came leaping and sparkling, some of them carried away in vapor before they could arrive at the bottom. We passed a spot where the slate was thrown up into high and jagged peaks, without finding a single place where we could land on this part of the shore, until our arrival at the mouth of the Tchoulishman, which has formed several small islands near the head of the lake: we encamped on one near some large and fine-looking birch and poplar trees, whence I had a magnificent view. During the latter part of our voyage we had been under some apprehension of another storm, as clouds were gathering thick over the mountains lower down on the lake. These continued to collect with astonishing rapidity; still, all was calm and sunshine with us. Hour after hour passed; the dark mass became black and descended upon the lower summits. It had a fearful aspect. Not a leaf quivered to the breeze; not a ripple was heard on the shore: it was one of those appalling calms which betoken a dreadful outbreak, and we all watched with feelings of deep anxiety. Shortly after dark this dense mass of black clouds was riven asunder by a terrific flash, which lit up lake and mountain for a few seconds with a glare of pinky light. The thunder rolled and echoed through the mountains with a most sublime effect. The lightning flashed in quick succession, sometimes descending into the lake, at others striking the mountain crags, among which we could see it leap from point to point. At last it became almost one continued blaze, affording me an opportunity of examining the thick clouds, which appeared almost solid before the flash.

This storm was not in one broad mass of clouds, extending over the heavens for many miles, but composed of innumerable pillars of electric clouds piled up in billowy masses, and vanishing off in endless perspective: some of them were lighted up with a vivid glow when the flash burst forth, while other parts remained in shade, and some stood out in inky blackness. This storm continued for several hours to rage on all sides, but without one drop of rain coming near us; a few miles farther down the lake, its effects must have been tremendous.

The next morning was sunny and beautiful, promising a fine day, and we started to ascend the River Tchoulishman, which enters the lake by several streams. We were obliged to try three of these before we could succeed in reaching the river in its single bed. When we did accomplish this, the stream was so rapid that it was with difficulty the canoes could be forced along.

The scenery on this river is worth all the toil of a long journey; in Europe we have nothing to compare with it. In some parts the roar of its waters is heard for many miles, and the rich foliage on its banks grows with striking picturesqueness amid fallen rocks; the stupendous mountains forming the gorge through which it runs, their various-colored rocks, with the patches of moss of almost every hue, and the sparkling waterfalls that come tumbling down their rugged sides, produce an effect impossible to be described by language. My portfolios will show how earnestly I strove to do them justice by means with which I am more familiar. Having spent a sufficient time in their delineation, I returned along the eastern shore of the lake, where I found much to occupy me. On one part, which is not so abrupt and wild as the west side, there are singular masses of conglomerate at a considerable elevation above the lake. Some stand near the edge of the precipice, others at a distance, and they frequently take the form of ruins.

Not far from this place we had a visit from a bear. After examining our camp, he very politely quitted it, leaving every thing untouched, and all our party fast asleep.

Near the point where a small arm of the lake turns directly east toward the Kamga the cliffs are limestone, in which is a large cave, and not far distant there is a noble waterfall on the River Karbou, about five hundred paces from the lake. The scenery on all the streams which fall into the Altin-Kool is very fine; on some it is exceedingly wild and grand. We continued our voyage toward the Kamga, which enabled me to obtain views of the high chain to the eastward; after which we crossed the lake, and proceeded along the north side about a verst from the shore. The attention of the Kalmucks was suddenly attracted by a sound in the mountains, which caused them to rest for a minute, when one of them gave orders to make for the shore. The canoes were instantly turned, and the men pulled for the land with all their might.

Kalmuck Resting.

The lake was perfectly calm, but these mountaineers knew that a storm was coming, and it was evident that they were exceedingly anxious. Our little boats were pulled along at a great speed toward a bay where there was a sandy shore, our only place of refuge. We were within a hundred yards of the beach when we heard the wind sweeping over the lake with a fearful sound. Looking out in the direction of the noise, I saw a streak of white foam coming toward us like a race-horse, and felt that if we were caught in this blast we were doomed; a few minutes more, and we should be safe. At last we touched the sand; to leap out was the work of a moment; simultaneously we seized the canoe, and ran with it up the beach; the other two crews performed the same operation. Now the gale swept past in its terrible fury, and a wave came dashing on to the strand four or five feet deep. Two of the canoes, being a little behind, were not out of reach of the wave as it rolled in, and were filled in a moment; the men, however, held on, and the boats were soon pulled out of danger.

We sought shelter in the forest under several large cedars, and while some of my companions brought our baggage, others began preparing a *balagan* as a protection against the storm. Just at this moment came a vivid flash, followed by a terrific crash of thunder, which appeared to shake the solid earth. The roaring of the wind and waves, and the heavy roll of the thunder, were appalling. It soon became a perfect hurricane; the tops of the waves were blown off as they rose, and the lake was covered as if with a sheet of snow. Had we gone even one hundred yards farther before turning toward the shore, we should never have been heard of again. Beyond this little bay there was not a spot on which we could land for fifteen versts. The perpendicularity of the shores and frequent storms render the navigation of this lake extremely dangerous, the more especially in a craft in which many persons would hesitate to cross the Thames.

Each canoe is cut out of the trunk of a tree; ours were made of poplar, which grows in some of these regions to a large size. Though the wood is very soft, it is a work of great labor for the Kalmucks with their implements. The sides are cut down to about three quarters of an inch thick, and the bottom is near double the substance, which is usually made flat and without a keel.

The storm continued until near evening and then cleared off. The Kalmucks proposed, although late, that we should take advantage of the calm and get out of the great basin, expressing their conviction that we should be detained in the morning, as the weather was breaking, and storms would now be frequent. I had already sufficient proof of their knowledge to induce me to adopt their suggestion; therefore the order was given to pack the baggage, and in a quarter of an hour we were on our way to seek another lodging. It was more than two hours before we turned the rocky point at the entrance of the smaller part of the lake. Even before doing so the rain began to pour down, and night came on apace, yet no place could be found where we could land and place our boats in safety. Nor was it until some time after dark that we discovered a favorable spot, and then we had to encamp "in thunder, lightning, and in rain," which continued nearly through the night. The following afternoon we reached our first encampment, near the outlet into the Bea, whence we started on our voyage round this lake, decidedly *one* of the most beautiful spots in the world.

CHAPTER XXII.

THE CHAINS OF THE ALTAI.

I NOW determined to visit the source of the Katounaia, though several of my Siberian friends considered it would be impossible to reach Bielouka with its glaciers at this season of the year, the winter commencing very early in this high region. During my journey I had collected jaspers and porphyries of great beauty, also several specimens of quartz and aventurine; and Kolyvan polishing works lying in my route, some of these I gave to be cut. The works here are not so extensive as those in Ekaterineburg, nor do they cut any of the precious stones. The articles made are often on a gigantic scale; and a walk through the Hermitage in St. Petersburg will sufficiently prove to every one the beauty and grandeur of the different vases, columns, and pedestals produced in this far-off region, where Europeans generally consider there is nothing but barbarism.

At the time of my visit there were about one hundred and twenty workmen employed in this Zavod. Many were engaged in cutting dark purple jasper columns fourteen feet in height; others were at work on vases of dark green jasper; both the design and material were exceedingly beautiful, and in some the foliage was equal to any I have ever seen, either ancient or modern. Were these artists free to exercise their talent for their own benefit, this wild region would soon produce men that Russia might be proud of; but the poor fellows are made to work for two shillings and ninepence and three shillings and eightpence a month. Let us hope that his imperial majesty will give these deserving men their freedom, and with it the privilege of putting a water-wheel on the stream which furnishes the moving power to the imperial works. Were this accorded to them, thiee or four artificers would join and erect a small wooden building and water-wheel, by which means they would be able to execute works of moderate dimensions, and find a ready sale at remunerative prices. The mass of materials on which they employ their talent is so enormous in the Altai that it will not be exhausted for ages to come.

From Kolyvan my road lay to the southeast. The director gave me his tarantass, in which I could travel about one hundred and thirty versts to a village on the River Tchurish, and at three o'clock we started with five horses over a hilly country. The first fifteen versts were uninteresting—rounded hills, with very few trees, to break the sameness of the landscape. After this we reached a more elevated part of the country, affording a fine view of the Tigeretzskoï chain. A little before dusk we arrived at a village where horses were ready to take us on. We had high hills to cross, which in some places were steep; this led us on to a plateau, with great blocks of granite standing up along several small ridges. From this spot I had a noble prospect of the Tchurish winding its course in a deep valley in the mountains. About ten versts beyond this point the road falls abruptly into the valley. It was no easy matter to descend: two wheels were locked, and the yemstchick begged me to walk down, he being afraid of his horses bolting. Night was fast covering hill and valley in gloom, which gave to many of the objects a mysterious aspect. Having, however, reached the valley in safety, we sat down in the carriage, and were soon fording the river, the water coming into the tarantass, but without doing us any damage. On reaching the opposite bank we had some difficulty in getting up; but, when once on the road, the men proceeded at a furious speed, regardless either of our necks or their own. The people of the village declared that it was impossible to go on in the dark, and, knowing nothing of the country, I reluctantly passed the night here.

The following morning a dense fog covered up every thing; but I found, on leaving the village, that we ascended rapidly. After about an hour we emerged from the fog into a brilliant sunshine, while all below was hid in a sea of white vapor. Having gained the summit, we had a fine view of the mountain chains to the south, among which I wandered in 1847. Many of their forms were familiar to me, so that it was like meeting an old acquaintance. No snow had yet fallen on their summits, which gave me hopes that I might still reach Bielouka. As we passed over the mountain, I saw some basalt columns in a deep ravine beneath. Stopping a few moments on the ridge before we descended, my man pointed out the River Tchurish in a deep narrow valley to the east, into which we were about to descend. From this point we had a fine prospect of the south part of the Cholsoun chain, with its high crags and snowy peaks glittering in the sun; other summits, still farther to the south, near the source of the Bouchtarma, could scarcely be distinguished from the clouds. The road down to the valley of the Tchurish was steep, and the country to the south well wooded with pine and birch trees. Our speed was a full gallop down a straight road for some five or six versts, when we turned suddenly round, forded a rapid stream, and in ten minutes were in the village. As my friend's tarantass was to stop here, horses were soon saddled, and a party of four men ready to accompany me to the next village, twenty-five versts distant.

The sun was sinking fast when we mounted and rode away. About two versts from the village we came to the Tchurish, a broad and rapid stream, which we must ford. One of the men rode in, I followed, the others came after us. The water was both deep and cold, but all passed in safety, when our horses were put into a sharp trot to enable us to reach Korgon before dark. The road was along the east bank of the river, close under the high granite cliffs, which rise in many parts from two to three hundred feet. In many places the scenery was very picturesque, and reminded me of some parts of the River Tom. Several deep ravines ran up into the mountains, down which small streams fretted and foamed over their rocky beds. We had a rough ride, and arrived at the village at dark. A boat was sent over to take us across, but our horses had to swim. The Startioner had been apprised of my visit, and was waiting to conduct me to his house. My horse was over in a few minutes, when I mounted and accompanied my host to his home, and this was to be my resting-place for the night. I was scarcely seated when the good man presented me with a plate of delicious honey, fresh from the hive.

It was seven o'clock in the morning before the men and horses were ready for our ride to Tchtchulika, the last village on the Tchurish. The rain, as my host had predicted, was pouring in torrents, and all the mountains were covered with a thick fog. We were going to ride along the valley of the river, in which, I had been informed, the scenery was beautiful, but I had very little chance of seeing it. In some parts it was well wooded, in others corn was growing and nearly ready for the sickle. After riding more than an hour the fog began to clear off, but the rain continued nevertheless. I was able to get some idea of the country we were traveling through. The valley at this place is about a verst and a half wide; portions were under cultivation, and in other parts there were good pastures, with clumps of fine trees. It is bounded on each side by high mountains, composed of purple and blue slate, broken into numerous ridges, with many small valleys and deep ravines running up toward their rocky crests. By ascending to the top of a rugged spur, which ended in a precipice sheer down to the river, not less than eight hundred feet, we obtained a view of the village, with the river winding through the little plain. In summer this is a beautiful spot, the ground being covered with wild flowers growing on a rich carpet of grass. On the mountain slopes wild strawberries, of a most delicious flavor, are found in great quantities, and game is abundant.

The descent into the valley was very abrupt, and rendered slippery and difficult by the rain. On reaching the bank of the river we found it somewhat swollen, but as we must cross it, we plunged in the water up to our saddle-flaps, and found it exceedingly cold. However, we all forded it in safety. I was taken to the house of a merchant evidently well off, most probably rich, who gave me a most hospitable welcome. Tea and *aladias* (batter fried in butter), with delicious honey, were placed before me. My host urged me to remain the night, as the rain poured down in streams, but this I declined, knowing the value of one day on a journey to the region to which I was bound. Here it was rain, there it would be snow. At noon the horses were brought into the yard, when one of them was honored with a precious cargo, consisting of four *vedros* of *wodky*, a quantity of tobacco, and sundry other articles, which received the greatest attention from my companions. Without this stock it would have been difficult to persuade any man to start in such weather; but when this provision for the journey was seen in the yard, I could have had any number of volunteers, rain, rivers, and snow losing all their terrors.

My party consisted of five men and nine horses. The Startioner and five other men accompanied us a short distance to aid in fording the river, which was rising fast; indeed, there were doubts of our being able to pass it. We succeeded, but our horses had to swim a short distance. Shortly after leaving the village the rain ceased, and a bright sun shone upon us, which soon became hot, and made our jackets smoke again. We had to follow a track up the valley of the Tchurish near to its source, and then cross a high chain to the valley of the Koksa. A change came over the aspect of the country; every thing was bathed in sunshine, and we passed through some most lovely scenery. The well-wooded valley of the Houekan, with the high mountains surrounding it, afforded some fine views, which I did not fail to add to my collection. I rode through the woods and beautiful glades, in some parts like park scenery; nor were the deer wanting to complete the illusion, several groups bounding past out of rifle-range. The red deer are numerous in this region, while higher up in the mountains the *alain*, a stag of a large size, may be met with. Crossing some low hills thickly covered with birch-trees, we descended upon the Yabagan Steppe, where many Kalmucks have their *aouls*, with large herds of horses and cattle, which find excellent pasturage on the steppe and in the small valleys among the mountains. The Tchurish runs across this valley. Here it is shorn of its woody banks; indeed, scarcely a tree is to be seen. Notwithstanding this barren appearance, the varied forms and colors of the mountains give a charm to the spot which would interest every beholder.

In the spring the Kalmucks offer up sacrifices to their deity: the rich give horses; those who are poor sacrifice sheep or goats. I was present at one of the ceremonies. A ram was led up by the owner, who wished for a large increase to his herds and flocks. It was handed to an assistant of the priest, who killed it in the usual manner. His superior stood near, looking to the east, and began chanting a prayer, and beating on his large tambourine to rouse up his god, and then made his request for multitudes of sheep and cattle. The ram was being flayed; and when the operation was completed, the skin was put on a pole, as shown in the accompanying sketch, raised above the framework, and placed with its head to the east. The tambourine thundered forth its sound, and the performer continued his wild chant. The flesh was cooked in the large caldron, and the tribe held a great festival.

Kalmuck Sacrifice.

The dress of the priest was a leather coat, over the laps of which are hung hundreds of strips, and leather tassels on the breast. He wears a girdle round his waist, with brass balls on his back; and scraps of iron hang on the front, producing a jingling sound. To accompany his other instruments, I added a key to his stock, which he received with great delight. His cap was of crimson velvet, with brass beads and glass drops hanging on his forehead, and feathers from the tail of the crane at the back.

Having completed these sketches, the lessening light warned us to seek a more sheltered resting-place for the night. A ride of

Kalmuck Priest.

somewhat over an hour brought us where the river runs through a small wood of fine larch-trees, and under these we encamped. It was, however, dark long before our strips of canvas were rigged up, and fuel collected for the fire, that was rendered absolutely necessary by the keen cutting blast whistling through the trees. At such times every man must do his duty; mine was to get up the blaze; and long practice had made me a good fireman.

The next morning at daybreak we left our resting-place and entered another branch of the steppe, running directly east. Over this we galloped at a good speed to a Kalmuck *aoul*, which we reached in two hours; we there changed horses and pushed on. The ride over these grassy steppes was exceedingly agreeable, constantly winding among picturesque ridges, where I found some beautiful specimens of red and green porphyry. The ascent hitherto had been gradual; but we had now reached the foot of the chain that forms the watershed between the Koksa and the Tchurish, and a rugged mountain rose up in front, on which there was no track to guide us on our course. About noon we came to a small stream, leaping and hissing over its rocky bed; and having remained here a sufficient time for both men and horses to be refreshed, we started again, riding up a very rugged ascent, rendered more difficult by a dense forest. In about an hour we were on the summit, or, as the men termed it, "the saddle." Thick clouds rolled over us, and a heavy pouring rain penetrated our clothing in a few minutes. Our position was both disagreeable and dangerous, for we could only see a few yards in advance; the descent, too, was steep, and no one knew whether we should find it gradual or abrupt. One of the men dismounted, and started off in the direction my compass told me we ought to go; in a few minutes he returned, led his horse down, and we followed. In less than ten minutes we were beneath the clouds, which were rolling fast over the top of the mountain. Although we were still in a drenching rain, we could see our way, which was very steep and difficult. As we rode down we passed three large larch-trees that had been struck by lightning, most probably in the storm of last night, as the splinters were quite fresh. Two of them were rent into thin pieces like laths, and strewn around, extending over a space twenty-three paces in diameter. The stumps were left standing, one five feet high, the other eight feet.

During my journey I have seen more larch-trees that have been struck by lightning than all other kinds taken together. What is the cause I can not tell, unless it is that they are more often found isolated than either pines or birches. Soon after passing these blasted trunks we got among a labyrinth of rocks over which it was impossible to ride. Every man dismounted, and after much trouble we passed this formidable barrier, and reached a steep grassy slope on which the horses could scarcely stand. After descending two or three hundred paces we came upon good ground, over which we could ride at a moderate speed; this soon brought us to the Abbaye Steppe.

We were now in a country quite familiar to me, for I had crossed part of it in 1848, and a few versts farther would place me on my old track, which we should follow some forty or fifty versts. I saw again "the old familiar faces." Each little rivulet was recognized; the lakes where hundreds of ducks were swimming, the picturesque masses of rock, and jagged outlines of the mountains, had left an impression which subsequent scenes had not obliterated, making me forget for a time the cold rain that was chilling me.

We had reached the Tschugash River, and a hard ride of two hours would take us to the Koksa. I put my horse into a gallop, and as all followed cheerfully, notwithstanding the plashing rain which beat in our faces, at a few minutes before eight o'clock we reached our intended camping-ground. While my tent was being pitched I aided in getting up a large fire, rendered doubly necessary by the piercing gusts of wind that swept through the trees and penetrated our wet clothing, making our teeth chatter again. A bountiful supply of dry wood created for us a blazing fire; and having partaken copiously of the contents of my *tea-kettle* (the tea-pot had been smashed), I walked to a more open part of the forest, which afforded me a view of the surrounding mountains. Those to the north rose up abruptly to a great height almost close to us, while to the south and east stood the Giants of the chain, their heads wrapped in eternal white, looking cold, grim, and ghastly; among them were the objects of my search. On looking up to the mountain near us I observed that the clouds were gathering fast in dark and lowering masses, while in another region of the heavens there was a great commotion; the clouds were whirling round, and huge piles were heaped up and tinged with a dusky red, apparently waiting an order for battle. I had now been long enough accustomed to a mountain life to know by these appearances that a storm was brewing.

My tent was pitched against the trunks of three large larch-trees growing close together, the foliage so thick overhead that the men said no rain could penetrate. In front of the tent a huge fire was burning brightly, and close by were other fine trees, which afforded shelter to my men, who had spread their saddle-cloths ready for their night's sleep. Within ten paces of our fire the Koksa ran over large rocks, making a great roar. The red glare from the blaze gave a warm tone to the trunks and branches, and rather a bandit-like character to our party.

Having written up my journal and placed my arms where they would be secure from wet during the storm, which I was certain would visit us, I turned down on my bearskin and was soon sound asleep; but this did not last long. Before eleven o'clock I was startled by a tremendous clap of thunder, which caused me to sit up and look around; the rest were sleeping soundly. The rain was pouring down, and came through my tent like water from a garden engine; every thing was wet. I had only sat up a few minutes, when a second crash came, followed by others in quick succession. Our fire was nearly extinguished by the torrents of falling water—it could scarcely be called rain—and between each flash of lightning it was utter darkness. I lay down again, trying to secure myself from the wet, and listened to the approaching storm. The noise of the river was lost in the roaring of the wind through the forest. Those who have never heard this sound can not form any idea of its power and awful effect. It comes rushing up these mountain valleys like a hurricane, wrenching off branches and uprooting mighty trees in its course.

I now began counting the time between the flash and the report, and found that the storm was coming on like a locomotive engine; when I could only count six after the flash, the bellowing was fearful. Every flash came nearer; the storm was soon directly over us, the lightning and the report simultaneous. It was awfully grand: a thick darkness at one moment, the next a blaze of light the eye could not look upon, at the same instant a terrific crash. The clouds appeared hanging on the trees in a black mass, while all around us was enveloped in a dense fog. Much as I like to see a thunder-storm, this made me fear its dreadful effects, more especially after seeing so many larches shivered during our day's ride. To remove was impossible; we must remain and trust in Providence for protection. In about half an hour the storm passed off toward the mountains, among which it echoed with fearful grandeur.

Soon, however, it was returning, when I marked the time between the flash and report with intense anxiety. Each few minutes brought these dreadful clouds nearer, until they were again directly over us, and the storm once more raged with all its fury. The lightning appeared to come from the tops of the trees, tinging the forest and all around with a pale blue light. This caused every man to sit up: the Russians were crossing themselves, but the Kalmucks sat smoking their short pipes perfectly calm. It was only when two of our horses broke loose that these men showed the slightest emotion; they then sprung up and secured the poor beasts while they stood trembling with fear. The flashes were now incessant; thick streams appeared darting through the branches, and the thunder positively shook the ground; I could feel it tremble with each crash. So long as memory lasts I shall never forget the effect of this fearful night. I doubt if any man slept.

At six o'clock we left our encampment, the thunder still rolling. From this place our track was down the north bank of the River Koksa to the Katounaia, forty versts away. Our ride was over a steppe for about thirty versts, having a chain of mountains to the south covered with snow, which gave a cold and winterly aspect to the upper region, while the forests and steppes beneath were clothed in their rich autumnal foliage.

The Kalmucks who inhabit these steppes have large herds of horses, oxen, and many sheep. Some of the men are fine fellows, and perfect Nimrods; they live by the chase, spending months in the mountains quite alone. I ever found these hunters faithful, honest, and brave. I have slept at their *balagan*, and partaken of their venison. A city alderman would be horrified to see the haunch of a fine buck cut into small pieces an inch square and half an inch thick, through twenty of which a sharp-pointed stick is run, and the thick end stuck into the ground in a leaning position near the fire. Every man here is his own cook, and attends to the roast. The upper piece is first done, when it is slipped off, dipped in salt, and eaten quite hot, without currant jelly.

Shortly after midday we reached the village of Kokstschinskoï, standing near the junction of the rivers Koksa and Katounaia, at the head of the valley of Ouemonia, a beautiful spot, through which the Katounaia rolls its rapid flood. High mountains surround this little plain, rearing their jagged peaks far into the clouds, and apparently shutting up the valley at both ends. Here is good pasturage for horses and cattle, and the mountain slopes on the north produce excellent crops of wheat and rye. Two villages in this valley are occupied by Russian peasants, who live by their agricultural produce and hunting, and many sable-skins are obtained in the neighboring mountains. Four years ago I visited this place, and the peasants recognized and were delighted to see me. Continuing our ride down the valley, we reached Ouemonia Lake in the afternoon, the last village in the Altai.

Immediately on my arrival I sent for the Startioner, and ordered him to provide me with a sufficient number of men and horses to go to the source of the Katounaia and the Bielouka, the highest point in the Altai chain. This was Monday evening; the men and horses were promised to be ready on Wednesday morning. It was arranged that I should have six Kalmucks and two Russians, one of them the great hunter of the village. During the evening several peasants came to advise me not to attempt the journey, as it was too late in the season. I admitted that it would have been better to have undertaken it earlier, but assured them that it was not only possible, but that it must be done, therefore any further arguments would be useless. This determination I perceived had become imperative, otherwise I should have had to endure a dozen different narratives of the horrors of the journey. Tuesday was rainy, with a strong wind, and snow was on the tops of the lower mountains. Though an unpromising day, I urged on the preparations. The hunter came to me; he, at least, was not daunted; indeed, thought we should have better weather. As he would command the party, I ordered him to have the men and horses in the yard at daybreak. When he saw the kegs of *wodky*, his eyes sparkled with delight, observing which, I gave him a glass, and it made him set about the work in good earnest.

On Wednesday, very soon after it was light, the Kalmucks rode into the yard with the horses. The rain had ceased, and at seven o'clock we sprung into our saddles and rode away, my little band consisting of two Russians from the village, six Kalmucks, my man from Barnaoul, and myself — in all, ten men, with sixteen horses and one dog; not a very jovial band, certainly, for several looked up at the snowy peaks over which we must ride with evident feelings of horror; indeed, my man would have bolted had not the fear of the birch conquered his dread of the snow above us. The people of the village gave us their prayers and a blessing, and the Russians stopped to cross themselves.

Our path was over a little steppe about five or six versts long, which runs up into the mountains toward the south. Having passed this, we entered a thick forest, which clothes all the lower region with magnificent timber, consisting of cedar, pine, birch, and poplar: here began our ascent of the first chain. After riding about four hours the rain commenced pouring down in torrents, with a strong wind blowing, which we only heard as it roared over the tops of the trees, while before us rose a rugged mountain quite destitute of wood, where we should have the full force of the storm without the slightest shelter.

Having reached the edge of the forest, we continued our ride up the bare mountain side. What a change! we had a strong wind, with rain and sleet driving into our faces, and penetrating our clothing in a few minutes. We pushed onward, and reached a small plateau five or six versts in length. Over this we rode at a sharp trot, with the gale blowing in our teeth, and reached the last straggling cedars, growing amid fallen rocks, that were thrown about in the wildest confusion. We were now at the foot of a very high mountain, over which lay our track. Its summit was covered with clouds, beneath which we could see the snow falling fast. Our guide pulled up his horse, and said it was quite impossible to cross the mountain in such weather, and proposed that we should seek a sheltered spot and dine. We therefore turned our horses, descended into a little glen, where grew some large cedars, under which we soon made ourselves comfortable by a rousing fire.

About three o'clock, the storm clearing off, I ordered a quick march, and we rode on again in a cold, cutting wind, which made our wet clothing feel any thing but comfortable. We reached the chaos of rocks and began to ascend; but our progress was very slow, in consequence of our having to wind among, and often over, huge masses of fallen granite and jasper. The cedars, which appeared small at a distance, were truly giants of the forest, their mighty trunks and branches towering up to a great height, while their gnarled roots were twisted about among the rocks like huge serpents petrified in the act of crawling from the ground.

After passing this belt of trees—the last struggling efforts of timber to maintain its place among rocks and snow—we began to climb the mountain in earnest. This was a most tedious operation, for great rocks, hurled down from the crags, appeared hanging so insecurely that the slightest touch would be sufficient to put them in motion and crush every one in their path. In some places we had to ride along narrow ledges, where a stumble from our careful and patient animals would have sent us many hundred feet beneath, when our lives and journey would be ended in a few moments. A ride of near two hours brought us to the summit, whence we had a magnificent view of the valley of the River Katounaia and the mountains to the north. We were now in a wintry region, while in the deep valleys there was summer in all her beauty of foliage and flowers.

Our ride was over a high plateau, on which rose up mighty rocks, rugged and picturesque, the remains of high peaks old Father Time is constantly mowing down. It is impossible to look upon these vast masses without wonder and astonishment. They are silent preachers, that carry the imagination back through thousands of ages to a period long before animal life had its existence on our planet, and make the mind reflect on the tremendous power which heaved up their rugged forms. They often, as already stated, present the appearance of ancient castles, well suited for the residence of genii and demons. Looking southward, we saw several high mountain peaks covered with eternal snow, and among them my guide said we should have to seek our track. They now appeared close to us, their white forms being cut out against a deep black sky.

A consultation was held between the hunter and the chief of the Kalmucks; then I was assured that we must ride fast, or we should be caught in a great storm, and not be able to find our way down into the valley on the other side. The appearance on the mountains denoted what was coming; therefore our horses were put into a gallop, rough as the ground was, and we watched with anxiety the approaching tempest. After riding about an hour without once drawing rein, we began to descend into the valley of the Tschugash. Even the animals seemed to perceive and dread the approaching tempest. We pulled up at the head of the valley, and it was only by holding the reins tight we could keep our steeds still; indeed, the moment my horse felt the reins slackened he dashed off, followed by the others.

All the high peaks around were now enveloped in dense black clouds, giving a fearful aspect to the scene before us. The forest was still several versts distant, and this both men and horses were anxious to reach. At length we heard the roaring of the winds as it came up the valley—a certain harbinger of a good drenching. We had not gone far when the tempest met us, nearly lifting us off our saddles, and the next minute the snow almost blinded us. Notwithstanding this, our horses hurried on, and soon brought us into the shelter of the trees near the banks of the river, along which we rode slowly, seeking a place on which to rest. We had not gone far when we found a thick group of cedars, affording ample shelter, and a good supply of firewood, with plenty of grass close at hand.

All hands went to work right willingly to house us for the

night, some making a fire, others fixing up our canvas coverings, unloading the horses, and sundry other matters necessary for our night's encampment. We had scarcely got the tent up when the rain poured down, not in drops, but in streams. After making every thing snug by stopping the wind out at one place with branches, at another with a wet coat, and at a third with my saddle-cloth, I sat down, enjoyed my usual refreshment, and listened to the roaring of the wind with a degree of satisfaction that can much more easily be imagined than described. The horses were picketed close to the encampment, as both the hunter and the Kalmucks thought the bears might pay us a visit, and leave us *minus* a steed in the morning. A good fire was kept up, and our rifles placed at hand in case of need. We slept, however, in peace.

A fog prevented our starting early, but about seven o'clock the sun's rays penetrated through the mist, and sent a flood of light into the hitherto gloomy valley. We were soon on horseback, wending our way toward the lake near the source of the Tschugash. It is a wild and gloomy spot; still, it had great charms for me, and I have endeavored to give the effect under which I have seen it just at dawn of day, when I have been out in search of the *alain*, or large stag. The opposite view will give an idea of this wild country.

After sketching the lake I continued my course, crossing another very high ridge, on which we found new snow up to the knees of our horses. Clouds were still hanging on the high summits to the southward; now and then floating masses rolled up the mountain sides, and exposed for a few minutes the wild and rugged scenery which lay hid under that misty veil. In short, the mountains became coquettish; at one moment the misty shroud was lifted sufficiently high to show all the beauties that peeped from the skirts of the hills, and then the fleecy garments were dropped with such a modest grace that fancy pictured innumerable hidden charms. After watching for several minutes with intense interest these curious effects, a gentle breeze wafted the misty veil from the forms it had concealed, and left them exposed in all their original beauty. Suddenly a gleam of sunshine lighted up these dazzling features; in a few minutes a shade as of sadness passed over them, and again the misty folds covered the objects I was longing to portray.

A LAKE NEAR THE SOURCE OF THE RIVER TSCHUGASH, ALTAI MOUNTAINS.

It was now time to proceed onward, and seek other scenes equally worthy of a place in my sketch-book, and fortune might perhaps favor me in the next valley. Our ride was over a lofty region, just below the line of perpetual snow, and above the region of vegetation. Not a blade of grass or a branch of moss was to be seen on this dreary place. Dark purple slate and patches of snow formed all the eye had to rest upon. A ride of somewhat more than an hour brought us to the brink of the abrupt descent into the narrow valley of the Arriga.

The clouds were rising from below and swept over us, obscuring every thing around; this brought us to a dead stand, for to proceed was impossible, as we were close upon precipices many hundred feet high. At last the sun burst through, and the clouds rolling off, a magnificent view lay before us, spread out like a map. Almost close under our feet lay the deep valley, with the little river Arriga winding along like a thread of silver; and high above us rose peaks of slate, sharp and jagged. To the westward we looked over many ridges to the Cholsoun, now clothed in its winter garment of pure white. On the south and southeast were the summits which are assembled round the Bielouka, all of which were decked in their mantles of snow. This was both curious and interesting: the deep valleys were still covered with grass and flowers blooming in all their beauty. Rich green and yellow foliage was waving on the trees, some not yet tinged with their autumn tints.

Looking over this sea of mountains, I observed the tops of the lower ranges colored with brown and green. The next summits also showed little vegetation, still they were tinted in brown, green, and purple. A little higher, and vegetation ceased; then came the line of snow perfectly level over the whole chain. Each region was distinctly defined, which enabled me to judge of the height of many summits over which I had traveled at different periods.

It was now discovered that we had struck upon the valley of the Arriga at a point where it was utterly impossible to descend; this compelled us to turn to the west; and after riding about three versts we found a deer-track, and succeeded in reaching the bottom in safety, although many parts were extremely difficult.

Having sketched two views on this picturesque spot, we crossed a low wooded ridge, and then turned up into a most rugged pass.

To the south the mountain rose probably twelve to fifteen hundred feet, very abrupt, and broken into crags, down which the water came tumbling in many a sparkling stream. Day was waning fast long before we reached the head of the pass. I had delayed our march by sketching, but all the men, except two Kalmucks, had gone forward to prepare our night's lodging. Just at dark we saw a large fire blazing at about a verst distant, which we were not long reaching; there a snug berth had been selected under some tall trees; the tents were pitched, and every thing made ready for my evening meal. The men were all cooking, and some venison chops were placed before me, our hunter having shot a fine deer near our resting-place. What with venison and *wodky*, the poor fellows made a glorious feast, singing songs until a late hour. Such savage scenery, with such wild music, would have satisfied a Salvator Rosa or a Callot.

Again day broke with a fog in the valley, but to go on before it cleared was impossible. As the sun rose we could see the vapor gradually diminishing, or, as the men said, "being eat up by the sun." About seven o'clock we rode up the bank of the Arriga, and in half an hour were at its source, which is a small circular basin of about thirty feet in diameter at the foot of a precipice seven or eight hundred feet high. The basin is deep, with white stones at the bottom; and the water, clear as crystal, rises from a spring, runs out in a good stream, and tumbles down in many little falls. In front of us a mountain stopped up the pass, rising very high, and the upper part deep in snow. To scale it was far from easy, but must be attempted. Our Kalmuck—Yepta—took the lead, and I followed on his zigzag track. It was curious to see us all in motion on the mountain side; our turnings far exceeded a hundred, I am certain, as we were more than an hour reaching the summit—a mere ridge, not twenty-five feet wide, having a descent even more abrupt. From this point a grand and wild scene was before us; high peaks of dark slate rose to a great elevation, with patches of snow and ice filling up the clefts, while far below us lay the little valley of the Mein, smiling in its summer garb. I met on the ridge blocks of a beautiful dark green jasper, and some in the crags we passed in our descent to the Mein.

Our ascent to the ridge was difficult, but this was much more so; indeed, it requires good mountain training to enable a man to sit coolly on horseback in such a place. After riding in a zigzag direction to the depth of more than a thousand feet, we found it less abrupt, and rode to the bottom without farther difficulty. The river has its source in a small lake at the foot of some black-looking crags, reaching far above the snow-line, and winds its course through a morass which has ages ago been a lake, formed by a mass of rocks that cross the valley more than a hundred feet above its bed. A narrow passage has been broken through these rocks, most probably by some convulsion, as the water could not have cut it down in such a manner. The little river rushes through this chasm, and forms a beautiful fall of about fifty feet in height. At the head of the diminutive lake there is a small waterfall, which comes down from the high precipices in one leap at least five hundred feet. When the wind is sweeping over the falling water it has a beautiful effect; sometimes it appears hanging over the dark rocks like a veil fluttering in the breeze.

Most of the rocks here are slate, some of a purple, and some of a greenish blue. I also discovered some splendid jaspers; one a deep green, with white or cream-colored veins, and another a deep red.

It was exceedingly hot among the rocks. While sketching I sat in the full blaze of the sun, and was almost broiled. In the height of summer the heat is fearful in most of these little valleys, and the vegetation becomes equally as luxuriant as in a tropical clime. Our horses having rested, we began to cross another chain, but this time rode over a mossy turf. Shortly after noon we reached a point whence we looked down upon the Kara-goll, or black lake, its waters appearing of a deep emerald green: this effect is not produced by surrounding verdure, as it is nearly encompassed by high mountains, and crags of yellowish and red granite, that rise up into the region of eternal snow, while at the upper end there is an enormous mass of dark basaltic rocks, and their deep gray color contrasts beautifully with the yellow castellated forms at their base. On the opposite side of the lake there are high precipices of granite, and beyond these are mountains with the snow of ages.

On reaching the shore the water appeared quite black, which agrees with the Kalmuck name, at the same time I observed that it was beautifully clear: we could see large fish playing at a great depth below the surface. The Cossacks come here from the pickets to fish in the winter, when the water is frozen, and large numbers of *talmane* are caught. The hunter told me that he was present with several Cossacks who had been sent to sound the lake; their lines, when united, were five hundred *sargens* (3500 feet), and with these they did not reach the bottom. That it is very deep I have no doubt, though not inclined to place confidence in their measurements.

Having finished my sketches and dined, we forded the Karra-sou, or black water, a large stream which runs from the lake, and then crossed a very picturesque valley, where the Chinese had formerly one of their pickets, now far removed from this spot. Our track was through a thickly-wooded region, extending over the lower range of mountains down to the Katounaia, and a ride of three hours brought us to the River Bi-tchuc-too. We had changed from summer to winter three times in the course of our day's ride; such sudden variations of temperature are far from agreeable.

On a bright sunny morning, after riding up the valley a short distance, we turned to the south, and began to ascend a very steep and high mountain, from which I expected to see the Bielouka. At first we rode over a fine grassy slope covered with flowers: red and yellow *primula*, deep blue *salvia*, yellow and purple *iris*, red and white *dianthus*, dark blue and white *gentiana*, with white and blue *aquilegia* in large patches. We passed through these beds, ascended to the region of moss and lichens, and in little more than two hours were riding over eternal snow, in some places solid and almost ice. Although very warm while in the sun, the moment we passed into the shade cast over us by one of the higher summits the wind seemed to cut through us. We pushed on and reached the summit, when I found we were standing on a rocky crest far above all the mountains to the west of the Katounaia; even the highest summits of the Cholsoun were far beneath our feet. A grand scene was spread out before us, the foreground, a ridge of gigantic granite crags, covered in part with mosses of almost every hue, contrasting finely with the snowy summits near us. Ridges and snowy peaks were rising in all directions, appearing like the waves of a stormy ocean suddenly congealed, and receding in beautiful gradations down to the steppes of Chinese Tartary, which at this distance looked like a sea of vapor.

Again we were disappointed; the Bielouka was not visible from the ridge on which we stood; other high summits intervened and shut out our view. We rode along the crest of the mountain for about two versts, and then descended into a little valley, in the bottom of which lay several small lakes. There were neither trees nor shrubs in this place; short mossy grass was growing in patches on the scanty soil, and sharp edges of slate were standing up, showing that the strata had been heaved into a perpendicular position. To the south rose *half a mountain* in a precipice of not less than two thousand five hundred feet above the lakes, while on the north side, at a distance of about nine hundred yards, are cliffs corresponding in outline to those opposite. Between these precipices, at the head of the valley, a vast dome-like form rises, and beyond are seen high snowy peaks, shooting up far into the clear blue sky. Huge fragments of slate, which have fallen from the south side, are lying scattered in wild confusion, forming a very appropriate foreground to this scene of desolation. This is one of the works of nature which must be seen to understand its vast and gloomy grandeur. Only a faint idea of this scene can be conveyed, even when painted on a large scale.

A ride of near an hour brought us to the head of the valley and to the enormous dome. From a distance the curve on its sides appeared regular; but we now found it consisted of huge blocks of slate and granite, over which it was utterly impossible to take our horses. By riding up the north side of the valley there appeared a probability of our getting over, as a grassy slope extended nearly to the top. Along the south side we could not proceed; one of our men had made an attempt, and was stopped by a precipice about fifty feet high. We therefore turned our horses up a steep ascent toward the cliffs on the north, and succeeded in reaching the top of the dome. It was a most singular place—a complete chaos of granite, slate, jasper, and porphyry, heaped up in the utmost confusion, over which it was impossible to take the horses. All the men, excepting Yepta and the hunter, were sent to try and get them along near the base of the cliffs, meeting us at the opposite side, while we three crossed this wonderful spot. After scrambling over large blocks, we stood on what appeared to be the outward rim of a vast circle, formed by a confused mass of rocks thrown together in the wildest manner, about twenty yards broad, from which the stones sloped down into a great bowl or crater, from three to four hundred yards in diameter, and about fifty feet deep. This was covered with blocks of stone of every size, from a cube of twelve inches to a mass weighing fifty tons. They were in such disorder that we found it difficult to cross; indeed, it was a work of time and of considerable risk to our limbs. Standing on the brim, I examined the precipices on either side, and could not help concluding that the mountain had been burst asunder by this mass of matter when heaved up. It took us near two hours to reach ground over which we could ride. It was not long before our horses arrived, when the men assured me that they had despaired of ever getting them safely over such a rugged place. To return by this route would have been regarded as madness; we had, therefore, to seek another track.

We continued our journey along the side of a steep mountain, still traveling southward, to strike on the Katounaia up toward its source, and, after riding eight or ten versts, began our descent toward the River Tourgan, passing over a bleak and desolate country. The river on which we intended to encamp we observed running like a small silver ribbon far away in a wooded valley, and at a great depth below us. Every half hour brought us into a warmer region; at length, after a long ride, we reached the woods, and found ourselves in a summer temperature, which both men and animals found agreeable, after a cold ride of such duration. The valley had long been in deep shade, but just as we reached the river the sun was tipping the snowy peaks with his crimson light; this gradually faded away, and all below was obscured in gloom. We pitched our tents in a sheltered spot on the bank of a roaring torrent, and it was not long before we lighted up the darkness by a glorious blaze, which spread its red glare on all objects around. The rocky crater over which we had passed was the subject of conversation round our camp-fire. The Kalmucks say that Shaitan inhabits this singular spot, which to them is a place of dread: they have an idea that something fearful has happened there.

From this place our ride was along a craggy summit with needle-like rocks rising out of the snow, the accumulation of ages

Over this we had to find our way, and many a weary verst we traveled. At length we were stopped by a deep mountain gorge, into which we descended with very great difficulty. There we found a torrent issuing from beneath ice and snow, and not far from this there was a hot spring bubbling up into a basin formed in the granite rocks. This was, indeed, a scene of desolation, for, as the sun never penetrates this chasm, there was not a blade of grass or a sprig of moss on the spot.

CHAPTER XXIII.

ASCENT OF THE BIELOUKA.

THE latter part of the night had been extremely cold, and the grass was now covered with a thick white frost, which made every thing look winterly. Before the sun's rays reached into the valley, we mounted and continued our journey down the bank of the Tourgan. This little river runs in a rocky bed, leaping and foaming in innumerable cascades. After riding about three versts, and making several vain attempts to ford, we succeeded. There is nothing either fine or picturesque in this valley, as the mountain slopes are gradual and unbroken. We had not gone far after crossing the stream when we came to a point which afforded us a peep at the mountains on the south side of the Katounaia, and the snowy peaks beyond. By this time the sun was sufficiently high to shine upon this valley in his full splendor, and the change was exceedingly agreeable in temperature—it was, in the space of a few minutes, from winter to summer. As we descended the valley the slate rocks began to appear, rising from fifty to one hundred feet above the green sward over which we were riding. Presently the river made a turn and flowed close at their base. Yepta, the Kalmuck, said that this was the only place at which we could ford the rapid stream, and here it was very difficult. We stood on the high bank a few minutes, and surveyed the boiling and rushing water beneath, while immediately above were a succession of small falls, varying from six to ten feet in height. At the bottom of the last there was a rapid extending about twenty paces down the river; then came another fall of greater depth; after which the torrent rushes onward over large stones until it joins the Katounaia. Across this rapid, between the falls, we had to make our passage, not one at a time, but five abreast, otherwise we should be swept away. As we could only descend the rocky bank in single file, and scarcely find room at the bottom for our horses to stand upon, it was no easy matter to form our party before plunging into the foaming water. Yepta was the first to descend; I followed; then came three others, with two led horses. To go straight across was impossible; we could only land on some shelving rocks a few paces above the lower fall. The brave Yepta gave the word, and we rode into the rushing water knee to knee. Our horses walked slowly and steadily on as the water dashed up their sides; instinct making them aware of the danger, they kept their heads straight across the stream. The distance we forded was not more than twenty paces, but we were at least five minutes doing it, and it was with no small satisfaction that we found ourselves standing on the rocks, some twenty feet above the water, wishing as safe a passage to our friends. When I saw them drawn up on the little bank, and then dash into the stream, I felt the danger of their position more than when crossing myself. Their horses breasted the torrent bravely, and all were safely landed; the dog was placed on one of the pack-horses, where he lay between the bags in perfect security. I am certain that every man felt a relief when the enterprise was accomplished, which would have been impossible had the water been three inches deeper.

While engaged sketching this dangerous spot, the hunter related to me the following anecdote, which gave a tragical character to the scene: I mentioned before that the Chinese had a picket near the Kara-goll, and it was by this route the soldiers came to relieve their companions and bring their provisions. On one occasion a party of sixteen men arrived here on their way to join their comrades at the Kara-goll. Six rode in abreast, but had only gone three or four paces when they found the water unusually deep, and the torrent swept them down. In a few moments five of them went over the fall; one man threw his long rein toward his comrades on the bank, which was caught, and by this means both man and horse were saved. The other poor fellows and their horses were dashed against the rocks and killed almost immediately; nor was there a single body of either found.

Continuing my ride down the valley, in about two hours I reached the River Katounaia, running in a valley about a verst broad, and covered with a rich grassy sward. Fine clumps of birches and pines are scattered about, while the lower parts of the mountains on either side are covered with a thick forest of picta and cedars. Some of these summits are bare rocks, and others reach far up into the snowy region. Our track was now up the banks of the river, and in about two hours we reached the Tourgan, which has its rise in the mountains to the northwest of the Bielouka. The view up this valley is very fine: a broad stream comes dashing over large rocks looking like snow; groups of magnificent cedars are growing on its banks, intermingled with graceful pendent foliage of the birch, colored in rich yellow and orange tints, while the poplar has put on every shade of color, from the most beautiful orange to the deepest crimson. Overtopping these are rocky ridges of brown and purple; the more distant mountains take a more aërial tone; and beyond, the snowy summits of the chain shoot far into the sky, looking like frosted silver against the deep ethereal blue.

Almost immediately after fording the Tourgan we were obliged to ford the Katounaia, high precipices rising from the bed of the river stopping our onward course. This stream was not difficult to cross, although five times as wide as the Tourgan. We pushed on toward a point where the valley makes a turn to the northward, and here I expected that we should obtain a view of the mountain we had traveled so far to see. I was the more anxious, as the sky was without a cloud, a rare occurrence in these regions at this season of the year. Yepta, the hunter, and a Kalmuck, rode on with me at a sharp gallop over very rough ground. Having proceeded about five versts, we reached the bend in the valley, where Bielouka stood before us in all his grandeur. I lost no time in seeking out a good point whence to sketch this monarch of the Altai chain. Adding this to my collection was something important gained, although I felt convinced other views might be met with of greater sublimity. Yepta and two other Kalmucks started with me on a sketching expedition across one of the spurs that run from the Bielouka toward the south. Even the lower part of it was extremely steep, which caused us to make many zigzag windings. When about half way up, we came to a most effectual barrier—

perpendicular rocks about a hundred feet high. We now turned toward the east, riding along the foot of these precipices, and shortly arrived at an opening, but so steep that it was doubtful if we could get up on foot. Leaving two Kalumcks with the horses, Yepta and myself started, and shortly discovered that it was almost impossible to keep our feet; one slip and a roll to the bottom would have been our fate. At last we reached the top, and found ourselves on a plateau rising gently for about half a verst to some rugged crags, crowned with dwarf cedars; beyond these rose the icy summit of Bielouka sparkling in the sun. Turning toward the southeast, we had a fine view looking down into the valley of the Biela, or White Beryl, which has its source among some high peaks of a very picturesque shape. The water in this little river has a most peculiar appearance; looking at it from this distance, it is like milk tinged with green. The rocks on this mountain are slate, of various colors—purple, blue, and light green. I have no doubt the latter gives the tint to the water.

Yepta.

The sky was now without a cloud; every mountain top was clear, and their outlines beautifully defined. While sketching the valley of the Beryl, the two Kalmucks arrived with our horses; they had continued their ride along the foot of the cliffs, and found by ascending one of the ravines that they could reach us on the little plateau. I was glad, as this would enable us to cross the mountain, and return by another route. Having finished my sketch, we rode on toward the cliffs, from which we could look down into the valley of the Katounaia. On gaining the crest we beheld the river running in its deep valley among dark pines, which gave a gloomy aspect to the scene. The sun no longer penetrated into these depths, although he was shining in full splendor on every thing around us. After riding a short distance, I attained a point which afforded me a fine view of Bielouka, a stupendous mass, whose mighty crags protrude through the snow and ice of ages. It has a singular effect when the sunlight falls on the different masses of snow, ice, and rocks. The summit of Bielouka is formed by two enormous peaks, shored up with innumerable buttresses, which form ravines or small valleys, now filled up with glaciers descending to the edge of some fearful precipices, which overhang the valley of the Katounaia.

The whole of the mountains around this giant of the chain seem to be composed of slate; on the lower spurs rich short grass was growing, which would have made a fine pasture for thousands of sheep. In this grass I found many spring flowers—the red *primula*, sweet-scented violet, and several sorts of anemones. Theirs will be but a short life, for in ten or twelve days deep snow will cover them for nine or ten months. It is a long winter. Three or four hundred feet higher the herbage had almost ceased; several varieties of mosses cover the stony ground and cling to the rocks. A little higher, and these are lost—long before we reached the top of one of the lower ridges separating the valleys of the Katounaia and Beryl. While sketching even in this high region I was attacked by legions of musquitoes: it is seldom they have any visitors in this region. Having finished my sketches, I was not sorry to move off into a more exposed situation, where the breeze dispersed my tormentors. During the time I had been occupied, Yepta had crossed the ridge, and discovered that it was utterly impossible for us to ascend to the Bielouka in that direction. We rode slowly down the mountain, that in some parts was exceedingly steep; and having gone more to the east, we had a fine view down the Biela Beryl, which at the lower end of the valley runs through a narrow and very deep gorge where there must be many falls, sounds of the roaring water being borne to us on the breeze. A little before dark we rode up to our camp, and found a large blazing fire; a fine deer had been added to our larder, shot by the hunter in one of the valleys not far distant. I gave the men a double quantity of *wodky*, and both Russians and Kalmucks feasted till a late hour.

About two o'clock next morning I was awoke by the hunter throwing logs of wood on the fire, when, to my great regret, I discovered that it was raining fast; the wind was blowing hard, and a thick fog driving along, obscuring every thing at a short distance from our fire. At nine o'clock the weather improved, the driving clouds rolled up the mountain sides, and the rain ceased, notwithstanding which, Yepta and the hunter said we should not be able to ascend the Bielouka. This induced me to order a march to the hot springs on the shore of Racmanskoï Lake, directly south from our present position. At ten we were once more in the saddle, started across a small ridge, and descended to the Biela Beryl. The stream is less than the Katounaia, the water thick and of a whitish green, appearing like a clouded beryl, many of which I have seen in large crystals. I found the slate in its bed of a light green color, some of it very soft; this is the cause of its peculiarity. A short distance from where we crossed the stream it enters a deep and wild gorge, through which it runs over many a fall, the roaring of the water being heard to a considerable distance; but these falls can neither be visited nor sketched. Not far from the view we came upon a rounded mass of purple slate, quite isolated, and about eighty feet high. As we approached it had the appearance of a huge Kourgan or tumulus; I sketched it, and then climbed to its dome-like summit; the crevices were filled with flowering plants, some still in bloom, and from others I collected seed. I discovered a small creeper, with a deep crimson flower of great beauty. A month earlier this must have been a lovely spot.

The clouds were gradually rising; all the lower range of mountains were clear, and the sun struggling to penetrate the thick canopy above us. Soon after leaving the valley we entered a dense forest covering the north side of the mountain which separates the Biela and Tcherney Beryls. Huge masses of slate had been hurled from its summit, forming a small chaos, about a verst in width, among which large cedars were growing. We made an attempt to ascend over this heap of ruins, but after an hour's trial were obliged to give it up. Yepta proposed that we should ride along the foot of the mountain to the westward; we did so, and shortly came to the bed of a mountain torrent nearly dry. Up this we turned our steps, and bad enough was the road; but, being free from trees and underwood, we could avoid the deep holes. It is wonderful to look upon the deep channel plowed through the mass of huge rocks that have been tossed about and piled up into heaps. Enormous trees have been uprooted, thrown across these pillars, and form bridges over which Bruin may pass when the torrent is raging without even wetting his paws. Other large trunks have been snapped asunder as if they were mere sticks. In about an hour we got over this difficulty, and continued our ride through the forest. At a short distance from the summit we passed over a small grassy hollow, and then crossed the ridge. Before descending we waited a short time, hoping the clouds would clear away from the top of Bielouka and let us have a peep at his snowy crest. But the mass of vapor continued to shroud him in its misty folds.

A keen blast made us desirous of a warmer berth in the valley, but this was not accomplished until we had had a ride of five or six versts over a high plateau, on which not a tree was growing, and here we found it bitterly cold. At last we began the descent, going for a short distance down a ravine, and then in a zigzag course down the mountain side, on which the horses had great difficulty in keeping their feet. It was so steep that even on foot no man could walk either up or down in a straight course. Having reached the bottom, we were soon on the bank of the Tcherney Beryl, which runs in a picturesque channel formed in the slate rocks. The water in this river is as clear as crystal, but with a greenish tinge; the deep purple mountains from which it comes, and the dark slate over which it runs, may perhaps have given it the name of Black Beryl. It has its source in a small black-looking lake between high mountains, shortly after flowing from which it is lost under some high rocks, and comes to daylight again on the opposite side of a spur from one of the mountains, which runs into the small valley; its subterranean course is several versts in length

After leaving this river we had a rugged and rocky mountain to pass, and the ascent was made with great difficulty over steep and stony places. About midday we reached some large rocks jutting out of the ground, among which I secured several choice specimens of jasper; blocks of considerable dimensions could be obtained here. On the summit I found some beautiful aventurine, equal if not superior to the best I have seen from Taganai in the South Oural. The top appears like a vast heap of ruins, not a block of stone lying in its original position. The devastation extends over a space half a verst in breadth, and not less than three versts in length; how it has been caused I am at a loss to conjecture. The horses were sent round, and I scrambled over these rocks on foot, shortly after passing which we began to descend to the lake. The warm springs were instantly recognized by the steam arising from them, and the water of the lake appeared black as it lay in the deep rocky gorge. There is rich pasture extending from these springs down the narrow valley for seven or eight hundred paces, when it is lost in a thick wood, through which the waters of the lake flow to the west, and ultimately into the Biela Beryl. Crossing this, near to the hot springs, we made our way through a thick wood, on the skirts of which, very snugly encamped, were four Kalmucks and a woman, from the upper valley of the Tschoulishman. It was with no little surprise they saw our party burst through the thick underwood. We merely saluted them and rode on to the shore of the lake, where we encamped under some fine picta-trees, in front of which there was a sandy beach eight or ten paces wide, stretching to the opposite side of the lake. Having flushed a woodcock near our encamping ground while the men were pitching the tent and making the other preparations for the night, I took my gun and the dog and rambled along the skirts of the forest, and in less than an hour I brought in five of these birds. The Kalmucks and the woman had joined our party, and were sitting cosily round the fire. About twenty paces from my tent and ten from the lake, two hot springs bubbled up, the water so hot that I could not keep my hand in it; from this I went to the bath which the Kalmucks have made: it is four feet deep, seven feet long, and five feet wide. Several springs run into it, from which the water overflows into the lake. At a short distance from the bath there is another place where the water rises rapidly; in a space of fifty feet in diameter there are more than a hundred little jets boiling up. I sat down on a stone near the middle of this spot, and soon found it would give me a vapor-bath. The Kalmucks from the Tschoulishman had been staying here thirteen days; when they arrived there were eight Kirghis from the steppe near Ilka Aral-Nor, but these had left two days before we arrived. I regretted this much, as I might have met some old acquaintances. From what I could learn, the bath is frequented by many people during the summer. Wild as the place is, I must own it is far more to my taste than the fashionable gambling mud baths of Germany.

As the day closed in dark clouds gathered round some of the high summits, betokening bad weather, and a cold wind rushed down the mountain ravines and swept over the lake in gusts. Yepta had a large quantity of fuel collected to keep up the fire through the night, as he said it would be cold and stormy, and every precaution was taken to secure the tents and afford us shelter. Soon after dark we could hear the roaring of the wind in the forest above; nor was it long in paying us a visit, and lashing the lake into a fury. The water was driven close up to our fire; presently it began to snow fast, and in a very short time all around was wrapped in a wintry mantle.

While sitting at breakfast next morning our neighbors called to announce their departure, fearing they might be stopped in the mountains by a heavy fall of snow. They advised us to leave as soon as possible, nor were we inclined to delay.

Five versts from the lake we came to the point where the Kalmucks turned to the east, and our route was directly north. We saw them upon one of the ridges about a verst distant. Both parties stopped for two or three minutes, then they descended below the rocks, and we beheld them no more. While crossing the high plateau we had a snowstorm and a great wind, rendering our ride very disagreeable, and almost blinding us. In six hours after leaving the lake we were sitting at our old encampment on the spur of the Bielouka, where we dined and made ourselves comfortable before a good fire; but a more pleasant resting-place having been proposed, we were once more facing the storm, which had now become sleet and rain, and about an hour before dark we arrived at a capital place, sheltered by rocks and trees.

The stormy night brought forth a bright morning, and as we left our encampment the white snowy peaks of Bielouka became brighter every minute, showing us that the sun was rising; nor was it long before they were tipped with his dazzling light, while we were obscured in a cold and deep gray shadow. The valley gradually became narrower as we advanced, the cedar and picta trees growing on the banks of the river in some places filling it up; the sides were abrupt, in some parts nearly perpendicular. On examining the water I found it was thick and of a whitish green, exactly like that in the Biela Beryl, proving that both are colored in the same way. A ride of an hour brought us to a point where the Katounaia is divided into two branches, one turning toward the northwest, the other to the northeast. The latter has its source among the glaciers of the Bielouka, and along this we continued our ride. We soon reached a point beyond the last straggling trees, even in the valley, while the little dwarfs on the mountains, which appeared forcing themselves into the region of snow, were left far behind us. A very scanty vegetation was growing in the clefts of the slate rocks, but this shortly ceased, and we entered upon a scene of desolation, rock and snow. The cliffs on both sides are a light green slate, some of it very hard and capable of receiving a fine polish; other portions are less hard, and in places are reduced to the consistency of a soft greenish clay, and this it is which colors the Katounaia and Biela Beryl.

It was impossible to proceed farther on horseback, and we were obliged to ascend on foot over the rocks, ice, and snow that blocked up the passage. Our party was now divided, the hunter, Yepta, and three Kalmucks accompanying me, all "good men and true." They carried with them three bottles of *wodky*, a bottle of *nalifka*, and some cold venison; bread we had none. Our rifles and all shooting apparatus were placed under some rocks to protect them from wet (we had no fear of thieves stealing our arms); above this point they would be useless, as no animals exist there. The horses were sent to a place where they could feed, and orders given to the two Kalmucks to return with them an hour before dark. The other two men were to go to the camp and make all ready for our night's lodgings. A little before ten o'clock we began to climb the mass ot ruin before us, the *débris* of an avalanche fallen from the Bielouka during the summer.

What an awful crash there must have been when this mighty fragment was hurled from near the summit of the mountain, cutting a broad and deep gap through one of the glaciers, the accumulation of ages, and carrying along in its course huge rocks, torn from their native beds by the crystal mass as it rushed on into the gorge, where they now lie in a confused heap, filling up the narrow space to the height of one hundred and fifty feet; while, extending about five hundred yards up the ravine, from beneath the blocks of ice and rock the Katounaia issues forth. After scrambling over this rugged spot we descended to the little river, or rather torrent, running among rocks, and often under ice and snow, that have formed natural bridges, beneath which the water rushes in many a fall.

We reached the foot of a glacier in a deep ravine, that extends very far up the mountain; from under two small arches in this mass of ice the Katounaia gushes forth in two streams, and is soon lost again under a bed of snow for a space of several hundred yards. This is the veritable source of the river.

So far one object of my journey was gained; but the mighty precipices of the Bielouka reared their rugged faces several hundred feet above us, and to ascend up the edge of the glacier was impossible. We sat down on some rocks, and while making our midday meal I scanned the towering crags with an anxious wish to plant my foot upon them. Presently we turned to the west, and entered a fearful-looking gorge, that appeared to lead up into the mountain; in this we found vast rocks and ice which had fallen from above. Over these we scrambled, often at considerable risk; at length a gleam of hope shot down upon us. The ravine terminated in a series of shelving rocks, forming almost an inclined plane, at the top of which one of the peaks of the Bielouka reared its lofty head. This gave us fresh vigor for the toil, and our cry was now "Excelsior!" Step after step was climbed up a vast stair of nature's own constructing, which at last landed us on the frozen snow. Over this we walked with much difficulty for about three hundred paces, when we stood at the base of the two high peaks of Bielouka, overlooking every summit of the Altai. To the west the vast steppes of the Kirghis stretched till lost in hazy distance. To the south were some high peaks, and many ridges descending toward the steppes on the east of Nor-Zaisan, and to the Desert of Gobi. Several lakes were visible in the mountains and on the distant steppes. Innumerable rivers were winding their courses in the deep valleys like a network of silver threads. It was a splendid vista, so many snowy peaks starting up from the purple ridges and green valleys around them.

While examining with intense interest the sea of mountains, and endeavoring to trace some of the routes by which I had traveled among them, the piercing blast intimated that it was time to move. Going about a hundred paces farther, we found ourselves at the head of another glacier, which descends by a deep ravine toward the west. Beyond this lay the great hollow between the two peaks. This we might reach, but to ascend either was impossible. They are cones from eight hundred to a thousand feet high, covered with hard frozen snow, with a few points of the green slate jutting through.

Hitherto the sky had been clear except to the northeast, where rolling masses of clouds were seen. Now the vapor commenced condensing into thick clouds around the peaks above us, which caused Yepta and the hunter to urge our immediate return. We began to retrace our steps, slowly at first, over the slippery ice and snow. After reaching the vast rocky stair our descent was rapid, but in some parts we found it much more difficult than climbing. When standing on the spot from which we had first seen the high peak, I stopped to take a last look at the loftiest point in the Altai; but this was denied me. The mountain had put on his robe of clouds, which were curling and waving in the breeze as the vapor gathered rapidly around his head. Notwithstanding some slipping and several tumbles, we came down in an hour; the ascent had taken more than three. The snow among the rocks enabled us to see our old tracks, and kept us away from some of the deep chains which would have rendered our descent more difficult, in some parts exceedingly dangerous.

We lost no time in making our way over the wreck of the avalanche, as the clouds were descending fast; indeed, most of the lower mountains were covered, and to be caught in this valley by a fog might prove a serious obstacle to our reaching the camp. Yepta showed more anxiety than I had ever observed before, and hastened us onward. We were not long in reaching the spot where the Kalmucks were waiting with our horses; then, having secured our arms, we rode rapidly toward our tents. With all our hurry, we were caught in a storm of snow, which almost blinded us; but it made our canvas home, with the blazing fire, look quite comfortable. Morning broke upon us through clouds of snow, and we rode slowly down the bank of the Katounaia. As the day advanced the storm became worse, which caused us to push on; still, our pace was slow, and not till six o'clock did we reach the Tourgan.

The hunter and Yepta advised our fording at the junction of the rivers, where the bed was broad and shallow. The water was deeper than my men had anticipated, but ford it we must, and that without delay. Our horses were drawn up in line on the bank, and then we rode slowly into the stream, which dashed up against their sides and on to our saddles. It was only by going in a close body that the animals could stand and force their way through the torrent. A party of three or four would have been swept away in a moment; nor did we accomplish the passage without considerable risk, and all felt a great relief when we stood on the western bank and looked back at the rapid flood. Yepta placed a stone near the edge of the water to see if it was rising, and in a very short time it was covered; had we been a few minutes later, we could not have crossed the torrent. The night continued stormy, with a cold wind howling through the forest, making the trees bend, and wrenching off their branches, which came tumbling down on our tents. All these were intimations not to be misunderstood, and the sooner we were among the Kalmucks on the Abbaye Steppe the better. Still, we had a long ride and many high mountains to cross before that warm and sheltered spot could be reached.

I awoke long before daylight, shivering with cold, and found the damp clothing frozen, and our fire nearly extinguished. Presently one of the men turned out and heaped up a large quantity of fuel, which was quickly in a blaze. Just as the day broke we were up and preparing for a long ride. In some of the pools the ice was half an inch thick, and the wind appeared to cut through us. About a verst from our encampment we entered upon a beautiful steppe, extending about ten versts, and the Katounaia ran in a deep channel close to the mountains on the south side. Along its bank fine clumps of trees were growing, giving to the spot a rich pastoral character, inclosed by mountains of greenish slate, the lower parts clothed with fine timber, their summits jagged and bare. After passing the steppe the valley becomes narrow, with a thick forest, through which we found it difficult to force our way. We had been struggling in this wilderness two hours nearly when we came upon an open space about five hundred yards broad, extending from the river to the top of the mountains on the north. An avalanche had swept over this spot only a few weeks ago, without leaving a tree standing, and very few lying on the ground. Beyond we found a morass, which caused us much trouble, and great toil to our horses. At this point the valley is bounded on both sides by very high slaty precipices, up which it was impossible to ascend, and get out of the quagmire that surrounded us.

Farther down the valley we came upon a bed of slate rocks extending quite across from one mountain to the other. Ages ago there had been a splendid waterfall on this spot, with a channel sixty feet deep; now the once magnificent fall has become a mere rapid. The slate in the mountains and in the valley is still the same formation as that on the Bielouka—soft, and of a pale green color. After passing these masses the scenery becomes much finer, and we enter upon the granite formation, which is thrown up and tossed about in a most capricious manner. Huge blocks are strewn over the valley, extending into the bed of the river, now become a broad stream dashing and foaming among the rocks, creating a terrible roar. For many miles the river is one rapid, which looks like snow when seen from one of the heights over which we rode. About an hour before sunset we arrived at the River Karaoul, which runs through a beautiful valley. Here we encamped on a most lovely spot—a fine green sward, with clumps of weeping birch-trees waving their golden foliage in the breeze; dark cedars and pictas extend far up the mountain sides, and these are overtopped by granite crags, covered with moss of every hue.

We had descended from the wintry region into summer. Many flowers were still in full bloom; the grayling were springing at the flies which sported over the pools, and several broods of ducks were swimming on the water. The Kalmucks soon procured us a dish of the finny tribe, while the hunter and myself supplied our larder with some of the feathered race, on which we all fared sumptuously. Large blazing fires were made, and a double allowance of grog given to each man, after the hard toil in the snowy regions we had just left. These troubles were now forgotten, and my companions made the woods resound with their wild songs. Yepta informed me that he had often hunted the *alain* on the mountains a short distance to the northeast of our encampment, and proposed to guide us over them, descending to the Katounaia at a point from which we should find a track down to the mouth of the River Koksa. By following this route we should save a day's ride and pass through a new region. I at once decided that this should be our line of march in the morning.

When we rose from our turfy beds the day was just breaking; long streaks of yellow rays were shooting up beyond the gray and purple crested mountains over which we must ride, while a gloomy twilight overshaded all the lower ridges and deep valleys. A very short time was spent in eating our frugal meal, when we mounted, forded the River Karaoul, and began to ascend the lower ridges. When these were crossed we got into a finely-wooded region, extending far up the higher slopes. Here we had no track to guide us toward the summit, and frequently we found the wood so thick that it was exceedingly difficult to penetrate; nor could we get a view of any of the peaks above us.

After riding about two hours we came to a more open place, and found a garden of raspberries extending along the mountain for three or four versts. The fruit was very large and ripe, and could have been gathered in enormous quantities. We had not ridden far when we came upon many well-trodden tracks, crossing in every direction, made by the bears, who are extremely fond of this fruit.

Having made a most delicious repast, we pushed forward toward the summit, still riding through a thick wood, and along the edge of a steep descent. The roaring of a mountain torrent was heard in the deep valley, but no traces of it could be seen. We had not gone far in this dense and tangled forest when other sounds greeted our ears, which brought some of our horses to a stand in a moment. At a very short distance in front of us we could hear some animals rushing through the brushwood. Yepta and the hunter said they were bears. Our steeds were left with the men, and we started on foot in pursuit. In a few minutes we found the track, when my two companions discovered that we had disturbed a female and her two cubs. They were running fast, and left us far behind. To continue the chase would have been useless, for it was impossible to come up with them before they reached the valley, where, among the slate rocks, broken into rugged crags and precipices, they would soon find a hiding-place out of our reach.

A call from Yepta brought our party to us, when we continued our journey up the mountain, and rode out of the forest. For about two versts our path was over a fine mossy turf; after passing this we entered upon a much more difficult track, through fallen rocks and large patches of snow. From this place we had a most dreary and tedious ride. Summit after summit was crossed, but not a tree presented itself to vary the dull aspect around us. We found several tracks made by the stags, but not a single animal. Yepta and the hunter thought we might find them in some of the lower valleys, as they had left this region for the winter.

We still kept riding on, and hour after hour was passed amid the rocks and snow. At last we began to descend toward the wooded region, and soon obtained a view of the Katounaia running in a deep valley three thousand feet below us, and through this forest we must descend to the river. We found a track made by animals, and followed it downward; but the path, which was easy for stags and deer, was difficult for our horses. In many places we had to pass over a narrow ledge, with deep precipices beneath our feet, often rising high above our heads. In one place we had to ride over what the Kalmucks call a "bomb;" this is a narrow ridge of rocks, along which but one horse can pass at a time. Should two persons meet on many parts of these bombs, one of the horses must be thrown over; they could not pass or turn around. As we had now reached the track by which the Kalmuck hunters ascend these mountains, Yepta ordered a halt, and sent one of his companions on foot to the other end of this fearful ridge, hid from our view by some high crags, round which we had to ride. In somewhat less than half an hour he returned, but without his cap; this had been left to signal to any hunters who might come up that a party were crossing the bomb.

Yepta and the hunter told me to drop the reins on my horse's neck, and he would go over with perfect safety. The former led the van; I followed, as desired, at three or four paces behind him. For the first twenty yards the sensation was not agreeable. After that I felt perfect confidence in the animal, and was sure, if left to himself, he would carry me safely over. The whole distance was about five hundred paces, and occupied us about a quarter of an hour in crossing. In some places it was fearful to look down; on one side the rocks were nearly perpendicular for five or six hundred feet, and on the other so steep that no man could stand upon them. When over, I turned round and watched the others thread their way across; it was truly terrific to look at them on the narrow and stony path: one false step, and both horse and rider must be hurled into the valley a thousand feet below! These are the perils over which the daring sable-hunters often ride. With them it is a necessity; they risk it to obtain food, and not for bravado or from foolhardy recklessness, like that of some men who ride their horses up and down a staircase. Kalmuck and Kirghis would laugh at such feats. I have seen men who would ride their horses along the roof of the highest cathedral in Europe if a plank eighteen inches wide were secured along the ridge; nor would they require a great wager to induce them to do it; theirs is a continual life of danger and hardship, and they never seek it unnecessarily.

After passing this slaty ridge, which runs across the deep valley, we descended rapidly through a thick forest of cedars, some of them of very large dimensions. Farther down we passed into a dense mass of underwood, among which were pines and a few larches of immense size, some one hundred and fifty feet in height. What splendid masts they would have made! Here they must grow and decay, or be shivered by the lightning; perhaps the hand of man will never be raised against them. Again we disturbed a bear: he was seen for a moment as he rushed across the narrow track into the thick forest. We could hear the cracking of the branches, but to follow him was impossible. Shortly after this we descended upon a beautiful grassy plot with clumps of birch and mountain ash. Just as we entered a fine buck bounded past, about fifty paces in front; the dog turned him, when Yepta and myself fired at the same moment, and he fell: he was pierced with two balls. The hunter and two Kalmucks dashed off at full speed toward the river. In a few minutes we heard the crack of their rifles: two other deer were swimming the river, but not one of the balls took effect. We had, however, secured a splendid buck, in prime condition. I need not say that my fellows made a sumptuous supper, and spent a glorious evening with their grog and tobacco.

This was a favorite haunt of the Kalmuck hunters: it was a fine green spot, about six hundred paces in length, formed by a circular indent into the mountains, with high rocks rising up perpendicularly from the river at both ends. The only path in or out was the small ravine by which we had entered, while in front of us ran the River Katounaia, at this point one hundred and fifty yards wide, deep and rapid. Immediately opposite the rocks at the lower end of this plot a great "parrock" (a succession of falls) commenced, extending for about half a mile. The water was tumbling and dashing over and among large rocks, making a tremendous roar. It was not pleasant music, knowing we must cross a short distance above it; but no advantage was to be gained by brooding over the risk. We enjoyed our supper, and slept as soundly as if the river were bridged with granite for our passage in the morning.

The Kalmuck hunters have a canoe here in which they row over, but it was secured upon the opposite bank under some bushes. The first thing to be done was to obtain the little boat, and carry all our baggage and saddles across. One of the Kalmucks undressed and walked as far up the bank as possible, then plunged into the stream. This was quite necessary, to avoid being carried down into the falls. The man was a strong swimmer; nevertheless, he was floated far down the stream before he reached the opposite shore. His companions had no fear for him, and in a short time he launched the canoe and rowed it across. A small quantity of baggage was placed in it and paddled over by two men, and they had to cross many times before all our traps were on the opposite bank. At last this was done, and then began the difficulty of getting our horses over.

One little Kalmuck, whom I had named "Chort" (devil) from his daring and antics, had been my companion on several different rides, and had given me ample proof of his courage. He was short in stature, and slightly built, supple in his limbs, and as active as a panther. He had a high round head, with a long tuft of jet black hair hanging from the crown far down his back, a pair of jet black sparkling eyes, and a face so characteristic that it must have been handed down to him through several generations. This little fellow had been selected by Yepta to take over the cattle. He stripped and mounted one of the horses, when all of them were driven up the bank to a place about three hundred yards above the falls; beyond this point the bank was too deep for them to walk into the water. There was many a run before they were all got together to the proper place; they evidently knew that the swim would be a difficult one, and were afraid. At last the whole sixteen were in the stream, and the little Kalmuck on the last horse, on which he kept to the lower side to drive them up. The moment a horse was carried below him, he slipped into the water, swam to him, laid hold of his tail, sprang upon his back like a monkey, and began shouting and driving the rest up the stream. This was repeated a dozen times or more before he got them across, and he was not more than twenty yards above the falls when he landed them all safely.

I have had much experience among the wild tribes of Asia; I have swum rivers with them, and have forded most dangerous streams in their company; many brave and daring spirits have been my companions, but I have never met the equal of my little "Chort."

Our path was now down the banks of the Katounaia, which runs in a narrow valley, with mountains rising above the line of vegetation on each side, and from many points the snow-capped summits of the higher chain were seen. I added several sketches to my collection from different positions in this valley, representing scenes of great beauty and grandeur. We had descended to a summer climate, in some parts the ground being covered with flowers, and the grass green and fresh, like spring. A week or ten days later, these valleys, now decked in all their summer beauty, will be swept over by the wintry blast, and scorched as if a fire had passed over them. So sudden are the changes, that I have seen the foliage cut down in one night. We have gone to sleep around our fire on a fine summer evening, and in the morning awoke under a coverlet of six inches of snow. Our ride today was not a long one, as I found much occupation for my pencil; indeed, one view looking down the valley to Tigeretzkoï Belock was exceedingly beautiful, the rich tints of the foliage on the lower mountains varying from the deep green of the pines to the pale yellow and orange on the birches, consisting of every shade of these colors to red, until they assume the deepest and most brilliant crimson. Above these rose up the brown and purple crests of the Tchurish Mountains, while beyond, and standing out from the rich golden sky, with its fleecy crimson clouds, was Tigeretzskoï, whose rocky and rugged sides were shaded into a misty purple, and its summit capped with snow, sparkling like a ruby as the sun went down. Even my Kalmucks were not insensible to the beauty of this prospect, but to the Russian it presented no charm. He has no love for Nature or admiration of her attractions.

A little after sunset we reached the mouth of the River Tschugash, where it falls into the Katounaia. This is also a most lovely spot; it is sheltered by some very high rocks of fine green and purple jasper, their tops fringed with birch and mountain ash, the latter covered with bunches of deep scarlet fruit, used in almost every dwelling throughout Siberia. The wealthy *housewife* makes a *nalifka* from it which is considered excellent: it has a fine bitter flavor. They make it into a preserve, and some dry the fruit in sugar. A delicious salad is also made by placing the bunches in large jars, filling them up with vinegar slightly sweetened with honey: this is found in most cottages. There are very few wild fruits which the Siberian does not turn to account, and, fortunately for him, his country abounds with them.

On this spot we were encamped about twenty-five feet above the water, and at the head of a great "parrock," or rapid, extending about half a verst. The river was narrowed at this point to about one hundred yards wide; the bed was a mass of large rocks, some of them standing eight or ten feet above the water. Against these the torrent rushed with such force that the water was thrown up in thick columns of white spray fifteen to twenty feet in height, breaking and falling in hundreds of little streams. Other rocks were covered, over which the flood rolled and surged in fearful eddies, in many parts forming whirlpools. The noise was deafening.

I was sitting sketching on a large rock overhanging the stream, when I perceived the little "Chort," divested of every rag of clothing, walking away from the river. The other Kalmucks were standing in a group on the edge of the bank, watching him. I could not understand what they were at, but was soon enlightened by observing the man run toward the bank and leap into the boiling flood. He plunged head foremost, the next moment rose to the surface, and was swept past like an arrow, but with his head well out of the water, to see the rocks before him. I expected to behold him dashed against some of the huge stones, or be sucked under by the eddies; but on he went, like a fish darting past. Two of his friends ran along the bank, and were soon left behind. I could see him float on for about one hundred yards; beyond this he was lost to my sight—I feared forever. It is impossible to describe my feelings during the few minutes I watched for him in the comparatively calm water at the bottom of the rapid. Presently, to my great relief, I beheld him climb the bank, where he sat down on a stone for two or three minutes, when, noticing my presence, he ran to me laughing. His friends were enchanted, nor did they seemingly think that he had run any risk, for they stood around him talking and laughing. Fearing, as he did not attempt to dress, that they were urging him to try the feat again, I walked up to them to prevent his risking his life a second time.

The hunter translated into Russian his reply to my remonstrance: "Eta nitchevo Barin; ya ochin lubit!" (It is nothing, sir; I love it.) Seeing they had all made up their minds that he should do it again, I walked back to the rock, taking out my watch to note the time occupied in passing the rapid. Again I saw him take the fearful plunge, but this time it was a little higher up the river. He shot up out of the water like a duck, looked forward, and the next moment went past me as if thrown from a catapult. In three minutes and twenty-eight seconds I watched him leave the water at the bottom of the rapid. Again the fearless fellow came running up to me laughing like a schoolboy.

We had a heavy storm of thunder in the night, with many fearful flashes of lightning, and the rain poured down in streams, against which our canvas and leafy covering formed no protection. These storms are certain harbingers of winter. Before daylight a council was held by Yepta, the hunter, and the other Kalmucks, when it was decided that we should take the shortest route to the village of Ouemonia. After a ride of six hours in rain and sunshine, we reached the village about noon, to the great joy of every one, the people having already become very anxious on our account.

I ordered a man to be sent to Kokstschinskoï to get horses and men in readiness for our arrival. The little old woman occupied herself in preparing me a dinner, consisting of eggs, potatoes, butter, and delicious honey, upon which I feasted most sumptuously, and then said adieu to my companions. They were brave fellows; I was sorry to part with them, and I think they will not soon forget me. Having crossed the Katounaia in a boat, I found men and horses ready to take me to Kokstschinskoï, where we arrived in about an hour. Here were fresh horses and new companions, and in less than half an hour we rode out of the village and crossed the little steppe. Our horses were put into a sharp trot, as I intended to sleep at our old encampment, where we had the terrible thunder-storm on my way hither. It was a long ride, but the animals were fresh, and carried us briskly over the grassy turf. We passed through the forest, then had a gallop over the steppe, and a little after nightfall were once more sitting under the larches, taking our evening meal. It was a calm night; the roaring of the cataracts on the Koksa was heard, sometimes with a deafening noise, then the sound came as if breathed in the softest sigh. This music fell most agreeably on the ear, and soothed our spirits.

Long before daylight the wind was blowing in squalls, accompanied by drenching showers, a state of things far from pleasing. As the morning broke we saw all the mountain tops enveloped in heavy clouds, which passed rapidly across their sides, sending down upon us a sort of Scotch mist, that dampened our clothing, but not our spirits. Our morning meal was quickly over, and once more we were on our road. At the commencement our ride was rather disagreeable, for a pouring rain was driving in our faces; but this did not continue long. The clouds began to rise like a mighty curtain, and one summit after another appeared, covered with its winter garments. We were now leaving the River Koksa several versts to the south, and following a track through a number of small steppes, lying between picturesque ridges of granite, and forming a beautiful landscape.

After a ride of nine hours a Kalmuck *aoul* was seen some seven or eight versts to the south. Two of my companions were sent to obtain horses for our whole party, and men to act as guides to the source of the Tchurish, while we went on to seek for a place on which to encamp for the night. A few versts brought us to the River Tschugash, tumbling and leaping in many a cascade down a small valley in the mountains which separate these steppes from the valley of the Tchurish. A nice wooded spot was selected for our resting-place, the tents were pitched under some pine-trees, and we were soon made snug for the night. The clouds were dispersed, and the evening sun was tinging every mountain top with his glorious rays, while all below was bathed in misty shadow. It was a beautiful calm evening; scarcely a leaf was moved; and the smoke from our fires rose up high into the air, far above our lofty pines. The thrushes were singing their evening songs on many a branch, while the call of the reptchick (tree-partridge) to its mate was heard in the neighboring forest. This proved fatal to many; I very soon shot sufficient for our supper, to the great gratification of my men. I had returned to our camp, and was sitting quietly drinking my tea, when five Kalmucks arrived at full speed, reeling on their horses, quite drunk. My two men, with other Kalmucks, followed quickly, bringing horses for our journey to-morrow.

My visitors had come with the hope of getting *wodky*, but this I would not give. I offered a tumbler of tea to the chief, which he rejected, and demanded *arrak* in a very insolent manner. He was sitting on the ground directly opposite to me, tall, thin, and apparently slight built, with a most unprepossessing countenance, rendered almost demoniac by the spirit he had drunk. His brother, a powerful man, sat beside him, also demanding *arrak*, but I took no notice of him: the other three were the great man's attendants, and crouched on their haunches close beside him, ready to do his bidding. My men were all engaged with the preparations for our supper—some plucking the reptchicks, others broiling venison, watching and turning each stick with its long string of chops, and every now and then burning their mouths while trying to ascertain if the former were cooked. I continued quietly drinking my tea, yet keeping a sharp eye on my swarthy visitors, who were becoming more clamorous in their demands for *arrak*. I knew full well, if their wishes were complied with, they would stay the night and give us much trouble.

The chief slipped his arms out of the sleeves of his kalat, letting it drop over his sash, which was tied round his waist. His brother and another of his associates followed his example, exposing their naked and brawny forms, that looked unpleasantly dark and greasy. Whether this was done to intimidate me or to cool themselves, I could not tell; but on one point my mind was quickly made up, that they should keep at a respectful distance, the inside of their garments swarming with filthy insects.

The two brothers now spoke together for a few minutes, then the chief again bellowed out for *arrak*, of which I took no notice. The man, however, having decided that the affair should not end thus, raised his hand and deliberately knocked my tea over, sending the glass to some paces distant. In a moment, dropping my saucer, I returned the compliment, sending him his full length on the grass. His bulky brother and myself simultaneously sprung to our feet, he trying to get his long knife out of its sheath; but before he could accomplish this movement, he also was sent sprawling on the grass. Seeing this unequal conflict, my men lost no time in securing the whole party. The chief was placed on his horse, and he and his fellows threatened with being tied to the trees till morning if they did not leave our camp at once. This had its effect; and, finding we were the stronger, they rode away, vowing vengeance. It was now decided that the fire should be moved into the forest, leaving our tents in the gloom, as a larger gang might steal upon us and fire at us from a distance, and their rifles were not to be treated with contempt. A sentinel having been placed in the shade, to be relieved every hour, we were soon sleeping soundly. Long before morning the rain poured down in torrents, while a strong wind threatened to rip open our tents and scatter the canvas in strips among the bushes. It was quite evident that the weather was breaking up, which disturbed me much more than the probability of a Kalmuck attack.

At last the morning broke, and all were busy with preparations for our departure; but the wind roared through the forest, and the rain and sleet fell thick. Even the lower hills were covered with snow, opposing a complete barrier to our journey across the high chain to the source of the Tchurish. I was therefore reluctantly compelled to give up this project, and turn in another direction toward the Yabagan. Having determined to reach Tchtchulika this evening, I began to ascend the mountain which forms the watershed between the Abbaye River and the Tchurish. In many parts this was stony and rugged, with large blocks of granite scattered over the surface, often rendering it difficult riding. From the summit of this high ridge we had a view of the mountains on the Katounaia, and those around the Bielouka, all deep in snow. It was fortunate that we left that wintry region, for a delay of two days might have detained us in the mountains, or at least have rendered our return both difficult and dangerous.

We descended through a thick forest, in about two hours reached the steppe, and shortly afterward found a Kalmuck *aoul*, where we got fresh horses. With them we galloped on at a dashing pace over a smooth grassy steppe toward the northwest, and in about two hours were on the bank at the Tchurish. Here we dined and rested our steeds, but only for a short time, as we beheld a heavy storm gathering in the mountains toward the source of the river. I added some splendid specimens of jasper and porphyry to my collection from the bed of this stream. Late in the afternoon we reached another Kalmuck *aoul* in the Yabagan Steppe, and while fresh horses were sought for, I sat down on a rock and sketched a beautiful view; but, before I had finished, the rain began to pour in torrents. When the men and horses arrived I was completely drenched; to my great surprise, only three saddle-horses were brought, but these were accompanied by two telagas with three horses in each. This mystery was soon explained: these little carts had been left here by the villagers, and some of my men preferred taking them instead of riding. As this was a matter which concerned themselves alone, I did not care to interfere. A splendid horse was brought for me; the other two were also good, therefore we should be able to go over the ground very fast.

My companions on horseback were a Russian peasant from Kokstschinskoï, and a young Kalmuck from the *aoul*, with three men in each of the telagas. As the rain was pouring down, we were anxious to cross the steppe as rapidly as possible, to reach the forest about ten versts distant, in which we should find some shelter. Our horses consequently started at a gallop, and soon left the telagas far behind. We reached the bank of the Tchurish, and were riding close to the river, when suddenly a great gust of wind carried the Kalmuck's cap into the stream. We could not recover it; it was lost among the rocks and whirlpools; so on we galloped to reach the forest, with the hope of finding shelter from the pelting storm. At length a clump of thick cedars stretched out their branches, protecting us effectually from rain and wind. Here we remained until the telagas came up; then, as my clothing was completely saturated, I deemed it prudent to be again in motion, therefore continued my course, listening to the howling of the wind among the higher branches. Our pace was a sharp trot, and the telagas kept up with us till we reached a torrent at the edge of the forest, over which we rode our horses without much difficulty; but the case was different with the little carriages, as the men had to seek a place where the banks were not so abrupt before they could cross. Here we left them, and proceeded, exposed to the full force of the storm. After riding a few versts the rain changed into snow, and began falling fast, with a great *bouran* blowing in our faces, rendering our progress almost impossible.

In about an hour we entered another forest, which afforded us shelter; and when our companions came galloping up, I ordered the Kalmuck boy into one of the telagas, as I knew it would be impossible to cross the river with the carriages. The peasant and myself left them and rode on, but the storm increased so much that we could scarcely make our horses face the blast.

After riding a few versts the man stated that it was impossible to proceed, turned his horse toward a large clump of trees, and said he would remain. I pushed on, and presently heard him following; in short, he dared not stop so long as I rode on. The snow almost blinded us, and was lying thick on our clothing, creating a chilling sensation whenever our speed was slackened. Our way was down the valley of the Tchurish, at about a verst distant from the river. On both sides of this valley high mountains ascended; those to the south were covered with a dense mass of cedar, while those to the north reared their rugged crests of slate, rendered exceedingly ghost-like by their clothing of pure white. As we were riding along we met a peasant, who inquired if we had seen a party of Kalmucks, five or six in number, that had stolen his horses. He was giving chase to the thieves, but with little chance of success. He told me that it was fifteen versts to the Kaier Koomin. I knew that it was about the same distance thence to the village; but the measure of distance given by a Russian peasant is very doubtful, and I suspected that this one was far from correct.

My companion had never been in this valley, so that it fell to my lot to be guide; no easy task with six inches of snow on the ground, and all traces of the track obliterated. We were compelled to ride with our heads bent forward, or the snow blinded us as it was swept along by the wind. We were proceeding at a trot, when I received a blow which laid me flat on my horse's back; for a minute or two I could see nothing but sparks gleaming before my eyes; but as soon as vision returned, I recognized my man holding up my hat, and the branch of a tree which had been broken off by a blow that had formed a bump on my forehead phrenologists would have found some difficulty in classifying. This made me keep a sharp look-out for trees ahead. Our progress was now very slow; the horses were floundering in a morass, nor could we tell which way to get out of it. As our route must be onward, turning to the right or left was only loss of time. At length we reached the forest, and got upon hard ground and into calm weather; still, the snow fell fast; but, in comparison, the temperature was like summer, while the trees were so thick we could only hear the blast as it roared over the topmost branches.

We had ridden more than two hours since the man told us it was fifteen versts to the Kaier Koomin. Although I had traveled over this country before, the snow had made such a change that it was impossible to ascertain our position. A little farther on in the forest we came upon two Kalmucks, who had made a fire and sheltered themselves, each having a piece of birch bark on his back toward the wind. We stopped, and my man had some conversation with them, after which he turned to me and said it was an hour's ride to the river, and useless going on, as the Kalmucks had declared that we could not ford the stream, the water being high. He proposed our encamping here for the night; to this I would not consent, and rode on; in a few minutes he followed, and very shortly afterward the two Kalmucks joined. Night was now drawing on apace, and the wind was exceedingly cold, but we pushed on fast toward the river. The Kalmucks were pretty correct in the time it required to ride the distance, and it was quite dusk when we reached the bank. We were now brought to a stand, for the water was much higher than usual. My man turned toward me and said "*Plavit nilza*" (We can not swim it). I answered him by riding into the stream, when at a few paces from the bank my horse began to swim; the other three followed, and we were carried two hundred paces farther down the stream than the usual fording-place before we reached the opposite bank, where we all landed safely. My man, wet as he was, avowed his satisfaction by exclaiming "*Dobery*" (Very good); even the Kalmucks expressed their approval, as they saw neither the weather nor the water deterred me from my object. We soon found the track leading to the village, and I pushed on at a sharp trot, as I began to shiver from the piercing cold, already freezing our clothing.

The snow ceased falling; the moon rose, giving light to our path; but it now became a dreary ride, and our poor horses were tired. Fortunately, I knew my way to the foot-bridge over the Tchurish, which we reached at a very late hour. Leaving our horses in the care of the two Kalmucks, we crossed, and arrived in my old quarters at the merchant's a few minutes before twelve o'clock. I sent for the Startioner, who ordered two men to go and bring our horses and the Kalmucks. I also told him about my companions left behind, when he instantly ordered five men and seven horses to be sent to their assistance. I now asked for some *wodky;* the merchant brought me a bottle; I drank two wine-glasses, and then sent it to the three men, who had got into snug quarters in a warm kitchen. The merchant brought me a kalat, or dressing-gown, and helped to strip off my wet things. My shooting-boots were filled with water from swimming the river, and now it was no easy matter to draw them off; however, after many efforts, I stood without them, and was soon divested of my other garments, sitting like a Kirghis, with only one covering.

One of my companions on a former journey in this region came to see me, and asked how far we had come; I told him from the River Tschugash; but I saw that neither he nor the merchant believed me, as they declared it to be one hundred and seventy versts —about 114 miles. They went and asked the peasant whence we had traveled; he also told them from the Tschugash. We had been seventeen hours on the road, and about fifteen on horseback, having changed our horses three times. My host now regaled me with tea, and, having taken sufficient to stave off the cold, I lay down on some rugs spread on the floor, and slept soundly till long after the cock had called the peasants to their day's labor.

On opening my eyes I observed that the sun was shining brightly through the small window, which caused me to leave my hard bed and prepare for another ride. The merchant brought my clothing dry and warm, and I was soon rigged up for the road. My first inquiry was about my companions left behind; but they had not yet arrived; this vexed me, as I was anxious to reach the Korgon without delay. About ten o'clock they rode into the yard, to my great joy. Before midday we started on our ride over the mountains, and in less than two hours came to the gorge of the Korgon. Entering this ravine at the Karaoul there is nothing particularly striking, but after riding five or six versts and turning an angle, the gorge bursts upon the traveler in all its grandeur. The precipices rise up two thousand feet, broken into rugged and picturesque shapes, while the torrent foams and roars beneath. This is, undoubtedly, the finest gorge in the Altai. Jasper of various colors is obtained here in very large masses. I saw the workmen cutting some blocks for columns fourteen feet long; they were obtained from near the summit of one of the highest precipices, and are lowered to the torrent with great difficulty. The labor of cutting out the large blocks of jasper is enormous; the workmen drill holes five inches apart the whole length of the block, and to the depth required; into these they drive dry birch-wood pins, which they keep watering till they swell and burst off the mass.

The workmen are sent to the Korgon from the different Zavods, of which some are as much as six and seven hundred versts distant. They arrive here in May, and remain till the end of September, when they all return to their homes. Small stone huts are built against the precipices at the bottom of the ravine, where they live, stowed away in filth and wretchedness, feeding upon black bread and salt, and receiving their poor pittance *of two shillings and ninepence a month.* Theirs is, indeed, a hard lot. Several vases from these jaspers were exhibited in the Crystal Palace in 1851, and the workmen are proud of the medal awarded to the works at Kolyvan. It is only in the palaces of St. Petersburg that the magnificent productions from the Korgon can be seen to advantage; there they are to be found in jasper, porphyry, and aventurine. I made several sketches of this mountain gorge, so rich in its varied rocks.

CHAPTER XXIV.

THE COUNTRY OF THE KALKAS—ANCIENT MONGOLIA.

My wanderings now led me to the Gobi, whose vast steppes, sandy deserts, and high mountain chains give a peculiar character to this region. The traveler who attempts to force his way into a land abounding with such striking scenery must be prepared for many difficulties and some risks. Perhaps before my visit these scenes were never looked upon by European eye, nor ever sketched by pencil. He who follows on my track will find that his rifle will be required for more purposes than obtaining a dinner. His courage and determination will be tested by men who seldom show fear, and are ever on the alert. It is only by a steady hand, a quick eye, and skill with his weapon, that he can remain safe from acts of violence. Plunder is the common trade; and, what is still worse, the traveler, if not murdered, is carried off into certain slavery.

My party consisted of three Cossacks—brave and honest fellows, who would have dared any danger. Long may they live, and be happy on their land near Kourt Choum. To these were added seven Kalmucks, four of them strong, sturdy hunters, and all accustomed to a hard mountain life. Powder and lead I had a sufficient store, and we mustered eight rifles. These Kalmucks had their hair cut close, except a tuft growing on the top of the head, plaited into a long tail, which hung far down their back, and gave them a Chinese appearance. They may, in fact, be considered Chinese subjects; but, unfortunately for them, Russia compels them to pay a tax also. The chief of my little band of Kalmucks was named Tchuck-a-boi, and was a very strong and powerful fellow, with a beautiful manly countenance, a fine massive forehead, and large black eyes. He was dressed in a horseskin cloak, fastened round his waist with a broad red scarf. When the weather was warm his arms were drawn from the sleeves, which were then tucked into his girdle, and the cloak hung round him in beautiful

ZABATA-NOR, MONGOLIA.

folds. This gave full effect to his herculean figure, while his manly bearing and graceful movements made him a fine study. He was born to be a chief, and his perfect good-nature rendered him a most agreeable companion. He was my faithful fellow-traveler through many a day of toil and hardship, and suffered hunger and thirst without a murmur.

We commenced our wanderings beyond the River Narym, and crossed the Kourt Choum Mountains toward what has been called the Great Altai. But this chain can only be found on our maps; in nature it does not exist. Numerous offshoots from the Altai run down to the desert of Oulan-Koum, in which direction we turned our steps, riding over many a rugged ridge and crossing numbers of picturesque valleys, threading our way eastward toward Oubsa-Noor. I had two objects in this journey—to visit the Tangnou Mountains, which I had seen from the Bielouka, and the large lake that receives so many streams and has no outlets. There are many peaks in the Tangnou chain rising far above the line of eternal snow, some more than eleven thousand feet in height. Our route was eastward, crossing the heads of several streams which run from the Tangnou Mountains into the Oubsa. The names of these rivers I could not ascertain, as none of my people had ever been in this region before, nor did we meet a single native to inform us. Game we found in great abundance in the higher region, and many a stag was broiled at our camp-fires and served up at our meals. In a few situations we observed the bare poles of the conical *yourts* of the Kalkas, indicating their hunting stations. After riding twelve days, and encamping beside various torrents that run from the Tangnou chain, we came upon a large and rapid stream, flowing from the northeast.

This could not be crossed at the point we struck upon it, and we were compelled to ascend toward its source. By following this river I was led up into the mountain wilds of the Tangnou, and at a great elevation we crossed the ridge and reached a plateau descending toward the north, on which I found the opposite scene "Zabata-Nor," a mountain tarn of great depth, surrounded by rugged precipices of granite. At this place the plateau has sunk, leaving perpendicular precipices around. To the east the rocks have the appearance of a wall five hundred feet deep, while picturesque granite mountains and snowy peaks rise up in the distance.

Having with some difficulty ascended one of the summits which pushed its head into the region of snow, I had a beautiful and most extensive view. Immediately beneath lay the Oubsa-Noor; far to the southwest was seen Oulan-Koum Desert and the Aral-Noor; to the south lay Tchagan Tala, and the ridges descending down to the Gobi; and to the southeast we looked upon the crests of the Khangai Mountains—several peaks covered with snow. This was a peep far into Central Asia, and over a region never beheld by any European. A dim and misty outline of Bogda Oöla was seen rising above the Gobi, and the vast desert stretched away till lost in haze.

Descending from this lofty peak, we sought a place to ford the torrent, and happily found one near a beautiful waterfall. Large blocks of fine white marble were lying in this torrent, and farther up the stream were very high precipices of this valuable material, untouched by man. Much of this country is extremely rugged and wild, and I sketched many beautiful scenes in the Tangnou chain. It is only in the deep valleys and ravines that trees are found; in most parts the mountains are even destitute of shrubs on their southern faces, but on many of the slopes there is a thick carpet of short grass, interspersed with a great variety of flowers. Three kinds of iris were blooming—a deep purple and white, a rich brown madder and white, and a very fine yellow. Large beds of pink *primula* were growing; a deep red and a pale yellow *dianthus* were scattered over the mountain sides, giving out a very delicious scent.

We continued our journey nearly due east, and in eleven days more crossed the head-waters of the River Tess. Following the mountain chain farther south brought us toward the sources of the Selenga and Djabakan, where it was expected we should find the Kalkas. The Kalmucks had often met some of these tribes on the Tchoui Steppe, and they now expected that we should be treated with hospitality; if not, our arms would at least command respect. During this ramble our camp-fires had burned on the banks of many a picturesque mountain stream, which had several times supplied us with fish speared by the Kalmuck knives. Hook and line fishing was too slow a process with these people; instead, three or four men went into pools, driving the fish up the stream, while the other Kalmucks speared them from the bank; and they

BOURIAT TEMPLE AND LAKE IKEOUGOUN, MONGOLIA.

were seldom more than half an hour in producing a fine dinner of fish.

After passing the River Tess we rode along the foot of the mountains, sometimes over a sandy plain, which often compelled us to ascend higher to obtain grass for our horses and secure game for ourselves.

In one of these rambles after a dinner I came upon the small and picturesque lake of Ikeougoun, which lies in the mountains to the north of San-ghin-dalai, and is held in great veneration by

San-ghin-dalai.

the Kalkas. They have erected a small wooden temple on the shore, and here they come to sacrifice, offering up milk, butter, and the fat of the animals, which they burn on the little altars. The large rock in the lake is with them a sacred stone, on which some rude figures are traced; and on the bank opposite they place rods with small silk flags, having inscriptions printed on them. Some of the snowy peaks of the Tangnou Mountains are seen from this spot. In eight days we reached San-ghin-dalai, a beautiful lake about fifteen versts in length, varying from four to six in breadth.

Here we encamped for two days to rest our horses and afford

me time to sketch the scenery. We were now near the source of the Selenga, and had not yet met with a Kalkas. Having accomplished my object in visiting this lake, we left it on a very rainy morning, and turned to the westward, intending to reach the River Tess about midway between its source and Oubsa-Noor. The Kalmucks began to fear we should find no people; at all events, we should cross a caravan track on our route, and might fall in with some of the tribes.

We had several days of drenching rain, which rendered our journey disagreeable and the country extremely uninteresting. The Tangnou Mountains were obscured by a dense fog, and our lodgings were on the wet ground, our saddle-cloths forming both beds and shelter. In the small ravines were found a few bushes, which enabled us to make fire for our cooking and tea-kettle; notwithstanding our hardships, not a man of my little band murmured at his lot. Late in the afternoon of the sixth day after leaving Sanghin-dalai we descended into a small valley covered with rich grass, which our horses appeared to look upon with delight. Many camels were feeding near us, and we could see several *yourts* in the distance—a most welcome sight to all. Across the valley we could also discern a herd of horses feeding on the grassy slopes beyond the *yourts*, and a large flock of sheep not far from them. We turned our horses and rode toward the Kalkas dwellings, and as we approached we saw two men mount and ride toward us. This indicated a peaceful mission, and presently we met. There was much conversation between them and Tchuck-a-boi, after which one of them galloped back to his friends, the other remained and followed with us. It was not long before we perceived three other Kalkas riding to meet and escort us to the *aoul*. On reaching the *yourts*, an elderly man took hold of the reins of my bridle, gave his hand to aid me in dismounting, and then led the way into his dwelling, in which were two women and four children.

This was Arabdan, the chief of the *aoul*, who received me, and was now preparing to be hospitable by handing me a bowl of tea taken out of a large iron kettle. It was brick-tea mixed with milk, butter, salt, and flour, which gave it the appearance of thick soup, but was not bad. The Cossacks and Kalmucks were also supplied with this beverage. While drinking mine I had time to examine my host. He was a tall, thin man, somewhere between fifty and sixty years of age, of a dark complexion, with high cheek-bones and small black eyes, a prominent nose, and a scanty beard. He was dressed in a long dark blue silk kalat, buttoned across his chest, with a leather girdle round his waist fastened with a silver buckle, in which hung his knife, flint, and steel. His cap was helmet-shaped, made of black silk, trimmed with black velvet, and had two broad red ribbons hanging down his back. A pair of high-heeled madder-colored boots completed his costume. One woman had a red and green silk kalat, the other a black velvet robe, and both were tied round the waist with broad red sashes. They also had similar caps; their hair was braided, and hung over their shoulders in a hundred small plaits, some of them ornamented with coral beads, which are highly valued by the Mongolian beauties. They wore very short, high-heeled boots of red leather, which prevent their walking with ease and comfort. The children were not overloaded with clothing, but to compensate for this deficiency they had been rolling on the bank of a muddy pool, that had covered them with reddish ochre, which contrasted well with their locks of jet-black hair.

The *yourts* of these people were constructed like those of the Kirghis and covered with felt, but the internal arrangements were different. Opposite the doorway a small low table is placed, on which stand the copper idols and several small metal vases. In some were grains of millet; in others, butter, milk, and *koumis.* On the left side of the altar-table stood the boxes containing the valuables, and near them the *koumis* bag and the other domestic utensils. Opposite were several piles of *voilock,* on which the family slept.

A sheep had been killed soon after our arrival, and was already cooking in the iron caldron in another *yourt.* This seemed to be the great attraction to every person in the *aoul,* and from where I sat I could see them busy with their preparations for the feast. The Cossacks were also engaged broiling a portion for me, and taking care to have enough for breakfast. The supper was not eaten in the chief's *yourt,* men, women, and children assembling in the adjoining one to eat the fatted sheep. Tchuck-a-boi had explained to our host that I intended crossing the plain to the River Tess, and asked him to give us fresh horses; the old man consented, promising both men and beasts should be ready for us at daylight to take us to an *aoul* not far out of our track. This would be the only one we should find before we reached Oubsa-Noor, and even there it was doubtful if any Kalkas would be met with.

A quiet night in the chief's *yourt* and a breakfast at dawn of day prepared us for a long ride. The sun rose brightly behind the Khangai Mountains, casting their long shadows over the lower hills and down to the plain. Faithful to his promise, Arabdan had four men and sixteen horses ready for our journey. How far distant this was to be, none could tell; but there appeared no doubt that we should have a long ride. When taking leave of my host I presented him with a strong hunting-knife made by Rodgers. He was delighted, and gave strict injunctions to his men to conduct me safely to the *aoul* of his friend. Our route was to the northwest, over an undulating plain covered with rough grass, which affords good pasture for the cattle. As we rode along, the Kalkas pointed out the track leading to the town of Ouliassotai, to which they said we could ride in less than twenty-four hours. At this place there were a large body of troops under a Chinese commander. Under these circumstances, it was not considered desirable to approach too near the town; indeed, our Kalkas guides objected to it.

During the morning the Tangnou Mountains had been enveloped in clouds; but as the sun rose the vapor rolled off, affording me a fine view of the chain. Seen across the plain from this distance, the numerous peaks form beautiful objects, their white snowy caps starting out from the deep blue sky like frosted silver. Five hours' riding brought us upon a stagnant water-course, with high reeds and bulrushes growing in its bed, some two hundred paces broad, with a wide space of clear water in the middle. The Kalkas seemed a little disconcerted, and, after a consultation, turned to the westward along the bank. In another hour we reached a spot where our guides proposed that we should swim our horses over this stagnant water. The fire-arms, clothing, and my sketches were secured against wet, and then the guide led the way, a Cossack and myself following. We were instantly in deep water, when our horses struck out, snorting and swimming with us across, but the soft and slimy nature of the opposite bank rendered it exceedingly difficult to get out. The others had remained standing on the bank till we were landed, and then the guide sent them farther down the stream, where at a short distance another place was found with a better bank to land upon. Our saddles, clothing, and fire-arms were carried over on the head of the Kalmucks and Kalkas, and kept quite dry. After landing we very soon dressed and continued our journey.

We had not gone far when we saw a fine herd of antelopes feeding not more than five hundred yards distant. Five of our party rode toward the north, apparently going away from them; but when at a proper distance they turned and spread themselves out in a line, to head the animals toward a bend in the river; we had also been gradually hemming them in. Our rifles were now unslung, and we slowly closed up toward the herd, while they retreated into the curve formed by the reeds. It became evident that they would make a rush to pass us; and in a few minutes the males turned round, stood for a moment, and then rushed toward a large opening between our lines. When sufficiently near, they received a volley from several rifles: two antelopes sprang high into the air, and then lay quivering on the steppe, and the report of the pieces frightened part of the herd back. A Cossack, Tchuck-a-boi, a Kalmuck, and myself, had fired; in a moment we were on the ground, reloaded our rifles, were ready, and in the saddle, moving up. Before we were within range the other men had fired at the herd as they rushed past, when two fell and another was wounded, which was followed by a Kalmuck and a Kalkas, and captured after a sharp ride. In this hunt we had obtained five animals, but no one could say which had been the successful shots.

The Kalkas were in ecstasies, and galloped from one group to the other of Cossacks and Kalmucks who were dressing the antelopes, the work of a very short time; the flesh was then placed on the pack-horses, wrapped up with the skins, and we continued our ride. Our guides intimated that it was necessary to push on, as it was still far to the *aoul;* the horses were good and the steppe smooth, which enabled us to gallop. We were not long in reaching a sandy plain, in some parts covered with a coarse reddish gravel, rising into low ridges, crowned with rocks toward the north. At length, in one of the slight depressions we saw a salt lake, on which many swans and hundreds of water-fowl were swimming; beyond this a grassy steppe, but no signs of any *aoul.* The horses kept up their speed, and made the pebbles fly as they went over the ground; this brought us to good pastures, but without any indication that would guide us to the Kalkas. We now came upon another herd of antelopes, but they were not disturbed; there was no time to spend in hunting, as the sun was sinking fast.

Having ridden a considerable distance farther, we ascended one of the ridges, from which the Kalkas pointed out what they supposed to be the *aoul*, very far away, on the shore of a small lake. This seemed to give our horses fresh courage, and on we went over hill and dale, for we were a two or three hours' ride from our resting-place. We saw several small lakes, but no indication of the River Tess, although we had been traveling toward the northwest several days. The Tangnou Mountains appeared much nearer, and from the shores of one of the small lakes I sketched a beautiful view. While occupied with this, all our party except two Cossacks and Tchuck-a-boi proceeded onward to seek the *aoul.* The sun sunk below the mountains to the west, and a glow of yellow light was beginning to spread over the sky. Presently the color changed to a deep orange, with crimson clouds stretching along over the mountain tops, and light fleecy masses scattered upon the silvery gray above. It was a lovely scene, and one quite common in this region, where no painters are found to contemplate these wonderful effects or admire their beauty. Having finished my sketch, I followed on the track of our companions, my mind deeply absorbed studying the effect of the scene before me. To the south, a few low and apparently sandy ridges extended east and west; beyond these it was one vast unbounded plain, where all the armies of Europe might be marshaled only to appear as a speck on this interminable waste, the steppe over which Genghis Khan had marched his savage hordes more than six hundred years ago. They too, perhaps, like me, had watched the sun sink below the mountains, thirsting to quench their savage appetites for rapine and slaughter beyond them. Probably the numerous barrows scattered so far over these wide plains contain the relics of nations these men exterminated.

Nature has here mapped out the conqueror's track from his birth-place on the Onon to the scenes of his terrible devastations on his course toward Europe, and it was to me a matter of deep regret that I had not the means of opening some of the large barrows I found along this route. Night was drawing on apace, and it was time for us to be at our encampment, but as yet we could see nothing to tell us where we should rest after a thirteen hours' ride. Not far before us there was a low stony ridge, and as we were ascending this three men appeared on its summit; they had come to guide us to our friends. While I had been sketching and thinking of Genghis Khan, the Cossacks and Kalkas gave up the idea of reaching the *aoul*, as nothing to indicate its whereabouts could be seen. They had found a nice little stream of pure water, and plenty of good grass, with bushes for a fire. We reached them in about half an hour, when I found all parties busy with their evening meal; mine was soon laid out on the grass, and hunger gave a fine relish to the venison and tea. Almost before we had finished eating day was gone, and night covered all around us. In a few minutes I was asleep.

We left our camp in the morning and continued our ride in search of the Kalkas, traveling over a barren plain almost without grass; in some places it was deep sand, in others sand and gravel, which rendered it rather trying for our horses. At length we reached some low hills, where we found grass and good pastures extended over valleys. Hour after hour passed away, riding over the same monotonous country till about two o'clock, when, to our great joy, we saw camels and horses feeding in a valley not far away. We now pushed on, and shortly came in sight of the *aoul*. Presently two men met us, and conducted us toward the chief's dwelling, greeting us civilly; and one rode on each side of me, leading the way to the *yourts*, which we found on the bank of a small stream running into a lake at a short distance. We rode up to a large one belonging to the chief, who was waiting my arrival. He laid hold of the bridle of my horse, gave me his hand to dismount, and then showed me into his *yourt*. A carpet was spread on which I sat down, when a bowl of tea-soup was presented to me, to refuse which would have been exceedingly impolite. I was in the *aoul* of a celebrated Kalkas, Darma Tsyren.

The chief sat down in front of me, and the two young men who had conducted me sat near him; they were his sons. Beyond these sat ten or twelve other Kalkas, watching my movements with intense interest. I was undoubtedly the first European they had ever seen. My large felt hat, shooting jacket, and long boots will be remembered for years to come; not that I think they admired the costume; theirs is far more picturesque. Presently a number of women came into the *yourt*, and at their head the wife of the chief. She sat down near him, and was joined by her daughter; the others got places where they could; but the gaze of all was upon me. No doubt it would have been highly amusing could I have understood their remarks, as they kept up an incessant talking.

At this moment a Cossack brought my *somervar* into the *yourt*, and these people were much astonished to see the steam puffing out, with no fire under it. One man placed his hand on the top, and got his fingers burnt, to the great amusement of his friends. My dinner of broiled venison was brought in on a bright tin plate: this and the knife and fork excited their curiosity, such articles being quite new to them. They watched me eat my dinner, and nothing could induce them to move till the plates were taken away. Darma Tsyren had ordered a sheep to be killed, which had now been some time in the caldron. When the announcement was made that it was ready, I was left to myself; the whole *aoul*, men, women, and children, were shortly enjoying the feast. It was my turn to be a looker-on, but I will not disgust my readers by a description.

After this meal was over I ordered Tchuck-a-boi into the *yourt*, and desired him to ask our host to give me horses for our journey next morning. He gave them willingly, saying all should be ready at daylight. He was told that I wished to go to the River Tess, and was asked how long we should be riding to it. In reply, he said it was a day's journey, and that it would be much better to leave our horses at his *aoul*, and go to the Tess with a small party of his people. To this I at once agreed, as our animals would be thoroughly rested for their long journey; and I ordered that two Cossacks, Tchuck-a-boi, and a Kalmuck should go with me, and the others remain at the *aoul* in charge of the beasts. Darma Tsyren gave me four Kalkas and twelve horses, and at daybreak we were in our saddles and away.

CHAPTER XXV.

PLAINS OF MONGOLIA.

From Darma's *aoul* our route was nearly due north, over grassy undulations, which gradually rose into hills, with broad sweeping valleys running east and west. This was a beautiful country for a gallop, and the Kalkas seemed inclined to try the mettle of their steeds in a chase after the antelopes, for we observed many large herds of these at a distance, but never within range of our rifles. About midday, while we began to ascend a high ridge, the view over the Oulan-Koum Desert spread to the westward as far as the eye could reach; many small lakes were also seen glittering in the sun. At one time I fancied I could perceive the Ilka Aral-Nor shining in the distant haze; but, on ascending higher, it proved to be a gleam of light stretching across the horizon. As we neared the top we had a charming prospect, extending throughout the country we had crossed, and the mountain chains to the southeast. The blue and purple haze now spread over them, declaring that we had left them far away in the distance. After gazing at this part of the landscape for a short time, I turned my horse and rode to the summit; then the Oubsa-Noor lay before me, with the River Tess winding in the valley beneath. The Tangnou Mountains were seen in all their grandeur, while the vast steppes stretched away to the west, till plain and sky seemed united in a misty tint. I hastened to sketch this scene, so peculiar with its lakes, mountains, and undulating plains. These latter have a character unlike all European scenery, and must have presented a grand spectacle when the vast host of that barbarian conqueror, Genghis Khan, were marching over them. They were now solitude, possessing neither man nor his dwelling.

The ridge on which I was standing was a deep red granite, in some places rugged and broken into singular masses. Thick veins of rose quartz crossed these rocks, running in parallel lines for two miles; some pieces of the quartz were semitransparent and of a beautiful rose color. Several of the veins were from nine to twelve inches thick, and many not more than three inches wide. Having finished my sketch, we continued our ride along the crest of the mountain for about an hour, and then descended into a narrow valley, following this down toward the River Tess. In about two hours we reached the river, at a part where it is a broad and

Cavern on the River Tess.

rapid stream, running between high rocks, with trees and bushes growing from the clefts. We turned to the westward, and followed the river toward the lake. I made several highly interesting sketches during our ride to-day, one of them looking from a cavern of large dimensions, and at a little before dark encamped in a small grassy valley not far from the river. A Cossack, Tchuck-a-boi, and a Kalmuck having been sent on a hunting expedition, joined us soon after dark, bringing a fine deer shot by the Kalmuck. It was not long before our fire was surrounded by small sticks broiling venison, and when I lay down to sleep the cooking was still going on.

The Tangnou Mountains were enveloped in a dense fog this morning, while on the Oubsa Lake and on the steppes the sun shone brilliantly. We started early toward the lake, and a ride of little more than an hour brought me to its banks, a few versts to the southward of the mouth of the River Tess, which at this point are flat and uninteresting; to the north they seemed more abrupt, but of no great elevation. The lake is more than one hundred versts in length from east to west, and thirty to thirty-five in width, with numerous bays running into the desert on the south. After making two sketches I continued my ride along the shore till we came to a river running into the lake from the south. This was a deep and sluggish stream, which it would have been very difficult to cross on account of the high sandy banks. From this place we turned southeast to make for the *aoul* of Darma Tsyren, keeping considerably to the west of our track. About two hours after noon we arrived on the banks of a small lake, the water of which was so exceedingly bitter that the horses would not touch it. We could see that a small stream entered the lake from the south; to this we made our way, and ascertained that it was drinkable. As no one could tell if we should find water in the direction we were going, it was decided that we should dine here and give the horses a rest. To cook a dinner was with us a short work; indeed, I have known the men make venison-soup in half an hour. They cut the meat into small pieces, and the moment it boils eat it. A little salt is thrown in; vegetables we had none.

We remained about an hour and a half, then continued our journey, and shortly reached a sandy steppe, almost destitute of vegetation, which appeared to extend over a considerable tract of country. Our Kalkas proposed a sharp ride, that we might cross this barren plain before nightfall; and as no one was inclined to delay our progress, on we went at good speed, hoping to find water and pasture before night. We continued our trot, sometimes across sandy valleys, and then among low hills. More than two hours had passed away, and we were still riding over this arid ground. The Kalkas, thinking we were going too far to the south, proposed that we should turn in a more easterly direction; and soon we got into a more undulating country, with tufts of coarse grass, which gave us hopes of finding pasturage. The sun was sinking fast, and lengthening our shadows over the steppe, when on the summit of a hill we observed a small lake in the next valley, with green herbage round its shores, and two small streams running into it; this was a gratifying sight; even the animals appeared to snuff the grass afar off, and went on quicker. A little before dark we reached the lake, and found rich grass for our horses. The water was fresh, a few bushes were soon got for a fire, and we soon made ourselves comfortable. While riding along the grass several double snipes were flushed; I therefore lost no time in getting my double-barrel and ammunition, and in less than an hour returned with snipes and ducks sufficient to form a supper for half a dozen people.

I gave the latter to the Cossacks; the birds and the venison were in a short time stewing, and sending up a savory smell equal to any from Soyer's kitchen. It was a beautiful night, the sky covered with brilliant stars, and not a sound heard save the crackling of our fire. The horses had been so secured that they could not stray far away; all hands were lying down, some even asleep, when suddenly we heard howling at a distance. The Kalmucks and Kalkas sat up in an instant: it was a pack of wolves following our track, and a distant howl every now and then told us that they were approaching. The men started up, collected the horses, and secured them on a spot between us and the lake. We had five rifles and my double-barrel gun, which I loaded with ball, at the service of these rapacious scoundrels, should they venture to come within reach, which the Kalkas thought certain, as they commit great ravages among their cattle frequently. Our fire was nearly out; but it was thought better that we should receive the robbers in the dark, or let them come quite near before a light was shown, when we should be able to see them, and, at a signal, pour in a volley. Again we heard them nearer, evidently in full scent of their game, and all lay ready on the ground watching their approach. It was not long before we could hear their feet beat on the ground as they galloped toward us. In a very few minutes the troop came up and gave a savage howl. The men now placed some dry bushes on the fire and blew it up into a bright flame, which sent its red glare far beyond us, disclosing their ears and tails erect, and their eyes flashing fire. At this instant I gave a signal, and our volley was poured in with deadly effect. The horrible howling which they set up declared that mischief had been done. We did not move to collect our game; that might be found in the morning. Our pieces were reloaded as quickly as possible, as the Kalkas warned us that the wolves would return. We could hear them snarling, and some of the wounded howling, but too far away for us to risk a shot. The fire was let down, and we remained perfectly quiet.

We were not long left in ignorance as to their intentions. Shortly there was a great commotion among the horses, when we discovered that the pack had divided, and were stealing up to our animals on each side, between us and the water. The Kalkas and Kalmucks rushed up to our steeds, uttering loud shouts, and this drove the wolves back. It was now necessary to guard our horses on three sides, as we could hear the savage brutes quite near, and the men anticipated that they would make a rush, cause the animals to break loose, and then hunt them down. If this happened we should be left without horses in the morning, as those that were not killed would be scattered far over the steppe. A Cossack and a Kalmuck turned to guard the approaches on each side, and I remained watching the front. The fire was now lighted and kept in a constant blaze by the Kalkas adding small bushes, and this enabled us to see as well as hear our enemies. Presently I discerned their glaring eyeballs moving to and fro nearer and nearer, then I could distinguish their grizzly forms pushing each other on. At this moment the rifles cracked to my right, and the fire sent up a bright light, which enabled me to make sure of one fellow as he turned his side toward me. I sent the second ball into the pack, and more than one must have been wounded, by the howling which arose in that direction. The other men had fired, I did not doubt but with equal effect, for I was certain they would not throw a shot away. In a few minutes the growling ceased, and all was still excepting the snorting of some of the horses. Both Kalkas and Kalmucks assured me that the wolves would make another attack, and said that no one must sleep on his post.

To increase our difficulty, we had few bushes left, and none could be obtained near us; therefore it must now be by a most vigilant watch that we could save our horses. The night became very dark, and nothing could be seen at a short distance excepting toward the lake, where any dark object could be observed against the dim light on the water. Sharp and keen eyes were peering out in every direction, but no wolf was seen or sound heard. The Kalkas said the wolves were waiting till all were still, when they would make a dash at the horses. We had been watching for a long time without the slightest movement, when two of the horses became uneasy, tugging at the thongs and snorting. The clouds rolled off, the stars shone forth, and reflected more light on the lake. Presently howling was heard in the distance, and Tchuck-a-boi declared that another pack of wolves was coming. When they approached nearer, those who had been so quietly keeping guard over us again began to growl, and let us know that they were not far away. As it was now deemed absolutely necessary to procure some bushes, four of my men crept quietly along the shore of the lake, two of them armed, and in about ten minutes returned, each having an armful of fuel. The embers were kindled, and material placed on them to be blown into a flame the moment it was wanted. The sound that we had heard in the distance had ceased for some time, when suddenly there was a great commotion; the other wolves had come up, and the snarling and growling became furious. How much I wished for a light to watch the battle which appeared likely to ensue! For a time there appeared to be individual combats, but no general engagements, and then all became calm as before. Again we waited, looking out for more than half an hour, when the horses began pulling and plunging violently; still we could see nothing. The man now blew the embers, and in a few minutes the bushes burst up into a blaze, when I saw a group of eight or ten wolves within fifteen paces, with others beyond. In a moment I gave them the contents of both barrels; at the same instant the other men fired, when the pack set up a frightful howl and scampered off.

Our fire was kept burning for some time, but we were not disturbed again during the night. At daylight we examined the ground, and found eight wolves dead. Others had been wounded, as we ascertained by traces left on the sand; and our men carried off the skins of the slain as trophies of the engagement. The Kalkas informed me that these brutes destroy many of their horses and cattle; that they are numerous to the westward, and would give us much trouble on our journey in that direction.

We started on toward the *aoul*, still to the westward of our former track, and were riding over a most uninteresting country. A heavy, sandy steppe delayed us much; but, after a three hours' ride, we were once more on a grassy turf, going at a good speed. It was not till late in the evening that we saw camels and horses wending their way toward home. After this we soon reached the *aoul*, and Darma Tsyren gave me a kind welcome; but when he heard of the attack of the wolves, and saw the skins, he was delighted. This circumstance afforded the tribe a subject for conversation long after our departure, nor will they soon forget me. I ordered two of the skins to be brought in, and presented them to the chief, to his infinite gratification.

I passed a good night with my host, and soon after day dawned mounted aud continued my journey over a grassy undulating steppe for six or seven hours, without seeing one living thing excepting our own party. The men desired that we should stop at the first fresh water, which we saw was not far distant—a small stream running across the steppe; to the south of us I observed several lakes, some of them of considerable dimensions, but I believe them all to be salt. Having reached the stream of fresh water, our horses plunged in and drank their fill. Here we dined, rested our animals, and then rode forward. A short distance beyond we entered upon a barren waste, stretching away for many versts. While riding along I collected numerous beautiful specimens of agate and chalcedony, and also a few pieces of sardonyx. Traveling south brought us to some low ridges of dark purple rock, spotted with red, extremely hard, and capable of receiving a very high polish. Crossing these gave us much trouble, as the rocks were sharp and pointed; indeed, it was exceedingly difficult for the horses to walk over them.

These stony ridges swarmed with serpents: they were lying coiled up, but we were quickly made aware of their presence by seeing their heads rear up and hearing them hiss as we passed. Some moved off, others were not inclined to make way, and many were killed with the heavy thongs of our whips. Any man who should be compelled to take up his quarters for the night on these ridges would soon have some unpleasant bedfellows. I observed four varieties of these reptiles: a black one, three feet eight inches long, and about one inch and an eighth in diameter: this fellow was very active. Another was of slaty-gray color, from two to three feet long, and smaller in diameter than the black snake. This breed was numerous, and often difficult to see, they so nearly resembled the color of some of the rocks. We had been obliged to dismount and walk, fearing to lame the horses; often I have nearly trodden on one without seeing it. My long shooting-boots were a complete protection to my legs, and I had seen too many of these reptiles to fear them; nevertheless, I have a great dislike to their company. We also found some of an ashy-green, and black, with deep crimson specks on the side: as they moved along in the sun the colors were most brilliant. None of these which we saw exceeded three feet in length, but we did not kill one of them.

A Cossack, Tchuck-a-boi, two Kalkas, and myself had walked on ahead, leaving the others to bring on the horses. I was occupied examining the rocks, and trying to obtain some greenish-yellow crystals, with the assistance of the Cossack and Kalmuck. But all our efforts were fruitless; the face and edge of my geological hammers turned like lead when struck with force against these rocks. While thus engaged we suddenly heard a shout, and looking round, I observed the two Kalkas run a short distance, then stop and look at some object. In an instant we were up and ran to them; the cause of their alarm was pointed out, about ten yards in front of us, in the shape of a large serpent coiled upon a rock, with his head elevated about eight inches, his eyes red like fire, and hissing furiously. They knew that his bite was exceedingly dangerous, and were afraid to approach too near to him. My rifle was unslung in a minute; I then lay down, getting a rest on a rock. Suddenly he lowered his head into his coil, peering over one of his folds; Tchuck-a-boi advanced two or three paces, when up it went again, hissing forth his defiance. I now got his head fair on the bead of the rifle, touched the trigger, and the leaden messenger performed its duty. His body sprang out of its coil, but headless, and wreathing in many folds. The men were upon him with their whips; but, notwithstanding their heavy blows, it was at least ten minutes before the reptile lay still. He was then stretched out, and measured five feet two inches and a half without his head, and four inches and a quarter round his body. His color was a dark brown, with greenish and red marks on his sides, and his aspect indicated, if I may so express it, deadly poison. We were obliged to continue our walk for a couple of versts farther, passing many of the slaty-gray reptiles, and two or three black ones, but the other two species we did not meet again. After crossing this stony tract we came upon a sandy plain, extending to a considerable distance.

The day was far advanced, which rendered a quick ride over this dreary steppe absolutely necessary. There was neither grass nor water to be seen in any direction, but they must be found, if possible, before night set in. Our route was in a southwesterly direction, and our pace a gallop. After riding a little more than two hours we got among tufts of steppe grass, associated with a thorny bush bearing yellow and deep purple flowers similar in form and size to the hedge-rose. We continued to push on, nor was it long before we began to descend toward a valley running to the westward, where a bright silvery band indicated the liquid we sought. Its presence was generally recognized, the horses pricking up their ears and extending their necks as we rode down into the grassy valley. We turned toward the nearest point, where we observed bushes growing on the bank of the stream, and in less than an hour were looking into the crystal flood with feelings of intense gratification. Both men and animals rushed to the water to quench their scorching thirst. The river was about twenty yards wide and about four feet deep, running sluggishly toward the west; but whether it found its way to the Djabakan or to the Kara-Noor the Kalkas could not tell, nor did they know its name.

A council was held by our whole band touching the probability of a visit from the wolves. The Kalkas thought they would scent our track and find us before many hours had passed; it was therefore agreed that the horses should feed until dusk, and then be secured on an open space between our encampment and the river; that three men should keep watch, changing every two hours, and a large fire be maintained through the night. Sufficient fuel for this purpose was collected, and all our other preparations made for defense; after this we supped, and many of us were soon sound asleep. Two watches passed undisturbed, but the third had not been long on their post when a Cossack shook my arm and told me the wolves were coming. In a few minutes we were up and ready to repel an attack should the brutes advance. A bright fire shed a strong light for fifty yards around us; beyond this was thick darkness, which the eye could not penetrate.

The horses were still; not a sound could be heard; and this continued for ten or fifteen minutes, when the noise of a distant howl was wafted over the plain; there they were, sure enough. It was so long before we heard it again, the men thought that the wolves had fallen in with a herd of deer, on which they were feasting. The watch was changed, the fire made up, and we lay down to sleep. A little before daylight we were again roused, when we heard the wolves quite near, but could not see one. A most vigilant look-out was kept up, but not one came within the range of our vision until day dawned, when a group of eight or ten were seen sitting and standing about four hundred yards distant from us. The Kalkas thought that they had not received a good share of the venison caught by the pack in the night. Two horses were unfastened and led over the plain, under cover of which we hoped to get within range of the depredators; but scarcely had we reached to within three hundred yards of them when they beat a retreat, going off at a slow pace. Three bullets were sent after them, which accelerated their speed, but did them no damage.

The horses were turned out to feed; then two Cossacks, with Tchuck-a-boi and myself, set off in quest of game. Our larder was very low, and, unless something was procured, we should have an insufficient dinner. We departed in pairs in different directions, and, after a walk of two hours, met again at the encampment, the whole produce of our rifles being two ducks, a swan, and a pelican. Large game we had seen none, the wolves having driven them off. On our arrival all hands were ready to depart, and in a few minutes we were pursuing our journey along the bank of the river. After riding about an hour the Kalkas discovered an object by which they knew the direction of the Kara-Noor. We left the river, riding more toward the northwest, and soon reached some higher ground, which gave us a view far over the country. The river we had just left, after running in a westerly direction for two or three versts, turned almost directly south. We could trace its course for a long distance, until it appeared lost in a bed of reeds extending over an immense tract, in which were seen small spaces of open water. About three o'clock in the afternoon we first caught sight of the Kara-Noor and the river which runs into it, and in an hour were on its northern shore. The lake is not large, nor is there any thing picturesque about it. We found good pasture for our horses, and observed hundreds of water-fowl swimming on the lake. We continued our journey toward the Kirghis, represented by the Kalkas to be a set of desperate banditti, worse than wolves, and constantly plundering; but I did not believe all the ill reported of them.

The east end of the lake and the river were surrounded by a thick bed of reeds, extending far into the steppe. As wild boars are usually to be found in such places, a Cossack, Tchuck-a-boi, and myself mounted fresh horses and sallied forth in quest of this game. In many places the reeds rose far above our heads, and often the horses were up to the saddle-flaps in water. Still we rode on in the hope of finding game, and saw indications of the ground having recently been turned up in many places in search of roots. Notwithstanding, however, all these traces, we were obliged to return after a long ride without having seen a single animal. One duck was cooked for my evening meal; the other, with the swan and the pelican, were made into soup, and eaten with great relish by my companions. Subsequently the same precautions were taken to protect our horses against any attack of wolves, but night passed and morning broke without our being once disturbed.

A thick fog was hanging over the lake and river, which gradually began to rise, betokening a hot day. Good-by was said, when the two little parties separated, the Kalkas returning to their *aoul*, the rest proceeding in search of the River Djabakan. I always felt a regret on parting with men who had shared the toil and danger of a journey. These men had stood bravely to their horses when the wolves made their grand attack upon us, and now we parted never to meet again. No one of our party had any knowledge of the country through which we were about to ride. I only knew that by following a southwesterly direction we should strike upon the Djabakan, but whether in one or two days I could not tell. Soon after leaving the Kara-Noor we entered upon an arid plain, extending far into the Oulan-Koum desert: it was a dreary waste, without either vegetation or water. Our larder again was nearly empty, and we could not expect to find game in such a region.

After riding several hours the country became rocky, with lofty ridges and narrow valleys quite destitute of vegetation. In one of these I found a small lake surrounded by high precipices; this was Oulunjour, with its caverns, described to me by the Kalkas. They say that Shaitan has his dwelling here; if so, he has shown good taste in selecting a most romantic spot; indeed, the view from one of the caverns is particularly wild and beautiful. This cavern is formed out of a compact yellow limestone, and extends into the rocks about two hundred feet; it is about sixty feet wide, and eighty feet high, and makes a magnificent natural chamber. Leaving the lake and ascending the opposite height, I got a view over the plain to the south, on to which we descended through a ravine.

Having traveled several hours, some low hills appeared many versts distant; we were, however, delighted to find a large lake stretching out far beyond them. As we approached nearer, trees and rocks appeared standing on its shores, casting their reflections on its surface, and giving me hopes of finding beautiful scenery.

We had ridden more than an hour, but appeared no nearer the lake; in fact, the water receded. I now saw that a mirage had caused this delusion; for, after riding a couple of hours more, it vanished, changing the appearance of a beautiful lake into a barren waste. At length, after riding many weary versts, we saw a small lake, with a little stream falling into it. Here we found a coarse grassy turf growing on the banks of the little river and around the lake. Long before the sun went down we reached the water, which proved to be good and sweet, and this decided us to remain the night. Noticing at no great distance several flocks of large birds feeding on the plain, a Cossack and myself started in pursuit, accompanied by two Kalmucks leading horses, by which means we hoped to get within rifle-distance of the game. The Kalmucks gradually approached the birds by going round in a circle, and we were all well sheltered by the horses. At length the men stopped, the Cossack and myself lay flat on the ground, and, having obtained a good sight, two of the flock were presently stretched dead on the plain. As the others did not fly far, our

CAVERN ON THE LAKE OULUNJOUR, MONGOLIA.

pieces were reloaded, and we again approached the birds with equal success; but this time the flock went far away. We now gathered up our game, and ascertained them to be four fine bustards. No cooks were ever more active in their occupation than our party were in preparing these birds for the pot, and when stewed they were delicious. Our usual precautions against wolves were again repeated; and as our safety depended on the horses, they were guarded with the utmost care. Again the night passed over in peace and quiet.

Four of us were off before day dawned in search of game, accompanied by two Kalmucks to lead the horses; this time we were more successful, for two deer and eight bustards were added to our larder. Breakfast was speedily dispatched, and we started again on our journey. At a few versts from our night's encampment we got upon some sandy hills that afforded a view far over the steppe. To the northwest I observed a large lake far away in the Oulan-Koum desert, but nothing could be seen to the south to indicate where we should find the Djabakan. Our route was still over a sandy steppe, with tufts of long grass reaching up to our saddles, which, the seeds being ripe, assumed at a distance the appearance of one immense corn-field just ready for the reapers. It was long past midday when we left these high tufts of troublesome grass, the seeds of which stuck fast to our clothing, and to the manes and tails of the horses, besides impeding our progress materially. We then got upon a plain covered with coarse gravel, among which short grass and numerous flowers were growing. A large herd of antelopes were feeding to the east of our track, but too far away for us to make any attempt to get near them. We now rode on at a sharp trot, fearing that we might not reach the river or find water before dark. In a little more than an hour we arrived at the edge of a broad valley, and saw the Djabakan winding its course at a few versts distant; a little later brought us to the river, which at this point is a deep stream, running slowly, and about two hundred yards broad. Three of us started in search of game, and returned after a long walk without firing a shot; but good grass for our horses was found in great abundance, and they fed well; at dark they were secured near us, and every precaution taken to keep off the wolves, for we were now in the region, according to the Kalkas, where we should find these brutes both savage and numerous. Another night passed without one being either heard or seen. We had a fine sunny morning, which made it pleasant to swim the river; Tchuck-a-boi crossed over first, and found the opposite bank good for landing upon. He then returned, secured my clothing on his shoulders, aud mounted a fresh horse, when four of us rode into the water, swam over, and landed without difficulty. Three others followed, bringing my sketches and arms fastened on their heads and shoulders. The men made several trips, and all our things were carried dry and safely over the river, which has its source far to the east in the Kourou Mountains, near the sources of the Selenga, and brings a large body of water to the Ilka Aral-Nor.

All our people being safely landed, we prepared for our ride over a very dreary-looking plain toward the region of the Great Altai, as laid down on our maps. We were now on a heavy sandy steppe—part of the Sarkha Desert, which extends into the Gobi—and vegetation was so very scant that even the steppe grass had disappeared. The *salsola* was growing in a broad belt around the small salt-lakes, its color varying from orange to the deepest crimson. These lakes have a most singular appearance when seen at a distance. The sparkling of the crystallized salt, which often reflected the deep crimson around, gave them the appearance of diamonds and rubies set in a gorgeous framework. I rode round several times, admiring their beauty, and regretting that it was impossible to stay and visit a large lake which I observed ten or fifteen versts distant, surrounded with green, orange, and crimson. I directed our course nearly due west, still riding over sand and gravel, and again I found many agates lying on the surface. The summits of the Tangnou Mountains were just visible to the north, but no high chain could be seen to the south. About an hour before sunset we reached the bank of a small river running from the south toward the Djabakan. Here we had fresh water and pasture for our horses, and determined to remain for the night.

We had not seen either animal or bird during the whole of this day's ride; from this I conclude that the steppe we crossed is uninhabitable, and never visited either by Kirghis or Kalkas. Under these circumstances, to seek game was useless, there being no cover or food either for bird or deer; indeed, it was with difficulty we found sufficient fuel to cook our evening repast. We thought neither wolves nor Kirghis would visit us here, nor did we make any preparation, believing the arid nature of the spot a sufficient protection. Our night passed without any attack, and morning roused us all to action. The horses had been feeding from the moment the gray dawn appeared, and were now ready for a march. After riding about ten versts we saw clumps of reeds, and shortly afterward had a view of the lake through an opening between these plants. On reaching the shore I found a thick belt of reeds, bulrushes, and other aquatic plants extending apparently round the lake, and growing far above our heads as we sat on horseback; even when standing on my saddle I could not see the water. Turning to the south, we continued our journey along the shore, hoping to find an opening through which I might obtain a view on to the lake, but rode for more than three hours without obtaining even a peep at the water. This brought us to the southern end of the lake, where I found a sandy shore, extending about half a verst, without a reed growing upon it. The sand was blown into round heaps, some of them fifteen and twenty feet high, and were of all sizes, extending far into the desert. Looking from one of the larger mounds, they had so singular an appearance one might have supposed that they formed a vast primitive necropolis, with its hundreds of tumuli. I obtained a view looking over the lake to the north; far in the distance I could see three small islands rising but a little above the water. The northern end of the lake was invisible, as the shore is very flat; a part of the western side, with its broad band of bulrushes, was visible till it diminished to a line, and was lost in the distance.

While sketching this scene I perceived that a storm was sweeping over the water, coming from the north directly toward us. The Cossacks and Tchuck-a-boi removed the horses under the shelter of the high reeds, while two of the men remained with me. The gale came on at a furious pace, lashing up the waves and bending down the plants as it passed. A long white streak was seen rushing over the lake, and when at about half a verst distant we could hear the roaring of the blast. The men urging me to be off, I took my sketch-book folio and other matters, and ran to join my companions in their shelter, and had scarcely reached the edge of the reeds when the storm passed, crushing the bulrushes and other plants flat to the ground. As the blast went on it licked up the sand, whirling it round in numerous eddies, and raised it high into the air as it passed along among the sandy mounds: it was now easy to understand how they had been formed. The storm was of short duration, for in a quarter of an hour it had passed, and all was calm again. We remained a short time longer, and while I made a second sketch, the Cossacks and Tchuck-a-boi searched for a wild boar, but without success. It was impossible for us to encamp on the shores of the Ilka Aral-Nor, for there was no grass for our horses, and the water was bitter. I determined that our course should be southwest, hoping to fall in with water and grass as we approached nearer the hills. We, however, continued our ride for many versts before we observed any change in the arid nature of the steppe. At length rough grass began to appear, and this gave us hopes. More than another hour elapsed, and no water could be seen in any direction. Horses and men were all suffering from thirst, and as night was drawing on fast, we urged on our steeds at a rapid pace. A small ridge rose before us, which we ascended, and in a broad sweeping hollow on the opposite side we descried a stream, glittering as it ran along among tall reeds and bushes. This was a glorious sight; our horses pricked their ears, snorted with delight, and dashed off down into the valley at a gallop. In a little more than half an hour we leaped from our saddles, when both man and beast rushed to the bank and cooled their parched tongues in the crystal stream. Hitherto our whole thoughts had been upon the water; we now turned to look for pasture for our steeds, and discovered that there was plenty of grass extending along both banks of the little river.

Bushes and willows for firewood were in abundance, but we had little in our larder to cook. This, however, was a place in which we ought to find game, and Tchuck-a-boi and myself started in one direction, and two Cossacks in another, while our companions were preparing our encampment. We had not gone a hundred paces when up sprang a fine cock pheasant; I sent a ball after him, which cut off two feathers from his tail: these, however, would make but a poor supper. I sent the man back for my double-barrel and game-bag while I reloaded my rifle, as we might find other game not so gentle as a deer; indeed, I had noticed a little in advance that the ground had been turned up, indicating the neighborhood of the wild boars. Tchuck-a-boi was soon back;

I gave him my rifle, and on we marched. We had not gone thirty paces when a pheasant rose up: this time he dropped about fifty paces from us, and before he was picked up a second bird was added to our bag. At no great distance we came upon my first acquaintance: he did not escape this time. Tchuck-a-boi knew him by the rifle-mark on his tail. We proceeded about half a verst without meeting with any thing, when we came upon some thick grass and bushes. Suddenly we heard a loud grunt and a rushing among the branches; about twenty paces from us a young sucking boar ran out of the grass. Tchuck-a-boi dropped down on his knee and gave a shrill whistle; the suckling stopped for a minute and looked round; this was fatal to him, for he fell without a scream. True to his craft, Tchuck-a-boi had shot him close to the eye. We had fallen in with a sow and her litter; but, not wishing to disturb them farther this evening, as we intended they should have our early attention next day, I turned toward our encampment through some small bushes, adding on my way two more pheasants to our bag.

When we reached our lodging in the bushes the Cossacks had not returned, but shots had been heard in their direction, which I felt sure would produce something, as these men seldom throw a shot away. Just at dark they came back, bringing in a young wild boar and a deer, with the intelligence that other deer and a large wild boar had been seen. The latter animal must be hunted on horseback; he is too swift to deal with on foot; so we determined to hunt him in the morning. The Kalmucks considered that there was no fear of wolves visiting us here, and that our horses were quite safe; their fore legs, however, were secured, to prevent them straying far away. I had a delicious supper of pheasant and tea; the Cossacks and Kalmucks preferred the young boar; and when I lay down to sleep, broiling was still going on.

Night had passed, and the rosy tints of morn foretold a glorious sunrise and a fine day. On looking round I observed a general cleaning of rifles. I, too, followed the example, and made preparations for the chase. Our breakfast was soon over, and all other arrangements having been made, it was decided that four men should remain at the encampment, two armed with rifles, in case any of the Kirghis should find them, while six of us, armed with rifles, and one Kalmuck, with my double-barrel gun, should rouse up the boars. The sun had been above the horizon about an hour, when we rode down the valley in the direction where the Cossacks had seen the boar. We had passed the point they reached the night before without observing bird or animal. Before us was a thick copse of low bushes and long grass; into this we rode, and very soon roused more than one from his lair. We could see their route by the motion in the grass, and followed, after riding some distance, when a small open space gave us a full view of our game. Two large dark grizzly boars were about two hundred yards ahead of us. We followed them fast, and after riding about a verst got clear of the long grass, with only a few bushes here and there. For a few minutes we lost all traces of the animals; suddenly one of the Kalmucks spied them running along behind some bushes a short distance in advance. Our rifles were now unslung, and our horses put to their speed. We gained upon them fast, and when within about fifty yards a Cossack and myself alighted from our horses, fired, and wounded one of the boars. While we reloaded our companions galloped on, and presently other shots were fired; we were soon remounted, and off again in pursuit. The boars had separated; one was leaving the river, and making across the valley, followed by two men, one of whom fired. We were now gaining on the animal, and had him in the open country: it was a splendid chase. As we came near I could see the foam on his mouth and his large tusks gnashing with rage; he was, however, dangerous to approach. Presently the Cossack gave him another ball, which took effect, but did not stop him. Giving my horse a touch with the whip, I was soon abreast of the animal, and about twenty paces from him. He was slackening his speed, which enabled me to pull up my horse and get a shot I intended for his head, but failed, and the ball took effect in his shoulder, stopping him for a moment. Slipping the strap of my rifle over my head, I then drew a pistol from my holster and galloped over to the left side.

Having practiced and become somewhat proficient in pistol-shooting at full gallop, I rode my horse alongside of the boar, within seven or eight paces. After my horse had made a few strides I fired the second barrel, when the boar staggered for a moment and fell. The Cossack and a Kalmuck came up immediately; we sprung from our horses, and saw that my last ball had entered just above his eye. He was a huge fellow; the Cossack said he weighed nine poods—about 324 lbs. His tusks were long, and as sharp as a knife, and two most formidable weapons they would have proved had he come to close quarters with either man or horse. A Kalmuck was sent to our encampment for a man, an axe, and horses to carry in our prize, while the Cossack and the other man began to dress him.

As this was an operation at all times disagreeable to me, I left —first reloading my arms—to seek the other men. After riding about half an hour, I heard shots fired, and observed my friends in full chase on the opposite side of the river, at least three versts distant from me. I hurried on, hoping to join in the chase; but, before I reached the stream, the hunt was ended, and a Cossack met me coming in search of our party. I now learned that they had killed a large boar, but not the one they had first hunted. He had escaped, and all trace of him was lost. Suddenly, while searching near some bushes and reeds, a large boar rushed into the middle of them and charged at the Cossack's horse. When within three or four paces of his intended victim a ball from Tchuck-a-boi's rifle stopped him for a moment, and horse and man escaped. So sudden had been his onset, that he got away before a second shot was fired; but very soon there were men on his track who were seldom foiled. The boar had led them a long chase, and had received several balls, but none of them stopped him. At length he rushed into the water and swam across the stream, where it extended into a broad and deep pool. The men crossed a little higher up, and were soon in full chase, when a ball from one of the Kalmucks wounded him severely. This made him furious, and he charged at the man who had just fired; the Kalmuck's horse bounded off, and a ball from Tchuck-a-boi laid the boar dead in the midst of the party. This was the larger boar of the two, and the most ferocious. We returned to the camp in triumph, having slain two large boars in less than three hours.

As it was near the middle of the forenoon, we decided on giving our horses a few hours' rest, to dine, and then continue our journey. The river flowing from the south, I decided that we should follow it upward and encamp on its bank before we attempted to cross the chain of hills which we could see in the distance. Early in the afternoon we commenced our journey, riding along at about two hundred yards from the river. Occasionally some of the men rode into the long grass and bushes to seek for game, when a brood of pheasants were met with, and several added to our stock. The valley had now become narrower, with low hills rising on each side, and, being desirous of obtaining a view over the country, I rode up one of them, accompanied by a Cossack and Tchuck-a-boi. From the summit we had a very extensive view over Sarkha Desert, and I satisfied myself that there was no Great Altai: a low chain of hills only extends to the south, till lost in the Gobi Desert. While taking a survey of the country, I saw at a long distance to the east of us a smoke: this could not be from the Kirghis; they are more to the west, and I could scarcely believe that there were any Kalkas in this direction; but as there were two or three fires, there must be people of some kind. We continued our ride along the crest of the hills for several versts, watching from time to time the wreaths of smoke. At length we came upon a well-beaten track, the caravan-road which crosses the Gobi. This accounted for the smoke; a caravan was halting for the night. From the summit of the ridge we had a view of the Ilka Aral-Nor as it lay shining in the setting sun; also another large lake was seen near the smoke of the caravan. We rode down into the valley and joined our companions, intending to encamp at the first desirable spot; and it was not long before one of the Cossacks who had ridden on in front pointed out a most convenient place for us to rest upon.

It was quite necessary to keep a sharp look-out, as we were coming nearer to the Kirghis, who have a very bad character in this region. As yet we had seen no indication of their being in the vicinity, but both the Cossacks and the Kalmucks thought they might have seen the smoke of our fires. The horses were turned out to feed until dark; they were then picketed near us, and two men placed on guard, to be changed every two hours. This was a most important precaution, and one in which every man of our little band was deeply interested, for we were quite sure, if once our horses were lost, that our capture would become easy.

Night, however, passed without any alarm, and a clear morning indicated a warm day. After examining my map, I still determined to continue our journey a day or two more in a southerly direction, then to turn to the westward and strike upon the River Ourunjour; by doing this I should enter the Gobi to the north of the great chain, "Thian-chan" on our maps, a name utterly unknown to the natives, who call this chain "Syan-shan," which I shall adopt whenever speaking of these mountains. They are the highest in Central Asia, and among them rises that stupendous mass "Bogda Oöla," the volcanoes Pe-shan and Ho-theou, to see which I was pushing my way into this dreary region. I had fully considered the risk before starting, and had determined that neither toil, nor hardship, nor the fear of banditti should deter me from drawing scenes no European eye had ever beheld, and from obtaining geographical information the value of which would, I trust, be acknowledged by future travelers.

CHAPTER XXVI.

CHINESE TARTARY.

I LEFT our encampment, still following the little stream for more than an hour, till it turned westward into the hills. Here we left its luxuriant and hospitable banks, which had supplied our larder so abundantly and fed our jaded horses. From this point our route continued over several small ridges, some of them destitute of vegetation, with dark green rocks cropping out to the eastward, and descending in huge steps to the plain. As we traveled I saw several small lakes to the east, but whether salt or fresh it is impossible to say. The country assumed a more sterile appearance the farther we got to the south; it was only in the small valleys that there was any pasturage, and this was short and scanty. We came upon several little rills of pure water, which was encouraging, as we should be able to encamp, and find both food and water for our animals. Hour after hour had passed away with the same monotonous hill and valley to ride over. Sometimes we had a view to the eastward over the Sarkha Desert, with its yellow sand, purple ridges, and numerous mounds scattered upon the steppe. At one point we could trace the River Djabakan by its dark green vegetation, as it was winding its course along the plain. These views we should shortly turn our backs upon, and cross the crest of the ridge, which would afford us a view on to the Gobi—that vast waste extending from Kessil-bach Noor (about 87° E. long.) to the Siotki Mountains (120° E. long.), more than two thousand miles in length, and varying from three hundred to seven hundred miles in width. Having reached the highest summit of the hills, I dismounted to examine the scene before me.

To the east stretches the Gobi, with its numberless ridges vanishing off into distance till lost in soft blue vapor. I now turned to the south, and saw the snowy summits of the Syan-shan, with Bogda Oöla rising far above all others. The sight of these white peaks excited a desire to gallop across the plain, and sketch the stupendous masses from the steppe. I stood some time trying to find out which of the peaks was Pe-shan, but it was impossible to decide unless the volcano had belched forth flame and smoke.

Subsequently we came upon the steppe over which the Asiatic hordes marched on their expedition to the west. Had De Quincey seen this spot, he need not have drawn so largely on his imagination for scenery like that through which he marches the Tartar hosts on their way to China. Nor was it necessary that he should make geographical blunders by placing the Lake Tenghiz close to the great wall, nor locate the emperor's hunting-box on the northern border of the empire, among the penal settlements of China. I have traveled over much of the country this distinguished author professes to describe in the "Exodus of the Tartars," and have lived among their descendants. I have read his story with intense interest and admiration, and consider the final scene, where Tartar and savage Bashkir rush together into the lake, fearfully tragic. I regret, however, to say that no Chinese guns belched forth flame or shot to check these savages of the Oural, nor did Kien Long look down on the scene of savage butchery.

The Cossack disturbed my musing on the Tartar exodus by pointing out a smoke very far to the west, which we knew was not from our people. Kirghis were undoubtedly there, and now we must keep a sharp look-out, as they were encamped to the west of our route, and would soon see the smoke of our fires. We mounted our horses and rode downward, following the track of our friends, whom, in less than an hour, we discovered in a small grassy valley, with a little stream of pure water leaping and foaming in its rocky bed. All was prepared for our sleeping, and a most vigilant watch was directed to be kept up throughout the night, as we might receive a visit from some of those roving bands who are constantly moving about the steppes. Just at dusk our horses were brought and secured close to us, and the first watch appointed: each man had his arms placed near at hand, in case of a surprise in the night. Every one knew that our safety depended on ourselves; that we should find no one to aid us here if taken unawares; that our fate would then be sealed, and that we should all be sold into captivity. These were strong inducements to bravery and vigilance, and all determined never to be taken alive. Our evening meal being ended, we were soon stretched on our saddle-cloths, and several sleeping soundly. For a time I was occupied in settling which should be our route; this done, I, like the rest, fell asleep.

Just as the day dawned I awoke, and saw a faint light rising in the east, which gradually increased, till the sun's rays were seen tipping the hills around us. The route was still to the south, among hills rising somewhat higher than many we passed yesterday. After riding about three hours, a singular dome-shaped hill was seen at some distance to the southeast, which reminded me of Kolmack-Tologuy. To pass this would not take us far out of our course, and I was very desirous of seeing what it was. As we approached the place I observed that the country was crossed by several ravines, and rode along the edge of one that led directly toward the great dome which had excited my curiosity. Having ridden about three versts, I perceived that the bottom of the ravine was covered with a dark substance of a peculiar character, which I immediately recognized.

Leaving our horses with the men, myself and three others scrambled down the rocky sides, when I found the dark mass was a bed of lava, which had flowed down the ravine. It was broken, rugged, and very difficult to walk over, and as we went along I ascertained that it had come from the dome-shaped mass before me. On reaching the spot I assured myself that the substance had gushed from several places on the side of the mount, and had run a short distance down the ravine. It was only a small quantity that had been ejected on this side. I now determined to ascend the dome and examine its summit. We found considerable difficulty in climbing the perpendicular face of the ravine, to reach what I shall term the springing of the dome. The whole mass was of a dark purple-gray color, with the appearance of having been forced up, in a soft or almost liquid state, into the shape of an enormous air-bubble. It was split and fractured in every direction, but not in regular strata. After examining the rock minutely, I concluded that the whole external covering was basaltic. I found olivine in small greenish crystals in two or three specimens; in some it appeared to pervade the whole mass, but only in small particles. That this was the commencement of a volcano is quite certain, but the melted matter had found an outlet at some other place. There was not a blade of grass growing on this dome, to the summit of which a Cossack and myself scrambled with great toil and difficulty.

I now observed that it was not a regular circle, but elliptical in form, the long diameter being about five hundred yards, and the other about four hundred yards. I spent several hours examining this singular place, and in sketching two views, which are highly interesting. While standing on the summit of the dome I observed another similar formation at a distance of twenty or twenty-five versts to the southeast; therefore, passing round the east side of the great dome, we turned our steps in that direction, riding over many small hills and gradually descending toward the plain. A sharp look-out had been kept to the westward in the direction of the Kirghis, and shortly after noon an *aoul* was seen among some low hills eight or ten versts distant. After a consultation, we deemed it best to proceed to it, and see how its inhabitants would treat strangers. In a short time we were riding through a large herd of horses and camels, when the Kirghis herdsmen came up, and asked whence we had come and whither we were going. They were told that we had come from the Oubsa-Noor, and that we were going to the Oulunjour. We now learned that the *aoul* was a very large one, and belonged to Sultan Baspasihan; also that we should find him with his tribe. Every Kirghis that we passed had his battle-axe hanging on his saddle, but whether this was adopted as a security against man or animals, we could not tell. After going on a few versts, a Kirghis came galloping up to point out the position of the *aoul*, then left us and rode fast toward it, as if the sight of our arms had caused him to hasten to afford the sultan an opportunity of giving us a warm reception.

A short ride farther brought us to the top of a ridge, beyond which we looked down upon the *aoul*, lying on the bank of a small stream in the valley. About a verst distant from the *yourts* lay a lake, probably four or five versts long and one and a half in breadth. On one side was a thick bed of reeds, and on the other a grassy shore, on which sheep and goats were scattered about in great numbers. We now observed several men spring on their horses and ride to meet us: this was certainly a mission of peace. When we met, one of the men rode up to me, placed his hand on my chest, saying "*Aman.*" I followed his example, and we rode on. As we approached there seemed to be a great commotion in the *aoul;* two Kirghis had mounted their horses and gone off at full gallop. Others were busy collecting bushes, and all seemed occupied. Our escort guided us to a large *yourt* with a long spear stuck into the ground at the door, and a long tuft of black horse-hair was hanging from beneath its glittering head. A fine tall man met us at the door. He caught the reins of my bridle, gave me his hand to enable me to dismount, and led me into the *yourt.*

This was Sultan Baspasihan, who welcomed me into his dwelling. He was a strong, ruddy-faced man, dressed in a black velvet kalat edged with sable, and wore a deep crimson shawl round his waist; on his head was a red cloth conical cap, trimmed with foxskin, with an owl's feather hanging from the top, showing his descent from Genghis Khan. A Bokharian carpet had been spread, on which he seated me, and then sat down opposite. I invited him to a seat beside me, which evidently gave satisfaction. In a few minutes two boys entered, bringing in tea and fruit. They were dressed in striped silk kalats, with foxskin caps on their heads, and green shawls round their waists. They were his two sons. The sultana was out on a visit to the *aoul* of another sultan, two days' journey distant.

The *yourt* was a large one, with silk curtains hanging on one side, covering the sleeping-place—bed it was not. Near to this stood a "bearcoote" (a large black eagle) and a falcon chained to their perches; and I perceived that every person entering the *yourt* kept at a respectful distance from the feathered monarch. On the opposite side were three kids and two lambs, secured in a small pen. There was a pile of boxes and Bokharian carpets behind me, and the large *koumis* sack carefully secured with *voilock*. Between us and the door sat eight or ten Kirghis watching my proceedings with great interest. Outside the door were a group of women, with their small black eyes intently fixed on the stranger. A conversation was carried on between the sultan, a Cossack, and Tchuck-a-boi; and by the scrutinizing glances of the sultan I soon perceived that I was the subject. My shooting-jacket, long boots, and felt hat were matters of interest, but my belt and pistols formed the great attraction. The sultan wished to examine them. Having first removed the caps, I handed one to him; he turned it round in every direction, and looked down the barrels. This did not satisfy him. He wished to see them fired, and wanted to place a kid for the target, probably thinking that so short a weapon would produce no effect. Declining his kid, I tore a leaf out of my sketch-book, made a mark in the centre, and gave it to the Cossack. He understood my intention, split the end of a stick, slipped in the edge of the paper, went out, and stuck the stick in the ground some distance from the *yourt*. The sultan rose, and all left the dwelling. I followed him out, and went to the target. Knowing that we were among a very lawless set, I determined they should see that even these little implements were dangerous. Stepping out fifteen paces, I turned round, cocked my pistol, fired, and made a hole in the paper. The sultan and his people evidently thought this a trick. He said something to his son, who instantly ran off into the *yourt* and brought to his father a Chinese wooden bowl. This was placed upside down on the stick by his own hand, and when he had returned to a place near me, I sent a ball through it. The holes were examined with great care; indeed, one man placed the bowl on his head, to see where the hole would be marked on his forehead. This was sufficiently significant. The people we were now among I knew to be greatly dreaded by all the surrounding tribes: in short, they are robbers who set at naught the authority of China, and carry on their depredations with impunity.

On looking round, I noticed that a set of daring fellows had been watching my movements; also, that the fatted sheep had been killed, and the repast would soon be given. Two brawny cooks were skimming the steaming caldron, and other preparations were in progress, while numbers of men, women, and children were seated around, waiting for the feast. As a Kirghis banquet is for any European an extraordinary event, I shall endeavor to describe one at which I was the guest of Sultan Baspasihan. The party were far too numerous to be accommodated in his *yourt.* A Bokharian carpet was spread outside, on which he placed me, taking his seat near. A small space in front of the sultan was left clear, and around this the men seated themselves in circles—the elder, or more distinguished members of the tribe, nearest his person: there were more than fifty men, women, and children assembled in front of their chief. The boys sat behind the men; the women and girls occupied the last place, excepting the dogs, who were standing at a short distance, apparently quite as much interested as the rest.

When all were seated, two men came into the inner circle, each having a cast iron vessel shaped something like a coffee-pot. One approached the sultan, the other myself, and poured warm water upon our hands; but each person must provide his own towel. This ceremony was performed for every man, from the sultan to the herdsman. The women and the girls were left to do it for themselves. The ablutions having been performed, the cooks brought in the smoking vessels—long wooden trays, similar to those used by butchers in London—piled up with heaps of boiled mutton. One was placed between the sultan and myself, filled with mutton and boiled rice. Each man drew his knife from its sheath, dispensing entirely with plates. My host seized a fine piece of mutton from the reeking mass, placed it in my hand, and then began on his own account. This was the signal to fall to, and many hands were soon dipped in the other trays. The Kirghis who sat nearest the trays selected the things he liked best, and, after eating a part, handed it to the man sitting behind; when again diminished, this was passed to a third, then to the boys; and, having run the gauntlet of all these hands and mouths, the bone reaches the women and girls, divested of nearly every particle of food. Finally, when these poor creatures have gnawed till nothing is left on the bone, it is tossed to the dogs. While the dinner was progressing, I observed three little naked urchins creeping up toward our bowl from behind the sultan, whose attention was directed to the circles in front. Their little eyes anxiously watched his movements, and when sufficiently near, their hands clutched a piece of mutton from the tray. They then retreated in the same stealthy manner behind a heap of *voilocks*, and devoured the spoil. I saw this repeated two or three times, and was highly amused by their cunning. Beyond the women, and surrounded by a group of dogs, there was a child about four years old sitting with a dry leg-bone of a sheep in its hand. This puzzled me at first, till I saw bones thrown among them, when there was a general rush of the canine race. The child was not daunted by their growls; his bony weapon fell heavy on their noses, and he frequently carried off the spoil. In a remarkably short time the sheep had disappeared, when large bowls of the liquid in which it had been boiled were handed round, and drunk with a great relish by the Kirghis. The dinner being ended, two men brought the water-vessels, and poured the warm liquid over our hands, after which all rose up and went to their occupations.

The sultan expressed a wish to see our rifles used, and ordered three of his men to bring out theirs. I gave them powder and lead, and induced them to fire at a target placed at sixty paces distant; each man fired two rounds, but not one ball touched it. They then removed ten paces nearer, and one man hit it, to their great joy. A Cossack and Tchuck-a-boi next fired, and sent both balls near the centre. I now desired one of the Cossacks to place the target at what he considered the best long range for their rifles. He stepped off two hundred paces—about one hundred and eighty-five yards. The sultan and his Kirghis looked at the distance with utter amazement. When the first shot was fired, and the hole pointed out not far from the centre, they were astonished. The target was a piece of dark *voilock*, with a piece of white paper, seven inches square, pinned on the middle. This I have always found much better than a black centre. We all fired, and not a ball missed the paper. When the sultan saw this, I fancied that it made a strong impression on his mind; the superiority of our arms, and the way they were used, could scarcely be without its effect. After this there was a general cleaning of arms, to have them in perfect order.

We were now in Chinese Tartary, in the country of the ancient Sungarians previous to their being conquered by the Chinese emperor Kien Long, near the middle of the eighteenth century. It was in this region that about four thousand men of the tribe of Prince Tsebeck Dordzi settled after the exodus of the Tartars from the Volga. We should most probably make an acquaintance with the descendants of these men before many days passed over.

The sultan returned into the *yourt* with me, accompanied by a Cossack and Tchuck-a-boi. I wished to ascertain if we should find Kirghis farther to the southeast, taking care at the same time not to hint that there could be any difficulty to retard our traveling in that direction, as I had learned that the Asiatics instantly take advantage of any doubt, and turn it to their own account: I have surmounted not a few of their impossibilities. In answer to my questions, Baspasihan said there were two chiefs in the country beyond his pastures, Oui-jass and Koubaldos; and at eight days' journey from his *aoul* we should find his friend, Sultan Sabeck, a very good man. He informed me that Oui-jass would treat us well, but he said that Koubaldos was a great robber. I desired to know if there were Kirghis about Kessil-bach-Noor. The sultan informed me that there were many *aouls* on the River Ourunjour, that Kessil-bach-Noor was six days' journey distant, and that the people were all robbers.

I desired the Cossack to inform Baspasihan of my intention to visit his friend Sultan Sabeck, and that we should start in the morning. He at once proposed to accompany me to another *aoul* of his own, nearly a day's journey distant in the direction we must travel. We were also to have a hunt with the bearcoote, that I might see their sport, as we should find plenty of game on our way. The gunpowder and the lead which I had given to his men had brought this about. He was also desirous of seeing a boar-hunt, and witnessing the effects of our rifles on the bristly animal. During the evening the sultan asked if I would permit two of his Kirghis to go with me to Sultan Sabeck. He wished to send a present of a fine young stallion to his friend, which he thought would be perfectly safe under our escort. The accuracy and range of our rifles had impressed upon him a very high notion of the power we possessed to repel the attack of any plunderers, and he thought it probable that we might meet with some of them. Several skins were spread for me in the sultan's *yourt*, on which I slept soundly, and forgot for a time both fatigue and robbers.

Soon after daybreak we were all up, and making preparations

for our departure. Horses were standing ready saddled, and every thing indicated a busy scene. I saw two Kirghis occupied with the bearcoote and the falcon. Having finished our morning meal, horses were brought for the sultan and myself. I was to be mounted to-day on one of his best steeds—a fine dark gray, that stood champing my English bit, which he did not appear to relish. All my party were mounted on the sultan's horses ; ours had been sent on to the *aoul* with a party of his people and three of my Kalmucks. When mounted, I had time to examine the party. The sultan and his two sons rode beautiful animals. The eldest boy carried the falcon, which was to fly at the feathered game. A well-mounted Kirghis held the bearcoote, chained to a perch, which was secured into a socket on his saddle. The eagle had shackles and a hood, and was perfectly quiet: he was under the charge of two men. Near to the sultan were his three hunters, or guards, with their rifles, and around us were a band of about twenty Kirghis, in their bright-colored kalats: more than half the number were armed with battle-axes. Taking us altogether, we were a wild-looking group, whom most people would rather behold at a distance than come in contact with.

We began our march, going nearly due east, the sultan's three hunters leading the van, followed by his highness and myself; his two sons and the eagle-bearers immediately behind us, with two of my men in close attendance. A ride of about two hours brought us to the bank of a stagnant river, fringed with reeds and bushes, where the sultan expected that we should find game. We had not ridden far when we discovered traces of the wild boar, large plots having been recently plowed up. This gave us hopes of sport. Our rifles were unslung, and we spread out our party to beat the ground.

We had not gone far when several large deer rushed past a jutting point of the reeds, and bounded over the plain about three hundred yards from us. In an instant the bearcoote was unhooded and his shackles removed, when he sprung from his perch and soared up into the air. I watched him ascend as he wheeled round, and was under the impression that he had not seen the animals; but in this I was mistaken. He had now risen to a considerable height, and seemed to poise himself for about a minute. After this he gave two or three flaps with his wings, and swooped off in a straight line toward his prey. I could not perceive that his wings moved, but he went at a fearful speed. There was a shout, and away went his keepers at full gallop, followed by many others. I gave my horse his head and a touch of the whip; in a few minutes he carried me to the front, and I was riding neck-and-neck with one of the keepers. When we were about two hundred yards off the bearcoote struck his prey. The deer gave a bound forward and fell. The bearcoote had struck one talon into his neck, the other into his back, and with his beak was tearing out the animal's liver. The Kirghis sprung from his horse, slipped the hood over

Bearcoote and Deer.

the eagle's head and the shackles upon his legs, and removed him from his prey without difficulty. The keeper mounted his horse, his assistant placed the bearcoote on his perch, and he was ready for another flight. No dogs are taken out when hunting with the eagle; they would be destroyed to a certainty; indeed, the Kirghis assert that he will attack and kill the wolf. Foxes are hunted in this way, and many are killed; the wild goat and the lesser kinds of deer are also taken in considerable numbers. We had not gone far before a considerable number of antelopes were seen feeding on the plain. Again the bird soared up in circles as before, this time I thought to a greater elevation, and again he made the fatal swoop at his intended victim, and the animal was dead before we reached him. The bearcoote is unerring in his flight; unless the animal can escape into holes in the rocks, as the fox does sometimes, death is his certain doom.

We returned to the river, beating the cover in search of other animals, and rode for a long time without success. At length we roused up some game which kept in the long grass and reeds. Subsequently we got sight of the bristly back of a large boar; several shots were fired, but no ball went near him. After running him about half an hour we came upon open ground, when we had the game in full view—two young boars and a very large one; and as they all made for the open country, they afforded us a good chase.

The animals bounded along at a great speed about four hundred yards ahead of us, but presently separated, the two young ones turning to the left toward the cover on the river farther down; and as the old boar went forward on his course, our party divided, some trying to head the young boars and force them out upon the steppe, while several of the sultan's Kirghis, two Cossacks, Tchuck-a-boi, and myself, followed the old boar, and were gaining upon him fast. I observed that he was a much nobler foe, and much more dangerous to approach than those we had shot before. The horses seemed to enter into the spirit of the chase, and dashed over the plain at a pace that was rapidly bringing us toward our game. A Cossack and myself had been gradually drawing ahead of the other hunters, and were now within fifty yards of the boar, though too much behind him to get a good shot. We could see his formidable tusks and the foam on his jaws as he gnashed them together in his rage. A few minutes more brought us abreast of him, and gradually closing nearer, when within about twenty yards the Cossack fired, and I saw that the boar was wounded. He turned his head toward us for a moment, and then rushed on. I was now within fifteen paces of him, and going at the same speed. Grasping the horse firmly with my knees, I dropped the rein and fired; I noticed with effect, as a red stream gushed down his shoulder.

He turned suddenly and made a rush toward me, but my horse

was too active for him, and in two or three bounds carried me past. A Kirghis, however, who was not far behind, was caught, and the chest of his steed torn open by one stroke of his fearful tusks. The horse sprung forward a few strides and fell. At this critical moment was heard the crack of two rifles, and the boar, again wounded, turned away from his intended victim. After this the Kirghis drew back, the Cossacks and Kalmuck remained to reload their rifles, and I followed alone. Opening both my holsters, I determined to try the effect of my pistols on the boar's tough hide, and keeping my horse well in hand, and ready for a bound, I rode alongside within a few yards, when I got a good shot, which stopped his progress. At this moment I heard the report of a rifle close behind me, when the boar gave a spring and fell dead. I turned round and saw a Cossack: his ball had inflicted the fatal wound. The people came up, the Kirghis who had been so unceremoniously dismounted riding behind one of his companions, his horse having been killed; he looked at the dead boar, spat at him, and called him "Shaitan."

Far away on the horizon we could see our other friends still engaged on their hunt. Leaving part of the men to bring in the animal, we returned slowly toward the river. When we reached the hunters I found that they had killed one of the boars, and that the other had escaped badly wounded, having, as we supposed, swum over the river. The sultan had remained with this party, and was delighted with the sport. I was informed that it would take us many hours to ride to the *aoul* where we were to have our night's lodging; also, that it was necessary to ride fast, or we should not reach it before dark. Baspasihan put his horse into a sharp trot, his hunters pushed on to their places in the van, and our march was continued in the same order as we left the *aoul* in the morning. Our route was in a southwesterly direction over a vast plain, extending far as the eye could reach, on which I could not discover any objects rising above the horizon, which greatly disappointed me, as I expected to see the summits of the Syan-shan. We had ridden for several hours over this plain, which in some parts was covered with rough grass, in others was a sandy waste, when at last we saw a smoke, and shortly afterward many dark spots on the horizon: these were the *yourts*. After riding another hour we came upon a large herd of horses and camels returning to the *aoul*. Our horses were now put into a gallop, and in a short time we were sitting in the sultan's *yourt*, when *koumis* was handed round in large bowls. I acknowledged a preference for tea, which was soon prepared; but as the Kirghis sat watching me drink it, I was convinced that they thought me a complete barbarian, and pitied my want of taste. Presently smoking platters of mutton were brought in, and, judging by the quantity, speedily consumed. Indeed, my impression was that it would be difficult to find hunters with better appetites. It was just dark when this meal was ended, and in a short time all were sleeping soundly.

Just as the day dawned I turned out to examine our position, when I discovered the snowy peaks of the Syan-shan. They appeared cold and ghost-like against the deep blue sky; presently they were tipped with the sun's rays, and shone forth like rubies. I sat on the ground watching the changes with much interest, till the whole landscape was lighted up. Immediately near me was a busy scene: on one side the men were milking the mares, to the number of more than one hundred, and carrying the leathern pails of milk to the *koumis* bag in the *yourt*, the young foals being secured in two long lines to pegs driven into the ground. In front and on the opposite side the women were milking cows, sheep, and goats, and at a little distance beyond these the camels were suckling their young. Around the *aoul* the steppe was filled with animal life. The sultan told me that there were more than two thousand horses, half the number of cows and oxen, two hundred and eighty camels, and more than six thousand sheep and goats. The screams of the camels, the bellowing of bulls, the neighing of horses, and the bleating of sheep and goats, formed a pastoral chorus such as I had never heard in Europe.

Bapasihan proposed sending three of his Kirghis—one possessed some knowledge of the country—as far as the pastures of the robber Koubaldos; beyond that point he had never been; the other two were to attend upon the young stallion. My host also desired that I would visit him on my return to Kessil-bach, as I should then find him more to the west on my route. He farther insisted on my riding during this journey his horse, a splendid animal, of great power and speed. After giving instruction to his Kirghis and the Cossacks, and cautioning them to keep a strict watch when we were with Koubaldos and his tribe, we parted and turned to the southeast, as our route lay in that direction. It was expected that we should find one of the *aouls* of Oui-jass late in the evening after a long ride. This anticipation prevented any attempt at hunting; indeed, the Kirghis urged us on at a rapid pace. After riding over a grassy steppe for near four hours, and crossing several dry water-courses, we came upon a stony track on which there was scarcely any vegetation. The aspect was exceedingly dreary in the distance, the prominent feature being some dark rocky ridges, toward which we were riding. Having gone about ten or twelve versts farther, we reached a depression in the steppe, at the bottom of which lay a lake, oval in form, and, as near as I could judge, eight to ten versts in length. The country around was stony and barren; even the shores of the lake appeared black and sterile; in short, there was not a patch of green to vary the dark purple coloring of the stony covering. It is into this deep hollow that the water-courses we had passed are emptied. The lake has no outlet; in the spring it must be much larger, when the snow-water from the vast plains is poured into it. During the summer in this dry region, the additional quantity of water is carried off by evaporation.

I wished to ride down to the shore of this lake, but the Kirghis objected, saying it was far to the nearest *aoul*. I was thus most reluctantly compelled to abandon my project. Our horses were urged on as quickly as the nature of the ground permitted, keeping along the southern edge of the valley. We had not gone very far when we came to the bed of another river, which was at this part cut into a ravine about fifty feet deep and three hundred feet wide. A small stream was running among the rocks, which at times must be a raging torrent. It was impossible to descend the abrupt rock on horseback; we therefore turned toward the lake and rode down into the valley. Here we crossed the bed of the river without difficulty, and ascended to the steppe, along which we could only ride slowly, as our path was over a layer of small stones, none larger than an egg, but not rounded by the action of water. They were all sharp and angular pieces; in fact, the country had been Macadamized, but by what process this singular effect had been produced I can not tell. We were closely approaching the rocky ridges—masses of stone thrown up to no great elevation—some several versts in length, with small steppes running in between. We soon reached one of these openings, and found it covered with sand, with occasional tufts of rough grass. Our horses were now pushed on at a rapid pace, when we shortly saw the steppe extending, till sky and plain mingled in blue and purple haze.

Before quitting these ridges, a Cossack, a Kirghis, Tchuck-a-boi, and myself rode to the summit of a high mound, hoping to see the *aoul* of which we were in search. We found the sandy plain extended a few versts farther, and then we could see grass and pastures, but neither cattle nor *yourts;* nevertheless, the Kirghis thought they were not far away. After descending, we pushed on again, galloping over the plain, and presently were on the grassy steppe. As we rode on, sharp eyes were looking out for any traces which might lead us to our destination. The sun was sinking fast, which made us all anxious; and although we had found grass, water had not been seen. Another hour passed, and the shades of night were creeping over the plain, when we came upon one of those singular depressions that have the appearance of a mighty water-course. This was about two versts broad, and covered with grass. Near to the opposite side we could see a small river reflecting the fading light, and on the banks *yourts* and large herds of horses. The Kirghis declared that this was the *aoul* of Oui-jass. While we stood looking at the delightful scene before us, several horsemen came riding from the encampment. We descended the steep bank and met them; and they were delighted when Baspasihan's Kirghis rode up, declaring that we were his master's friends, and not robbers. One of the Kirghis rode back at full gallop, and we followed slowly. We were not long in reaching the *aoul*, when a fine old man took hold of my bridle and led my horse to a *yourt*, which had been moved bodily to a clean piece of turf, where the women were busy spreading *voilock* and carpets on the ground. *Koumis* was brought in bowls; but I preferred waiting for my tea, which the Cossacks immediately prepared, adding some slices of broiled mutton for my evening meal. Not far from the dwelling I saw a fire blazing under a great caldron, and other preparations in progress for a feast, to which, I have no doubt, all my party did ample justice.

When I turned out the next morning I found that most of my people were still asleep; but they were not long left so, for as soon as the Kirghis observed me outside the *yourt* they roused them. My host and his people had not been idle, for I noticed a troop of fresh horses picketed near our own. The chief insisted on giving us his own horses for our ride, and Kirghis to take charge of ours to the encampment of Oui-jass. The old man said it was far away, and that we should not reach it until the evening of the second day; that a Kirghis would guide us to a pasture and water, where we could remain for the night. He declared that it would be a long ride, and most of it over a sandy plain. He gave us six Kirghis, one as our guide, and five to take charge of our horses and bring his own back: each carried his battle-axe. We were now twenty-one in number, and a wild-looking band.

After saying "*Aman-bul*" (farewell) to Tursum—such was the chief's name—the guide led the way in nearly a southeasterly direction. In due time we reached the bank, forming one side of the depression, and ascended to the steppe, which was covered with coarse dry grass. Again I could see the snowy peaks of the Syan-shan, and anticipated, by continuing our present course, that we should in a day or two have the whole in view. The guide put his horse into a trot, and away we went over the plain. The track of dry grass was soon passed, when we entered upon a sandy waste almost without vegetation. But this was not wholly unproductive, for we presently reached a part which produced a fine crop of tarantulas. The ground was quite covered with their webs and holes; and as we rode over it, many of these venomous insects were killed by our horses. I was curious to see them in their little dens, and dismounted to make a nearer acquaintance. I quickly came upon a large web, indicating a manufacturer on a great scale. I drew my long knife and touched it, when out he rushed, fixed his fangs on the steel for a moment, and then retreated into his hole. When the Kirghis observed me begin to dig him out, they were afraid that I should be bitten, but I took especial care to keep my fingers beyond his reach. I rolled him out of the sand, and again he sprung at the blade, evidently much enraged at being disturbed. His body was dark brown and black, and very ugly. Leaving him to seek or dig another dwelling, I mounted my horse and left this venomous spot. The Kirghis have a great dread of these little reptiles, but the sheep eat them with impunity and relish.

After this delay our guide urged us on, pointing to the misty outline of some ridges as the place for our night's encampment. The sun was shining down upon us with great force, but tempered by a strong breeze from the west, which rendered our ride pleasant. We had been many hours crossing this sandy plain, with nothing to vary the scene. About two o'clock we came upon a small stream, where our guide proposed that we should rest for an hour, as there was plenty of pure water, and a little grass for our horses. The men were provided with smoked horseflesh, which they all ate with great relish. The Cossacks had brought me a little broiled mutton, and this, with a few glasses of tea, made me an excellent dinner. Our horses having been changed, we now rode our own, and pushed on at a very rapid pace, fearing that we should not reach our destination before dark. Several hours had passed, and we were still on the sterile steppe. The ridges had assumed a deeper tone, and I could perceive the natural colors of the rocks shining through the misty vapor. This told me we were approaching them fast; and just at dusk we saw a golden line of light stretching across the plain, caused by reflection of the gorgeous sky on a long narrow lake. We soon reached the shore, and found, as the Kirghis had predicted, good pasturage and fresh water, with bushes for a fire.

No sound or sign of animal life was seen or heard during the night excepting from our horses, and they fared sumptuously; and while the ridges were still casting long shadows over the plain, we sprung into our saddles and left our resting-place. Our route was along the margin of the lake, to the westward, for a distance of about ten versts; we then turned round the head of the lake, and came upon a small river which flowed into it from the west. Here we found several pheasants, some of which I bagged; but of other game we saw no traces. I believe, however, that we should have found both wild boars and deer, could we have spared the time to beat the bushes and reeds on the opposite side of the lake.

The guide continued a route toward the southeast, which I knew was taking us away from the mountains, but this was necessary to find the *aoul* of Oui-jass. A ride of little more than an hour brought us to the ridges which had appeared so small as we approached. On examination they proved to be red granite, and some rose seven or eight hundred feet from the ground. They were broken into very rugged and picturesque shapes, and many had a singular appearance as they stood out on these vast steppes, like ruined castles of colossal dimensions. No wonder the tribes of Central Asia fear to pass many of these places, and invest them with superstitious horrors. To-day we passed a ridge more like the ruins of some vast city than a mountain; there were isolated pillars—huge masses like the broken shafts of columns; walls rising up to a great elevation, pierced with large circular apertures, and enormous blocks heaped around, forming a complete chaos. I proposed to stop and explore this wonderful scene, but the Kirghis stood aghast; and when they saw me sketch it, they looked as if they expected to see Shaitan and his legions threaten us from the mighty walls.

Having passed the ridges, we came once more upon the steppe, and discerned the outline of other hills in the southeast, toward which the guide informed me we must look for Oui-jass. We had now reached a part of the plain on which the *salsola* plant was growing, and in the distance I could see salt lakes: I knew them to be salt by the crimson margins which encircled them. After a few hours' ride we passed near one, and observed all around its shores a crystallization of salt, sometimes more than an inch thick, and perfectly white, that sparkled in the sun like diamonds.

Presently our Kirghis guide descried a summit to the south of our route; by this he was able to direct our course, and he now made it more easterly, assuring me that, by continuing in this direction, we should be certain to strike on the pastures of Oui-jass, which he hoped to accomplish before nightfall. I felt satisfied that without the aid of this man it would be exceedingly difficult for us to discover the *aoul.* We rode on, in full confidence that we should find both pastures and water, even if we did not find Kirghis, and in less than two hours came upon a part of the plain covered in many places with patches of grass, while in the distance we could see that the country had lost its sterile appearance. Our animals began to prick up their ears, an intimation that water was not far off. It was not long before I observed dark objects dotted over the plain, but at a considerable distance; these were camels, and we were proceeding directly toward them. Having gone some distance, we could see men riding about hurriedly, and driving the herd away: this was accounted for in a moment. Our party had been seen approaching, and were considered banditti.

The guide ordered a halt, and sent one of his men forward. The Kirghis saw him, and one of their party approached to meet him; still, they continued to drive in the camels, as if not quite satisfied of our intentions. At length the two Kirghis met, conversed a few minutes, and then separated; one galloped off to his friends, and the other waited for us. We rode sharply onward, and shortly reached the camels, which were now left to feed. Intelligence of our arrival would soon reach Oui-jass, as one man would carry the news to another, galloping at full speed. We came up to the herdsmen, who pointed out the direction of the *aoul*, and on we went at a sharp trot. A short distance brought us among a herd of horses, having passed which we beheld a group of Kirghis approaching. As both parties were riding fast, we were not long before we met, when we learned that they had been sent by Oui-jass to welcome us to his encampment. We could see the *yourts* not far off, on the bank of a lake, which was stretching out much beyond them. This was a most delightful scene after our dreary ride. It was plain that the chief was rich in flocks and herds, and had a large *aoul* around him.

The Kirghis led me up to a *yourt* where a spear, with a tuft of red hair, was stuck in the ground, and a fine-looking old man was standing near, dressed in a rich silk kalat, striped with crimson and yellow, tied round his waist with a green scarf. He had a deep crimson silk cap, fitting close to his head, embroidered with silver, and very high-heeled red leather boots. This was Oui-jass, who took hold of the reins, and held up his hand to help me to dismount. He then placed first his right hand, and then his left, on my breast, after which he led me into his *yourt*. The carpets were already laid down opposite the door; on these he placed me, and would have retired to a *voilock* had I not insisted on his sitting beside me. In a few minutes a brass tea-pot was brought in; then some small china tea-cups and saucers were put on a low table, and placed before us; a basin with sugar-candy, and several plates of dried fruit, were added. A youth, about seventeen years old, came in, knelt down before the table, poured out the tea, and handed a cup to me, and then some of the fruit. He performed the same office for my host, and replenished our cups the moment they were empty; and we had the tea-pot filled several times.

The guests had crowded into the *yourt* the moment we were sat down. Several were dressed in silk *kalats* and foxskin caps; the youth handed tea to these men, partaking of it himself, and I was now informed that he was Oui-jass's son. Besides the visitors in the *yourt*, I saw that there were many outside peeping in at us, and frequently changing places, that all might get a view. The costume of all my party had some similarity to that of the Kirghis in fashion, but not in quality and color; but the difference between the Kirghis costume and mine was so marked that they had never seen any thing in the smallest degree resembling it. I wore a shooting-jacket of rifle-green, a checked waistcoat and trowsers—but very little of the latter were seen, as my legs were inserted into a pair of long shooting-boots—a pink calico shirt, with the collar turned down over a small neck-tie, and a large-brimmed felt hat that would accommodate itself to any shape. For a period of four years no barber had touched my silvery locks, and they were hanging down in heavy curls. This was a great wonder, as all male heads with them are closely shaven.

I wished to get some information about the country we had yet to pass through to reach Sultan Sabeck. A Cossack and Tchuck-a-boi were my interpreters. I learned that it would require two days' hard riding to reach the *aoul* of Koubaldos; that we should find a small grassy valley where we could encamp, and a sandy waste on our second day's march. My host said Koubaldos would not molest us at his *aoul*, but that some of his bands would be set on our track, and try to plunder us on our march. I also ascertained that we were only six days' journey from Tchin-si or Barkoul, lying near the eastern end of the Syan-shan, on some of the lower slopes of the mountain.

Sultan Baspasihan's young stallion being placed under my care proved of great assistance. What his Kirghis reported to my host I can not tell, but Oui-jass also desired to forward a mission to Sultan Sabeck. He wished to send three Kirghis with me, and proposed to give us fresh horses, which he said we should require farther on, while he would take charge of ours till we returned to his pasture-ground, three days' journey to the westward, where his *aoul* would be removed to in a few days. This, he said, would be our route back. All these matters having been settled, a Cossack brought me some broiled mutton, and the great feast was served in another dwelling. In a few minutes I was left quite alone, excepting a dog, who probably expected to fare better with me than in the crowd at the banquet.

So soon as the first streak of daylight appeared on the steppe, the Kirghis were in motion, and very shortly the horses were brought in. Our preparations having been made, before the sun rose we said "*Aman-bul*" to Oui-jass and our late companions, and sprung into our saddles. We were now seventeen in number, and all were armed, eight with battle-axes. Before we started I desired one of the Cossacks to ask if any of the Kirghis were afraid to visit the *aoul* of Koubaldos. Their reply was "*jock*" (no), swinging their battle-axes round their heads. Our guide pushed to the front and led the way, followed by three fine dogs. Again we rode in a southeasterly direction, passing through large herds of horses and cattle, which had not yet been driven to the pastures. Our route was over a level plain for many hours, and it was not until about noon we got a view of some ridges that extended far to the southward. Our guide directed his course toward the north end of these hills, saying that the place for our night encampment was near them. The change from rich pastures to barren steppes, from a scene so full of life as that we had left in the morning to the perfect solitude which surrounded us now, afforded matter for much speculation. Here were little communities nearly shut out from each other, and quite so from the rest of the world, engaged in rearing their flocks and herds; and many of these people become old and die without ever seeing the face of man, excepting their own tribe.

To-day we had a beautiful mirage—an enormous lake appearing stretched out across the steppe, with a large city standing on its shore. Tall trees and extensive forests were pictured with so much fidelity that it was really difficult to satisfy the mind that the whole was an illusion. Hour after hour passed away as it kept receding before us, and constantly changing its forms, till at last it vanished. Two of the Cossacks and the Kalmucks had never seen this phenomenon before, and were much astonished when they found the lake dry land. We had been nearly ten hours on horseback when we came upon a small stream running sluggishly toward a lake some five or six versts distant. It was decided that we should rest for an hour, and let the horses drink and feed. We had come upon a spot where a number of horses had been picketed, the Kirghis thought, only two or three days before, from which they conjectured that some of the bands of Koubaldos were out on a roving expedition. After an examination, it was found that they had gone toward home, and it was decided that we should follow their track. Having eaten some cold mutton and washed it down with a draught from the stream, we resumed our journey.

Leaving the river in our rear, we rode over a sandy soil, possessing very little vegetation, on which we found the track of horses distinctly visible—an excellent guide—and we pushed on with increased confidence. The ridges we had seen at midday had lost their hazy appearance; they now stood up boldly from the plain in rugged masses of purple gray rocks. They were beautifully lit up by the setting sun, which developed many singular forms. Beyond these, and far in the distance, other mountains were seen; and not far from these our guide said that we should find Koubaldos. As we journeyed on, our shadows were lengthening fast along the plain, and as yet we had seen no signs of pasture or water; but in less than an hour we arrived at the edge of a little valley, beautifully green, with a small lake in the middle, reflecting the golden tints of the sky. We were not long reaching its shore, and a place possessing all the proper requisites was soon found for our encampment, almost close to the water's edge.

We had lost all traces of the Kirghis who had preceded us, but before it was dark several of the men started along the shore of the lake in both directions to search for their track, and the party that had gone to the westward found their encampment about a verst distant. The embers of the fire were still hot, and the men thought they had slept there last night.

At dark our horses were brought close to the camp, and well secured; a guard of three men was appointed, to be changed every two hours; besides which, the Kirghis said the dogs would give mouth if any thing came near. Tchuck-a-boi proposed that the fire should be extinguished, as the light would be seen to a long distance over the steppe; this having been done, we lay down to sleep, with our arms close at hand. In an hour after sunrise we were on our march, and soon found the track of the Kirghis' horses on the sandy waste. It turned more to the south than our guide intended to go, but after a consultation we decided on following it. As we rode along I saw the white summits of Syan-shan, but none of the lower range. Having passed by the northern end of the rocky mass, which descended abruptly to the plain, we entered a desert of sand and gravel quite destitute of herbage. We had not gone far when the track we had been following turned more to the east, and continued straight toward a gap in the distant mountain. This accorded with the opinion our guide had expressed, and convinced me that he could take us to the *aoul.* Hours passed over, and sand, with a few pebbles, was all we saw; neither beast nor bird was met with. In some parts we found the tarantula, but not very numerous.

Soon after noon we observed a change of color on the plain in the distance; this indicated the position of the pastures we were seeking. In another hour we could distinguish the green color, which showed us that we were drawing near to this land of robbers. We pushed on and reached the turf, where it was struggling to maintain its ground against the sandy intruder, and in a short time were riding over good grass, but no cattle could be seen feeding upon it. We examined the steppe in every direction, but nothing was visible: this induced us to ride nearly due east toward the great rent in the mountain. After proceeding in this direction some time, I could distinguish some dark object on the plain. Stopping our horses, I pointed them out to my companions, not one of whom could see any thing but the grassy steppe. Feeling certain that I was right, I turned my horse and rode toward the objects, followed by all. In less than half an hour we could see the camels and large herds of horses feeding, but not one man was visible within the range of my vision. Still, we were now sure of finding the *aoul*, and on we rode.

When within about a verst of the herd several men were seen riding toward us, and one galloping off in the opposite direction. We had been observed, and our arrival would shortly be made known to the chief, if this was his *aoul.* It was not long before four Kirghis met us; and when *Aman* had been said, they began a series of questions, desiring to know who we were, and where we were going. It would have been difficult for any individual among us to say who we were, but their last question was answered by asking to be directed to the encampment of Koubaldos. They instantly turned their horses and rode with us, going more to the south. A conversation went on between our guide and them for a short time, after which two of them started off at a gallop, and we followed slowly. After riding about two versts I saw the *aoul*, whence several men were riding fast to meet us; and our horses being put into a canter, shortly brought us together. They pulled up and greeted us, then two of them rode toward me, and taking a place at each side, led the way. The distance was not great, and I observed that the encampment was a large one: I counted twenty-seven *yourts*, several with spears standing at the doors. The Kirghis guided me to a large one, at the door of which stood a tall man dressed in a black velvet kalat, a crimson cap trimmed with fur, and a crimson shawl round his waist. He stepped forward, took hold of the reins, and in the customary manner gave me his hand to dismount. When I had alighted, he touched my breast with his right and left hands, and then led me into his dwelling.

I was now sitting face to face with the great robber-chief Koubaldos, of whom I had heard so much, and whose fame has spread far throughout Central Asia. When standing, I thought him tall; I now observed, when sitting, that he was reduced to about my own stature—five feet eleven inches. The heels of his boots were two inches high, and this had deceived me. Having placed me on the carpet, he seated himself opposite, and ten or twelve of his people sat beyond him. I could see that my face, figure, and dress were being scanned by these men with a most rigid scrutiny; nor was I less interested in the group before me. At this moment tea was brought into the *yourt* by two boys, a small low table was placed before us, and I invited my host to sit beside me. We were now equals in honor, and his people had a full view of both chiefs, for they looked upon me as the head of my band. The tea was served in small china cups, and sugar-candy and several sorts of dried fruits were placed on the table on china plates. My host selected fruit for me, was very attentive, at the same time partaking of it largely himself, and I followed his example.

Two Cossacks and Tchuck-a-boi were sitting at a short distance from me. The youths handed tea to my men, and to three or four of the Kirghis sitting in front. Sugar-candy was given to them, but no fruit. When these had finished, the other Kirghis were regaled with the beverage. Koubaldos now began inquiries concerning my visit, and asked where I was going. I desired a Cossack to say that I was traveling to Tchin-si, and could not pass near his country without paying my respects to a chief so famed; adding that I also intended to visit Sultan Sabeck, and then continue my journey to Tchin-si. He inquired if I had any thing to sell, and was answered in the negative. He next asked if I was going to buy goods at Tchin-si; the answer "*jock*" appeared to astonish him. He then wished to know why we had so many rifles and arms. My reply was, "To kill game for food, and defend ourselves." He expressed a wish to buy my pistols, the double-barrel gun, and two rifles. Again the Cossack rolled out the word "*jock*" with great force; and to his requests for powder and balls, he received the same answer. The Cossack turned to me and said, "The *chort!* let him have these, and he would soon kill us."

I opened my folio and sketch-book, and showed him some colored sketches. He looked at a view with *yourts* and camels in the foreground, which interested him greatly, but he would not consent to have his own portrait taken. While the two sheep were being cooked, Koubaldos was very anxious to see my double-barreled gun used. He evidently thought both barrels would be fired at the same moment. Perhaps he also deemed it an imitation of a Chinese sword which he had shown me, having two blades in one hilt half an inch apart. This was drawn from its scabbard with much care, and exhibited to me as a terrible weapon; but it did not produce the expected effect. As we rode down to the *aoul*, I had observed a lake at a short distance beyond, on which many water-fowl were swimming. Taking my gun, I went toward it, followed by Koubaldos and his Kirghis; when I got near, several ducks rose; I fired, and one dropped upon the water; the others wheeled round and came back, flying over our heads. I fired again, and shot a second duck, which fell dead within a few yards of the chief.

He now examined the gun, watched me reload, and evidently would have liked me to shoot for hours had the ducks remained. We returned to the *yourt*, when I desired the Cossack to inquire how many days' journey it was to Tchin-si. The chief said four days, and to Sultan Sabeck three days. He proposed that we should go a more southern route, and visit his friend Ultigun, as from his *aoul* we should find our way easier. The Cossacks and Tchuck-a-boi thought it better to let him believe that we should take his advice, and then his plans would be formed in that direction, but in the morning we could take our own course more to the eastward; by doing so we were certain to strike upon the pastures of Sabeck.

The mutton was boiled and was dishing up when Koubaldos rose and led me to a carpet on the outside. The ablutions performed, the smoking platters were placed before us. The Cossacks had broiled some of the meat for me, as the entrails had been boiled in the caldron without having been particularly well washed, an ordinary process in Kirghis cookery; indeed, I had seen lumps of masticated grass floating on the bubbling liquid and in the soup-bowls at other places. There were about fifty men grouped in front of their chief, some of them desperate-looking fellows, who would not stand at trifles to attain any object. About half this number of miserable-looking women were sitting around, and many children were among them. Most of the men had fur coats on—many of horseskin, with the mane down the centre of the back—and wore fur caps. This gave them a wild and rather ferocious aspect, which was somewhat heightened by the savage manner in which they dined.

I had no fear that we should be molested while staying in the *aoul*. Koubaldos had already invited me to remain another day and rest our horses, but none of my people liked this, and the Kirghis were anxious to continue our journey in the morning. Our horses were picketed near the *yourt*, and each man had orders to take especial care of his arms. Just before dark it was a busy scene round the encampment; the men were milking the mares, the women the cows, sheep, and goats. Near to us stood three large iron caldrons, placed over furnace-holes dug in the ground. The women brought their leathern pails of milk and poured them into these vessels, when three boys set a light to the bushes beneath, and tended the fires until the contents in the caldrons were boiling. This was the preparation of "*hyran*," composed of the milk of cow, sheep, and goat, which by boiling becomes very thick.

It is then cut into pieces four inches long and two inches square: these are laid upon reed mats and dried in the sun, which makes it a sort of cheese, that forms a considerable article of food with the people in these regions. When dried it has the appearance of yellow limestone, and is almost as hard. They pound it in a mortar, then steep it in milk, and dine upon it. I have eaten this food, but I can not say that it is good.

I slept in the *yourt* of Koubaldos. Two Cossacks and Tchuck-a-boi spread their furs near me. Having secured my arms, I lay down, and was soon fast asleep within a few feet of the robber-chief. A man must be a sound sleeper if he be not roused up at daybreak in a Kirghis *aoul*, the noise of the animals being quite sufficient to awaken the most drowsy of mortals. In a few minutes after awaking I was out in the air, where I found one of the Cossacks waiting for me. He had been up some time, and had seen Koubaldos leave the *yourt* very quietly, and had also heard men speaking to each other, mount their horses, and ride away. He instantly went out, and observed the chief and four men leave the encampment. I directed him to call Tchuck-a-boi, and tell the other Cossacks to stay in the *yourt;* also to bring my gun. This was instantly done, and we then went toward the lake to look for ducks. When far enough out of ear-shot, the Cossack repeated to Tchuck-a-boi what he had told me.

We all agreed that there was something strange in the conduct of the chief—after inviting me to remain, then going off in this manner; and while continuing our walk to the lake, we settled our plans, and decided to ask no questions. I shot a duck, and the report of the gun brought out several Kirghis, who had most probably been watching us. We then returned to the *yourt*, and ordered the Cossack to let me have breakfast, and tell the other men to take theirs. All this was done, and at the end of two hours our horses were brought up saddled, and in a very short time we were ready to march. After putting fresh caps on my pistols, I stuck them in my belt, the Cossacks did the same, and we then left the place.

I desired the Cossack to ask for Koubaldos of one of the Kirghis who had sat near me in the *yourt;* the man replied that he had gone to look at some horses, and would return by midday. I then requested my compliments to be given to him, adding my regret that I could not wait for his return. The Kirghis said that he had received orders to conduct us to the *aoul* of Ultigun in case we wished to start before his chief's return, but he was informed that his aid would not be required, as we should not go there, which appeared to astonish him. He assured me that Koubaldos had arranged for our visit to his friend, and would be angry if we left without going to see him. I desired him to say that I thanked the chief for his kind intentions toward us, and should be sorry if he were angry at our departure, but that we did not fear his wrath; we could and would defend ourselves, if necessary. After this we left the encampment, rode past the head of the lake, and directed our course southeast.

We passed several Kirghis tending the horses and camels, and they asked our Kirghis why we were traveling in a direction where no *aouls* would be found; but we wished them good-by and rode on. One of our men called my attention to three Kirghis who had just left the encampment, and were riding fast toward the south: this was significant. The pastures extended many versts in this direction, and after riding about three hours we noticed some *yourts* three or four versts distant, a little to the north of our track. Two Cossacks, a Kalmuck, and a Kirghis rode toward them, hoping to get some information, while we continued our course, and in little more than an hour they joined us. They had found an old Kirghis, three women, and two boys at the *yourts*, which belonged to Koubaldos, and ascertained that four men had gone to his *aoul* very early this morning. There were a large herd of horses and a few camels. A Cossack questioned the old man about water and pastures farther on. He said that we should find a small river if we rode fast before the sun set, and plenty of grass on its banks for our horses, but he did not know how far it was to the *aoul* of Sultan Sabeck.

The Kirghis succeeded better; he discovered that one of the women had been stolen from his master's *aoul* several years ago, and that the two boys were her children. He gave her information about her friends, and she told him that Koubaldos had sent for the men, a Kirghis having come in the night, and that they were out on a plundering expedition, but she did not know where. She also said that we should find a river and good pastures where the old man had described; and at a day's ride beyond we should come upon a lake and pasture. She had been there, and had remained while the band had gone to the pastures of Sabeck. She added that we should see a pointed mountain, near which we should find the sultan. The pointed mountain agreed with the description Baspasihan had given me; nor did I doubt the woman's veracity. It was thus Providence had given us all the information we required.

Our horses were now put into a sharp trot, and in about two hours we left the grassy steppe and entered on a sandy waste. The sun was still high, and we pushed on; another three hours passed, and then we could see a dark line crossing the steppe: these were the bushes on the river. Several rocky ridges appeared to the north; to the south it was a plain as far as the eye could reach—a sterile and most uninteresting country. It was not long before our horses pricked their ears, having scented the water afar off, and we reached it half an hour before the sun sank below the plain. I watched him go down; it was a glorious sunset. A reddish haze extended along the horizon, spreading over steppe and sky, and obscuring the dividing line between earth and heaven. Golden clouds were scattered in fleecy masses above the spot where the sun was last seen, and extended far up toward the zenith. They first assumed a bright flame-color almost too dazzling for the sight; then a reddish burning glow, gradually changing into a deep crimson. The upper part of the sky was a deep blue gray, passing with beautiful gradations into a greenish hue; then to a pale yellow, which became stronger in tone as it descended, until the color was a brilliant orange, shadowing into a deep red on the horizon, now distinctly marked by the purple and misty plain. It was a beautiful and calm scene, and my little band must have looked like a speck on the vast desert.

A council was held on this spot, now so calm, which would probably become the scene of strife and bloodshed before the sun cast his morning rays over the steppe to cheer our solitude. The Cossacks, Tchuck-a-boi, and some of the Kirghis thought the band would follow us. We all knew that it was not our horses alone that Koubaldos wanted; if they could only rob us of them, we must become an easy prey; we could not escape on foot from these vast sandy deserts, and the robbers would be able to secure our arms without much danger to themselves. It was probable that they might make an attack upon us, hoping to succeed by numbers, but we made up our minds that it should cost them much blood before they obtained possession of our weapons. Koubaldos would hear of us from the herdsmen, and at the small *aoul*, where he would most probably get fresh horses, and follow. It was thought that his band might reach us soon after midnight; but before dark our rifles were all examined and put in good order. I drew the charges from my gun, and loaded with ball cartridge, ot which I had a plentiful supply. Just at dusk the horses were brought in and secured, and the watches appointed. It was arranged that a Cossack, a Kalmuck, and two Kirghis should take the first watch, two Cossacks and two Kirghis the second, that myself, Tchuck-a-boi, and two Kalmucks should go on duty at midnight, and the dogs would give us notice of the approach of either man or beast.

All except the watch were soon asleep, and no one feared that they would slumber on their post. Subsequently, when a Cossack touched me, I sprung up, and was surprised that the hours had passed so quickly. My three companions were at their posts, and the other men left us; they had not heard a sound save the rippling of the stream, nor had the dogs given a growl. The night was beautiful; not a cloud was to be seen; the stars shone forth with great brilliancy, and a perfect stillness reigned over this vast region. All nature seemed sleeping; even our own footsteps were hushed as we paced the grassy turf; nor could any thing be seen when we peered into the deep gloom spread over the steppe. We were quietly pacing on our different posts, each occupied with his own reflections, when suddenly the whole plain was lit up with a pale blue light. This gave me a start for a moment, and on looking up I saw a large meteor passing slowly across the sky, from the south to the north, of a beautiful blue color. After moving along for about thirty seconds it burst with a great flash, and shortly followed a sound like the booming of a distant gun. The noise awoke some ot our people, who started up, thinking that we had fired our rifles. I was much interested with this phenomenon. Presently other meteors appeared; they were small, of a bright flame color, and rushed down with great speed, frequently leaving a long train of white sparks behind them. Our watch had passed without being disturbed by robbers; other men were called on duty, and I sat watching the meteors. About half past two o'clock they became very numerous, and still more beautiful. Some were a bright crimson, others a deep purple; they fell in various directions, but principally toward the northwest, and continued to fall for more than an hour, during which period I counted one hundred and eight. I frequently saw three and four at the same moment. This happened on the morning of the 11th of August, New Style.

While this was going on I forgot both Koubaldos and his band, and was sitting musing over the scene I had just witnessed, when a dog lying near me gave a growl; we remained perfectly still; shortly he repeated it, when the other dogs also began to give forth low growls. Tchuck-a-boi and a Cossack who were lying near declared that the dogs heard something on the steppe. A long narrow streak of light was already breaking along the horizon on the northeast, therefore we should shortly have light to see around us. Presently the dogs commenced to bark, which roused up the whole camp. The Kirghis stopped their barking and kept them still, as the noise would guide the band toward us, should they be approaching. They, however, could not take us by surprise, as all were on the alert. I now told the Cossacks that not a shot was to be fired until I gave the word, and then only four were to fire, each one selecting a Kirghis, beginning from the right, and making sure of his man; and while they were reloading, the other four were to fire.

The gray dawn was creeping fast over the plain, and we could see objects at some distance. The dogs were let loose, and they left us, going along the side of the river; very soon they set up a furious barking, and we saw a small herd of deer bound over the plain: their neighborhood had made the dogs uneasy. The horses were now turned out to feed; a fire was lighted, and two men only left on duty; but nothing could be seen on any part of the plain to indicate that we were pursued. Four of us started down the river in search of game. We had not gone far when we found a brood of pheasants, of which several of the young ones were carried back with us. They were well grown; and I can answer for their flavor, as one of them afforded me a breakfast.

The morning was delightful, with a bright sun and a fine breeze. About half a verst from the little river we came on to the sandy waste which stretched away to the eastward beyond the reach of our vision. As we rode along we congratulated ourselves on having passed one night without an attack. The Kirghis, however, thought that we had not yet done with Koubaldos. From what the captive woman had stated, we had a long day's ride before we should reach the pastures on the lake. For five or six hours our route was over a level sandy plain, with the *salsola* plant growing on many parts. After this it became slightly undulating, and very far in the distance we could see the summits of apparently high ridges. We were now riding over a country covered with tufts of long grass; still, it had a dry and sterile appearance; farther on we came upon dwarf bushes, the green foliage of which improved the country.

About the middle of the afternoon we first got sight of the lake, which appeared to be of considerable dimensions, and was surrounded by pastures that formed a green belt along its shores. To the south there were some high ridges, which branched off and extended westward. We were within about fifteen versts of these, riding straight toward the centre of the lake, which was not less than forty versts in length, and it was necessary to decide to which end we should take our course. After some consultation we determined to go to the south, as we thought that route would lead us more directly toward the sultan's *aoul.*

Having traveled on about ten versts, and approached nearer the mountain ridges, the face of the country became quite changed. Immense blocks of granite were strewn over the surface, and small ravines were extending up toward the rocky ridges. Rough as this was, it varied the scene, and was so far agreeable. We had not gone far when the dogs came upon a large herd of wild goats, which bounded off toward the mountain. After a short run they caught a kid, and it was carried off with vast satisfaction by the Kirghis. We continued our ride nearly south, having ascended considerably toward the foot of the mountains, which gave me a view over the country beyond the lake to the north and east: in both directions it was steppe, with very small elevations. There were no pastures in these regions within the reach of my vision, which satisfied me that Sabeck must be sought still more to the south. Having ridden a few versts farther, the mountain ridge suddenly terminated, and a broad valley extended to the ridge on the east. Between these lay a portion of the lake, stretching twelve or fifteen versts up the valley, and about four versts broad; immediately opposite to us a long narrow neck of land or rocks ran out into the lake, terminating in a bold mass.

While I was engaged sketching this scene, one of the men observed smoke about half way up the mountain on the opposite side of the lake, which, when pointed out, attracted the attention of the whole party. The Kirghis said that Koubaldos and his robbers had arrived before us, knowing that we must pass in this direction. As it was now late in the afternoon, we decided to encamp on the shore of the lake. The party on the mountain would see us as we rode down into the valley, as they were sure to have men on the look-out. In a short time we reached the shore, and found a beautiful spot for our encampment among bushes and good grass, about a verst to the south of the neck of land. The lake was good fresh water, and at a little distance to the south there was a long line of sandy shore. Whoever the people were whose fire we had seen, they would soon know that they had neighbors, as the smoke from our encampment began to rise in thick wreaths.

While the men were preparing our suppers, I wished to examine the narrow neck of land jutting out into the lake, and a Cossack and Tchuck-a-boi accompanied me. I found it was a ledge of rocks, in some places four paces wide, and in others twenty. In parts the causeway was covered with a thick grassy turf; elsewhere it was bare rock, with deep water on each side. At the other end were curious masses of dark purple rocks; one of large dimensions, with a deep recess on each side. Other pillars were standing near it: from this point it is about eight hundred yards to the shore.

While I was engaged sketching this curious and picturesque scene, my two companions had been examining the spot, with the intention of making it our encampment during the night. They said there was no doubt that a great number of Koubaldos's men were at hand, and they thought that an attack would be made in the night by the whole band rushing down upon us when it was supposed that we were sleeping—their usual mode of war and plunder. Here was a spot on which we could defend ourselves against five hundred. One part of the ledge was not more than twelve feet wide: it was broken up, and large stones were scattered over it; and this narrow passage was about one hundred yards from the shore, and forty in length. We could shoot with our rifles every man who ventured upon it, and our expected visitors had not been trained to face a deadly fire. It was arranged

Our Night Encampment.

that we should remain at our camp till it was quite dark, then remove the horses to the farther end of the rocks, and secure them there for the night, guarded by four Kirghis, who should take charge of the dogs and prevent their barking. The Kirghis have these animals so well trained that we had no fear of their betraying us. Having agreed on these matters, we returned to the camp, when our plan for passing the night was explained, and orders given for carrying it into effect.

During the evening, several men had been seen on the mountain watching us: they could see whatever was done with our horses, which, just at dusk, were brought up and picketed (as if for the night) between us and the lake. The fire was piled up with fuel, which threw up its bright flame, and showed the robbers that we were preparing for sleep; but when the night was sufficiently dark, our steeds were saddled in readiness to depart for our new abode in the citadel. Two Kalmucks were left to keep up the fire, with orders to remain until Tchuck-a-boi recalled them.

We now rode slowly to our place of security; and having reached the end of the narrow part, we dismounted, two of the Cossacks going on with the Kirghis, and taking all our horses with them; the former were to see that they were well secured, then return to us, after giving the Kirghis strict injunctions to keep the dogs quiet. The saddle-cloths were brought, when we at once pitched upon a spot for our night's lodging, at about twenty-five paces from the end of the narrow pass. A Cossack and a Kirghis were stationed at the opposite end, nearer the shore, to listen for the approach of the robbers, with orders to creep along the rocks and join us when they heard the band coming near. Tchuck-a-boi had called in his Kalmucks, and one was appointed sentinel. We now felt perfectly secure in our position, and lay down to sleep. The fire of our old encampment sent up a strong glare of light. I watched its flickering on the water for a short time as I lay on the bank, and then fell fast asleep.

Before the first watch was over, the two men from our advanced post had come in, announcing that the villains were at our encampment. Bushes had been thrown on the fire, and the flames springing up enabled our sentinels to see men on horseback. I now ordered that three men only should fire at a time; this would give us three volleys, and my gun would do good service in defending the narrow pass. Two Cossacks and myself would fire first, then Tchuck-a-boi and his Kalmucks; lastly, the others. This being thoroughly understood, we waited patiently for the approach of the enemy. Presently we heard the tramp of horses on the shore, but it was too dark to distinguish any object. The robbers were riding slowly along, and shortly stopped at the neck of land; many were talking fast, but the Kirghis could not hear what was said. A party presently advanced along the ledge, and we could hear them coming nearer, and they soon reached the narrow part where not more than three could ride abreast. This brought them to a stand; on our side every rifle was ready, but we could not see a man; they stood and spoke, but no one attempted to ride over.

Every word they uttered could now be distinctly heard, and we presently recognized the voice of Koubaldos. The band remained talking on this spot for about ten minutes, then returned to the shore, going off at a trot to the northward. The Kirghis explained what they had heard. Koubaldos was very angry that we had escaped, calling us cowards, and he told his band that we could be easily taken. He was certain that we had gone to the north end of the lake, and by following quickly he would be up with us at daylight, and have us fast in the morasses. Even if we succeeded in passing these he was equally confident of being able to drive us on the steppe, from whence we could not reach Sultan Sabeck's *aoul* in less than three days, before which we could easily be cut off when our horses were exhausted for want of water.

The Kirghis wished to leave as soon as possible, and ride to the southward; but to this plan none of my men would consent. It was finally arranged that we should leave the moment day dawned, without stopping to feed our horses or ourselves; for when it was daylight, Koubaldos would discover his mistake, and probably be forty versts away from us with tired horses. A vigilant watch was kept up, but we were not disturbed again till the horses were brought to be saddled. This was done in the dark, and when the first faint gleam of light was seen in the east the animals were led over the rocky ledge. We now turned to the south, following the shore of the lake, and it was soon light enough for us to see the track on the sand. The Kirghis thought that there were forty or fifty men with Koubaldos, who doubtless felt certain that with this band we should be easily secured. Having reached the end of the lake, we followed their track and forded a narrow part. This placed us on the east side; and we rode toward the mountain, where our enemies had been lurking, and skirted along its base.

Daylight was spreading fast over mountain and steppe, giving a rich velvet appearance to the herbage round the lake. We were still on the track of our enemies, and now found that they had come from the opposite side of the mountain. The smoke we had seen was from a fire which their men on the look-out had made, and so most fortunately gave us warning. A ride of two hours brought us to a small lake with good grass, where we found plenty of evidence that this had been their resting-place; we decided to let our horses feed here, breakfast ourselves, and then push on in search of Sabeck. As it was necessary to give our animals sufficient time, I proposed to a Cossack and Tchuck-a-boi that we should ascend the mountain and look out for the sultan's *aoul*;

and in about an hour we stood on the summit, although the ascent in some parts was rather difficult. The rock was a deep red granite, with thick veins of quartz crossing the mass from east to west; there was scarcely any vegetation, and it had a very rugged and sterile aspect. No *aoul* could be seen, nor a living thing of any kind on the whole expanse of this vast plain. We examined the shores of the lake, but no one could be seen there. After crossing several large rocks we reached a point which afforded a view more to the south, and there we saw the pointed mountain described by the Kirghis woman.

This was an excellent guide for us, and we descended to the plain in less time than it occupied in going up, and found every thing ready for a march. We left the pastures, and entered upon a barren waste of sand and pebbles, among which I discovered several fine agates and a few cornelians; had there been time, many good specimens could have been obtained. It was not till after a ride of more than five hours that we saw the summit of the mountain toward which we were bound. If the *aoul* was there, we could not reach it before dark, and now we began to be apprehensive as to not finding water. The snowy peaks of the Syan-shan were observed to the southwest, much nearer than we had ever seen them before, and a cool breeze blowing from that direction enabled us to push on without distressing our horses. A few more hours, and the conical mountain stood boldly up from the plain. Pointing to certain dark lines visible in the distance crossing the steppe, the Kirghis said we should reach the pasture before sunset, and, to make sure of the fulfillment of their predictions, they put their horses into a sharp canter. They were right; an hour before sunset we saw not alone pastures, but horses and camels feeding. This was a joyful sight to man and beast, and we presently reached the herds.

We soon came upon some Kirghis, who told us that these were flocks belonging to Sultan Sabeck, who was at his *aoul* seven or eight hours distant. They looked at us with some alarm until the Kirghis explained their mission to the sultan, when they led the way and brought us to a few *yourts* in a small valley. Here we found other herdsmen, and two of their dwellings were given up to us and a sheep killed, while two men were sent to carry the news to the sultan, and say that we should follow in the morning.

Our Kirghis having informed our new friends how Koubaldos had followed us, they called him Shaitan, and spat toward him. The night was spent without our watching, and early in the morning fresh horses were ready to take us to the sultan's *aoul*, to which four Kirghis accompanied us, the route being southwest, leaving the conical mountain to the east. Most part of the way was over good pastures, which our tired horses seemed desirous of enjoying. Before we reached our destination we had a beautiful view of the Syan-shan, taking in the lower chain. Shortly after midday a party of six Kirghis met us: they had come to conduct us to the encampment, still several versts distant. They were dressed in rich silk kalats of very bright colors; some had embroidered silk caps on their heads, and others had caps of foxskin.

We soon obtained a view of the *aoul*, standing on the edge of a lake, with high reeds and long grass growing on its banks. As we rode on, I observed that this encampment consisted of many habitations; while at the distance of a verst, and beyond, were other large ones, as well as several scattered along the shore, on the opposite side of the lake, which appeared about two versts broad. In answer to my inquiries, I was told that they all belonged to Sultan Sabeck and his tribe. As we drew near the *yourts*, I was guided toward one of considerable size, standing alone on the edge of the lake, where a group of Kirghis were waiting in their richly-colored kalats. When we reached them, a tall man stepped forward, took hold of the reins, and gave me his hand to dismount. To refuse such assistance would be a mark of disrespect, and I had by this time reconciled myself to the custom. This was Sultan Sabeck, who saluted me in the usual manner, and then led me into his dwelling, the floor of which was covered with *voilock* and with two Bokharian carpets. On these he placed me, and sat down on the *voilock* in front, giving me all the honors; but these, I, as usual, insisted should be divided. The place was shortly filled by Kirghis, taking their seats in circles, according to their grade, before us. One of the Cossacks, who spoke Kirghis well, and Tchuck-a-boi, were always my attendants on these state ceremonies, and places were always given to them in the first circle near me. Several of the Kirghis from Baspasihan and Oui-jass were seated near, as they were also distinguished guests.

A small, low table having been placed between the sultan and myself by a young Kirghis, two others deposited on it Chinese dishes filled with dried fruits; to these were added plates of small cakes, and sweetmeats, the productions of Chinese confectioners, which gave an aspect of variety and elegance to the repast. Then tea was served to the sultan and myself in beautiful Chinese cups. The fruit, cakes, and sweetmeats were delicious. When we had finished the company were regaled with the beverage. Sultan Sabeck was a tall man, with a ruddy, intelligent countenance, black eyes, and a dark beard. His kalat was of *kanfa* (Chinese satin), of a deep purple color, with flowers embroidered in various-colored silks, which produced a beautiful robe. A rich yellow crape scarf was tied round his waist; his cap was sable, turned up with crimson silk; and he wore light green boots and yellow over-shoes. The other Kirghis were dressed in silk kalats, some of which were exceedingly beautiful. The *yourt* in which we sat had been prepared especially for me, and such of my people as the Kirghis thought were in attendance; for the others, another was placed near.

After tea the sultan asked many questions about his friends Baspasihan and Oui-jass; also if I had seen Koubaldos. The Cossack gave him an account of the proceedings of the robber-chief, when he apprised me that his bands would be watching for our return, and stated that we must take care, or they would plunder and kill us. I inquired how far we were from Tchin-si, a Chinese town, and was told a two days' journey; but on our way back we should be much nearer. My host advised me not to go there, as we should have much trouble with the Chinese officers, and perhaps be taken prisoners, assuring me that there were five thousand soldiers in this garrison, commanded by two generals.

The sultan rose to depart; his horse, and those of his attendants, were brought to the door, and they rode to his *yourt*, although the distance was not more than fifty yards. He was going to receive the Kirghis sent by Baspasihan and Oui-jass. The Cossack told me that horses were waiting to take us to the sultan; that he had been my guest, and that I must now return his visit, as tea was being prepared for me. In a short time a messenger came to say that all was ready, and we mounted the horses and rode to his dwelling. The sultan received me, and placed me on the carpet, taking a seat opposite. The sultana and her daughter were sitting near us—the former was not handsome—she was clad in a black velvet kalat embroidered with colored silk, and wore a crimson crape scarf round her waist, and a white muslin head-dress. Her daughter was pretty; she had a kalat of crimson and yellow silk, reaching a little below the knee; white cotton drawers and a white silk turban, with her long black curls hanging beneath.

Again I was regaled with tea, and this time in the company of ladies, who did not officiate at the table, the beverage and fruit being handed to us by the attendant. The young stallion sent by Sultan Baspasihan was now led to the door, and one of the Kirghis who had accompanied me knelt before the sultan, and delivered his master's message, which appeared to give great satisfaction both to him and to his tribe. A Kirghis sent by Ouijass delivered in the same manner a small packet, which was received by Sultan Sabeck with evident delight. What it contained I can not tell, as it was not opened; my Cossacks said it was *altin* (gold). When this was over, all rose and went out to look at the young stallion. He was examined by many critical eyes, and pronounced perfect; we then returned to my *yourt* on horseback.

In a short time dinner was brought to me—a large platter heaped up with broiled mutton and boiled rice, which I found very good. A sheep was served in the other *yourt*, on which they feasted joyfully. After dinner my host paid me another visit, when I announced my wish to depart in the morning; but he proposed that I should remain till noon the next day, as he wished to send presents to his friends; moreover, that he would give me horses and Kirghis to guide me to another *aoul* of his, eight hours distant, where we must sleep, whence three of his own Kirghis and several others of the tribe, with fresh horses, should accompany me two days' journey across the desert, as without such assistance we should not be able to find either water or pasture. To this arrangement I willingly assented. The sultan said it would be dangerous to approach near the foot of the Syan-shan Mountains, as we should be sure to meet with large bands of Chinese robbers, who often committed great depredations, and murdered the Kirghis. His own guide was to accompany us, who knew the country, and would point out the mountains over which we must pass on our route to the *aoul* of Oui-jass, which he supposed we should reach in eight days. Beyond the pastures of Sultan Sabeck to the south and east there are no more Kirghis: the country is a sandy desert, destitute of water for many hundred versts.

In the evening it was a busy scene round the *aoul;* the plains were covered with camels, horses, oxen, sheep, and goats; and great numbers of the latter were being milked. My host estimated the number of his horses at eight thousand, and his camels at six hundred: these are sold to the Chinese; but he had no idea how many oxen, sheep, and goats belonged to him. Here we had no thought of robbers; we therefore determined to take in a store of rest, and, like good Kirghis, lay down to sleep at dark.

Early in the morning all were in motion making ready for another march. The sultan had prepared the presents for his friends: they consisted of Chinese silks and tea; and some of the latter, of a very fine quality, he presented to me. Before midday we had dined, after which I took leave of my host and his family, and then left, accompanied by six of his Kirghis. He had given me for this journey one of his best horses, that possessed great strength and speed, and had ordered that another equally good should be provided for me at his *aoul.* Our route was to the southwest, over a grassy turf for many versts; after which we came upon a gravelly soil, but not destitute of herbage, rising into gentle undulations, and forming several small valleys. In one of these we found a stream of pure water, its banks clothed with rich grass and bushes. Not far from this we saw a large herd of antelopes. Here the dogs had a sharp run, but were too far behind at starting to succeed.

Every hour gave me a better view of the lofty peaks of the Syan-shan, and the effect was beautiful as they glittered in the evening sun, while the blue and misty summits of the lower range were seen rising above the brown and yellow steppe. As we rode on the sun sunk fast, till at last he set below the snowy peaks, throwing up a flood of golden light into the clear blue sky. Our horses were now urged on rapidly, nor was it long before we saw herds of camels and horses going slowly toward their home, when two of the sultan's Kirghis galloped on to announce us. Just before the Syan-shan was lost in the gray twilight we reached the *aoul*, and found the Kirghis busy preparing a *yourt* in which they intended I should lodge. This was a large encampment, and had several others around it, all belonging to the tribe of the sultan. A stream of clear water was winding in many a turn along the steppe, and thousands of cattle were scattered about on its banks, giving me a most vivid idea of the days of the patriarchs; many Kirghis were galloping about in their wild costumes, adding much interest to the scene. I was ushered into my new dwelling by the chief of the *aoul*, when tea was served. The *yourt* was soon filled by both sexes, who crowded in to take a peep at the strangers. In due time the substantial repast was ready, and a Cossack having brought me my supper, all left the place to take their own. Mine was soon ended, when I turned down on the *voilock* and slept.

In the morning fresh steeds were neighing and prancing round the *yourt*, and one having been led up for me by the chief, I mounted. In a few minutes all my party were in their saddles, and after saying "*Aman-bul*" we turned to the south, rode across the stream, and left these pastoral people forever.

CHAPTER XXVII.

TCHIN-SI AND SYAN-SHAN.

A BRIGHT sun was rising behind us, but his rays had not yet touched the snowy peaks in our front. As we rode on I watched for the first bright gleam that lighted up the ice and snow on Bogda Oöla, which one of the men had pointed out to me. Presently his crest was tipped with a crimson glow, gradually descending and changing into yellow, and then to a silvery white. The sun shone upon his head for many minutes before any of the lower peaks were touched by his rays. After this new peaks were shooting into light every few seconds, till at last the whole chain was a mass of dazzling white, while all the lower ranges were clothed in hazy gloom. There is something marvelously grand in these effects, and in the changes which pass over such stupendous mountain masses. Having observed them, I examined the addition to my band, which now consisted of twenty-five men and forty-five horses. Four of the sultan's men carried long lances and battle-axes, the others battle-axes only; and their horseskin coats, with the flowing manes and helmet-shaped caps, gave them a singularly savage aspect. The Kirghis selected as my guide across the desert was a man about forty years of age, with a good, intelligent face, and a strong, athletic frame. He always accompanied the sultan on his journeys, knew the routes in every direction, and had led several expeditions against Koubaldos and other plundering bands, that, he said, were in retaliation for robberies committed on their tribe. In these enterprises they had taken several men and women, which the sultan kept as slaves.

We had traveled many hours over the sandy plain, when the guide pointed out a green spot a few versts to the south, and as it possessed water and grass, we turned our horses in this direction, and soon reached it. The water was brackish, nevertheless the horses drank it; but the guide would not let them feed, as we were far from the pastures selected for our night's encampment. He informed me that we were now only eighteen hours from Tchinsi, adding that if I wished he would take me to some pastures six hours nearer the town, where I could see the mountains better, as well as a neighboring lake. He acknowledged that we might meet some Chinese robbers, but thought that they would not like to attack us, and advised that good watch should be kept over our horses in the night. By taking this route, he told me, we should pass nearer the Syan-shan, and be one day more crossing the desert. Neither Chinese robbers, nor the additional day in the desert, had any weight with me; I instantly ordered our march in the direction he pointed out, which was directly south. Again we were on a sandy plain, riding fast, as it was necessary to reach the pastures before sunset, that our horses might feed before dark.

I now observed that the mountains terminated rather abruptly on the plain, some low hills only extending to the southeast. We kept up our speed, and reached the pastures and a small lake in good time. Our guide directed his course to the farther end of this piece of water, where thick clumps of bushes were growing. We stopped close to the mouth of a small river, flowing from the southwest, where we found a delightful spot for our encampment; there were thousands of water-fowl flying and swimming on the lake. My gun was soon in readiness, when I sallied forth to procure a supper, accompanied by Tchuck-a-boi and the Kirghis guide. The latter was greatly interested in my proceedings, as he had never seen a gun fired. We had not gone more than fifty paces along the shore when several large snipes rose up: they were in great numbers, and many fell; twice I killed two with one barrel. Ducks were also lying in the grass, and as they rose I added several to our bag—one as large as a young goose, with beautiful plumage. His neck and breast were a bright orange, with black feathers on the top of his head; the back was a deep reddish-brown, with a bar of black across his yellow wings. The feathers on his belly were a yellowish cream-color, and his bill and legs red. His Kirghis name is "Turpan:" many were swimming on the lake. The guide was delighted when he saw the birds fall, and I believe deeply regretted that the gun had not been as well used against the Chinese bands, who give his people much trouble. We supped this evening upon snipes, ducks, and tea. Our guide arranged the watches, placing four men on duty at a time, to whom he gave instructions to wake us quietly if there was any alarm. We were not once disturbed, and I slept soundly till morning.

The horses had fed early, and soon after sunrise we started, riding along the bank of the little stream for a considerable distance, to a point where it made a sharp turn to the southeast. We continued our ride to the south for several versts, and reached a large tumulus, around which there were many of smaller dimensions. We were now within a three hours' ride of Tchin-si, and nearer the guide would not go: he had never been in the town, and had no wish to visit it. I could see the lake he had mentioned, which is a short distance from the town to the eastward. The buildings were also distinctly visible on the declivity of a hill; but there are no striking edifices or large architectural masses in a Chinese town. The houses are small, and of no great elevation.

To the northwest of Tchin-si the Syan-shan rises into large peaks, but they do not reach the snow-line. After taking my last look at the town we turned to the northeast, and rode along the plain parallel to the mountain chain, the rugged and riven tops of which were in full view. I believe these stupendous masses were then seen and sketched for the first time by any European. We had ridden over the sandy steppe for several hours, when we reached the first elevation of this great mountain mass, which runs far out into the desert to the northeast. Ascending this, we observed a smoke about ten versts distant in a southwesterly direction.

The guide said that there were no good people in that region, and that if they discovered us we might be sure of a visit. Our route was now over undulating ground, formed into broad sweeping valleys, partly covered with tufts of steppe grass, growing about four feet high, and looking in the distance like rye ready for the reapers. It is so coarse that horses will not feed upon it, nor is it pleasant to ride among, as the seed pierced through our clothing.

After crossing several of these valleys, we ascended a much higher ridge covered with small stones, which rendered our ride very tedious. From the summit we looked down upon a steppe apparently twenty or thirty versts in breadth, the yellow sand giving it a sterile aspect. It extends in a northeasterly direction for a long distance, till it joins the great plain. At the foot of the hill we had to descend to a small lake twelve or fifteen versts in length, and varying in width from one to three versts. Its shores were covered with green herbage to a considerable distance from the water, and it was fed by two streams entering from the southwest, but there was no outlet. Here we stopped to rest, and feed our horses on the rich grass which covered the shore. I made another sketch of the Syan-shan, but Bogda Oöla is not well seen from this, though many other snowy peaks were visible. Early in spring this lake is much larger; the water extends far over the grassy plain, which is carried off by evaporation during the summer. As far as any moisture reaches, there we found herbage.

Having passed this, we were on the arid steppe, on which not a blade of grass was growing, nor was there one living thing to be seen excepting our party. To the northeast it had the appearance of a vast sandy ocean, with a purple ridge rising up in the distance like an island on a yellow sea. It was a long ride before we reached the opposite ridge, and when on the top I observed that a narrow stony valley lay before us. This we crossed, and ascended another hill, from which we looked down upon a lake not a verst distant, and, greatly to the astonishment of our Kirghis, beheld two small *aouls* with camels, a large number of horses, and a few sheep. Our guide declared that we had fallen upon a band of thieves, and proposed that we should cross the valley without stopping, and seek another place to encamp, some hours distant from these men. I did not agree to this plan, telling him that it would be running away, which would give these people courage.

I ordered that we should encamp on the lake, which the Cossacks and Kalmucks thought the best plan, and we rode down toward the *yourts.*

View looking down upon the Lake.

We had not proceeded far when a man galloped off toward the other *aoul*, and all the people at this one were in great commotion. As we came nearer the *yourts* the women began to scream, and the men sprung on their horses, brandishing their battle-axes. It was now quite clear that they thought us robbers like themselves. Shortly two old men rode out and met us, and, seeing that we were well armed, they began to beg of us not to plunder their *aoul.* A pledge to this effect was instantly given, when one of them galloped back to his friends, and we slowly followed. A *yourt* was instantly given up to me (the supposed robber-chief), but when we reached it half a dozen women were carrying it bodily to a clean piece of grass. At this *aoul* there were thirteen men, and wild-looking scoundrels they were; nor would they have shown us much consideration had we been the weaker party.

Deeming it desirable to know how many men there were in the other *aoul*, the guide, two Cossacks, Tchuck-a-boi, and a Kalmuck accompanied me, and the two Kirghis who had met us led the way.

As we approached, the women were running about from *yourt* to *yourt*, making great lamentations. The men were on horseback ready for fighting; but when they saw Kirghis of their own tribe riding beside me, they came to meet us in peace, and were assured by the guide that we were not going to plunder them. Here were five *yourts* and eleven men besides those who were with the cattle: thus they outnumbered us; they would, however, have had no chance against our weapons. As we returned along the shore, I observed two pelicans standing on a small grassy island about two hundred yards distant. As this was a good opportunity of showing the Kirghis the effect of our rifles, I told a Cossack to shoot one of them. He instantly dismounted, and returned back a short distance till he got both birds in a line, or till the body of one covered the other. The prongs of his rifle were then thrown forward, he knelt, and as the leaden messenger sped on its errand, one fell dead, and the other sprung up and fell on the water a few yards distant. Two Kirghis rushed into the lake, rode to the spot, and brought back the game, when I perceived that the lake was very shallow. This shot produced a wonderful effect on the minds of these wild fellows: they examined the wounds on the birds, and looked at each other with great astonishment.

When we reached the *yourt* the sheep was preparing; nor was it long before a Kirghis rode up with one from the other *aoul*, to feast the formidable robber-chief and his band. My tea having been prepared and placed before me, with three tumbler glasses, I ordered the Cossack to fill them, give one to each of the old Kirghis who first met us, and hand me the other. This gave great satisfaction. I also desired him to give a sufficient quantity of brick-tea to feast all the people in the *aoul;* after which I was established in the good graces of both sexes. I wished to obtain some information about the country we had yet to travel through, and desired a Cossack to ask how far we were from the *aoul* of Ultigun; also, if any one could guide me to him. The old Kirghis said we could ride there in two days, promising that some of their tribe should go with us a day's journey and point out the route; but no one would guide us to his den. I then inquired for the *aoul* of Oui-jass, also about his horses and camels, which they felt sure we intended stealing. They most willingly gave me full information on all these points, and said it would take four days to ride to his *aoul*. The two chiefs of these encampments were Kirghis from the great horde, whose faces bespoke familiarity with crime. Several Chinese, with a few Mongolians, and Kirghis who had escaped from different hordes, composed this band of cutthroats and plunderers. A strict watch was kept over our horses, and a sentinel placed on duty where we slept, for we could not trust these men too far. The rest of us lay down with our arms close at hand, and shortly nothing was heard in the *aoul* except the bark of a dog and the cry of the watchman.

When we turned out in the morning only three Kirghis were left; the others had gone before daylight, driving off the horses and cattle, thinking that we had stolen our horses from Sultan Sabeck, and that we should do the same here on our departure. We were not long in preparing for our ride; the Kirghis had given us instructions about our route, telling us that we should find one or two *aouls* on our way, and probably meet Syren and his band, and other plundering chiefs of extraordinary daring. They knew he was in the country over which we must pass, and this had induced them to move to the southward.

The sun was shining brilliantly when we left the lake, and to cross the valley and ascend the opposite hill was but a short ride. Beyond this, our route was over a grassy undulating steppe, in many places covered with reeds. Early in spring there are many large shallow lakes, which render the country swampy; but the water was now nearly dried up, and reeds and bulrushes occupied their beds. Through these we had to wend our way for eight hours, when we crossed another ridge and descended into a small valley, with a river in the bottom running toward the northeast, and feeding the lake on which we slept the night Koubaldos missed us. This was to be our encampment for the night, and Sultan Sabeck's Kirghis would leave us and return toward their home in the morning. It was necessary to obtain all the information we could from the guide relative to our route. For this purpose four of us rode to the top of a high ridge, from which we had an extensive view far over the country, whence the guide pointed out several summits which would be landmarks for us. I took the bearings, made a few notes, and then had no fear of not finding Oui-jass.

We spent the night in peace, and early in the morning said

Aman-bul to our friends and separated. Both parties reached the top of the ridges nearly at the same time, when we stopped a few minutes, waved our caps, and rode on, never to see each other more. I now took upon myself the duty of guide, and pointed out the route to Tchuck-a-boi and a Kirghis, after which we entered a more fertile region. The hills and valleys were covered with short grass, among which many beautiful flowers were growing—several unknown to me. As our horses were in good condition, the Kirghis wished to push on fast, and leave the region belonging to Koubaldos behind us.

As we rode on this morning we had a beautiful view of Bogda Oöla and some of the other peaks to the west, but shortly afterward clouds began to gather around his head, and soon obscured him in surging vapor. The lower range of the Syan-shan is exceedingly picturesque; jagged peaks stand out in bold relief against the snowy masses, which tower up from eight to ten thousand feet above them, while the rich purple and misty tone spread over these mountains produced a marvelous effect. About midday we saw a great smoke near the foot of one of the mountains to the southwest, rising in dense black columns, and extending over a considerable space. The Kirghis thought it was one of the Chinese towns on fire; we could not, however, see any flames, as some high hills intervened. Shortly afterward we reached a river, flowing rapidly over a rocky bed, where we stopped to feed our horses and refresh ourselves.

It was now discovered that there was only one bird left, which was cooked, and I made a good dinner; the men, having been provided with plenty of smoked horseflesh by Sultan Sabeck, fared well. While we rested the clouds gathered thicker on the mountains, which indicated a coming storm, and made us hasten onward. Our route was still over grassy hills, with broad sweeping valleys running down to the great plain. These, and the Syan-shan Mountains, being obscured, rendered the journey exceedingly monotonous. It was not till the evening of the third day that the clouds rolled off, when the mountains stood out in all their majestic grandeur. We were near the high ridge which had been our landmark for the last three days—and hungry ones they had been to me—and had arrived at the end of a narrow valley extending up toward the mountains, and forming a deep gorge through the lower chain: the place possessed many bold and picturesque scenes.

Here we decided to encamp, having found all the requisites of grass, wood, and water. A small river was winding along between banks thickly covered with trees and high bushes. While our camp was preparing, and the horses sent out to feed, four of us started in search of game. We had not gone far when I shot a pheasant, and a Kalmuck was sent back with it to the cook. We proceeded down the valley; in a short time I procured two others, and then returned to our camp. My tea was ready, the pheasant was cooking, and the scent gave an additional zest to my hunger. The men were sitting at their suppers, and the horses were feeding about a hundred paces distant, when suddenly our dogs set up a furious barking. The Kirghis had warned me that tigers were found in these mountains, and that sometimes they came to their *aouls* and carried off cattle. We all thought that there must be one approaching, and in a moment were on our feet, rifle in hand, when we observed over the tops of the bushes the cause of the alarm—a group of men on horseback coming down the valley. They were within about one hundred yards of us, looking intently at our horses.

At first they did not see us till several of the party stepped out on to the open space. I noticed that they were seven in number—three armed with long spears, the others with battle-axes, and had with them two savage Mongolian dogs. They stood still for three or four minutes, unslung their spears and battle-axes, and then slipped their dogs, which came at us furiously, while they prepared to charge when their four-footed allies should be tearing some of us down. We let the dogs come within thirty yards; a Cossack and myself then fired, when one fell dead, and the other was wounded with shot from my gun, which sent him howling back. Their masters, now within fifty yards of us, pulled up their horses in a moment, and the Kirghis told them that if they moved they should be killed like the dog. Their battle-axes were instantly put down, and four of them dismounted. A Cossack, two Kirghis, and myself met them, and exchanged salutations. The Cossack asked why the dogs were set upon us, and, without any hesitation, they said it was done to occupy our attention while some of the men drove off the horses, believing that we were a party of Kirghis, and knowing that when our animals were secured they could take us at their leisure. I invited these men to our camp, to which I returned, the other three following with their horses.

When these men saw our whole party and observed our arms, they seemed greatly astonished, and evidently considered that they had fallen into a trap, as we were again taken for a powerful band of robbers, very dangerous to meet. They told us that their *aoul* was in a valley on the west side of the mountain, to which we could ride by midday if we started early in the morning. I received most pressing invitations to visit their chief Syren, who, they said, held great power over all the tribes to the westward of the mountains. I told them that my present engagements rendered it impossible for me to visit Syren on this occasion, but it was probable we might meet in his western dominions, when I hoped he would order his followers not to set their dogs upon me, or I would shoot both the men and animals. In answer to our questions about the locality of the pastures of Oui-jass, they gave us full information, stating that they had also been on the look-out for the *aouls*, and that the tribes had arrived two days ago. We were advised to ride to the second river, and follow its banks to the plain; this would take us to their encampment, and within a three hours' ride of the *aoul*. Their chief intended visiting it soon, to get a supply of horses.

These fellows remained with us till morning, when they departed for their den of thieves, and we to seek our friend. The route they had pointed out led us over the mountains, where from one point we had a magnificent view of Bogda Oöla, with its rocks, snow, and glaciers. It is, indeed, a stupendous mass, and the inhabitants of these regions have a saying "that it hides both the sun and the moon." As the sun goes down the shadow extends a long distance over the steppe. After sketching this wonderful scene, I rode on, and descended to the first river, which we crossed with great difficulty. The torrent is very rapid, and rolls over large blocks of stone. We now began to ascend the last mountain, from which we expected to see the *aoul* and tribe of Oui-jass.

In many parts this was rugged, steep, and difficult to ride over, and it was not till long after midday that we reached the summit, consisting of a mass of dark purple slate, among which there was very little vegetation. The view from this high ridge extended across the vast steppe to the Tangnou Mountains, but these were lost in haze. The plain was spread out like a map, on which I counted fourteen lakes, some of them of large dimensions. I saw many of the streams running along the steppe like lines of silver. Not far from one of the lakes I observed the *aoul* of Oui-jass, which made us feel quite at home. The descent was more difficult, and much of it had to be done on foot; but at last we reached the robbers' encampment, from which we rode soon to the plain. The Kirghis was delighted; our horses were put into a good speed, and shortly after sunset Oui-jass again welcomed me to his encampment.

The evening was spent by the Kirghis relating all that had happened on the journey, including an account of Syren's intention to visit them early. While delivering the presents from Sultan Sabeck and his messages, I learned the object of the missions from Baspasihan and my host. A plan had been proposed for an attack upon Koubaldos by their united forces, to strip him of his plunder, and kill or carry off his people, break up his *aoul*, and, if he escaped, to render him powerless for a long time to come. My visit had been a God-send, and thus their friendly assistance is explained. Sultan Sabeck had named the twenty-seventh day after our departure from his *aoul* for the attack on the robber-chief.

Oui-jass made me very liberal offers of spoil if I would remain with my men and aid them in their expedition, saying that, with our assistance, few of the robbers should be left alive, as our rifles would do most of the execution. I, however, declined the honor of joining in the anticipated massacre. Early in the morning our own horses, which were left to enjoy the rich pastures of my host, were brought fresh and in good condition for a journey; nevertheless, Oui-jass insisted on sending us to Baspasihan on his own horses, for the service I had rendered by obtaining from the robbers a knowledge of their intention to plunder him, and expressed his deep regret that we had not shot the seven men instead of the dogs.

About two hours after sunrise I exchanged salutations with my friend and departed. Our route was in a northwesterly direction, toward one of the lower ranges, running nearly parallel with the Syan-shan. The Bogda Oöla rose up in all his sublime grandeur, and the volcanic peak, Pe-shan, with dark crags jutting out of the snow, was seen still farther to the west, while beyond these a long line of snow-capped summits receded into distance. On our ride we crossed several streams which find their way down to the plain; some are lost in the sands, while others form lakes and marshes, extending for fifty or sixty versts to the east up to a chain of hills, which renders traveling over this country extremely dangerous. I and two of my men had a narrow escape; for, being a little in advance of our Kirghis guides, we rode on to one of these morasses, believing we could cross. Having gone about ten paces from the hard ground, we suddenly perceived the surface begin to move like waves on a lake, extending far from where we stood. We instantly turned our horses gently round, reached the solid ground, and were thankful for our escape. The Kirghis said that, had we gone a few steps farther, the turf would have broken, when we should have sunk to rise no more, assuring me that they frequently lose horses and camels in these places. I now determined that the men sent by Oui-jass should be our guides through this dangerous labyrinth of reeds and quagmires.

On these lakes there were thousands of aquatic birds—pelicans, swans, cranes (a beautiful black variety), flamingoes, with their crimson plumage; geese, ducks, and divers; besides millions of musquitoes, which rendered the ride rather disagreeable. We had not been long winding our way among the reeds when the dogs gave mouth a short distance in front. Riding to the place, we observed, by the fresh rooting in the ground, that a herd of wild boars had been disturbed, and had escaped into the high reeds. We found these animals very numerous in the swamps, but to follow them into the reeds was impossible. The dogs were kept back, and each opening in the reeds examined, but not a boar was seen, although we had heard them.

One of the Kalmucks was riding about a hundred yards distant along the edge of some reeds, when he suddenly called out. We thought he had found a herd, but on reaching him he pointed to the soft ground, covered with footprints and gore, where a terrible conflict had evidently taken place. At first we thought the boars had been fighting, but a closer inspection showed us that one had been measuring his strength with a more formidable foe—a tiger! whose footprints were stamped around the field of battle. The boar had been slain and carried off: it was easy to trace the crimson track, which led toward a mass of high reeds, into which the tiger had carried his prey. A well-trodden path or reedy tunnel formed the approach to this lair, which was about two feet six inches wide, and three feet and a half high, thickly matted over into an arch. The tiger had put down his burden at the entrance of this covered way, the red marks being distinctly visible. The men thought the battle had been fought three or four days ago; from this they concluded that a tigress and her cubs were in their den not far off; and, in confirmation of their opinion, the dogs barked furiously. In a conflict with robbers none would have shrunk, however unequal the contest; but not one of us had courage to enter this place, and seek honor "at the *tiger's* mouth." The Kirghis proposed setting fire to the reeds; but in such a labyrinth it might have been fatal to ourselves, so we left the brutes in peace. During our ride we found a tiger's track in several places; but there is so much shelter it is impossible to hunt him here. The Kirghis say that, wherever the wild boars are numerous, there the tiger takes up his abode, as he is fond of pork.

Having passed the swamp, we ascended the high hills, which afforded me a view over this place of torment and ague. In length it extends about sixty versts, and is twenty-five in breadth, and still farther to the east there is a lake of large dimensions. About an hour before sunset we had crossed the mountains, and reached the banks of a thickly-wooded river, running and leaping over rocks in numerous waterfalls. The valley was covered with rich grass, and our guide proposed to encamp: he thought it possible we might find the tiger in the valley, as they often descend to the plains and destroy the horses. While the arrangements for sleeping were being made, and the supper cooked, four of us started up the valley, and four others down the bank of the stream, in search of the animal, but after a long ramble we returned to the camp at dusk, without finding any trace of him. Those who descended the valley were more fortunate: they had found his track and the remains of a stag on which he had dined the day before. They also brought back a buck, shot by a Kalmuck; from this we expected some sport in the morning. The men made a glorious feast, cooking and broiling venison till a late hour, when a large fire was made, and the horses picketed close to us. Two Kalmucks mounted guard with their rifles, attended by two Kirghis. It was thought the tiger might pay us a visit; nevertheless, after the watch was set, all the rest of our party were soon asleep.

During the early part of the night we remained quiet till near the end of the third watch, when there was a great commotion. The dogs had frequently growled, which made the men on duty keep a sharp look-out; at last there was a burst of furious barking. The horses began to snort and plunge, and tried to break loose, when every man was on his feet in a minute. Before we could seize our rifles, two shots were fired by the sentinels, which were followed by a savage growl, and the Kirghis threw blazing branches at the intruder. The Kalmucks had seen the glaring eyeballs of some animal crouching in the grass. For a short time the dogs continued to bark, and then all became still, which assured us that our visitor had retired. On looking at my watch, I saw that in less than two hours we should have daylight: this induced me to sit up, and Tchuck-a-boi followed my example.

Before sunrise all were in motion, preparing for our journey, when several of the Cossacks and Kalmucks examined the grass, and found that a large animal had crept along to within fifteen paces of our horses. They also observed that he had been wounded, there being marks of the crimson dye on the grass. Soon after this we started down the valley, with our rifles ready for slaughter, but had not ridden more than two hours when we reached a spot where the valley narrowed into a rugged gorge, with high precipices on each side. The river had now become a roaring torrent, and it was with considerable difficulty that we rode along the ledges of rocks overhanging the boiling flood. At last we reached a point which barred our farther progress, where huge masses of rock had fallen, and were piled up so high that it was impossible to get our horses over. We decided that a party should return and cross the mountain with the horses, while five other men and myself should descend the ravine on foot, and meet them on the steppe. This was soon found to be impossible; for, on climbing over the fallen rocks at great personal risk, we discovered that the torrent washed the foot of a perpendicular precipice seven or eight hundred feet high.

By this time the men with the horses were on their way and far out of hearing; we therefore turned back and ascended one of the narrow ravines. This was also difficult, but, after an hour's climbing, we reached the ridge and observed our horses three versts distant, trotting toward the steppe. Our route was along the ridge, and we shortly had a splendid view over the steppe. Several streams were winding their course along the plain, some lost in morasses, and others fed several large lakes. Nowhere could I see any thing to indicate the *aoul* of Baspasihan. A walk of near four hours brought us to the foot of the mountain, where our horses had been some time waiting our arrival. It was past midday when we forded the river and put our steeds into a gallop. Our guide was anxious to reach some low hills before dusk, which we saw far in the distance, as he expected to find an *aoul* there. After a hard ride of more than four hours we were at the hills, but no *aoul* could be seen in any direction. It was now getting dusk and time to encamp. Presently we found a suitable place on the bank of a small stream, where we passed the night undisturbed.

Early in the morning, and before the sun had tipped the snowy peaks of the Syan-shan, we were crossing the hills in search of Kirghis. After a ride of four hours we came upon a herd of camels and horses in one of the valleys, and saw thousands of sheep and goats feeding on the opposite ridges. In a short time our Kirghis met their brother herdsmen, very much gratified at having reached their homes. We were not long reaching the *aoul*, where all were delighted to see us. The sultan received me with great kindness, and the *yourt* was soon filled with the heads of his tribe, listening to the accounts the Kirghis gave of the journey. When the presents from Sultan Sabeck were placed before Baspasihan, he looked upon the rich silks and kalats with much pleasure. But when the Kirghis announced that Sultan Sabeck had named the time for the attack on Koubaldos, there was a shout of defiance and savage satisfaction, which boded no good to Koubaldos. My host made several efforts to induce me to remain and join in the enterprise, but, in order to avoid all farther importunity on this subject, I determined to depart in the morning.

My next point was Kessil-bach, not two days' journey to the northward, and soon after breakfast my host had horses and men ready to take us to the lake. They were to remain there as long as I wished, and then accompany me to the Tchernoy Irtisch. I accepted this act of kindness with pleasure, received the parting salutation, and rode away, leaving many friends among this tribe. To gain the esteem of the Kirghis a man must be a daring rider. If he have a quick eye and an unerring hand with his rifle, they will respect and obey him; but if he once flinch at any danger, or show fear, he is lost.

Our route was over low hills covered with rich pastures, on which large herds were feeding; these we soon left behind, and entered a sandy steppe. After a dreary ride, we arrived on the evening of the second day at a stony ridge, from the summit of which we beheld the lake. Kessil-bach-Noor is about one hundred versts long, and in some parts twenty to thirty versts broad. It has a flat shore to the southwest, and has hills on the northeast side. There are extensive beds of reeds and bulrushes growing on many parts of its shores, with some good pastures; but we found no Kirghis. A little before sunset we encamped on the bank of a small stream a few versts from the western end of the lake, where we passed the night in quiet.

Early in the morning I made two sketches, then continued my ride in a northeasterly direction toward the Tchernoy-Irtisch, which has its source among some low hills in the region where the fabulous Great Altai is placed on all the maps of Asia. A range of hills extends to the northwest, and joins the offshoots of the Altai. We crossed several hills, some almost without vegetation, while many of the valleys were sandy and sterile. From some of these ridges we had an extensive view to the southwest, in which direction I saw the picturesque summits of the Barluck Mountains, while to the west rose the rugged crests of the Tarbogatai. Late in the afternoon we reached the river, where it was running over a rocky bed fringed on each side with small trees and bushes. After following its course for seven or eight versts, we discovered an *aoul* at a few versts distance, in one of the valleys. We very soon reached the herdsmen, who told us it belonged to Sultan Dulembie: the Kirghis were delighted, as he was their master's friend. One of Baspasihan's Kirghis and a herdsman went off at a gallop to announce my arrival, nor was it long before I saw a party of Kirghis galloping to meet me; they conducted me to the *yourt* of Dulembie, whom I found standing at the door of his dwelling ready to give me a welcome. He was an old man, with a short gray beard, a ruddy complexion, and friendly expression of countenance. There was no remarkable difference in the dwellings or costume from those of the other sultans I had visited. A large bowl of *koumis* was handed to me. I drank a little as a compliment to his brewing, and then gave the bowl to a Cossack, who speedily put the contents under his belt. In due course tea and supper were served, when I made an excellent repast. To my inquiries concerning our route to the Barluck Mountains and the Tarbogatai, the sultan said I could cross the steppe and reach the Barluck in nine days, and he promised to give me Kirghis guides to the *aoul* of Sultan Ishonac Khan, which we should reach in five days.

The time had now arrived when I must part with my brave Kalmucks, who had been my faithful companions through many a day of hard toil, and in some dangers. Their route was north to their homes in the Altai, which they would reach in eight or ten days, while mine was southwest, through the country of the ancient Sungarians. Having supplied them with a good store of ammunition, I had no fear for their safety; and in the morning, after shaking hands and expressing mutual regret, we turned our horses and rode in opposite directions. My route was over low hills covered with grass, that extended about twenty versts; then we descended to the plain, which we found a sandy desert, over which the Kirghis proposed to ride fast. Sultan Dulembie had sent to accompany me eight of his men, well mounted and armed with battle-axes; therefore, with the three Cossacks and myself, we still formed a strong party. The new-comers were wild-looking fellows, evidently ready either for fight or plunder.

CHAPTER XXVIII.

THE SULTANS OF THE STEPPE.

After a rapid gallop over the dreary waste, late in the afternoon of the fifth day, after having suffered much for water, we reached the *aoul* of Sultan Ishonac Khan, who gave me a friendly reception. He was stout, with strongly-marked Kalmuck features, and as he claimed his descent from Genghis Khan, the owl's feather hung from the top of his cap: his costume was of Chinese silk, richly embroidered. About fifty versts to the southward of this *aoul* rise the Barluck Mountains, lying between the Tarbogatai and the Alatou Mountains, and eastward of the Ala-kool, a small rocky chain extending about sixty versts from east to west; its breadth is about twenty-five versts, and the highest summit is three thousand feet above the plain. On the lower slopes there is pasturage, but the upper parts are bare rocks. From this *aoul* my route was westward, over a sandy steppe. I obtained horses from the sultan, and eight of his Kirghis to be my companions to the Tarbogatai—a four, or perhaps six days' journey. Soon after daylight I left my host, and shortly his pastures, when we entered upon the dreary waste, and rode over sandy hills and valleys, on which not a blade of grass was growing. On many parts there was a thick saline incrustation, which was thrown up in dust by our horses' feet, filling our mouths with its bitter particles, and causing intolerable thirst. The Kirghis said we should have great difficulty in finding fresh water, as all the streams were dried up.

Again the Kirghis were armed—I could not understand for what reason, as we were traversing a desert where no man can dwell. They said we should have to travel near the worst region in the whole steppes, as the country to the east of the Ala-kool is inhabited by large bands of robbers, whom they called *Byjagat:* these are composed of Kirghis from the different hordes who have escaped after committing great crimes, and Chinese convicts from the penal settlements on the Ila. They live in security in this region, and carry on their depredations with impunity. The Kirghis kept a sharp look-out as we rode along, evidently expecting to see smoke or some other indication of their encampments. Hour after hour passed, and still I rode over the same saline plain; at length our horses began to flag for want of water, of which not a drop could be seen. The sun was now descending fast below a sandy ridge a short distance in front of us. On reaching the top of this, we were overjoyed by the sight of a lake stretching eight or ten versts across the steppe, and were not long in reaching it. Here were grass and water, which made the eyes of man and horse sparkle with delight. A Cossack sprung from his horse and stooped to drink; but the liquid had scarcely touched his parched lips when he rose and exclaimed "Gorkie"—bitter. This was a terrible blow; the horses, however, drank the water with great zest. The

A LARGE BARROW IN A VALLEY IN THE TARBOGATAI, CHINESE TARTARY.

Kirghis declared it was impossible to proceed farther, as we should find no other pastures. I now tasted the water and found it brackish; still, as no other was attainable, ordering some to be boiled, I made tea, which turned the water into a milky-looking fluid, exceedingly disagreeable to drink.

We left this bitter lake with the first gray dawn, going to the northwest, still over the sandy desert, where no fresh water can be found. Late on the evening of the fifth day we reached the River Eremil, to the infinite gratification of both man and beast, for tea made with stinking brackish water is poor fare after a hard day's ride. Having slept and refreshed ourselves and horses, we proceeded onward, and night brought us to the Tarbogatai, along which we must continue our journey, passing about ten versts to the north of Tchoubachack, a Chinese town, in which Russia has, since this period, established a consul, and now carries on a considerable trade with the inhabitants of his Celestial majesty. We passed the Chinese pickets about noon on the second day, and reached a rocky valley just as the sun was setting behind a large barrow, which gave to the scene a peculiar and striking effect. After fording a mountain torrent at considerable risk, just above the falls, we encamped for the night at its base. It is about one hundred and fifty feet high, steep, and regular in its form. I ascended to the top, and found the tomb of a Kirghis sultan, with many of those of his followers around him. The opposite view will give an idea of this singular scene. The tumulus has been thrown up by a people of whom we have no trace; and in this part of Asia such ancient works are numerous.

Many of the rocks in this valley are a deep red jasper; and one mountain, a little to the north, possesses a bright crimson color, which, when seen lit up by the setting sun, has a brilliant effect. Early in the morning we began our ride to the south, crossing low ridges, which extended far down toward the plain. A little before dusk we observed, much to our satisfaction, a large herd of horses feeding on the grassy slopes; nor were we long in reaching the *aoul*, which we found belonged to Sultan Iamantuck, and a most excellent man I found him. He had arrived here three days before, and was now encamped near the place where his forefathers were buried. High conical tombs of sun-burnt bricks were erected over their ashes, and once every year the sultan and his tribe visit this spot, remaining eight or ten days. Below are the portraits of the sultan, his daughter, and his son, who is making a communication to his father, which is always done on the knees.

Sultan Iamantuck and Family.

The sultan and his family are by far the most intelligent people I have met with in this part of Asia. The Kirghis from the Gobi Steppe returned to their *aoul*, and I procured eight other Kirghis and horses from the sultan to be my companions toward the Ala-kool. After spending a day at the sultan's *aoul* we left, crossing the plain to the south. A ride of two hours carried us out of the pastures, and we entered upon a sandy steppe. We were now riding directly toward the Alatou (Variegated Mountain), and saw the snowy summits of the Actou (White Mountain), which forms the crest of the chain, some of whose peaks rise fourteen thousand or fifteen thousand feet above the sea. We came upon several rocky ridges which rise out of the steppe, several of them three hundred feet high. About noon I rode to the summit of one of these, and got my first peep at the Ala-kool, still very far away. No *aoul* was within the range of our vision, and the Kirghis were anxious to ride on, as neither water nor grass could be obtained on this inhospitable soil. The only living things we found were scorpions and tarantulas—bad food for a dinner. We passed several groups of ancient tombs, which induced me to believe that this steppe had once afforded pasturage for large herds of cattle, when inhabited by a race who probably irrigated the soil. It was near sunset when a white smoke was seen curling up beyond a low sandy hill; on gaining the top of which we saw a small stream of water, with grass covering a little valley, with plenty of cattle feeding thereon. A ride of half an hour brought us to the *aoul*, where we caused much alarm. The Kirghis were soon assured that we were not robbers; then the sheep was cooked, and the feast spread before us, to which every one did ample justice.

Before leaving we were informed that it would take a day to ride to the Ala-kool; also that we should have some broad and deep places to swim in crossing between the large and small Ala-kool. It was deemed desirable to take two men with us from this *aoul*, who knew the track, as without them the journey would be difficult and dangerous in such a labyrinth of reeds and bulrushes. We were soon on a sandy plain, into which the horses sunk deep, which rendered our ride very tedious.

Late in the evening we found a small *aoul* on the bank of a little river, and here the Kirghis proposed that we should stop the night. Early in the morning we were on our way; about midday we reached the Tarsakhan, a very deep, rapid, and dangerous stream, flowing between high sandy banks, rushing past like a torrent. The great danger was that the horse, when swimming, would be carried below the path, and then there was no chance for man or horse. As the passage could only be accomplished by one person at a time, a Kirghis went first, then a Cossack, and both got over well; I followed, then came the others, and all landed safely. The Kirghis say that accidents often happen here, when both man and horse are drowned; nevertheless, these people never attempt to make a bridge.

Soon after crossing the river we skirted the edge of a bed of reeds for several versts, and while riding on I noticed a cloud of sand rising high into the air; but this was so common an occurrence that I paid no attention to the matter till we passed the bed of reeds, when we had a view over the steppe for fifty or sixty versts. I now saw that a dense black mass, of fearful appearance, was rolling straight toward us, extending about a verst in width. The moment the Kirghis beheld it, in the greatest alarm they turned their horses and galloped back under the shelter of the reeds; I and the Cossacks stood watching it approach for a few minutes, and then made for the shelter. The Kirghis led the horses into the cover, securing them fast, and urged me to lie down. It was not long before we heard the roar of the hurricane; on it came, obscuring the sun, and casting a deep, gloomy shade over the country. In a few minutes a terrific blast rushed by, laying the reeds and bulrushes flat over us. To look up was impossible: we were shrouded in a thick cloud of dust. In five minutes the storm passed, and then I saw that we had only been visited by the edge of the cloud, as it rolled on with fearful rapidity. Fortunately, we were not caught on the steppe, or every man and animal would have perished. As it went off into the distance it looked like a dense black cloud.

After this escape from wind we were soon on the bank of the Yeljin-sa-gash, a broad and deep stream, over which we must swim our horses. We undressed and took off our saddles; my clothing, and my sketches and fire-arms, were carried over on the heads of the Kirghis, some of whom swam their horses four and five times across the river. Between the lakes we had three deep rivers to pass. This being accomplished, we reached the shore of the large Ala-kool, which is about sixty versts in length and twenty-five in width, with a small rocky island, that rises about one hundred feet out of the water, standing at a distance of two versts from the north shore. A narrow ledge of rocks runs far out into the lake, and nearly joins the island. About ten versts from each end of the lake, narrow reefs of rock run across from one shore to the other, over which it is possible to pass. Eight rivers empty their contents into this lake, which has no outlet, and the water is carried off by evaporation. In summer it is intensely hot: we had 45° on the sandy steppe extending along the south shore.

Baron Humboldt has stated that a volcano exists on an island in the Ala-kool—so the baron had been informed by Tartar merchants who cross the steppe with the caravans. But no volcano has ever been in action in this region; the one nearest to this place is that shown on my map in the Gobi Desert, and Pe-shan

SULTAN BECK AND FAMILY.

in the Syan-shan. In all my wanderings in the Karatou, Alatou, and Actou, I did not discover one crater.

We now turned toward the west in search of the *aoul* of Sultan Beck, the largest man and most wealthy Kirghis in the steppes. He has ten thousand horses, and camels, oxen, and sheep in proportion to this vast herd. It was late in the evening when we found him: perhaps we disturbed his slumbers, and by so doing ruffled his temper, as he was exceedingly uncivil, and sent us a sheep that was diseased. This was quickly returned to him with my compliments, and a message stating that we did not eat such food, nor did we require any thing from him. I desired the Cossack to say that he was the first sultan who had behaved so ungentlemanly toward me, and that, notwithstanding his large body, he had the heart of a mouse. This roused him into a fury, and he ordered us away, threatening that if we did not move instantly his men should drive us into the lake. The Cossack replied that if either he or any of his men came near our camp, we would shoot them; which having said, he left the *yourt*, and told us what had passed. It was not long before we perceived two girls coming toward us leading a sheep, which the sultan had sent, begging me to accept it, as it was one of the best in his flock: they assured me that he wished to pay me a visit, had offered to let me stay as long as I liked, and had promised to give me men and horses when I left.

His mutton having been accepted, and a message returned saying I should be glad to receive him, it was not long before we saw his huge bulk approaching our camp. He saluted me by touching the chest in the usual manner, after which we sat down and became friends. He drank tea with me, and remained to partake of his own mutton; and while this was preparing, he ordered his poet to sing for us. The man obeyed, and chanted forth songs, describing the prowess and successful plundering expeditions of my host and his ancestors, which called forth thunders of applause from the tribe. After spending more than two hours in the company of the sultan and his bard, we separated on friendly terms. Next morning before starting I sketched Sultan Beck and his family. He is feeding his bearcoote, hunting with the king of birds being his favorite sport. Early in the forenoon I said *Aman-bul* and departed, attended by ten of the sultan's men; good horses had also been provided.

From this *aoul* our route was in a southwesterly direction, about twenty versts from the foot of the Karatou, a chain of mountains rising abruptly from the steppe. They are composed chiefly of a dark purple slate, are destitute of vegetation, and in no part rise to more than six thousand feet; but there are several magnificent gorges here, through which the rivers find their way to the steppe. Again we had to ride over a sandy plain, stretching westward to the shores of the Lake Tengiz; and after a two days' journey found the Kirghis more numerous. Their *aouls* and dwellings resemble each other so much that it would be repetition to describe them.

On the fourth day after leaving Sultan Beck's *aoul* we were in search of Sultan Boulania. If the first was the largest man in the steppe, the one I was now seeking was reported to be by far the most enlightened and talented among the Kirghis. Having slept the night at an *aoul* on the River Lepsou, the inhabitants told me that we should find the sultan's *aoul* a two days' journey up the river; and soon after daylight we left these people, and rode in the direction indicated. The Lepsou is a large stream, running between high sandy banks, in some parts extending into broad shallow pools covered with reeds and bulrushes, while in others it has a rapid current. We presently reached undulating sandy hills, into which our horses sunk deep at every step, and this materially retarded our progress. By noon we had not traveled more than twenty versts, when we came upon a plain covered with hundreds of sandy mounds: it was, indeed, a perfect labyrinth. As we were winding our way through these hillocks, we met a party of Kirghis armed with rifles, the advance guard of the sultan, who was following at a short distance. We soon met, when he invited me to accompany him to his *aoul*.

A few years before the sultan had visited the Governor-General of Western Siberia, who had most kindly given me a letter recommending me to his care. It was written in the Tartar language, which the Mulla could not read. When the contents had been explained to Boulania, he ordered the Mulla to write me a passport which would be respected in the middle horde; it would also aid me with two of the sultans in the great horde. While I remained at the *aoul* I sketched a portrait of this sultan.

At daylight we left, attended by ten of the sultan's Kirghis,

RIVER TERRIC-SOU, KARATOU, AND KIRGHIS STEPPE.

Sultan Boulania.

who had orders to escort me to the next *aoul*, which we found, after a long ride, just at nightfall. The country we now traveled was covered with good grass, and thousands of horses were feeding on these vast plains. During the journey I got several good views of the Alatou, with the high snowy peaks of the Actou shooting far up into the sky. When seen from these plains, which stretch out like a sea, the chain has a most imposing effect. The yellowish green of the grass, and the red and orange color of the sand, extending along the base of the Karatou, form a beautiful contrast with the deep purple rocks, while above these the high ridges of the Alatou are seen receding in almost every shade of color, their misty summits overtopped by the snow and glaciers of the Actou. Here I found inestimable studies of the mountain scenery, and, I hope, profited by the opportunity. There are seven rivers running from the Alatou down the steppe, and three find their way to the Lake Tengiz; the others are lost in the sands of the steppe, on which they form extensive and dangerous morasses.

There are many, and some very large tombs scattered over the steppe, built at different periods and by different races. The great tumuli are the most ancient. One of these was composed of stone; it is a circle of three hundred and sixty-four feet in diameter, forming a dome-like mound thirty-three feet high. The stones have been rounded in the Lepsou, and were brought from that river, which runs through the valley about eight versts distant. None exceeded twelve inches in diameter, but most of them were smaller. To whom this tomb belongs the Kirghis have not even a tradition; they attribute all such works to demons, and say their master Shaitan has been the chief director. Another kind of tomb, of more recent date, is circular on its plan. I examined one which was twenty-five feet in diameter, with walls of stone four feet thick. It was carried up to the height of fifty feet, taking the form of a blast-furnace, with an aperture at top, and an opening on the side two feet square and four feet from the ground. Through this I obtained access to the interior, where I found two graves covered with large blocks of stone, proving beyond all doubt that the superstructure has been erected over them. The Kirghis assured me that these were built by the people who inhabited the country before the Kalmucks. The third kind, which they say were built by Timour Khan and his race, are of sunburnt bricks, and in design possess a Mohammedan character; even now some of these are in excellent preservation.

Not far from several tombs I found Sultan Alie Iholdi, a distinguished man, who claims his descent from Timour Khan; indeed, his son bears his name, as though destined to march the wild men of these regions across the Himalaya, like his ancestor. Below is a sketch of the sultan and his family; behind him stands the chair of state, which is carried before him on a camel when

Sultan Alie Iholdi.

the *aoul* is removed from one spot to another. The plumes of peacock's feathers are a mark of great distinction among these people. The sultana is sitting on a pile of carpets, and the son behind the great iron caldron, standing on an iron frame, in which the sheep are cooked.

After a night at the sultan's *aoul* Boulania's men returned, and we proceeded onward with others obtained from my host. We shortly entered upon a sterile plain extending to Lake Tengiz. The Kirghis declared that only on the banks of the streams should we find pasturage. This was the great horde, and the country had a most desolate appearance. We were approaching the western end of the Karatou, which descended in many low hills down to the plain. Having passed these, we continued our journey nearly due west, and rode over several deep and troublesome morasses. In the evening we encamped on the bank of a small stream, where we found good pasturage for our horses. We had four days of a most uninteresting journey, and arrived on the afternoon of the fifth at the *aoul* of Sultan Souk. He and his family are figured in the frontispiece. A greater robber could not be found in the steppe; and though at this time, being eighty years of age, he could not join in the *barantas*, many were planned by him. On another occasion, when I was staying at his *aoul*, some Kirghis came from the middle horde to beg of him to give up their wives and children, who had been carried off by his banditti—they formed part of his share of the plunder—but the old scoundrel would not restore one. He received a pension from the Russian emperor, sold his country, and deceived his imperial majesty. In one of his *barantas* a battle-axe had cut his nose and rendered it crooked; and when I was sketching him, he desired me not to copy his present nose, but put in a proper one, or the emperor would discover his plundering habits. When sitting for his portrait, he had on a scarlet coat, a gold medal, and a sabre sent him by Alexander the First, of which he was wonderfully proud.

After leaving the sultan's *aoul*, accompanied by himself and nine of his people, we turned to the south, ascending the first ridges of the Alatou. On first approaching them they appear low hills in comparison with the stupendous masses that rise above them, and are cut through by numerous deep and rocky ravines, in which foaming torrents were rushing down to the plain. On reaching the first summit I saw a large tumulus, built of rough stone, on which many staves were standing, decorated with horse-tails, tufts of long hair, and small pieces of silk that fluttered in the breeze. The Kirghis hold this tomb in great veneration, and have a tradition that it is the grave of a mighty Kalmuck, who ruled over his people with so much justice that all were happy. They believe that he still watches over those who inhabit his kingdom. At this place, after adding an offering, Sultan Souk gave me the usual salutation, and departed to visit some friends, a two days' journey over the steppe, where a large party were to assemble for horse-racing and other sports.

Leaving the old tomb, we traveled to the south over a table-land, from which rose the high summits of the Alatou. A ride of a few hours brought us to the River Balicty, which crosses the plateau in a deep rocky gorge, into which we had great difficulty in descending. In the bottom, along the bank of the stream, poplars of great size were growing; also birches, aspens, and several flowering shrubs. Here were a number of birds—some with beautiful green plumage on the neck and breast, shaded into brown on the back and tail; others with black heads, a deep crimson on the neck and throat, and the rest of the body a bluish gray. Pigeons were also numerous. Having sketched a view looking up the gorge to the snowy peaks of the Actou, I continued my ride, and before evening reached a large rent in the mountains, and encamped. Early next morning we began to ascend the Alatou by this ravine, in which runs the "Tchim-Boulac" (pure spring). This was, indeed, a wild place to ride up, and we had often to find our way along ledges of rock two and three hundred feet above the torrent. In some places the water rested in deep pools, then it leaped over two or three falls, and rushed down the gorge with a mighty roar.

A ride of ten hours brought us to the spot from which I made the accompanying view. The rocks on the left are porphyry of a deep red shading into brown, with flecks and veins of white. Their coloring, as well as that of many others found during my journey, is so exceedingly vivid, that the fidelity of my pictures would have been doubted had I returned without specimens. The singular columnar mass in the centre is basalt, and the precipices to the right are slate and jasper. Beyond the large rock over-

TCHIM-BOULAC, ALATOU MOUNTAINS, CHINESE TARTARY.

hanging the fall it was impossible to proceed on horseback. I, however, succeeded in ascending a ravine on foot, and reached the top of the high crags, whence I had a splendid view of the Actou. Having transferred this scene to my paper, we descended, and retraced our steps down the gorge. We found returning much more difficult than going up, but at length reached a ravine running to the west, which enabled us to ascend the mountain above.

From this place we crossed a high ridge, and continued our ride toward the Actou, entering one of the upper valleys that was rich in grass; a good pasture and dwarf trees grow in the ravines. This valley is far too high for the Kirghis to visit with their flocks, and too difficult to approach. The grass, therefore, is only cropped by deer, wild goats, and wild sheep; we observed several of the latter, but at a great distance, for they are exceedingly difficult to approach. Our encampment was in a beautiful spot, under the shelter of high granite rocks; a carpet of thick grass, with a little stream in front fretting and bubbling on its course, added much to its attraction, while to the south rose the high peaks near the source of the rapid river Tschad-jscha.

During a ride of ten days I made many sketches of the sublime scenery in these mountain regions, each view possessing some remarkable feature. I had now reached the western end of the Alatou, and turned toward the south, exploring several valleys. On the Terric-sou I found a large tribe of Kirghis in their summer pastures. The valley is broad and rich in grass, and was now covered with herds of horses, camels, and other cattle. Here there are many tumuli, some of them large, which are held in great veneration by the inhabitants. From their numbers, I am induced to believe that at one period this country has been densely populated. I also met with numerous canals, which had been formed by these ancient people to convey water from the mountains to irrigate the land; and some display considerable engineering skill. They have not been executed by a pastoral people like the present race. There are also several large earth-works, which have formed their fortified camps or settlements. The Kirghis look upon them with dread, under the belief that they have been constructed by Shaitan and his legions.

Shortly after our arrival at the *aoul* on the Terric-sou a Tartar merchant came and invited me to drink tea at his *yourt*. He was bartering his wares with the Kirghis for their cattle, which he takes to China, returning again with Chinese produce. Every sultan and chief has his merchant, as well as his mulla, or priest, and both are very important personages in the tribe. The men had just returned from a successful *baranta*, and were constantly drinking and feasting. It was evidently considered a great event, and the plunder must have been enormous; indeed, the merchant said that they had carried off near two thousand horses and four hundred camels, besides many men, women, and children, whom they would keep as slaves. It had, however, cost them several lives, for two *yourts* were pointed out to me where the killed were then lying.

We were not sorry to leave a people among whom robbery, murder, and dissipation are carried on with impunity. They expect a retaliation as soon as the tribes who have been plundered can muster a sufficient force; thus the entire population is constantly at war. Leaving the *aoul* early, we arrived about midday at the River Cora, which we crossed, and half an hour brought us to the Tschad-jscha, where we had *yourts* built in a very pretty spot close to the water. After tea I began sketching where the river had cut a channel through a high granite mountain. With considerable difficulty I scrambled through this great gorge, and obtained a fine view of the snow mountains towering many thousand feet above me, and apparently near, yet they are so steep and rocky that it is impossible to ascend them. In the lower part there are many tigers—at least so the Kirghis say—but I did not see any in my rambles. I observed their footprints, and should have been glad to have found one within rifle distance.

We ascended a mountain to the north, which proved rugged and difficult, and after riding about an hour gained a mass of rock jutting out nearly perpendicular down to the river. Over this point we had to ride, and most frightful it was to look down into the roaring torrent, nearly a thousand feet below. From this place we soon gained the summit, which gave me a view over the plain of the Karatal, and as far as the Lake Tengiz, till it was lost in a blue mist. Looking southward, we had the high mountains on the road to, and not far from the Chinese town of Kulja and the River Ilia. One high summit in this range is called Ugentasch. The people have a tradition that one of the Chinese emperors lost a golden saddle on this spot, from which this name is derived. Leaving early the *yourt* in which I had slept, I ascended to the east by the mountains which run along the south side of the River Tschad-jscha. From the first summit I had a splendid view of the junction of the three rivers that form the Karatal, and of the plain through which it runs. The River Tinteck and the mountains near the Ilia were also visible. These I sketched, then continued my ride along the crest of the ridge, and in two hours arrived at the snow-line, and found it difficult to ride where the snow was melting. I had now gained a point which afforded me a view looking across the valley of the Tschad-jscha to the Actou, with a torrent rushing down over the rocks with a frightful noise. I was far above the line of perpetual snow: to the east the mountain peaks rose in long succession, their white crests cutting against a sky of a blue so intense, that, on looking up, it appeared almost black. Turning to the west, I saw lake Tengiz shining like a plate of polished silver in the blue and misty distance. During my ride along the crest of the mountain I found a great variety of flowers—iris (blue, purple, yellow, and a pink one spotted with brown), the peony, cowslip, and many others. Having finished my sketch, I began to descend by a new track to the River Tek-el-airik, which afforded me a scene perfectly new; then a ride of three hours brought me to the Tek-el-airik, a rapid and roaring torrent. I also crossed the dry bed of what had been, some ages since, a great river, the course of which may be traced by the deep channel and rounded stones that formed it. No water runs in it now, but what has caused the change it is impossible to say. The rocks which I passed to-day were principally slate—in some parts porphyry. In the little ravines I found bushes and several flowering shrubs, while the ground was covered with flowers up to the snow—indeed, the white crocus was in many places growing close to the snow.

My next ride was to the River Cora; its outlet into the plain is truly grand, for it runs through a rent in a high mountain chain where the rocks rise several thousand feet. As I determined to explore this mighty gorge and sketch the scenery, our horses were left at the mouth of the chasm, it being impossible to ride up the gorge, and track there was none. We had to climb over huge masses of rock; some we were obliged to creep under, they being much too high to climb over; in other places bushes and plants were growing in tropical luxuriance. A scramble of five hours brought me to a point I could not pass. Here the rocks rose quite perpendicularly from the boiling flood, making ascent to the summit impossible. Nor can this be accomplished either in spring or summer, while in winter the chasm is so deep in snow—there being no *aoul* within several hundred versts—that it would be madness to attempt it at that time: thus these grand and wild scenes are closed to man, and the tiger remains undisturbed in his lair, and the bear in his den, and the maral and wild deer range the wooded parts unmolested. A very large bearded eagle was found among these crags, which I shot. After making several sketches, I returned to the horses and ascended toward the great plateau between the mountains, where I arrived in the evening tired and hungry. The dark clouds which had obscured the mountains cleared off, and gave me a most splendid view of the Actou, which runs up toward the Ilia, the snowy peaks shining like rubies in the setting sun, while all below them was blue and purple, with the shades of evening creeping over the lower range. In the foreground was my *yourt*, with the Kirghis cooking the sheep in a large caldron, while the camels and horses were lying and standing around. Tired as I was, I could not resist sketching the scene, which will ever be impressed upon my memory, as well as the splendid sunset over the steppe. To the south of this high plateau the Alatou rises into lofty and picturesque peaks, many of them robed in eternal snow, while the plateau itself is covered with fine grass, which affords good pastures for the flocks of the Kirghis, who will soon take up their quarters here for two or three weeks. Here I found many tumuli, one was two hundred feet in diameter and forty feet high, with a trench all round it twelve feet wide and six feet deep. There is a circular hollow on the top ten feet deep. After examining this great mound, I came to the conclusion that it has been a fort as well as a tomb. On the west side, close to the trench, there are four masses of large stones standing in circles; these I suppose to have been the altars on which the victims have been sacrificed to the manes of the dead. But to whom they belonged, or when they were deposited, no one can state. The Kirghis have a tradition that they belonged to a nation who (for some cause they can not explain) determ-

FALLS ON THE RIVER KOPAL, CHINESE TARTARY.

ined to put each other to death, and that the mounds were raised to receive the bodies before the work of destruction began. They say that the father killed his wife and all his children excepting the eldest son, whose lot it was to kill his father and then himself. The name the Kirghis give to this people means self-killing.

After leaving this scene, which called up many melancholy reflections, we continued our ride toward the River Kopal. This stream afforded me many striking views, the opposite engraving being one which I took at a point where the water leaps over a precipice into a deep gorge, whence it rushes along with a deafening roar. The singular forms of these rocks, and their brilliant coloring, render the locality remarkably attractive. I made several attempts to reach the foot of the fall, but found it impossible, owing to the slippery surface of the rocks over which I had to climb. Not far below this point I discovered the "Arasan," or warm spring, which rises in a ravine formed of yellow and purple marble of striking beauty. From this point the snow-capped summits of the Alatou were seen towering up to a great elevation.

The spring gushes up among dark marble rocks about four hundred feet above the bed of the torrent, and has 29° Reaumur winter and summer. The Kalmucks built a bath here many ages ago, which is still resorted to by Tartars, Kirghis, and Chinese. For scurvy and other cutaneous eruptions, the Kirghis say that bathing a few times effects a cure; they consider it holy ground, and will not allow it to be defiled. Having sketched this rugged and picturesque spot, I descended the gorge, passing over fallen rocks and through splendid scenery for about ten versts. We then crossed the mountains, and from the top of one I got several beautiful views. A valley, about thirty versts broad, extends from the foot of the Alatou to the Karatou, while to the east rises the holy mountain called by the Kirghis "Byanjarouk," after some fair saint of theirs whom they highly reverence.

The steppe extends quite round Byanjarouk, and beyond it rise the lofty peaks near the source of the Actou. Still farther off are seen the highest summits of the chain, a mass of rocks, snow, and ice among which the River Sarcand has its source. Hence we traveled toward a large cleft in the mountain: here the rocks have been torn asunder, and the strata laid bare to an enormous depth. This chasm was about two hundred yards wide, and in some parts more than twice that depth. With great difficulty I descended to the bottom, where I found a rich carpet of grass studded with flowers; in some parts immense cedars were growing. It was a most romantic spot, in which I made several sketches. The horses had been sent down the mountain, to meet us at the mouth of the ravine; and after a walk of several hours, I found them feeding near a small mountain rill, where all had been prepared for our night's encampment.

Early next morning we crossed another spur of the chain, and reached the eastern branch of the Kopal. Following this upward, it led me to the higher parts of the Alatou, among scenes wonderfully grand, many of which were added to my folio. Late in the evening we reached a waterfall, which comes tumbling from beneath a mass of ice formed into an arch, with snow-covered mountains rising above it. At a short distance is a conical mass of slate rock, rising eight or nine hundred feet above the fall. In this region vegetation had almost ceased, but short moss was still struggling upward.

After spending three days in this elevated locality, we returned toward the plain by another route, and visited Tamchi-Boulac, or Dropping Spring, and a magnificent one it is. It lies at the foot of the Alatou, and the opposite view gives but a faint representation of its beauty. The water comes trickling out of the rocks in thousands of little streams that shine like showers of diamonds, while the rocks, which are greatly varied in color, from a bright yellow to a deep red, give to some parts the appearance of innumerable drops of liquid fire. There are several small grottoes in these rocks, and the water drops into a large basin, which runs over fallen masses of stone in a considerable stream.

From this place our route was to the eastward, and after traveling many days we reached the River Acsou. We entered the gorge in the mountains, and found it very difficult to ride up from some high rocks. Having sketched a fine view up the river, I proceeded on foot, and made another sketch, after which I went a short distance, but soon found it utterly impossible to proceed: the river runs between perpendicular rocks, without leaving a place on which man can set his foot, while beneath lies a roaring torrent, rolling over great rocks with frightful speed, by which large trees are snapped asunder like twigs on their passage down. No man has

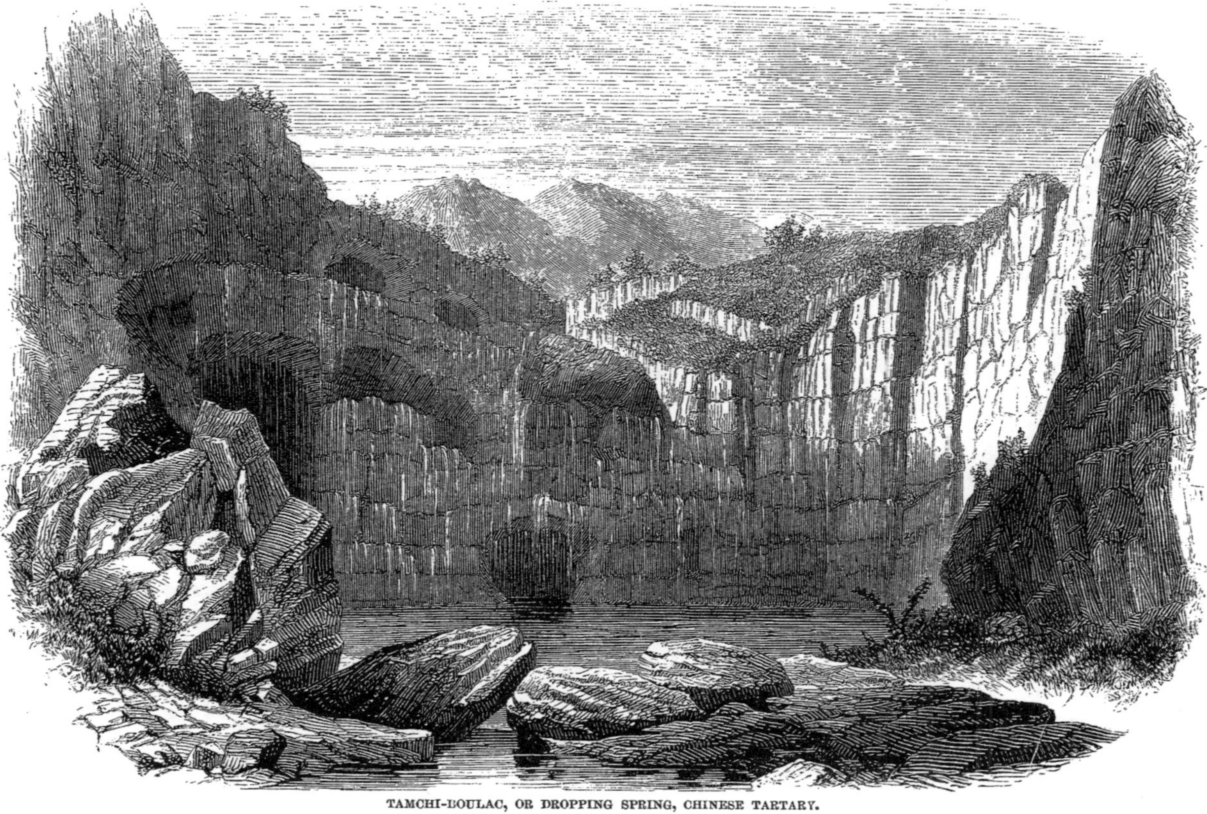

TAMCHI-BOULAC, OR DROPPING SPRING, CHINESE TARTARY.

ascended higher than this. If this river is ever explored, it must be in winter, when the stream is frozen; but then the gorge will be blocked up with snow, and thus rendered impassable. In all probability, man will never see the full grandeur of this mighty chasm. The Kirghis say that the mountain may be crossed in two days, but at no point can any one descend to the river. The snow on the Actou, including the lower parts, is at this time too deep to admit of a journey on that side, even after a most difficult ride over the mountains. Perhaps at the end of July it might be possible to ascend to the foot of the mountains in which the Acsou has its source, but this even is doubtful. At some very distant period there must have been great convulsions here, the rocks being elevated with so many different angles of inclination; nevertheless, I found no signs of volcanic action. Earthquakes are frequent, and I felt the effects of two in this region. This evening I made a sketch of the Acsou, with Kirghis passing over their flocks and herds, which was a work of great difficulty. The men remind one of the Greeks, as they sit naked on their horses, which they manage with skill and courage, frequently plunging into the water, at considerable personal risk, to save a sheep or a goat.

We encamped in a most beautiful situation, commanding a view along the mountains to the east and west, and looking over the valley of Ghilder-a-gar-a-ghi, but we shortly found that we had done this at the expense of our comfort, as the wind threatened every moment to carry away our *yourt*. At last it was secured with ropes and stakes, and then we considered ourselves safe. I started early into the mountains to sketch the Ghilder-a-gar-a-ghi, a beautiful waterfall in the Actou. For about a verst our track was over the plain, and subsequently the mountain rose abruptly, with deep chasms cut into its sides. Along one of the ridges, which were narrow and sharp, we began to ascend, and after riding three hours reached a point beyond which it was impossible to take our horses. From this place we had a splendid view: the water is seen leaping over the precipice in one fall eight hundred feet high, and reaches the bottom in vapor, after which it is again collected, and rushes down the gorge in white foam. To obtain a good sketch it was necessary to descend into this mighty gorge, which was a work of great risk. The Cossacks accompanied me, and we reached the bottom without an accident. When standing beneath, the fall appeared stupendous, and the roaring of the water prevented the sound of our voices being heard.

At a short distance from the fall there is a natural arch in the slate rocks which spans the torrent. Beyond, the water rushes on in many a fall till it reaches the plateau five thousand feet below, which is at a distance of about two versts. The savage effect of this spot must be seen to be fully understood; the opposite view conveys but an artist's impression of the scene.

With this view I shall take my leave of the Alatou and Mustou Mountains, among which I wandered for one hundred and twenty-three days, visiting scenery of the most striking character, which contributed one hundred and nine sketches to my folio. In these regions I encountered many dangers; Providence, however, preserved me. Once a Kirghis sent a ball from my own rifle, which struck the rocks three inches above my head. Though this was accidental, he immediately threw down the rifle, sprung into his saddle, galloped away, and we saw him no more. I often experienced hunger, and when I departed from the neighborhood it was almost without clothing, and without a serviceable pair of boots; notwithstanding which, as I rode away I looked back with regret upon the purple summits and snowy peaks, remembering only the happy days I had spent among their wonderful scenery.

CHAPTER XXIX.

SAIAN MOUNTAINS—ORIENTAL SIBERIA.

After leaving the eastern end of the Alatou, a ride of seventeen days over hill and steppe brought me to the Russian frontier and a post-road at Semipolatinsk, when I appeared once more among my Siberian friends, who had given me up, believing that I was killed. I shall now cross Siberia from its western boundary on the Irtisch to its Oriental capital Irkoutsk, but shall not inflict the monotony of a post journey on my readers.

It was not dragged on at the rate of three or four stations a day, for in the twenty-four hours I often traversed two hundred and ninety, and sometimes as much as three hundred and four versts. If any person traveling to Irkoutsk by the great post-road will

GHILDER-A-GAR-A-CHI, ACTOU MOUNTAINS, CHINESE TARTARY.

keep awake for three stations after passing the Irtisch, ne may sleep the remainder of the journey, and on his arrival may describe the whole country. Where the soil is sandy, the pine-tree is spread over the land, and where it is swampy, there grows the birch. Having reached Atchinsk I left the post-road, and turned directly south toward the Saian Mountains, through which runs the Yenissey. This river is one of the largest in Siberia, and has its source in a high valley lying between the Tangnou and Saian Mountains. I have followed its course in a small boat for about

Singular Formation.

thirteen hundred versts, sketching many fine scenes. I visited the Tas-kill Mountains, through which it rolls its mighty waters, and have seen it in the volcanic region near its source. In one part it runs through a limestone chain, with many singular masses of rock standing in the river: some are peculiar, and show curious formations in the strata.

I came upon cliffs of white marble, as fine as any obtained at Carrara, and the quantity is enormous. Here it rests untouched, near a large river whose waters are lost in the Arctic Ocean: thus it can not reach Europe. From this place I crossed the Tas-kill Mountains, and visited the higher region of the Saian, of which several of the summits rise far above the line of perpetual snow. Having ascended one of the high peaks, I had a peep at old friends, the snowy crests of the Tangnou Mountains, that were seen far to the south. I retraced my steps by another route, and ascended the Abakan River nearly to its source, which led me into regions to the east of the Altin-kool, and through some of those miserable convict colonies that are there scattered about. One day we were greatly surprised by meeting forty Cossacks all armed with rifles: they had been chasing four men who had committed several daring robberies. The den of these rascals was in the higher part of the Saian chain; but up to this time they had evaded their pursuers, which greatly annoyed the Cossacks, who would have shot them all had they got them within range of their rifles.

After a long ride I commenced my ramble in the valley of the Oka, a most romantic spot, in which I spent several days sketching. On one occasion I came upon the opposite scene, where the small river Djem-a-louk falls over a bed of lava eighty-six feet deep. The view was peculiarly striking at the back of the fall, a large cavern having been formed by the action of the falling water. It is dark, almost black; indeed, the eye can not penetrate its shade and depth, while in front huge masses of lava are piled up. The scene had a dreary aspect, but the coloring was exquisitely beautiful. From this dark-looking basin the water escapes into the River Oka, that has cut a passage through this immense bed of lava, which here covers the whole valley. Having finished my sketch, I crossed to the foot of the mountains, where our horses were waiting, and then we continued our ride toward the north. After going about ten versts I found that the lava terminated abruptly, and that I had reached the farthest point to which it had flowed. My companions were three Cossacks and three Bouriats; the latter, though natives of the valley some twenty versts distant,

RIVER DJEM-A-LOUK, ORIENTAL SIBERIA.

had never visited this place before. I desired to cross the Oka, and trace this bed of lava toward a great ravine in the mountains which I saw to the south; but, having reached the bank of the river, we found it a broad and deep stream, over which it was impossible to swim our horses.

A few versts farther down the river we saw a Bouriat *aoul*, that the men said belonged to a lama, who had a canoe, with which we could cross the flood. On reaching the habitation we were informed that the lama was absent; but his son, a youth of eighteen, instantly consented to aid us with the canoe, if we could cross with safety, though he seemed to fear that the river had swollen so much by rain in the mountains as to render our passage impracticable. There was only one spot where it was possible to paddle over, and he ordered some men to take the canoe and accompany us. The river at this point was about a hundred yards broad, with a rapid rushing over the bed of lava above us, and another large one about one hundred and fifty yards below. It was over this small space that we must cross; and as it was by no means in smooth water, not one of the lama's men would consent to take us. Another Bouriat was sent for. He soon arrived, and, after looking at the rushing waters a few minutes, said he would do it, but on no account would undertake to swim the horses across. The young lama assured me that this was of no consequence, as we could obtain horses at an *aoul* on the other side.

This being settled, the man proposed to take me over first, and instantly began to strip off his clothing, insisting that I should do the same, which having been done, and a part only of my dress, shirt and trowsers, secured in the canoe, he extorted from me a promise that I would not move when seated in the little craft; then he stepped into the canoe, and I sat down in the bottom. The Bouriats hauled us near to the foot of the rapid, when my Charon called out to let go, and in an instant we were in the rushing water, which carried us fast toward the falls. The man handled his paddles well, and managed his little craft beautifully, landing us only a few yards above the place where the water passed the brink. It was with no slight relief I stood on the granite rocks and put on part of my dress; for, had a paddle broken, destruction was inevitable. After resting a few minutes, the man dragged his canoe up to the falls, recrossed the river, and brought over a Cossack; in a little more than an hour all the party, with our arms and saddles, were safely landed. Horses were then procured, when I rewarded the man, and, having watched him across the river, we rode up the valley. The lava rose like a wall, in some places forty feet high; in others it was heaped into enormous masses, and great chasms crossed the bed, looking as if formed by the mass cooling. This volcanic matter interested me greatly, and I determined to seek its source, for during my ride I had ascertained that it had flowed down the valley of the Djem-a-louk. At dusk in the evening we reached a Cossack picket, when I made known my wishes to the officer, who told me that the Bouriats had great dread of that valley, and never ascended it except by compulsion. He ordered that seven good men should be collected, and be ready to accompany me in the morning.

Soon after daylight they had assembled. We were eleven in number, and the Cossacks had no fear of Shaitan, whom the Bouriats thought we should be sure to find. About ten versts from the picket we entered upon the dreaded region, and wended our way close to the edge of the lava, frequently through a dense forest, amid fallen rocks and detached heaps of volcanic matter. I am not surprised that these men have a superstitious dread of this place, for a more savage and supernatural-looking valley I never saw. The River Djem-a-louk was lost under the lava for ten or fifteen versts, and then we found it rushing and roaring over its bed of the same material. The ride was a difficult one, often along the foot of various precipices 1500 to 2000 feet in height, from which huge blocks had been thrown into the bed when in a fluid state, which was clearly perceptible by the current dividing on each side of the rocks, like water at the pier of a bridge. About noon on the second day we reached a point where another deep and narrow valley joined the Djem-a-louk from the south, and in this there was also a bed of lava evidently produced by the same eruption, which was so rugged, and intersected by such deep fissures, that it was impossible to take our horses across to explore the valley. Our difficulties became greater as we proceeded forward; in some places the lava filled the valley up to the perpendicular face of the precipices, which compelled us to take our horses over its broken surface. In one part we came upon a beautiful waterfall, flowing over the top of one of the high cliffs. The

VOLCANIC CRATER, SAIAN MOUNTAINS, MONGOLIA.

strata were perfectly horizontal; the water fell in a thin stream, about twenty-five feet wide, and all the forms of the rocks could be seen through it. After dropping thirty feet, it was wafted about by the breeze like a piece of the finest gauze, and before reaching the bottom it was lost in vapor, but we found it again collected into a stream at the bottom of the rocks.

On the evening of the third day we beheld the Kara-Noor, which I at first supposed to be the crater, but on reaching its shore I found that it must be sought in another direction in a deep valley running directly to the south, which was done on foot. We started at daybreak the following morning, and crossed the bed of lava in the valley of the Djem-a-louk. In doing this we had to descend into chasms sixty and eighty feet deep, where the volcanic matter had cracked in cooling. After a day of extraordinary toil, we slept on blocks of it at night. On the afternoon of the second day we beheld the top of a huge cone, and, as the sun was setting, stood on its summit, looking upon the terrific scene around. I at once began sketching a view of this wonderful region, and gave orders to a Cossack to have a fire and preparations made for our night's encampment. Large trees were growing on the sides of the cone, wood close at hand, and water could be got at no great distance. He left me to communicate his instructions, and shortly returned, informing me that the Bouriats were in a state of great alarm. They begged of me not to attempt to sleep on the cone, as, should I venture to do so, Shaitan, with his legions, would certainly pay us a visit, and probably hurl us into the fearful abyss in the crater. So great was their dread, that the Cossack assured me the men would run away and leave us. I desired him to tell them to prepare our camp where they pleased. The cone is about 800 feet high, is exceedingly abrupt and deep in the interior, and formed of lava and red ashes. It stands at the northern end of the crater, which is elliptical in form, but very irregular, extending from north to south nearly two miles, and in some parts more than three quarters of a mile in width; toward the southern end of the crater rose another cone of more recent date and of greater magnitude. Beyond this is the opposite scene—a small stream which comes from the snowy mountains above, dashes over the brink of the crater, and rushes on among masses of lava till it takes its last leap into a fearful abyss. This crater is not on the summit of a mountain, as high peaks and ridges surround it on every side. Its eastern side is bounded by rocks probably not less than two thousand feet high, which are not perpendicular, but overhang their base, their faces bearing marks of intense heat. A few are gray, others purple, and some of a deep red. To the north-east these high precipices have been rent asunder into a tremendous chasm, through which the lava has flowed into the valley which joined the Djem-a-louk, where I observed it when making the ascent. No scene with which I am acquainted conveys such an impression of the terrible and sublime as the prospect from some parts of this wonderful region, in which I spent many days.

We returned by another route, crossing the high mountains to the north. When ascending, I found many large stones and other matter that had been ejected from the crater during the eruptions, of which there have been three at distant periods, and the cones are still more recent. From one summit we looked down into the crater, and could see the valleys through which the igneous matter has flowed. When the volcano was belching forth its lava, flames, and thunder, with the molten mass surrounding the mountain, it must have appeared like an island in a sea of fire.

In the country of the Kalkas, to the south of Oubsa-noor, exist other volcanic indications, which would connect this volcano with Pe-shan in the Syan-shan.

Leaving the wild volcanic region, we commenced our journey up the valley of the Oka, on our way to visit a black-lead mine discovered and worked by a Frenchman, M. Alebere. The route led us through some fine mountain scenery, which I found well worth a visit, and we had to pass many mountain torrents, now much swollen by the snow melting in the higher chains, which not only delayed us, but frequently rendered our ride dangerous. After a journey of three days we reached the mine, which is on the summit of a mountain perfectly dome-shaped; there are others all around it rising considerably higher, while to the east rise great cliffs of granite, which appear falling into ruins as they are tumbled into the valley beneath. M. Alebere received me with great kindness, and I found him a most intelligent man. The mine was a shaft about twenty feet in diameter, and at that time about twenty feet deep; I descended it by a wooden staircase, and found the sides covered with a thick coating of ice, that rendered it impossible to distinguish one mineral from another. Some large pieces of black lead were shown to me of an excellent quality, which M. Alebere considered superior to the best Cumberland lead. Having tried it, I think it is equal to any now produced, and much better than most black lead in use. He has invested a large sum in the mines, and I most sincerely wish him success.

My journey was now southward, toward the higher parts of the chain, which extends far into Mongolia. Our route was over a lofty ridge, from which I had a splendid view to the west, where a high plateau runs up to the snowy peaks, while to the north are seen the white summits beyond the Oka. Leaving this, we descended into a deep valley, in which runs a branch of the River Buch-a-sou. On reaching its bank we found it a mountain torrent, that gave us much trouble to cross, but we succeeded at a point where it was bridged over with ice, under which the water rushed with a great roar. The ice was in many parts twelve, fifteen, and even twenty feet thick, with channels cut through it in every direction. In some places the river undermines these icy masses, and we were obliged to cross from one side to the other several times. As we rode over at one place a part fell with a tremendous crash, which echoed among the rocks like thunder. This was a most difficult and dangerous ride, and occupied us many hours; at last we turned up a ravine which led us to a higher valley between two mountain ridges. Having ascended the one to the south, we looked down upon a lake in a deep and beautiful valley, with snow-capped mountains in this direction, while to the eastward were seen the high peaks near the sources of the Oka and Irkout.

Before night we had descended to the lake, and discovered the whole valley to be a morass. Having selected the best place we could find, our saddle-cloths were spread at the roots of some birch-trees, where we spent a most uncomfortable night. We left as early as possible, and crossed the mountain to the River Korolgo. It was by following this river that I hoped to penetrate to the higher part of the chain. I was led into many a wild and desolate scene among mountain peaks covered with eternal snows. In this region there was much work for my pencil; from one summit I obtained a view of the misty crests of the Tangnou chain; also of another, which branches from the Saian in a southerly direction, and joins the mountains near Saugin. Thus I was enabled to see and sketch the whole of the mountain chains in this vast region. The best idea I can give of the magnitude of the mountain masses that run through Asia, separating Siberia and Mongolia, is by a comparison with the Alps, which can be crossed in four or five days: the wanderer among the Asiatic Alps has lost no time if he contrives to cross them in thirty-five.

Having sketched many views, and satisfied myself about the direction of the chains, I ordered that our route should be to the eastward. We continued our ride for several days along the valleys to the south of the highest ridge, where the water runs to the south, and ultimately finds its way into the Yenissey. The Bouriats proposed that we should turn to the north, as they could guide me by a route used by the Cossacks and Mongolians when they meet to exchange small quantities of the produce of the two empires. The representatives of his Celestial majesty bring tea, silks, and a few other Chinese articles, which they barter with the Cossacks for some of their valuable furs. These are small fairs held at stated periods, when the little bands of traders assemble in these wild and desolate regions, and conduct their transactions on strictly honest principles, spending a few days in such enjoyments as their camp can afford. They then separate and return to their homes. I have been present at one of these little gatherings, and have observed the intense gravity with which they enter upon their mercantile transactions.

We had a rough ride for three days, when at length we reached the pass by which we had to recross the chain. The snow-capped summits rose far above us. We began to wind our course upward, and in a few hours had ascended considerably above the line of perpetual snow. In some parts we found it soft, causing our horses to sink and flounder rather uncomfortably, and more than one man left his portrait on the snow. Having passed the snowy region, and descended some distance to the north, I saw a large rounded hill in one of the valleys, of a beautiful light green color; that it was not grass or herbage I was certain. I ordered our march in that direction, and on reaching the spot discovered that the whole mount was a mass of beautiful green talc—some transparent, other portions opaque. During our ride to-day I procured from one of the mountain torrents some beautiful pieces of nephrite, which could, no doubt, be found in large quantities if a proper search were made for it. One of the specimens was of a deep green, with yellow veins crossing in various forms; the other was a light green, with veins of a white metallic appearance. This country is rich in aquamarine and other stones, and some of considerable value are to be met with in the granite, and in the rivers lower down. I saw both men and women searching for lapiz lazuli, which in some of the streams has been found in considerable quantities. I ascertained that it contained a great deal of quartz, which reduced its value; nevertheless, they offered it to me at sixteen shillings a pound, and the peasants sell it to the Chinese. Although this mineral, like the precious stones, belongs to the crown, the people carry on their searches almost without molestation.

After many a day of toil over mountain and morass, I at last reached "Nouk-a-daban" (a mountain over which it is possible to ride). We began our ascent in heavy rain, following the valley of the Oka, now dwindled to a small rill. About midday we reached the lake in which it has its source; seven or eight versts from this there is another lake, the source of the Black Irkout, and between these two there is a morass, a thorough "slough of despond," almost impassable—indeed, the mud and water were sometimes over our saddles. At length it was passed, and every man felt a relief; but we had not ridden far when the rain poured down in torrents, accompanied by a cold, piercing blast. This made us push on as fast as possible, as there was not a tree to shelter us —not even a shrub. We were now ascending fast, when we beheld a worse enemy than either rain or morass. The clouds were settling fast on the higher summits, causing serious alarm to all, as we should shortly be among the precipices near which we had to ride. Both Cossacks and Bouriats observed the fog approaching with great dread. At length we reached a torrent, and without hesitation several of us rode in, and got over with great difficulty. Some of our men were a little behind; they came up in a few minutes, but were too late. The water was rising fast, and not a moment was to be lost; they turned their horses, and galloped toward a bend in the torrent, about a verst distant. Fortunately they succeeded, but the passage across was attended with great danger; two minutes later it could not have been accomplished. As the fog was settling down upon us fast, I took the bearings with my compass of the high rocks at the head of the pass by which we were to descend to the White Irkout. Our horses were then pushed on at a gallop, but we were soon obliged to pull up by the fog. At some distance to the south we knew there were tremendous precipices, and our chief object was to keep clear of them. One of the men thought he could guide us, and we proceeded slowly for a considerable time. Suddenly he stopped us, when we could hear falling water evidently near at hand. Two of the men rode toward the sound, and when they returned stated that the water was falling from some rocks rising far above us. They advised us to turn to the northeast, believing that we had got up to the edge of a deep valley, which they knew ran along the south side of the mountain; but we had not proceeded far when the clouds began to break, which enabled us to see objects around us. We presently perceived that they were right in their conjectures, and they now found an object by which they were able to guide us to the head of the pass.

After descending about two hundred yards we were beneath the clouds that were rolling up fast. In a short time the rain ceased, when we obtained a fine prospect of the white summits of "Monko-seran-Xardick" (eternal snow and ice). It is a huge mountain mass rent asunder by deep ravines; down them were rushing many torrents, the thundering sound of which was distinctly heard. The pass was not difficult to descend, and we presently reached a small chapel built by the Cossacks on the brink of a deep ravine. Our horses were stopped, the men dismounted, and the Cossacks entered the little building to offer up their thanks for our preservation, and prayers for our farther safety, as we had yet some dangers to encounter before reaching the Irkout. The Bouriats also make this a sacred spot; and ours hung up a few small pieces of silk on several rods secured on the edge of the rocks. From this place the descent into the ravine is very abrupt, and after riding some distance I came upon the opposite scene. The arch is a natural one in a great mass of limestone; farther down there are several caverns, but of no great extent. Part of the men went on to the Irkout, and two remained with me while I sketched. My work was nearly completed when we were startled by a rushing sound far above us, which continued for the space

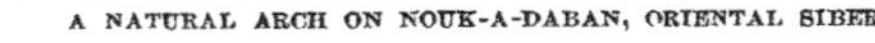

A NATURAL ARCH ON NOUK-A-DABAN, ORIENTAL SIBERIA.

K k

of two minutes, when it suddenly ceased, followed some moments after by a terrible crash. One of the Cossacks sprung up, and said a mountain had fallen. It was an avalanche which had swept down the side of Monko-seran-Xardick, and leaped into one of the gorges.

Long before dusk we had passed over the difficulties on Nouk-a-daban, and joined our friends at the encampment on the White Irkout. Our night's quarters were on the bank of this mountain torrent, fronting its fearful gorge, and on a triangular piece of land, two sides formed by the Black and White Irkouts at their junction, the other by the precipices of Nouk-a-daban: each was about four hundred yards in length, and in parts studded with large larch-trees, under some of which we encamped. A bright sun cast his rays into the deep gorges, which induced me to start early on my sketching expedition in the valley of the Black Irkout, accompanied by three men. We forded the river without difficulty, and I shortly found subjects for my pencil. At one point the river flows through a narrow chasm, and the mountain appears to have been rent asunder. Through the opening the water rushes with fearful force. Though it proved a barrier to any farther progress, I was well repaid for my ramble, and my folio was enriched by several striking scenes. The next morning I started with five of my companions to explore the gorge of the White Irkout, a river rolling down the side of a mountain in a deep rent in the rocks. To ride here was impossible, for in front of our tent the bed of this torrent was about one hundred and fifty yards wide, with huge masses of rock and small stones brought down by the water heaped up in great confusion. These divided the channel; the one portion near to us was dry, but the water was thundering down on the other side of the gorge. Having ascended about three hundred yards we came to a part where the stream was bridged over with ice, which in some places was broken through, and I found it twenty feet thick. It was not agreeable to hear the rushing water under our feet; but in a little time we reached a scene that filled us with wonder. The chasm was here narrowed to fifty feet wide, and the rocks were overhanging, suggesting the idea of a portal leading to the halls of Eblis. The rock rose seven or eight hundred feet, casting a deep gloom over the green icy floor. This and the thundering of the water beneath created a feeling of dread I had never felt before, which I could perceive was shared by my companions. When we had passed through it into a gleam of sunlight, I felt a relief it is impossible to describe. We ascended by this gorge far up into Monko-seran-Xardick to the great glacier which supplies this fearful torrent. The locality afforded me many subjects for my pencil, and I spent five days exploring and sketching its extraordinary scenes.

Subsequently we descended the valley of the Black Irkout, which skirts the high precipices of Monko-seran-Xardick. Some of these are limestone, others are beautiful marble—white, with deep purple spots and small veins. In another part I found a rich yellow marble, equal, if not superior, to the best Sienna; but these valuable materials remain untouched by man. As we descended the high bank of the river, we came upon a deep ravine, nearly filled with ice, in which there were many chasms. This compelled us to ascend, and try to cross at a higher point. At length we reached a part of the ravine filled with snow and ice, where large poplars were growing, with only their tops above the icy mass; the branches were in full leaf, although the trunks were imbedded in the snow and ice to a depth of twenty-five feet. I dismounted, examined several, and found that there was a space around the stem nine inches wide, filled with water, the only parts that appeared to be thawing. I have often seen flowers penetrating a thin bed of snow, but this was the first time I had found trees growing under such circumstances.

Having descended the river about fifteen versts, we turned to the south, and crossed one of the lower ridges of Monko-seran-Xardick, that brought us to a part of the mountain which afforded me a view of Kosso-gol, a lake extending from the foot of the ridge on which I stood into Mongolia: it is about one hundred versts in length, and probably thirty in breadth. A picturesque chain of mountains runs along its western shore, many of the summits reaching far above the snow-line. There is a large island near the northern end of the lake thickly wooded, and the Kalkas come here in the winter to hunt. Far to the south, and nearly in the middle of the lake, there is a conical island, most probably ot volcanic origin. I found three great volcanic hills, from the sides of which lava had issued; one, at the north end of the lake, is of large dimensions. There was much to interest me here, and the

BAIKAL, ORIENTAL SIBERIA.

geologist would find this a country where he could study some of Nature's grandest works.

From this place we rode directly east, over a country crossed by several low ridges of mountains, in many parts densely wooded with pines and cedars. Here, also, I found both men and women engaged in seeking for lapis lazuli; they had been successful, having discovered it in the mountains near the source of the little river Koultouk. Our route was down the bank of this stream to the Baikal, which we reached on the seventh day after leaving Kosso-gol.

The village of Koultouk stands at the western end of the Baikal, or, as the natives call it, the Holy Sea, which is said by them to be unfathomable, and subject to terrific storms. Here I obtained a small boat, and a crew of seven men to row her. It was now the last week in August, rather late for a voyage on these dangerous waters; but the men were hardy, sturdy fellows, who knew the risks and perils they would incur in conveying me to the River Angara. We left the village about noon, when numbers of the peasants assembled to wish us a good voyage. In the night there had been a great thunder-storm, and they feared that we should have bad weather. After rowing about two hours we passed a rocky headland, which shut out the view of the village. Nor was there any other along the shore, which had now become rugged and extremely wild. The evening was calm, with scarcely a ripple on the water, and the sun went down in a blaze of crimson light, which can only be seen in this part of the world, or in tropical regions. Our steersman proposed that we should run into a deep bay and encamp, and landed us at the mouth of a small river, where we slept on a sandy beach, the boat having been drawn far out of the water.

Again we had a fine calm morning, with a prospect of a good day, and the men pulling well, we glided beautifully over the glassy water. The cliffs along the shore were high and rugged, with occasional breaks, where a mountain torrent found its way to the lake. It was near one of these that I sketched the accompanying view, looking toward the mountains on the opposite shore, among which is Amar-daban. I had heard a description of this mountain from a high official, who had been sent on a mission to the Trans-Baikal. When relating the perils of his journey far away from the district, I will not repeat the nonsense he talked, but merely state that he concluded his marvelous story by saying it was not decided by geographers whether Amar-daban or Chimborazo possessed the higher elevation, but his opinion was that "*nasha gora*" (our mountain) had the advantage. In reality, Amar-daban is rather more than four thousand feet above the sea: it does not reach the line of perpetual snow.

Our voyage to-day was a splendid one, and the lake was like a mirror; indeed, we could see into its depth, and watch the fish sporting round the rocky points far below the surface. We encamped on the bank of a small river, which flows through a wild glen leading up into the mountains, and is a celebrated hunting-ground for bears. Our steersman, who was a great Nimrod, related a circumstance which happened to himself on this spot a few years before. Three of the villagers came here to hunt in the forest above. They got separated, two of them following a bear, and the third another, which turned toward the upper part of the glen, where he pursued him until dusk, but without success. After this he returned to the camp, expecting to find his friends, but they had not arrived; hour after hour passed, and they did not appear. He was under no apprehension about their safety, and sat down to his evening meal. When this was ended, he piled several logs on the fire, and was soon fast asleep. Two or three hours had passed, when he was awoke by something near him, and, turning his head, he observed, by the light of his fire, a large bear going down the bank to the little stream. He divined the object of the brute in an instant. Bruin was going for water to put the fire out, then intending to devour his victim. It was the work of a moment for the hunter to seize his rifle, which was at hand, and wait for his return. Presently he was heard in the water, was watched ascending the bank, and when fairly in the light of the fire he received a bullet that rolled him down the bank dead. It is a fact well known that the bear will not attack a man when sleeping by a fire, but will first go into the water, saturate his fur, then return, put out the fire, and devour his victim at his leisure.

In three days more I passed the Angara, the only outlet for this great body of water. Again I had Russian peasants for my boatmen, who pulled me along at a short distance from the shore.

There was great monotony in the high cliffs, nevertheless I found a few points of extraordinary beauty. After rowing about 150 versts I had Bouriat boatmen; but these are not the men to navigate the Baikal in a gale, and I not only encountered bad weather, but was often in great danger. Having spent twenty-eight days on this Alpine sea, I left these people and the risks of the voyage, crossing the country on the north of the Baikal to the great post-road, and reached Irkoutsk the 3d of October. Here I spent the winter in the capital of Eastern Siberia, where I made a few friends and many acquaintances. I deeply regret that want of space prevents the expression of my feelings toward those whose kindness has not been forgotten.

INDEX.

C.

D.

E.

L.

M.

N.

O.

THE END.

Fresh Books of Travel and Adventure.

PUBLISHED BY

HARPER & BROTHERS, NEW YORK.

HARPER & BROTHERS will send either of the following Works by Mail, postage paid (for any distance in the United States under 3000 miles), on receipt of the Money.

South Africa. Missionary Travels and Researches in South Africa; including a Sketch of Sixteen Years' Residence in the Interior of Africa, and a Journey from the Cape of Good Hope to Loando on the West Coast; thence across the Continent, down the River Zambesi, to the Eastern Ocean. By DAVID LIVINGSTONE, LL.D., D.C.L. With Portrait, Maps by ARROWSMITH, and numerous Illustrations. 8vo, Muslin, $3 00.

North and Central Africa. Travels and Discoveries in North and Central Africa. Being a Journal of an Expedition undertaken under the Auspices of H.B.M's Government, in the Years 1849–1855. By HENRY BARTH, Ph.D., D.C.L., Fellow of the Royal Geographical and Asiatic Societies, &c., &c. Profusely and elegantly Illustrated. Complete in 3 vols. 8vo, Muslin, $7 50; Sheep, $8 25; Half Calf, $10 50.

Western Africa: Its History, Condition, and Prospects. By Rev. J. LEIGHTON WILSON, Eighteen Years a Missionary, and now one of the Secretaries of the Presbyterian Board of Foreign Missions. With numerous Engravings. 12mo, Muslin, $1 25.

Southwestern Africa. Lake Ngami; or, Explorations and Discoveries during Four Years' Residence in the Wilds of Southwestern Africa. By CHARLES JOHN ANDERSSON. With numerous Illustrations, representing Sporting Adventures, Subjects of Natural History, Devices for Destroying Wild Animals, &c. New Edition. 12mo, Muslin, 75 cents.

A Hunter's Life in the Interior of Africa. Five Years of a Hunter's Life in the Far Interior of South Africa. With Notices of the Native Tribes, and Anecdotes of the Chase of the Lion, Elephant, Hippopotamus, Giraffe, Rhinoceros, &c. A new Edition. With Illustrations. 2 vols. 12mo, Muslin, $1 75.

Boat Life in Egpyt. By WILLIAM C. PRIME, Author of "The Old House by the River" and "Later Years." Illustrations. 12mo, Muslin, $1 25.

Tent Life in the Holy Land. By WILLIAM C. PRIME, Author of "The Old House by the River," "Later Years," &c. Illustrations. 12mo, Muslin, $1 25.

Atkinson's Siberia. Oriental and Western Siberia: A Narrative of Seven Years' Explorations and Adventures in Siberia, Mongolia, the Kirghis Steppes, Chinese Tartary, and part of Central Asia. By THOMAS WITLAM ATKINSON. With a Map and numerous spirited Illustrations from Drawings by the Author. 8vo (Uniform with Livingstone's Travels), Muslin, $3 00.

European Acquaintance: Being Sketches of People in Europe. By J. W. DE FOREST. 12mo, Muslin, 75 cents.

Washington Territory and the Northwest Coast. Three Years' Residence in Washington Territory. By JAMES G. SWAN. Map and numerous Illustrations. 12mo, Muslin, $1 25.

Virginia Illustrated: containing a Visit to the Virginian Canaan, and the Adventures of Porte Crayon and his Cousins. Illustrated from Drawings by Porte Crayon. 8vo, Muslin, $2 50; Half Calf Antique, $3 50; Half Calf, extra gilt, $4 00.

Random Sketches and Notes of European Travel in 1856. By Rev. JOHN E. EDWARDS, A.M. 12mo, Muslin, $1 00.

Explorations and Adventures in Honduras, comprising Sketches of Travel in the Gold Regions of Olancho, and a Review of the History and General Resources of Central America. With Original Maps and numerous Illustrations. By WILLIAM V. WELLS. 8vo, Muslin, $2 00.

Stories of the Island World. By CHARLES NORDHOFF, Author of "Man-of-War Life," "The Merchant Vessel," "Whaling and Fishing," &c. Illustrations. 16mo, Muslin, 75 cents.

El Gringo; or, New Mexico and her People. By W. W. H. DAVIS, late United States Attorney. 12mo, Muslin, $1 25.

Doré. By A STROLLER IN EUROPE. 12mo, Muslin, $1 00.

New Granada: Twenty Months in the Andes. By I. F. HOLTON. With between 30 and 40 Illustrations, Maps, and a Copious Index. 8vo, Muslin, $2 00; Half Calf, $3 00.

The Araucanians; or, Notes of a Tour among the Indian Tribes of Southern Chili. By EDMOND REUEL SMITH, of the U.S.N. Astronomical Expedition in Chili. 12mo, Muslin, $1 00.

A Journey through the Chinese Empire. By M. HUC, Author of "Recollections of a Journey through Tartary and Thibet." With a new and beautiful Map. 2 vols. 12mo, Muslin, $2 00.

Travels in Europe and the East. Being Sketches and Incidents, with graphic Descriptions of Men, Places, and Things, as seen by the Author in England, Scotland, Ireland, Wales, France, Belgium, Holland, Germany, Austria, Italy, Greece, Turkey, Syria, Palestine, and Egypt. By SAMUEL IRENÆUS PRIME. 2 vols. Large 12mo, Muslin, $2 00.

Jarves's Parisian Sights, First Series. Parisian Sights and French Principles seen through American Spectacles. By JAMES JACKSON JARVES. With Illustrations. 12mo, Muslin, $1 00.

Jarves's Parisian Sights, Second Series. Parisian Sights and French Principles seen through American Spectacles. Second Series. By JAMES JACKSON JARVES. Numerous Illustrations. 12mo, Muslin, $1 00.

Jarves's Italian Sights. Italian Sights and Papal Principles seen through American Spectacles. By JAMES JACKSON JARVES. Numerous Illustrations. 12mo, Muslin, $1 00.

Ida Pfeiffer's Journey Round the World. A Lady's Second Journey Round the World; from London to the Cape of Good Hope, Borneo, Java, Sumatra, Celebes, Ceram, the Moluccas, &c., California, Panama, Peru, Ecuador, and the United States. By IDA PFEIFFER, Authoress of the "Lady's Journey Round the World," &c. 12mo, Muslin, $1 25.

Beckwourth's Life and Adventures. The Life and Adventures of JAMES P. BECKWOURTH, Mountaineer, Scout, and Pioneer, and Chief of the Crow Nation of Indians. Written from his own Dictation. By T. D. BONNER. Illustrations. 12mo, Muslin, $1 25.

Mexico: its Peasants and its Priests; or, Adventures and Historical Researches in Mexico and its Silver Mines during Parts of the Years 1851–52–53–54, with an Exposé of the Fabulous Character of the Story of the Conquest of Mexico by Cortez. By ROBERT A. WILSON, late Judge of Sacramento District, California. With Engravings. 12mo, Muslin, $1 00.

Baird's Modern Greece. Modern Greece: A Narrative of a Residence and Travels in that Country. With Observations on its Antiquities, Literature, Language, Politics, and Religion. By HENRY M. BAIRD, M.A. Illustrated by about 60 Engravings. 12mo, Muslin, $1 25.

Vagabond Life in Mexico. By GABRIEL FERRY, for Seven Years Resident in that Country. 12mo, Muslin, 87½ cents.

Madeira, Portugal, &c. Sketches and Adventures in Madeira, Portugal, and the Andalusias of Spain. By the Author of "Daniel Webster and his Contemporaries." With Illustrations. 12mo, Muslin, $1 25.

Life and Travels of Herodotus. The Life and Travels of Herodotus in the Fifth Century before Christ: An imaginary Biography founded on Fact, illustrative of the History, Manners, Religion, Literature, Arts, and Social Condition of the Greeks, Egyptians, Persians, Babylonians, Hebrews, Scythians, and other Ancient Nations, in the Days of Pericles and Nehemiah. By J. TALBOYS WHEELER, F.R.G.S. Map. 2 vols. 12mo, Muslin, $2 00.

Ewbank's Brazil. Life in Brazil; or, a Journal of a Visit to the Land of the Cocoa and the Palm. With an Appendix, containing Illustrations of Ancient South American Arts, in recently-discovered Implements and Products of Domestic Industry, and Works in Stone, Pottery, Gold, Silver, Bronze, &c. By THOMAS EWBANK. With over 100 Illustrations. 8vo, Muslin, $2 00.

Squier's Central America. Notes on Central America; particularly the States of Honduras and San Salvador; their Geography, Topography, Climate, Population, Resources, Productions, &c., &c., and the proposed Interoceanic Railway. By E. G. SQUIER, formerly Chargé d'Affaires of the United States to the Republics of Central America. With Original Maps and Illustrations. 8vo, Muslin, $2 00.

The Mosquito Shore. Waikna; or, Adventures on the Mosquito Shore. By SAMUEL A. BARD. With a Map of the Mosquito Shore, and upward of 60 original Illustrations. 12mo, Muslin, $1 25.

Ross Browne's Yusef. Yusef; or, The Journey of the Frangi. A Crusade in the East. A new Edition. By J. ROSS BROWNE. With numerous Illustrations. 12mo, Muslin, $1 25.

Kendall's Santa Fé Expedition. Narrative of the Texan Santa Fé Expedition: comprising a Description of a Tour through Texas, and across the great Southwestern Prairies, the Camanche and Caygüa Hunting-grounds, &c. A new Edition. By G. W. KENDALL. With a Map and Illustrations. 2 vols. 12mo, Muslin, $2 50.